SUKHDEV SANDHU has a doctorate from Oxford University and has taught at New York University. His work has appeared in a wide range of publications, including the *London Review of Books*, *Times Literary Supplement* and *Modern Painters*. He is chief film critic for the *Daily Telegraph*. He lives in Whitechapel.

Praise for *London Calling*:

'This is that rare and welcome thing – a book about immigration to London which isn't a chronicle of doom and gloom ... [Sandhu] tells a fascinating story, rich in detail, in which he rescues some fine writers from comparative oblivion ... Sandhu's vigorous deep-mining teems with discoveries. He makes it clear how much London owes to its migrants.'   *Evening Standard*

'Like the city itself, *London Calling* is a monumental work ... Although at core a serious literary study, it revels in unearthing whores, pornographers, playboys, beggars, boxers, circus performers ... A brilliant book.'   *Independent*

'Sukhdev Sandhu's 389-page trawl through four centuries of storytelling about the capital city, through the eyes of black and Asian writers, is a clarion call for an over-looked literary tradition ... This cocktail of literary archaeology, social critique and storytelling reopens a window on a marginalized world.'

Observer

Writers, especially "minority" writers, cannot do it alone. They need wise critics too. Step forward Sukhdev Sandhu, a young critic who doesn't want for ambition ... This is a fine, usually insightful and stylishly written piece of work, a valuable, zesty contribution to the growing body of literature on black writers by black writers.'

Daily Telegraph

London Calling

How Black and Asian Writers
Imagined a City

SUKHDEV SANDHU

HARPER PERENNIAL

Harper Perennial
An imprint of HarperCollins*Publishers*
77–85 Fulham Palace Road
Hammersmith
London w6 8jb

www.harpercollins.co.uk/harperperennial

This edition published by Harper Perennial 2004

1

First published in Great Britain by HarperCollins*Publishers* 2003

A catalogue record for this book is available from the British Library

ISBN 0 00 653214 4

Set in PostScript Linotype Janson by
Rowland Phototypesetting Ltd, Bury St Edmunds, Suffolk

Printed and bound in Great Britain by
Clays Ltd, St Ives plc

For – and because of –
Puran Singh and Jagir Kaur Sandhu

Contents

List of Illustrations

Introduction

Lo, lovely London, rich and fortunate,
Famed through the world for peace and happiness[1]

THESE FLORID SENTIMENTS were ascribed to a 'stranger from the parching zone' by the playwright George Peele in 1585. They divert and confound: did an African really speak these lines? It seems scarcely credible for black people to have been living and working in London as far back as the sixteenth century. Yet they curiously anticipate the lyrics of 'London Is The Place For Me' which the calypsonian Lord Kitchener freestyled upon disembarking from the SS *Empire Windrush* at Tilbury Docks in 1948, the year commonly thought to mark the arrival of dark-skinned foreigners to England.

The words were actually delivered by a white actor. Peele was writing for the Lord Mayor's Pageant, a festival of London's merchant capitalists held annually throughout the sixteenth and seventeenth centuries to mark the investiture of the incoming Mayor. Many merchants, as brash and exhibitionist as City traders and early dot-com entrepreneurs, used the occasion to show off. In particular, they liked to flaunt their success by draping negroes in fabulously expensive silks, pearls and jewels. At one pageant a pair of elaborately dressed Moors were mounted on leopards, waving the banners of the Skinners' Company and the City of London. At another, a black youth was transported through the capital on top of a life-size model of the Grocers' Company crest – an elaborately carved camel – while he hurled raisins, almonds and prunes at the thousands of cheering spectators. On his head he wore a feathered wreath. At his sides stood two goddesses representing Plenty and Concord.[2]

This cavalcade – extravagant, absurd, oddly affecting – is by no means an isolated example of how black people have been enlivening the life of the capital over the centuries. For the African presence in London spans the millennium. Writing with that strange mixture of churlishness and chiliasm, relish and repugnance, to which critics of the metropolis have often resorted, Richard of Devizes claimed in his twelfth-century *Chronicle* that the city was a hive of perversity and attracted 'Stage players, buffoons, those that have no hair on their bodies, Garamantes [i.e. Moors], pickthanks, catamites, effemoinate sodomites, lewd musical girls, druggists, lustful persons, fortune-tellers, extortioners, nightly strollers, magicians, mimics, common beggars, tatterdemalions'.[3]

During the sixteenth century more and more black faces could be seen in the capital. A trumpeter from Africa, known as John Blanke (i.e. John White), played for both Henry VII and Henry VIII. A painted roll belonging to the College of Arms shows him blowing his horn at the 1511 Westminster Tournament held to celebrate the birth of a son, the short-lived Prince Henry, to Catherine of Aragon. In the summer of 1555 a merchant's son called John Lok imported five Africans to London. He hoped that they might learn sufficient English for them to be able to return to the West African coast and act as interpreters for metropolitan traders eager to challenge the Portuguese control of slave-trafficking.

By the 1570s black people were being brought to England fairly regularly. They were employed as household servants, prostitutes, and court entertainers. Their visibility far exceeded their numerical presence and allowed Queen Elizabeth I to make political

capital in 1601 by issuing a proclamation ordering their expulsion. In doing so she announced that she was

> highly discontented to understand the great numbers of negars and Blackamoores which (as she is informed) are crept into this realm ... who are fostered and relieved here to the great annoyance of her own liege people, that want the relief, which those people consume, as also for that the most of them are infidels, having no understanding of Christ or his Gospel.[4]

Writing *Othello* just two years later, Shakespeare was undoubtedly influenced by the black bandsmen he'd seen in London, as well as the growing number of African prostitutes on the capital's streets.

As 'Londinium', the metropolis had prospered because it was a port city that was ideally located for exporting British slaves, both household chattel and prisoners of war, to other provinces in the Roman Empire. Now, in the seventeenth and eighteenth centuries, the traffic was reversed: it began to import slaves from Britain's colonies in the Americas and the Caribbean. Soon thousands lived and worked here. Not only could they be spied in menial environments – serving food at lordly tables, on the streets tailing their masters and opening carriage doors for them – but they could be found embroiled in aristocratic sex scandals, niggering it up on the Drury Lane stage, servicing peruked noblemen in Covent Garden male brothels, running coal mines in Kingston upon Thames, helping to free the Newgate Gaol inmates during the Gordon Riots of 1780. Fear of their growing numbers, a lurking racial hostility, and the need to stop runaway slaves from becoming skilled and economically self-sufficient led the Lord Mayor to issue a proclamation as early as 1731:

> It is Ordered by this Court, That for the future no *Negroes* or other *Blacks* be suffered to be bound Apprentices at any of the Companies of this City to any Freeman thereof; and that Copies of this Order be printed and sent to the Masters and Wardens of the several Companies of this City, who are required to see the same at all times hereafter duly observed.[5]

Intermarriage between blacks and whites, and also between lascars from the Asian subcontinent and whites, was so rife that a correspondent for *The Times* in 1867 wrote, 'There is hardly such a thing as a pure Englishman in this island. In place of the rather vulgarized and very inaccurate phrase, Anglo-Saxon, our national denomination, to be strictly correct, would be a composite of a dozen national titles.'[6] In 1900 – the heyday of an Empire often assumed to have been a foreign affair, thousands of sweltering miles away in the malarial jungles of darkest Africa and the heat-and-lust shimmer of the Raj – black and Asian people were common sights in London: peddling religious tracts in Whitechapel; walking, law books in hand, to the Inns of Court where they were students; operating on sick patients at teaching hospitals; collecting fares on the city's omnibuses; performing as nigger minstrels at children's parties or church halls; campaigning for Parliament (in 1892 Dadabhai Naoroji became the first Asian to be elected to the House of Commons); advocating decolonization from behind lecterns at The Reform Club and Westminster Town Hall; serving cheap coffee in East End cafés to their fellow countrymen who had just finished long shifts at dock warehouses.

At Trafalgar Square, perhaps the best known landmark in all of London, a young couple from Singapore are wearing smiles and woolly hats and having their photo taken in front of the fountains; schoolchildren whoop with delight as they feed the pigeons; a lone activist protests human rights violations against the Kurds. No one stops to look at Nelson's Column, far less the bronze relief at its south-facing base. Sculpted by J.E. Carew, it is called 'The Death of Nelson' and shows the Admiral stricken and dying. All around him is flurry: cannons are being loaded, the rigging tugged at, the injured carried away. At the very edge of the relief is a black mariner, rifle in hand, still busy doing battle. Who was he? HMS *Victory*'s master book doesn't supply his name, but it does reveal that he was one of a small number of foreigners amongst the crew, and that at least one other was born in Africa. 'England Expects Every Man Will Do His Duty' reads the inscription. Many black men during the eighteenth and nineteenth centuries did exactly that. They were often maimed or killed in the process. After abandoning life at sea, a number of them, as this book will show, ended up in London where they sank into destitution and were forced to choose between beggary and the workhouse.

Close to Nelson's Column can be found a statue of Sir Henry Havelock who in 1857 put down an uprising in Lucknow with barbaric savagery. Having forced villagers to lick up the blood of the relatives his troops had just killed, he then made Muslims, on pain of being whipped, eat pork, and Hindus eat beef. They were further bludgeoned and then hanged. He was honoured for his efforts in 1861 when a memorial was erected in Trafalgar Square, paid for by public subscription. On its back can be found the exhortation, 'Soldiers! Your Labours Your Durations Your Sufferings And Your Valour Will Not Be Forgotten By A Grateful Country'. Clearly they have. In October 2000 Mayor Ken Livingstone proposed that the statue be removed and admitted that he did not know who Havelock was. If the role of black and Asian people in shaping English history, both its high and its low points, can be so easily overlooked even at so visible and central a location as Trafalgar Square, is there any point in trying to draw attention to it in relation to less exalted parts of London?

Part of the problem may be that blacks and Asians tend to be used in contemporary discourse as metaphors for newness. Op-ed columnists and state-of-the-nation chroniclers invoke them to show how, along with deindustrialization, devolution and globalization, Englishness has changed since the end of the war. That they had already been serving in the armed forces, stirring up controversy in Parliament, or, as *The Times* suggested, through their mere bedroom arrangements helping to change the way that national identity is conceptualized, often goes unacknowledged. In contrast, New York defines itself through such symbols of newness and ethnic multiplicity as Ellis Island and the Statue of Liberty.

Popular culture encourages the conflation between London, ethnicity and newness. The very category 'urban', signifying a range of musical styles from garage and drum'n'bass to glossy r'n'b, is used as shorthand for black, or at least a certain version of it, one that is associated with a kind of in-yer-face, street-real nowness that is highly valued by advertisers and media planners who have always been eager to tap into – and exploit – youth culture's desire for the next 'next thing'.

Certainly, walking through the streets of London today, it's hard not to be struck by the omnipresence of 'colour', and its importance in giving tang and immediacy to the city. Strange aromas flume out of North African side-caffs and foodstalls; puffa-clad man-bwoys slouch along with barrio-hustler gaits and practise throwing shapes; Nike billboards enjoin us to buy boots endorsed by the latest soccer sensation who, according to that morning's tabloids, is as lethal a striker in the bedroom as he is on the pitch; a riot of badly-xeroxed fly-posters plastered on to a defunct internet café big up Nation of Islam rallies and lecture series in Highgate to be delivered by ludicrously-monikered Indian holy men; a would-be It Girl sports a ludicrous bindi on her forehead as she flicks through the cheap sari fabrics on display outside 'Qasim Cloathes'; a Bangladeshi cornershop offers cheap calls to Dakar and Accra; telephone kiosks are plastered with cards announcing the dominating charms of a 48DD Brand Nubian Beauty; a straggle of interestingly-coiffured clubbers queue to see if there are any returns for tonight's soundclash between two Dalston-based dark-side glitch-fiends; a sleek young courier poised at the traffic lights sings to himself, 'We're loving it loving it loving it'; flush with his first salary cheque from a German multinational, an expensively-suited young Asian leads his broken-backed mother into an upscale salon for the first beauty treatment she has ever had.

None of this is heinous, but neither, except in terms of scale, is it especially new. Black people, whether as horn players, percussionist-beggars, touring gospel singers from the American South, or cash-in-hand jazz musicians at illegal basement clubs, have long introduced new and eerie sounds to the metropolis. During the eighteenth and nineteenth centuries they bonded with the white underclasses at wharf taverns where they glugged down ale and sang sea shanties, and at bawdy mixed-race hops where people of all colours roared and danced together. As retailers, too, they have hawked anything they had to hand – bits of cloth, hankies, toys, foodstuffs. Sometimes they hawked themselves. The Georgian version of telephone cards were the directories of 'Covent Garden ladies' which listed prostitutes available for hire. Mrs Lowes, of 68 Upper Charlotte Street in Soho, was a West Indian who charged clients three guineas for a whole night and one guinea for a short visit. She was described, in the tersely reductive terms that were also a feature of slave advertisements during the eighteenth century, as having 'a sweet cheerful disposition, fine dark hair, and eyes of the same friendly hue; fine teeth'.[7]

My central concern in this book is not just to highlight the presence of dark-skinned people in bygone London, but to tell the story of the black and Asian people who have told stories about black and Asian London from the eighteenth century to the present day. I want to show how they have depicted the city rather than how they have been depicted; Olaudah Equiano, V.S. Naipaul, Jean Rhys, Salman Rushdie, Frederick Douglass, Claude McKay, Wole Soyinka, Mary Seacole, Hanif Kureishi, Sam Selvon and Wilson Harris are just some of the authors who have written about the English metropolis. They have employed a wide variety of genres – short story, TV poem, journal, travelogue, radio drama, cinema screenplay. They have also had utterly conflicting responses to the capital. Some have sought to reverse European literary classics by depicting the metropolis as a heart of darkness or composing volumes entitled *A Passage To London*. They have drawn on – and crucially diverged from – the visions of London painted by Jonson, Blake, Dickens, H.G. Wells and T.S. Eliot.

Contemporary novelists increasingly understand and prize the fact that their metropolitan chronicles are part of a longer, deeply sedimented tradition of black London writing. Some – Mike Phillips and David Dabydeen, for instance – have themselves contributed to the upsurge in black English historiography over the last two decades. S.I. Martin has even been sponsored by the London Arts Board to organize literary walks pointing out the sites and landscapes that informed many of the eighteenth-century authors whose lives he wittily dramatized in his 1996 novel, *Incomparable World*. Other writers, such as Salman Rushdie and Bernardine Evaristo, have been inspired to put on their walking boots by reading history books which recount the intimate relationship between London and Empire: at a pivotal stage of *The Satanic Verses*, the anglophiliac and horn-sprouting Saladin Chamcha visits Club Hot Wax where he is confronted by a black literary London hall of fame – Ukawsaw Gronniosaw, Ignatius Sancho, Mary Seacole. This attempt at historical connection signals a living, *felt* tradition of black metrography – one that infuses the imagination of today's writers. They are engaged in constructing a heritage, one that makes the city more navigable. They are also doing something that all immigrants from time immemorial have sought to do – to give shape and meaning to a metropolis that at first terrifies them in its noisy chaos and formlessness. Writing about the Sylheti natives who settled in the East End during the 1920s, the historian Caroline Adams observes:

> It was not easy to find their way around in the big city and various ingenious systems were devised. For example, a man would arrange bricks along the pavement to mark his route to work through the confusing streets around Brick Lane . . . and get hopelessly lost if they were moved. Then there were the codes for identifying the buses to the West End: the number 8 was 'two eggs', the number 22 'two hooks'.[8]

That this is the first book to be written which looks at black and Asian accounts of London is rather surprising. After all, many historians and anthologists have commented on London's accretive and polyglottal nature.[9] They point out that it has flourished through invasion and immigration. From the Romans and the Saxons, to the Huguenots, Russian Jews, Italians, Cypriots and the Irish, the capital's energy, wealth and aura of infinite possibility have been fuelled most ardently by successive waves of outsiders. And yet these newcomers – especially those from the colonies – are rarely themselves heard. Their stories are considered ancillary, of minority interest. A.N. Wilson's *Faber Book of London* (1993) excerpts Lord Scarman's *Report into the Brixton Riots of 1981*, but not a single passage from a black writer.

Even in the academic sphere, where questioning the traditional canon is the rage, there has been little interest in the relationship between colonial writers and the metropolis. Certain areas such as eighteenth-century slave memoirs and Anglo-Caribbean writing of the 1950s have been covered relatively well. No one, however, has attempted to pull together this disparate scholarship, and identify some of the tropes and motifs that have recurred down the centuries. It's been left to creative writers to take up the challenge. Fred D'Aguiar and S.I. Martin have drawn parallels between late Georgian and 1990s black London; Caryl Phillips and Gbenga Agbenugba both hark back to the post-war period. Braiding past and present, reaching out for personal and social linkages, what Grace Nichols calls 'webs of kin', these authors' books resonate with, and are underscored by, histories all too often absent from black literary criticism.[10]

What becomes clear from reading Nichols's work, and that of her forebears, is how slippery the term 'metropolis' is. It encompasses millions, arrivants from a thousand different places, aliens to one another, who, even if they live in the same streets and districts, often barely see – yet alone know – one another. This book will illustrate how the Petticoat Lane loft where Gronniosaw first spotted his future wife held none of the social cachet of Charles Street, the small Westminster side-road in which Sancho –

also black, also an ex-slave – opened his grocery in 1773. Those lascars who froze to death in nineteenth-century Limehouse glue-boiling factories had nothing in common with the Indian travellers who, fifty years later, stayed in expensive West End hotels and consorted with leading politicians and royalty.

Not only have colonial authors lived and worked in a variety of different boroughs, but they have also imagined, perceived and described the city in very different ways. London is variously portrayed as epicurean banquet, luminescent centre of the imperial world, mazy labyrinth in which self and sanity are lost track of, moral abattoir, ontological catwalk, redemptive culmination of life's travails, inferno. Class, race, gender, historical context and personal psychology have all inflected their descriptions of the capital in large and unpredictable ways. There is no single black or Asian London. Like the city itself, the way in which it is imagined and depicted changes over time. And a good thing too. It's not even obvious that the relationship between colonial writers and London has to be vexed or agonistic. The 'metropolis', contrary to critical cliché, does not always feel imperilled by, or hostile to, 'marginal' culture. On the contrary, as this book shows, individuals (such as Laurence Sterne) and institutions (such as the BBC) have traditionally been very keen to encourage marginal voices.

The role of 'imagination' is central to this book. For too long black literature has been considered in extra-literary terms. It is treated primarily as a species of journalism, one that furnishes eyewitness accounts of sectors of British society to which mainstream newspapers and broadcasters have little access. Given that interest in black and Asian people tends to be at its highest when they are attacked, rioting, or the subject of official reports documenting prejudice in some tranche of daily life, it is hardly surprising if black writing comes to be viewed as a kind of emergency literature, one that is tough, angry, 'real'. It was ever thus:

in 1787, two years before the first African-English autobiography was published, a trader-turned-Abolitionist called John Newton described in cold print what he had seen when he first poked his head below the deck of a slave ship:

> the Slaves lie in two rows, one above the other, on each side of the ship, close to each other, like books upon a shelf. I have known them so close, that the shelf would not, easily, contain one more.[11]

It is an astonishing metaphor – domesticating the inferno of the Middle Passage, week after week of shitting, starving, shrieking hell, to the status of an over-stocked personal library. And it was against this context that ex-slaves kick-started the history of black writing about London. Yet, even then, as we can see from reading the letters of Ignatius Sancho, imagination and idiosyncrasy kept spilling out of every page. The metaphors and allusions pile up. The tone of his correspondence, far from being strait-laced, is comic and highly stylized. Not only does Sancho elicit a good deal of pleasure from writing about London, he imparts it to his readers. So, I believe, does the work of many of the authors I discuss in this book.

My goal, then, is partly archaeological: to uncover and expose the sheer variety of works about London that have been written since Ukawsaw Gronniosaw's slave autobiography in 1772. Indeed, almost every author whose roots lie in the former colonies has produced work, fictional or non-fictional, focusing on life in the English metropolis. To embark upon a study of this vast corpus of writing is, in effect, a decision to write a history of black British literature. At the risk of conflating the word with the world, the textual with the social, it's also a history of black and Asian London itself. Read properly, the printed page is actually a very good place to turn to for an insight into coloured immigrants' relationship to the capital. Cities have always been imaginative as well as physical

places. We mythologize and fantasize about them. We create mental maps. Sometimes they're created for us. This is particularly true
for colonial writers, many of whom were taught about London and
its 'correct meaning' in tiny village schools thousands of miles away
from the actual city whose reality proved to be rather different.

It could be argued, of course, that the literary history I am
about to narrate could also be told about other ethnic groups who
arrived in London during the past few centuries. There would be
a good deal of truth in this, and the likes of *Children of the Ghetto*
(1892) by Israel Zangwill or Emanuel Litvinoff's *Journey Through
A Small Planet* (1972) certainly do have a lot in common with many
of the books looked at in *London Calling*. Not only do they cover the
same benighted urban locales and totter-down social milieux, but
they share with black and Asian accounts what the critic Raymond
Williams called a 'structure of feeling'. This includes a keen interest
in labour (both its dignity and indignities); an uneasy relationship
with what is perceived as 'mainstream' culture – and an attendant
refusal to neglect marginal sectors of society; and, most of all, a
hunger to find a literary voice capable of evoking the hopes and
fears, the din and chatter, of people who speak in tongues dissonant to the ears of longer-resident Londoners.[12]

Yet the simple fact of not being white in London matters a
great deal. It means black and Asian accounts of the capital cannot
be conflated with those of writers from other immigrant groups.
Three centuries of imperial history also make a difference: authors
in this book often bridle at the social roles they feel Londoners,
victims of shoddy education, are asking them to inhabit.

I have, as will become apparent, a soft spot for rhapsodical
writers, those who are not embarrassed to talk about having fun
in the city. Black and Asian writing is often seen as worthy, rather
than enjoyable. Reading histories of immigrants in London one is
often left with the impression that if they weren't being bruised and

harried by hostile whites, then they spent all their spare time agitating and organizing. Many immigrants were harried. And a not-insubstantial minority did agitate. But feel-good (or should that be feel-angry?) narratives which impute to their subjects ceaseless radicalism tend to overlook the fact that, throughout the centuries, the primary struggles for most black and Asian Londoners have been domestic, not political. They wanted to have a bed to sleep in, food on the table, friends with whom to banter, someone to cuddle up to at night, their kids to be safe and happy. The pursuit of pleasure and comfort overrode the pursuit of political equity.

Not that the two are mutually opposite goals. Nor would I want to downplay how challenging life in the capital has been for black and Asian Londoners. The numerous racially-motivated killings in recent years, of young men like Stephen Lawrence and Ricky Reel, attest to that fact. And yet I would still argue that London has been good to people coming from the old Empire, just as they have been good for London. That's why so many of them live here rather than, say, in Taunton or the north-west of England. They have never had to reside in segregated ghettos as in the United States. Riots have been few. Inter-racial contact has been common. Year after year, decade after decade, from one century to the next, they have come here, from abroad as well as from other parts of England, by various means – from slave ship to the freezing undercarriage of a jet plane – in order to flee poverty, apartheid, ordinariness. They found in this old, old city a chance to become new, to slough off their pasts. London gave them the necessary liberty. It asked for very little in return. Certainly not for loyalty: newcomers were able to rail against slavery, dictatorship, imperialism, London itself. They had free congress. They were emotionally and intellectually unshackled. And so, for all the bleakness and hard times recounted in it, this book is, as are many of the books it discusses, a love letter to London.

CHAPTER ONE

'In Our Grand Metropolis'

Sale of a Negro Boy. – In the account of the trial of John Rice, who was hanged for forgery at Tyburn, May 4, 1763, it is said, 'A commission of bankruptcy having been taken out against Rice, his effects were sold by auction, and among the rest his negro boy.' I could not have believed such a thing could have taken place so lately; there is little doubt it was the last of the kind.

Poet's Corner   A.A.
(Letter to *Notes and Queries*, 1858)[1]

it is wrong for 20th-century multi-culturalists to invent a spurious history for black settlement in Britain before the Fifties and Sixties.

(Geoffrey Littlejohns, letter to *The Independent*, 1995)[2]

A.A. WAS WRONG. In the years following his letter of baffled disgust, many of the antiquarians, genealogists and men of letters who made up the readership of *Notes and Queries* wrote in to provide subsequent examples of African men and women being parcelled off to the highest bidder at public auctions held in the centre of the English capital. A.A.'s question, the ensuing lost-and-found advertisements, and the details of slave auctions which were reprinted in the journal, are evidence of the speed and ease with which London's malodorous past had been forgotten in some of the most learned quarters of English society. Although slavery had only been fully abolished as recently as 1838, it required archivists and antiquarians to fill in the large chinks that were already emerging in the public memory.

The most cursory glance at the paintings, the prints and the literature will prove how myopic it is to insist on a culturally homogeneous conception of the eighteenth century. Empire not only underpinned the swelling British economy during this period, but was crucial to the capital's well-being. The Thames allowed London to become one of the world's leading trading centres. Tea, sugar, cotton, cloth, spices, coffee, rum, fruit, wine, tobacco, rice, corn, oil were just some of the products ferried into London from India, Africa and the Americas. Nearly all of these goods depended on slave labour. Not for nothing did a coin – the guinea – derive its etymology from the West African region of that name, the area from which hundreds of thousands of natives were seized in order to work on plantations across the Atlantic. In the seventeenth and eighteenth centuries the African became literally a unit of currency.

By 1750 London was the second most important slaving port in the country. Alderman Newnham, one of the capital's MPs, and a partner in a banking firm who had formerly worked as a sugar merchant, as well as the head of a grocery business, claimed Abolition 'would render the city of London one scene of bankruptcy and ruin'.[3] Between 1660 and 1690 fifteen Lord Mayors, twenty-five sheriffs and thirty-eight aldermen of the City of London were shareholders in the Royal African Company, the trading operation that held a monopoly on shipping Africans to the colonies. Many MPs were either West India planters or their descendants. Sir Richard Neave, a director of the Bank of England for forty-eight years, was also Chairman of the Society of West India Merchants.[4]

One consequence of this transatlantic trade was the rising number of black Africans who began to enter the capital. They were brought over as servants by planters, returning Government officials, and military and naval officers.[5] They were used as reassuring companions to comfort their masters on their long voyages back to an island from which some had been absent for decades. Other blacks had been offered as perks for the commanders of slaving vessels:

> The post of captain of such a craft was a lucrative one, and those who gained it were prone to make display of their good fortune by the use of gaudily-laced coats and cocked hats, and large silver or sometimes gold buttons on their coats. A special mark of distinction was the black slave attending them in the streets.[6]

These naval captains were allowed to sell their slaves in the capital. Auctions were by no means secret affairs: slaves 'were sold on the Exchange and other places of public resort by parties themselves resident in *London*'.[7] That this was possible, despite the long-standing belief that the air of England was too pure for slaves to breathe, and the assertion in 1728 by Lord Chief Justice Holt that, 'As soon as a negro comes to England he becomes free', was confirmed by two legal rulings. The first, in 1729, was issued by the attorney-general Sir Philip Yorke and the solicitor-general Charles Talbot; their counter-opinion was that the mere fact of a slave coming from the West Indies to Great Britain or Ireland did not render him free, and that he could be compelled to return again to the plantations. The second, in 1749, was a judgement by Lord Hardwicke, that runaway slaves could legally be recovered.[8]

Many Africans found themselves working as butlers and attendants in aristocratic households. Their duties were rarely onerous and their chief function seems to have been decorative and ornamental. They served as human equivalents of the porcelain, textiles, wallpapers, and lacquered pieces that the English nobility was increasingly buying from the East.[9] These slaves were often dressed in fancy garb, their heads wrapped in bright turbans. Owners selected them on the basis of their looks and the lustre of their young skin much as dog fanciers today might coo and trill over a cute poodle.

Oil paintings of aristocratic families from this period make the point clearly: artists such as John Wootton, Peter Lely and Bartholomew Dandridge positioned negroes on the edges or the rear of their canvases from where they gaze wonderingly at their masters and mistresses. In order to reveal a 'hierarchy of power relationships', they were often placed next to dogs and other domestic animals with whom they shared, according to the art critic David Dabydeen, 'more or less the same status'.[10] Their humanity effaced, they exist in these pictures as solitary mutes, aesthetic foils to their owners' economic fortunes.

Yet, on the whole, black people were well-treated by the nobility. Relationships flourished, not only in the kitchens and the pantries where blacks and working-class maids flirted and fondled, but between black servants and the aristocracy itself. Owners often took it upon themselves to educate their possessions and gave them lessons in prosody, drawing, musical composition. Dr Johnson famously left his Jamaica-born employee Francis Barber a seventy-pound annuity and, much to the disgust of his biographer Sir John Hawkins, made him his residuary legatee.[11] Johnson was happy to pray together with Barber and refused to let him go and buy food for his cat as he felt that 'it was not good to employ human beings in the service of animals'. His politics both shaped and were shaped by this friendship: 'How is it', he once roared about America, 'that we hear the loudest yelps for liberty among the drivers of negroes?'[12] Over two hundred years on, Barber's descendants still

live in the Lichfield area where he moved after Johnson's death. They are all white now, and the name will die out with this generation: the last male descendant's children are all daughters.

Less well-known than Barber is Julius Soubise who was born on the Caribbean island of St Kitts in 1754. Brought to England as a ten-year-old, he was fortunate enough to be taken under the wing of Kitty, Duchess of Queensberry. She tried to bribe one Dominico Angelo Malevolti Tremamondo, an Italian fencing master based in Windsor, to teach him to fence and ride. Reluctantly he agreed but refused to take her money. Soubise was an adept student and soon became an accomplished equestrian and fencer. He also learned to play the violin, compose musical pieces and, with the help of the elder Sheridan, improve his elocution.

Soubise's self-regard burgeoned dramatically and he began to claim to all and sundry that he was an African Prince. Never shy of an audience, he sang comic songs and delighted in amateur dramatics. According to Henry Angelo, 'his favourite exhibition was Romeo in the garden scene. When he came to that part, "O that I was a glove upon that hand, that I might touch that cheek," the black face, the contrast of his teeth, turning up the white of his eyes as he mouthed, a general laugh always ensued, which indeed was not discouraging to his vanity, and did not prevent him pursuing his rhetorical opinions of himself.'[13] He goes on:

> I remember seeing him, when presenting a chair to a lady, if from some distance, make three pauses, pushing it along some feet each time, skipping with an *entre-chat en avant*, then a *pirouette* when placed. One of his songs, truly ridiculous, his black face and powdered woolly head not suitable to the words, was a Vauxhall song then, 'As now my bloom comes on a-pace, the girls begin to tease me'; when he came to tease, making a curtsey to the ground, and affecting to blush, placing his hands before his face, an encore was sure to follow.[14]

Soubise excelled as a fop and doused himself with such powerful perfumes that members of the audience attending the same theatrical performance as him had been known to exclaim, 'I scent Soubise!'[15] He was also a serial philanderer and was often spotted at the opera surrounded by aristocratic women. Even during the time he worked as an usher to Dominico Angelo at Eton he often drove up to Windsor 'with his *chère amie*, in a post-chaise and four. There, *Madame*, waiting his return from the college, he would meet her, dine in style at the Castle-inn, take his champagne and claret, entertain half a dozen hangers on, and return to town by the same conveyance.'[16]

A member of fashionable London clubs, and accustomed to

riding fine horses in Hyde Park, the increasingly cocky Soubise also fancied himself not only as a poet – composing chiefly romantic sonnets – but as an accomplished letter-writer. His notoriety flourished, no doubt to his satisfaction, and it was rumoured that the Duchess of Queensberry was besotted – and possibly sexually involved – with him. In 1773 William Austin produced an engraving that showed her and a dandified Soubise fencing.

His fall from grace, though it had been long forecast, was sudden. The Duchess, upon learning that one of her maids had been raped by Soubise, tried to dissuade her from going to court. The young woman was adamant, and in July 1777 the Duchess paid for Soubise to flee the country. Two days later she died. Soubise sailed to Calcutta where he established a riding and fencing academy and trained Arab horses. He died in August 1798 after falling from a horse and damaging his skull.

The following letter originally appeared in the anonymous *Nocturnal Revels* (1779). Lascivious and strategically self-abasing, it is unfortunately the only piece of Soubise's writing known to have survived:

> Dear Miss,
>
> I have often beheld you in public with rapture; indeed it is impossible to view you without such emotions as must animate every man of sentiment. In a word, Madam, you have seized my heart, and I dare tell you I am your Negro Slave. You startle at this expression, Madam; but I love to be sincere. I am of that swarthy race of Adam, whom some despise on account of their complexion; but I begin to find from experience, that even this trial of our patience may last for a time, as Providence has given such knowledge to man, as to remedy all the evils of this life. There is not a disorder under the sun which may not, by the skill and industry of the learned, be removed: so do I find, that similar applications in the researches of medicine, have brought to bear such discoveries, as to remove the tawny hue of any complexion, if applied with skill and perseverance. In this pursuit, my dear Miss, I am resolutely engaged, and hope, in a few weeks, I may be able to throw myself at your feet, in as agreeable a form as you can desire; in the mean time, believe me with the greatest sincerity,
>
> Your's most devotedly,
My Lovely Angel,
Soubise.[17]

Soubise's letter did not elicit quite the response he hoped for. The recipient, a wealthy young lady known to us as 'Miss G—', broke into hysterical laughter before writing back sarcastically:

I acknowledge a Black man was always the favourite of my affections; and that I never yet saw either OROONOKO or OTHELLO without rapture. But lest you could imagine I have not in every respect your warmest wishes at heart, I have inclosed a little packet [a parcel of carmine and pearl powders] (some of which I use myself when I go to a Masquerade), which will have the desired effect, in case your nostrums should fail. Apply it, I beseech you, instantly, that I may have the pleasure of seeing you as soon as possible.[18]

It's not hard to see how, educated and smothered with the kind of love that Soubise was, blacks might identify with their masters and begin to assume their airs and graces. Some even adopted their methods of conflict resolution. In 1780 *Lloyd's Evening Post* lamented that

The absurd custom of duelling is become so prevalent that two Negroe Servants in the neighbourhood of Piccadilly, in consequence of a trifling dispute, went into the Long-Fields, behind Montagu-house, on Thursday morning, attended by two party-coloured Gentlemen, as their seconds, when on the discharge of the first case of pistols, one of the combatants received a shot in the cheek, which beat on some of his teeth, and the affair was settled.[19]

Good treatment was no substitute for liberty. To be treated as a clever pet was not much of an existence. Many wore metal collars, inscribed with the owner's name and coat of arms, riveted round their necks. The numerous 'lost-and-found' advertisements in London newspapers during this period attest to the high incidence of slaves running away:

a Negro boy by name Guy, about 14 years old, very black, with a cinnamon colour'd serge coat, waistcoat, and breeches, with a silver lace'd black hat, speaks English very well, hath absented himself from his master (Major Robert Walker) ever since the 4th instant. Whoever shall bring the above said Negro boy into Mr Lloyd's Coffee-house in Lombard-street London, shall receive a guinea reward, with reasonable charges.[20]

Highly visible on account of their colour and their loud dress, it wasn't easy for runaway blacks to escape detection and capture:

Mary Harris, a black-woman of the parish of St Giles in the Fields, was indicted for feloniously stealing a pair of Holland sheets, three smocks, and other goods of Nicholas Laws, gent, on the 30th November last. It appeared that she was a servant in the house, and took the goods, which were afterwards pawned by the prisoner; she had little to say for herself and it being her first offence, the jury considering the matter, found her guilty to the value of 10d. To be whipt.[21]

Runaways tended to flee in the direction of St Dunstan's, Ratcliff and St George's-in-the-East, areas blighted by poverty which had comparatively large black populations.[22] Here, amongst over-crowded and unhygienic houses located in stenchy, ill-paved alleys full of brothels, rundown lodging houses and dens for thieves, sailors and the dregs of society, they eked out illicit, subterranean livings. They had to. Few of them had marketable skills. Nor did they have contacts in the provinces or in the countryside to whom they could turn. They scraped together piecemeal lives – begging, stealing, doing odd jobs, going to sea – alongside the white under-classes of the East End who extended the hand of friendship to them. So much so, in fact, that Sir John Fielding, a magistrate, and brother of the novelist Henry, complained that when black domestic servants ran away and, as they often did, found 'the Mob on their Side, it makes it not only difficult but dangerous to the Proprietor of these Slaves to recover the Possession of them, when once they are sported away'.[23]

Africans and English sang and danced together at mixed-race

hops. Inevitably they also slept with each other – much to the disgust of the literate middle classes: the narrator of Defoe's *Serious Reflections* (1720) spots a black mulatto-looking man in a London public house speaking eloquently and intelligently. During their conversation, the mulatto, whose colour had precluded him from entering the kind of respectable profession his education merited, curses, to the obvious approval of the narrator, his father who 'has twice ruin'd me; first with getting me with a frightful Face, and rhen [sic] going to paint a Gentleman upon me'.[24] Over half a century later in 1788, Philip Thicknesse bemoaned that 'London abounds with an incredible number of these black men [...] in almost every village are to be seen a little race of mulattoes, mischievous as monkies and infinitely more dangerous'.[25]

Demographics, as much as the easy-going tolerance of the pro-letariat, shaped the high levels of intermarriage. Throughout the eighteenth century barely twenty per cent of the black population was female. Most men – including the likes of Francis Barber and the writer Olaudah Equiano – married white women. This challenges the common assumption that the high percentage of black-white relationships in Britain today is a recent phenomenon, one that is a by-product of multiculturalism or increased social liberalism.

It also shows how misleading is talk of 'the black community' in eighteenth-century London. Certainly slaves did meet up when-ever possible to gossip, reminisce and exchange vital information. When two of them were imprisoned in Bridewell for begging they were visited by more than 300 fellow blacks. And in 1764 a newspaper reported that

> no less than 57 of them, men and women, supped, drank, and entertained themselves with dancing and music, consisting of violins, French horns and other instruments, at a public-house

in Fleet Street, till four in the morning. No whites were allowed to be present for all the performers were Black.[26]

But such occasions seem to have been exceptional. The black population, even in big cities such as Liverpool and London, was simply too small for its members to try to isolate themselves from the white English majority. Of course, it was itself racially diverse: black Londoners hailed from different tribes and regions of Africa. Some had been born or spent long stretches in the Caribbean or in North America; others had spent most of their lives in the United Kingdom. They spoke different Englishes: some, brought up by their aristocrat owners, used language that was refined and decorous; others, educated at sea, preferred jack tar lingo, a stew of Cockney, Creole, Irish, Spanish and low-grade American. Class mattered at least as much as colour in how they dealt with day-to-day vicissitudes.

Recent studies indicate that there were probably never more than about 10,000 blacks in eighteenth-century England at any one time.[27] This out of a population that had swollen rapidly to over nine million by 1800. Even in London, where swarthy men and women were most commonly found, they made up less than one per cent of the citizenry. Numbers did rise, however, in the early 1780s when, following the War of Independence, hundreds of black Americans who had been promised their liberty in return for supporting the Loyalist cause fled to London. Lacking money and education, many starved or froze to death on the city's streets. Their plight attracted widespread public sympathy. Money for food and relief was contributed by all sections of society. The philanthropists and Abolitionist Evangelicals who sat on the Committee for the Relief of the Black Poor decided that the best long-term solution for their charges was to offer them assisted passages out of England.

Influenced by the naturalist Henry Smeathman's arguments that Sierra Leone offered warmth, a fertile climate and a fine harbour, the Committee arranged for the blacks to be shipped there. Many members were keen for the black settlers to have an opportunity to run their own community. This, they believed, would be an effective rejoinder to the anti-Abolitionists who claimed Africans were incapable of self-government. After months of delay and prevarication, in April 1787 a small fleet of ships carrying 459 passengers finally set sail as part of the first 'Back To Africa' repatriation scheme in history. Unfortunately they had the misfortune to arrive at the start of the rainy season; about a third died, and the rest quarrelled with their African neighbours who, refusing to see them as 'brothers' or 'sisters', burned down their settlement.

In the eighteenth century, as has been the case since the Second World War, the notion (however insecurely founded in reality) that too many black people were entering the country animated a number of critics. In 1723 the Daily Journal wrote, ''Tis said there is a great number of Blacks come daily into this city, so that 'tis thought in a short time, if they be not suppress'd the city will swarm with them'.[28] And in 1731, long before the build-up of a sizeable African presence in the metropolis, the Lord Mayor of London issued a proclamation decreeing that blacks could no longer hold company apprenticeships.

Foreign travellers were startled (and Americans appalled) by how cosmopolitan the streets of London appeared. As early as 1710 one German visitor noted that, 'there are, in fact, such a quantity of Moors of both sexes in England that I have not seen before'.[29] In a city whose increasing prosperity meant its streets were awash with noble women wrapped in costly shawls and dazzling pearls and shops which displayed exquisite jewellery and exotic fruit, black people embodied a new kind of globalism. Sitting down to compose the 'Residence in London' section of The Prelude

(1805), William Wordsworth recalled his thrill upon emerging from three years of blanched provincialism at Cambridge:

> Now homeward through the thickening hubbub [...]
> The Hunter-Indian; Moors,
> Malays, Lascars, the Tartar, the Chinese,
> And Negro Ladies in white muslin Gowns.[30]

Black faces could be seen, if only in isolation, in most quarters of London society. Many turned to music: black bandsmen – particularly trumpeters, drummers and horn players – served with army regiments; others mustered meagre livings by fiddling on street corners and around taverns. Non-melodians begged, swept crossings, or turned to prostitution. Johnson's biographer, Boswell, even recorded the existence of a black brothel in London in 1774.

Black Londoners had a visibility far in excess of their small numbers. Images of them cropped up everywhere. They often featured in the prints of Hogarth, Cruikshank, Gillray and Rowlandson, as well as on countless tradesmen's cards – particularly those of tobacconists. They were used to advertise products such as razors: 'Ah Massa, if I am continued in your service, dat will be ample reward for Scipio bring good news to you of Packwood's new invention that will move tings with a touch.'[31] Huge pictures of negro heads or black boys were ostentatiously displayed on the signs outside taverns, shops and coffeehouses. Attractively painted and gilded, these extruded on to the streets, cutting out daylight on account of their size and, occasionally, falling and killing those people unfortunate enough to be passing below.

Swarthy Londoners also fleet-foot their way through much of the century's metropolitan literature. In Thomas Brown's *Amusements Serious and Comical* (1702), a quizzical Indian accompanies the narrator on his ambles through the city's byways and sly-ways.

One of the first people they see is another 'sooty Dog', who 'could do nothing but Grin, and shew his Teeth, and cry, Coffee, Sir, Tea, will you please to walk in, Sir, a fresh Pot upon my word'.[32] African characters were familiar to theatre-goers, with Southerne's adaptation of *Oroonoko* (1696) being performed at least once a season until 1808. Stock characters with names like Mungo, Marianne or Sambo were especially popular; they functioned as comic and mangled-English-speaking versions of the black servants found in aristocratic households.

After the Abolitionist movement began to flourish in the 1770s and 1780s, it became difficult to avoid the constant gush of anti-slavery poems, songs and broadsheets flooding from the printing presses. Black men and women were cast as heroic leviathans, their teeth of finest ivory, their brows set most nobly, their souls

ride and vigour. Yet, despite such epic stature, they rarely
.e. Their enslavement and death were drawn out with the
maximum of Latinate polysyllables and pathos. It's no surprise
that almost all of these poems – florid, well-intentioned, and
crammed with formulaic pieties – have been long forgotten. They
deserve the scorn cast upon them by the literary historian Wylie
Sypher: 'The slave and his wretched lot were a poetical *pons asino-
rum*: the worse the poet, the more he felt obliged to elevate his
subject by the cumbrous splendor of epithet, periphrasis, and apos-
trophe, even at the cost of dealing with the facts only by footnotes
and appendices.'[33]

Africans were represented rhetorically as well as visually.
Despite being cherished by their aristocratic owners and blending
relatively seamlessly into underclass society, a cluster of negative
clichés about black people developed and calcified over the course
of the century: they were portrayed as stupid, indolent and libidinous. Violent and untrustworthy, they were said to lack ratiocination. They were wild and emotional. Often compared to
orang-utans,* their simian propensities encouraged audiences to
believe that enslaving them in no way contradicted the laws of
humanity. Such tropes peppered cartoons, stage plays, private
journals, plantocratic tracts, coffeehouse pontification, parliamentary invective, and the thick-skulled, blue-blooded pomposities
bandied about over the clink and gleam of crystal decanters in
noble dining rooms. These views were also confirmed by textbooks – the *Encyclopaedia Britannica* of 1810 described the negro
thus:

---

* 'Orangoutangs do not seem at all inferior in the intellectual faculties to many of
the Negroe race; with some of whom, it is credible that they have the most intimate
connexion and consanguinity. The amorous intercourse between them may be frequent; the Negroes themselves bear testimony that such intercourses actually happen;
and it is certain that both races agree perfectly well in lasciviousness of disposition.'
Edward Long, *History of Jamaica* (London: T. Lowndes, 1774), vol. 2, p.370.

Vices the most notorious seem to be the portion of this unhappy race; idleness, treachery, revenge, cruelty, impudence, stealing, lying, profanity, debauchery, nastiness, and intemperance, are said to have extinguished the principles of natural law, and to have silenced the reproofs of conscience. They are strangers to every sentiment of compassion, and are an aweful example of the corruption of man left to himself.[34]

It's clear, then, that black people were almost inescapable in eighteenth-century London. Yet though they're often spoken about in this period, they're rarely heard to speak for themselves. Ukawsaw Gronniosaw, or James Albert as he was christened, is an exception to this rule. His memoirs, ghost-written by Hannah More 'for her own private Satisfaction', were published in Bath in 1772.[35]

Gronniosaw, whose grandfather was the King of Baurnou in the north-eastern corner of what is now Nigeria, was sold on the Gold Coast to a Dutch captain for two yards of check cloth. After a long sea journey to Barbados, he eventually found himself in New York serving a young man called Vanhorn. He was soon sold again, this time to Theodore Frelinghuysen, an evangelical Dutch Reformed pastor who tried to educate him.[36] Mental collapse ensued: having been introduced to Bunyan's writings, Gronniosaw became so convinced of his own wickedness that he tried to kill himself with a large case-knife. His master died, forcing him to become a cook on board a privateer's ship in order to pay off his outstanding debts which an unscrupulous friend of Frelinghuysen had promised to clear. He came through countless adventures at sea before arriving in England where he was immediately robbed of his savings by a corrupt landlady. Eager to visit the Methodist evangelist George Whitefield, whose sermons he'd been enthralled by in New York, he headed for London where the minister greeted him warmly before directing him to a lodging house in Petticoat Lane. While eating breakfast the next morning,

Gronniosaw heard a clatter coming from above his head. Curious, he climbed upstairs to discover a loft full of women crouched over their looms weaving silk. One of them (never named) besotted him instantly. Despite learning that her errant husband had died, leaving her in debt and with a child to raise on her own, he decided to marry her.

Difficulties soon arose when Gronniosaw left London to earn money for his new family. Following a brief spell as a servant in Holland, he and his wife settled in a small cottage near Colchester. It was a hideously bleak winter. Gronniosaw had been discharged from work, his wife was sick and bedridden, they had no money. At one stage, they had only four carrots (given to them as a gift) to last them four days. As there was no fire the carrots had to be eaten raw. To make them digestible for her infant child, Gronniosaw's wife chewed them before passing on the mulch to her baby. Gronniosaw himself went without.

Help arrived unexpectedly from a local attorney, and shortly afterwards they decided to move to Norwich where weaving work was easier to find. However, hours were long, wages irregular, their landlady was inflexible about rent payments, and their three children contracted smallpox. When one of the daughters later died of fever, the Baptists refused to assist with the burial. Nor did the Quakers help. The Gronniosaws had begun burying her in the garden behind their house when a parish officer relented. Even then, he declined to read a burial service for her.

The narrative ends with Gronniosaw, aged sixty, pawning his clothes to pay off his family's debts and medical bills, and moving to Kidderminster where he tries to make a living by twisting silks and worsteds:

As Pilgrims, and very poor Pilgrims, we are travelling through many difficulties towards our HEAVENLY HOME, and waiting patiently for his gracious call, when the Lord shall deliver us out of the evils of this present world and bring us to the EVER-LASTING GLORIES of the world to come. – TO HIM be PRAISE for EVER and EVER, AMEN.[37]

Gronniosaw's brief narrative is a depressing start to the history of black English literature. He had headed for England believing it to be a cruelty-free nation. London, in particular, appealed to him because he was 'very desirous to get among Christians'.[38]

In the years following his arrival in London, Gronniosaw's life mirrored that of many of his black compatriots in a number of respects: his enduring marriage to a white woman; the poverty and bereavement which dogged them at every turn; their need to scuttle constantly between different parts of England. Scholars have tried and failed to assemble a detailed biography of Gron-niosaw. This isn't surprising. In his enforced mobility, his depen-dence on handouts, his inhabitation of seedy lodging houses and freezing cottages both in London and on the edges of other Eng-lish towns, Gronniosaw, like so many ex-slaves in the eighteenth century, relied both on his long-suffering family and on his sorely-tested religious faith for survival. The pilgrimage motif on which the narrative ends tempers Gronniosaw's despair with what is only a partially convincing vision of future repose. The journey across the Atlantic to America, the passages to England and, finally, to London, may have been fruitless. However, when earthly cities are so inhospitable to the transplanted African, it's understandable if the goal of migrating to a heavenly city becomes the only redeeming alternative.

Gronniosaw is still a largely unknown figure. The same cannot be said of Olaudah Equiano (c. 1745–1797). Born (or so he claimed) to Ibo parents in Essaka, a village in what is now Nigeria, he was the youngest son of an aristocratic, slave-owning family. At the age of eleven he was kidnapped and sold into slavery. After surviving the Middle Passage, he found himself working in a plantation house in Virginia before being sold to Michael Pascal, a lieutenant in the Royal Navy. Pascal christened him Gustavus Vassa after a sixteenth-century Swedish freedom-fighter, a name which, as personal inscriptions and his letters to the press reveal, Equiano used for most of his life.

Coming to England for the first time in 1757, Equiano stayed in Falmouth and London where he slowly learned to read and write. He spent much of the next five years aboard British ships fighting the French in the Mediterranean. At the end of 1762 he was sold to Captain James Doran who, five months later, sold him on to a Quaker merchant named Robert King. Equiano worked for four years as a small goods trader in the West Indies and various North American plantations; the money he earned during this period allowed him to purchase his freedom for forty pounds in 1766. The following year he returned to London where he practised hairdressing before his maritime twitchings got the better of him and pushed him towards the oceans where he adventured away the next few years serving under various ship captains. An intensely ambitious man of 'roving disposition', he was the first black to explore the Arctic when he joined Lord Mulgrave's 1773 expedition to find a passage to India, sailing on the same ship as a young Horatio Nelson.[39]

Equiano spent much of the final two decades of his life campaigning against the slave trade. In 1783 he was responsible for notifying the social reformer Granville Sharp about the case of the 132 Africans who had been thrown overboard from the Liverpool slave ship, the *Zong*, for insurance purposes. The incident, though hardly unprecedented in the miserable annals of slave history, provoked mass outrage and was later the subject of one of

Turner's finest paintings, 'Slavers Throwing the Dead and Dying, Typhoon Coming on' (1840). His growing status amongst London blacks was rewarded by his appointment in November 1786 as Commissary of Provisions and Stores for the 350 impoverished blacks who had decided to take up the Government's offer of an assisted passage to Sierra Leone. It made him the first black person ever to be employed by the British Government, but the job did not last long. Angered by the embezzlement perpetrated by one of the official agents, he notified the authorities but was dismissed from his post. The affair did not curtail his political activities: he fired off letters to the press, penned caustic reviews of anti-Abolitionist propaganda, and became an increasingly effective speaker for the Society for the Abolition of the Slave Trade as well as the more radical London Corresponding Society.

Equiano published his autobiography in 1789. Over the next five years it ran to nine editions and was translated into Dutch, Russian and German. He was a canny businessman and held on to the copyright of his book after its initial publication by subscription. This meant that he reaped all of the profits that accrued to him when he toured the United Kingdom inveighing against slavery and hawking his narrative. By the time he died in 1797, his literary success allowed him to leave an estate worth almost a thousand pounds to Susan Cullen, the white Englishwoman he'd married in 1792, and their two daughters, Anna Maria and Johanna. It was a far cry from the single half-bit with which he had bought a glass tumbler on the Dutch island of St Eustatia, a transaction that had kicked off his career as a small trader.

Over the course of the last two decades Equiano has become one of the most famous black Englishmen to have lived before World War Two. His memoirs were issued in 1995 as a Penguin Classic and have sold tens of thousands of copies on both sides of the Atlantic. Films, documentaries and cartoons have been based on his adventures. His life and travels have inspired a growing amount of academic research into eighteenth-century maritime culture. Of the millions of people who flocked during 2000 to the Millennium Dome in Greenwich a good proportion would have seen a video about him that was screened in the 'Faith Zone' there.

This level of fame is in part a belated – and hence amplified – recognition of his distinction in being the first African to write rather than dictate his autobiography, an achievement which confounded pro-slavery ideologies and led various newspaper critics to question the book's authenticity. *The Interesting Narrative* is also one of the earliest slave narratives, a genre more normally associated with nineteenth-century American figures such as Frederick Douglass. It offers a rare – and, for a black writer, unprecedented – account of life below the deck of a slave ship. Long before the golden period of anti-imperialist activity in the metropolis – the first half of the twentieth century when Marcus Garvey, Kwame Nkrumah and George Padmore railed against colonialism – Equiano, in tandem with a cabal of black revolutionaries who had named themselves the 'Sons of Africa', fought tirelessly for the abolition of slavery. His autobiography is also, inadvertently, a fascinating account of life in black London in the final decades of the eighteenth century.

To Equiano the capital seemed a place of liberty, a shelter from the storms that slavery had rained down upon him since he was a young boy. Throughout the time he was chained below deck or toiling in plantation fields, London lingered stubbornly in his imagination as a city that, far off and possibly unreachable, might be an asylum from the immiseration in which he and his fellow blacks found themselves. It was a dream, one that inspired hope. He had seen friends dashed to pieces in battles at sea. He had seen female slaves raped, men tied to the ground and castrated before having their ears chopped off bit by bit. In Georgia he himself had been randomly bludgeoned and left for dead by one Doctor Perkins. And when he was in Montserrat he

> knew a Negro man, named Emanuel Sankey, who endeavoured to escape from his miserable bondage, by concealing himself on board of a London ship: but fate did not favour the poor oppressed man; for being discovered when the vessel was under sail, he was delivered up again to his master. This Christian master immediately pinned the wretch down to the ground at each wrist and ankle, and then took some sticks of sealing-wax, and lighted them, and dropped it all over his back.[40]

The Interesting Narrative is invaluable as a book about witnessing. It is a record of horrible things seen, horrible events from which the author would rather have averted his gaze, which, he hopes, might be brought to an end as a result of his describing them. London, in contrast, is a place where looking is a pleasure, not a duty. A place full of entertaining spectacle, not evil: 'Though I had desired so much to see London, when I arrived in it I was unfortunately unable to gratify my curiosity; for I had at this time the chilblains.'[41] Equiano found himself unable to stand up and had to be sent to St George's Hospital where his condition deteriorated. The doctors, fearing gangrene, wanted to chop off one of the twelve-year-old boy's legs. He recovered just in time only to find that, on the brink of being discharged, he had contracted smallpox. By the time many months later he had regained his health he was needed to sail to Holland and then on to Canada, having seen almost nothing of the capital except the inside walls of a hospital dormitory.

Such dismal experiences didn't turn Equiano against the city. When he returned two years later in 1759 he had a much better time. While serving three sisters in Greenwich, the Guerins, he decided to learn skills that might hasten his liberty. He attended school to improve his English and got himself baptized at St Margaret's Church in Westminster. He watched how the nobility comported themselves and what made them tick. For a while he became rather besotted by them: 'I no longer looked upon them as spirits, but as men superior to us.'[42]

As he attended Miss Guerin around town, 'extremely happy; as I had thus very many opportunities of seeing London, which I desired of all things', he also saw many sights – public executions, a white negro woman – that imprinted themselves on his memory.[43] No doubt he would have seen other blacks, in situations not dissimilar to his own, working as coachmen and footmen for the aristocracy. Such sightings would have alerted him to the fact that some black people in London were not as blessed with good fortune as he was, and that not only could he strike up friendships with them, but he could also help to improve their lots.

On Equiano's own daily perambulations, though, danger and delight were never far away. Once, hanging around a press-gang inn located at the foot of Westminster Bridge, he was playing with some white friends in watermen's wherries. Along came two 'stout boys' in another wherry and started abusing him. When they suggested that he should cross over to their boat, Equiano, eager to placate them, tried to do so but was pushed into the Thames, 'and not being able to swim, I should unavoidably have been drowned, but for the assistance of some watermen, who providentially came to my relief'.[44]

Equiano never forgot London. Through the years he spent at sea it stuck in his memory as a brief interlude of joy. The moment he gained his freedom in 1766 his thoughts turned back to the grey, sportive city across which he had once ranged. At dances in Montserrat his freshly purchased clothes caught the attention of pretty women: 'Some of the sable females, who formerly stood aloof, now began to relax, and appear less coy, but my heart was still fixed on London, where I hoped to be ere long.'[45] Over the course of the next fifteen years Equiano's 'roving disposition', his attraction to the 'sound of fame', and the poor wages that domestic service offered in comparison to seafaring led him back to the ocean time and again. Yet he always returned to the capital.

Perhaps the pivotal moment in Equiano's life came in 1773 after his return from Lord Mulgrave's Arctic expedition. Arriving in London he went to a lodging house in the Haymarket near the Strand. He had stayed in this area before, during which time he had learned to dress hair and to play the French horn and had persuaded a neighbouring Reverend to teach him arithmetic. Now he felt much less resourceful: 'I was continually oppressed and much concerned about the salvation of my soul, and was determined (in my own strength) to be a first-rate Christian.'[46] He began to go up and talk to anyone he thought might be able to succour him in his hour of spiritual need. When this proved to be useless he wandered dejectedly around the streets of central London. Soon he was visiting local churches, including St James's and St Martin's, two or three times a day, always searching for fresh answers. He approached Quakers, Catholics, Jews. Yet 'still I came away dissatisfied: something was wanting that I could not obtain, and I really found more heart-felt relief in reading my bible at home than in attending the church'.[47] He fled to Turkey. In 1779 he resolved to become a missionary in Africa, but, despite visiting the Bishop of London to seek permission, was refused ordination.

Equiano's memoir is couched as a spiritual autobiography, a genre that was hugely popular during the eighteenth century. It required its authors to talk at length about their sinful lives and about how, just before they decided to surrender themselves unto Christ, they experienced extreme guilt and self-abasement. The phrases they used to do so were often tired and hackneyed. In contrast, Equiano's account of this troubled period in his life is far from formulaic. It also seems somehow implausible. Black people who roam London's streets in this period usually do so because they're panhandling or because they're on the run from their masters. That they would dizzy themselves searching for faith is especially noteworthy given that throughout history most chroniclers of London have tended to dwell on its venal and secular aspects. Those who chart the immigrant experience associate faith with faith in the motherland or see it as a metaphor for resilience during hard times. In Equiano's narrative the capital becomes a crucible for transformation, one that hoists him from servitude to freedom, from the choppy waves of agnosticism to the pure shores of Christian salvation – a double emancipation. This rebirth acted as a prelude to his decision to begin campaigning on behalf of his fellow black Londoners. The city was worth enskying – not just because as sailor, servant and activist he had flourished there – but because all those experiences had added up to make him a figure of such public importance as to merit an autobiography, one that helped accelerate the abolition of slavery, under which system he had been brought to the metropolis in the first place.

Equiano may be the most famous black writer of the eighteenth century but his is by no means the most substantial, nor the most astonishing chronicle of exilic London. That accolade belongs to Ignatius Sancho (1729–1780), whose life, perhaps because it wasn't quite as buffeted as that of Equiano or of Gronniosaw, has often been discussed in rather dismissive terms. He has been described as a Sambo figure and as 'one of the most obsequious of eighteenth-century blacks'.[48] Yet those who compare him unfavourably to the more 'righteous' Equiano rarely mention the fact that not only did the latter come from a slave-owning family, but that he gained his freedom through purchase rather than escape and, in so doing, 'implicitly acknowledged the legitimacy of slavery'.[49] Moreover, he later went on to buy slaves whom he set to work on a Central American plantation.

Sancho was born aboard a slave ship heading for the Spanish West Indies. His mother died before he was two years old; his father committed suicide. Soon after, he was brought over to England where his master gave him to three maiden ladies who lived in Greenwich. Like wicked sisters in a fairy story, they refused to educate him and bestowed, as did many wealthy families who owned blacks in the eighteenth century, a preposterous surname upon their new possession in the belief that he bore a passing likeness to Sancho Panza, Don Quixote's much put-upon squire.

Fortunately, a godfather in the form of the eccentric John, second Duke of Montagu, soon emerged to offer Sancho an escape from what would have been a life of servitude and illiteracy. The Duke, who lived nearby at Montagu House in Blackheath, London, was famed for his philanthropy and had been known to rescue from penury total strangers whom he had seen wandering about in St James's Park.[50]

The Duke was passionately interested in theatre and in opera. He devoted much of his energy to promoting both arts, though the size of his financial outlay was usually in inverse proportion to the artistic success it reaped. In 1721 he even brought a company to the Theatre Royal, Haymarket. Sancho found in his household a refuge from the cold philistinism he faced daily at the sisters' home. Ever the cultural evangelist, Montagu fomented and helped to feed the African teenager's growing appetite for literature and art. The Duke, so full of humanitarian zeal in his personal behaviour, also proposed constructing a seaport and depot in Beaulieu Creek – where he owned land – in order to profit from the slave trade by means of 'grandiose schemes of exploitation'.[51]

These plans were never realized. John died of pneumonia in 1749. His death panicked Sancho for he longed to leave his mistresses' home, but Lady Mary Churchill, the Duke's widow, 'never associated herself with [John's] drolleries', and was reluctant to allow him to serve as butler in her home.[52] Sancho threatened to commit suicide before she finally relented. She died in 1751, leaving him seventy pounds and an annuity of thirty pounds.

Flushed with his new-found fortune, Sancho felt liberated and headed for central London where, like many eighteenth-century servants who had been granted their freedom, he frittered his allowance on aping aristocratic excesses such as gambling (he once lost all his clothes playing cribbage), boozing, women, and the theatre. His money exhausted, he returned to Blackheath in 1758 with his new wife, a West Indian named Anne Osborne, who bore him seven children. In November 1768, Sancho, who had attained a degree of celebrity two years earlier after a letter he had written to Laurence Sterne had been published, became the first definitively identified African in England to have his portrait painted when, following in the footsteps of Sterne, Garrick and Dr Johnson, as well as many members of the Montagu family, he sat for Thomas Gainsborough.[53]

Between 1767 and 1770 he had at least three pieces of music published which the musicologist Josephine Wright has described as revealing 'the hand of a knowledgeable, capable amateur who wrote in miniature forms in an early Classic style'.[54] He also wrote an analytical work dealing with music theory, no copy of which has survived. Towards the end of 1773, having become too incapacitated to continue work at Blackheath, he moved with his family to 20 Charles Street, Westminster, which lay close to another Montagu House, built by the second Duke at Privy Gardens in Whitehall. Here he opened up a grocery selling imperial products such as sugar, tea and tobacco. The shop lay on the corner of two streets, making Sancho – almost two centuries before the retailing revolution effected during the 1960s by an array of Patels, Bharats and Norats – the first coloured cornershop proprietor in England. Parish rate books show that his premises had one of the higher rents in a street that chiefly housed tradesmen such as cheesemongers and victuallers as well as surveyors, barristers and watchmakers.

The majority of Sancho's extant correspondence stems from this period, a busy one during which he also composed harpsichord pieces, imparted literary advice to writers such as George Cumberland, socialized with the likes of Garrick, Reynolds and Nollekens, and succeeded – albeit with difficulty – in juggling both commerce and connoisseurship. For much of the 1770s, he paid the penalty for his youthful dissolution. Racked by constant stomach pains, he was also frequently gout-ridden, and died on 14 December 1780. Two years later one of his correspondents, Frances Crewe, took advantage of the rising tide of Abolitionism and published as many of his letters as she could track down in a two-volume edition that was also prefaced by a short biography by the Tory MP Joseph Jekyll. The book was a huge success, attracting 1182 subscribers (a number apparently unheard of since the early days of *The Spectator*) and selling out within months. It raised more than five hundred pounds for his bereaved family and was followed by another four editions over the next two years.

The letters themselves are of variable quality. Many are homiletic and filled with social and religious advice to his correspondents. Others contain literary and art criticism, accounts of illness-torn domestic life at Charles Street, political commentary, descriptions of election hustings and London's pleasure gardens, requests for financial aid. Some are just business chits, workaday notes dealing with grocery matters, and are accordingly rather dull. Some, too, are clotted with the rhetoric of social decorum: cordiality, cultivation, civility, sincerity and gratitude are the key – and endlessly invoked – virtues. He lauds people excessively and claims they are 'deservedly honoured, loved, and esteemed'.[55] At his best, though Sancho can also be scatological and biting, as well as learned, tender and deeply moving. The letters brim, to an extent unparalleled for almost two centuries, with comedy, familial devotion and an unembarrassed love of London. They also display an obsession with literariness, a quality not especially prized by Equiano or Gronniosaw, or, indeed, those who would value eighteenth-century black English writing for its historical rather than its aesthetic significance.

A major reason for the success of Sancho's book was that he was already known to a large section of the metropolitan elite. This was because of his friendship with Laurence Sterne (1713– 1768), country pastor and author of *Tristram Shandy*, a nine-volume novel that is in equal parts philosophical treatise, family saga, shaggy-dog story, anatomy of melancholy, and proto-Modernist experimental fiction with a memorable cast of characters that includes the grandiloquent and crazed autodidact Walter Shandy, placid Uncle Toby who only ever gets animated by the thought of military fortifications, and the waspish and incompetent Dr Slop. Standing alongside Henry Fielding and Samuel Richardson as one of the three most important novelists of the eighteenth century, Sterne has been a major influence on twentieth-century writers such as Salman Rushdie and Milan Kundera.

Sterne was at the height of his considerable popularity when Sancho first contacted him during the summer of 1766. He had been reading a copy of Sterne's theological tract, *Job's Account of the Shortness and Troubles of Life* (1760), when he came across a passage which dealt with 'how bitter a draught' slavery was.[56] Wanting to thank the author for such progressive sentiments, and perhaps also to establish contact with so distinguished a man of letters, Sancho introduced himself in his note as 'one of those people whom the vulgar and illiberal call "Negurs"', before going on to praise Sterne's character Uncle Toby: 'I would walk ten miles in the dog-days, to shake hands with the honest corporal.'[57] The bulk of the letter, though, picked up on the reference to slavery in *Job's Account*. Why not, he asked,

> give one half-hour's attention to slavery, as it is this day practised in our West Indies. – That subject, handled in your striking manner, would ease the yoke (perhaps) of many – but if only of one – Gracious God! – what a feast to a benevolent heart.[58]

Sterne – whose own father had died of fever in 1731 after his regiment had been sent by the Duke of Newcastle to put down a slave uprising in Jamaica – was delighted to receive this letter.[59] A benighted negro – known in the Georgian period merely as a trope of literary sentimentalism – was here communicating to him in person, confronting the author. In his reply, Sterne mused on the 'strange coincidence' that he had been 'writing a tender tale of the sorrows of a friendless poor negro-girl' at the very moment Sancho's letter had arrived, and promised to weave the subject of slavery into his narrative if he could. Picking up on Sancho's conceit of walking a great distance to meet Toby, he declared that he 'would set out this hour upon a pilgrimage to Mecca' in order to alleviate the distress of African slaves. Sterne ended his letter by congratulating Sancho on his academic diligence, and promised that, 'believe me, I will not forget yr Letter'.[60]

The ninth volume of *Tristram Shandy* (1767) contains Trim's account to Toby of how he once went to visit his brother and a Jewish widow. He entered their shop only to find there a 'poor negro girl' whose behaviour as well as her colour captivated him. She was so sensitive to the idea of pain that she made sure never to swat flies, but instead slapped at them with a bunch of soft white feathers.[61] Hearing the tale, Toby was moved that a girl who had been oppressed on account of her colour from the day she was born was, nonetheless, loth to 'oppress' flies. He insisted to his sceptical friend that the story proved categorically that black people, like Europeans, possessed souls. This being the case, Africans could not be the inferior, sub-human brutes that plantation owners and pseudo-scientists in the late eighteenth century claimed they were.

Sterne's and Sancho's friendship wasn't confined to the epistolary sphere. In a letter from June 1767, Sterne hoped that his 'friend Sancho' wouldn't forget his 'custom of giving me a call at my lodgings'.[62] He was writing from Coxwould near York having temporarily left the Bond Street home in London at which Sancho frequently used to call. The letter's tone is one of intimacy, both in revelation and in register; Sterne bemoans his ailing health, his weary spirits and his equally weary body. In another letter he asked Sancho to urge the Montagus to subscribe to his book.[63] The idea of a successful white author in the middle of the eighteenth century asking a slave's son for financial assistance is startling. It certainly testifies to their closeness for, as one biographer has observed, 'A person has to be quite secure of his position to ask and receive such favours, especially from a man who could not afford a subscription himself.'[64]

Sancho always loved Sterne. One of his most prized possessions in his Charles Street grocery was a cast of the novelist's head that had been made in Rome from a bust by the sculptor Joseph Nollekens. It's unlikely that he knew much about where it had come from. The truth emerged when Lord Justice Mansfield, the man whose 1772 court ruling played an important role in outlawing slavery in England, later had an appointment to sit for Nollekens. The sculptor pointed to Sterne's bust and confided to

Mansfield that he had used plaster casts of it to smuggle silk stockings, gloves and lace from Rome to London.[65]

Sancho was drawn to Sterne's writing not because of its avant-garde trickiness, but because of the religious values it expressed. These can be found (though they are rarely emphasized) in all of the pastor's work. For instance, in the sermon, *Philanthropy Recommended* (1760), Sterne recounted the parable of the Good Samaritan who, unlike the wealthier travellers who had preceded him on that route, had been prepared to deflect his attention and compassion towards the stricken victim lying at the side of the road down which he'd been travelling. Sterne used this story to attack the bogus and solipsistic theology of a certain kind of Christianity:

> Take notice with what sanctity he goes to the end of his days in the same selfish track in which he first set out – turning neither to the right hand nor to the left – but plods on – pores all his life long upon the ground, as if afraid to look up, lest peradventure he should see aught which might turn him one moment out of that strait line where interest is carrying him.[66]

Linearity equals selfishness. We must be prepared to look around us, to halt, to be diverted by what's going on in the corners, the crevices, the byways of life. These side-routes are full of value, pleasure, goodness. Here, in Sterne's work, sermons pop up in military textbooks; young negro girls are found to have souls and compassion. This is a religious doctrine that commands us to be concerned for the defective, the maimed, the incapable, those unable to hasten along the straight paths of economic or social success. Indeed, *Tristram Shandy* is a novel characterized by disability: Toby has a wounded groin, Trim a creaky knee, the narrator a flattened nose. Sterne allowed these characters to talk, to yarn, to smuggle their way into our affections. He achieved this by means of digressions, hobbyhorses, and by procrastinating and shilly-shallying rather than by kowtowing to the narratory imperative. Tristram, the novel's narrator, was literally – and morally – correct when he asserted: 'my work is digressive, and it is progressive too, – and at the same time'.[67] Sterne himself eschewed a rigidly linear, sequential unfurling of plot. In *Tristram Shandy* he approvingly reproduced Hogarth's line of beauty: it dips, rises, fluctuates rather than heading straight into the future.[68] By choosing to incorporate dashes and marbled pages within his novel, Sterne requires us to read more deeply into the text, to recognize that smooth-talking eloquence is less important than empathy, solidarity.

Sterne most valued the empiric, the contingent, the immediate. He prized practical virtue over metaphysical abstraction and admired Tillotson's Latitudinarianism. As a vicar he was known to be most fond of his humbler parishioners. He had great regard for 'the house servants whom he portrayed so lovingly as Susannah, Obadiah, Jonathan the coachman, and the fat foolish scullion'.[69] Sancho, who had spent most of his life as a domestic servant for the Montagus, would undoubtedly have appreciated the value of such personal kindnesses in daily life. He was also stirred by Sterne's warmness towards the socially marginal. As someone who was handicapped by both colour and class, and who had gained literacy and an education only as a result of being taken up by an eccentric aristocrat, he had to be.

Sancho, then, grew up around – and was the beneficiary of – people who espoused a social creed that stressed the importance of looking out for and helping those struck down by misfortune. He imbibed their values. Generosity, toleration and philanthropy were to become key words in his ethical lexicon. As a small-scale grocer whose business frequently suffered from downturns in trade, Sancho often relied on the kindness of friends and acquaintances to keep his ailing business afloat.

It's hardly surprising that he distrusted merely metaphysical theology, and forms of Christianity which, he felt, were 'so fully taken up with pious meditations [. . .] that they have little if any room for the love of man'.[70] In a letter from 1775, a depressed Sancho, writing about the poorliness of his wife and his four-year-old daughter, Lydia, claimed, 'I am sufficiently acquainted with care – and I think I fatten upon calamity. – Philosophy is best practised, I believe, by the easy and affluent. – One ounce of practical religion is worth all that ever the Stoics wrote.'[71] Lydia died six months later.

Issues of race and philanthropy come together in a letter praising the verse of the young black American poet, Phillis Wheatley, who had arrived in London in 1773 and whose first collection, *Poems on Various Subjects, Religious and Moral*, had created a literary and political sensation that same year:

> the list of splendid – titled – learned names, in confirmation of her being the real authoress. – alas! shews how very poor the acquisition of wealth and knowledge are – without generosity – feeling – and humanity. – These good great folks – all know – and perhaps admired – nay, praised Genius in bondage and then, like the Priests and the Levites in sacred writ, passed by – not one good Samaritan amongst them.[72]

Sancho's belief that linearity and eyes-on-the-prize straight-aheadedness were morally dangerous re-emerges in a letter about his friend Highmore who, he claimed, 'rides uneasily [. . .] he is for smoother roads – a pacing tilt – quilted saddle – snaffle bride, with silken reins, and golden stirrups. So mounted we all should like; but I query albeit, though it might be for the ease of our bodies – whether it would be for the good of our souls.'[73]

Sancho wasn't merely a passive recipient of acts of Christian charity; he helped others unstintingly. For instance, he played the Good Samaritan to Isaac de Groote, writing to Garrick and newspaper editors in an attempt to stoke up support for this myopic and paralysed octogenarian who was a descendant of the legal theorist Grotius. Even as he performed good deeds such as these, however, Sancho felt rather uneasy; he knew that some people would feel ashamed about relying on the beneficence of an ex-slave: 'I have wished to do more than I ought – though at the same time too little for such a being to receive – without insult – from the hands of a poor negroe.'[74] On other occasions he wrote coyly ironic letters of introduction on behalf of his black friends: his reference for the bandsman, Charles Lincoln, pastiched the rhetoric both of contemporary pseudo-science and of newspaper lost-and-found ads: 'a woolly pate – and face as dark as your humble; – Guiney-born, and French-bred – the sulky gloom of Africa dispelled by Gallic vivacity – and that softened again with English sedateness – a rare fellow!'[75]

At least two other aspects of Sterne's novel – naming and decrepitude – spoke directly to Sancho. Walter Shandy believed that names had a direct relationship to a child's future success. Christening was, he felt, a form of branding and a means of determining social rank. He was understandably mortified to learn that his servant, Susannah, had been unable to get her tongue round 'Trismegistus', the mighty and winning name he had chosen for his son, and, instead, plumped at the baptism service for the paltry and demeaning 'Tristram'. Sancho, like many of his fellow blacks in England at this time, was given his name because his owners believed that he would never – could never – attain sufficient status in society for his name to become a source of embarrassment to him. But Sancho far outstripped his anticipated destiny. Like Tristram, he exhibited such winning talent in both his life and his letters as to discredit theories that claimed people's abilities could be predicted even before they were born.

Again, the preoccupation with weakness and illness in *Tristram Shandy* could hardly fail to resonate with the declining Sancho. As Gainsborough's oil painting shows, his nose was as flat as that of the novel's stricken narrator. Like Toby, and like Sterne himself whose bout of tuberculosis left him with a weak, cracked voice, Sancho had some speaking problems; Jekyll claims he harboured an ambition to perform on the stage, but 'a defective and incorrigible articulation rendered it abortive'.[76] It was ill-health that cut short his service with the Montagu family and led him to open a grocery. As the years passed and Sancho was increasingly tortured by gout, dropsy, corpulence and asthma, he continued to draw strength from Sterne's belief in the need to struggle on in the face of physical debility.

Contemporary criticism focused on Sterne's peculiar style and his rather salacious humour. It took Sancho, an ex-slave, to pinpoint immediately the moral core of Sterne's work and, more than that, to glean how his form and subject matter were so intimately connected. In a lengthy letter comparing Sterne, Fielding and Swift, Sancho explained that his criterion for greatness was the diffusion and generosity of each writer's moral vision. So Sterne surpassed Fielding in the 'distribution of his lights, which he has so artfully varied throughout his work, that the oftener they are examined the more beautiful they appear'.[77] Swift was a greater wit than Sterne, Sancho claimed, but Swift excelled 'in grave-faced irony, whilst Sterne lashes his whips with jolly laughter'. He went on to argue that

> Sterne was truly a noble philanthropist – Swift was rather cynical; – what Swift would fret and fume at – such as the petty accidental sourings and bitters in life's cup – you plainly may see, Sterne would laugh at – and parry off by a larger humanity,

and regular good will to man. I know you will laugh at me –
do – I am content; – if I am an enthusiast in any thing, it is in
favour of my Sterne.[78]

It was these thematic and ethical parallels between Sterne's work
and his own life that led Sancho to use Shandean literary devices.
On the most superficial level, this involved creating comic neologisms: 'bumfiddled' for befuddled; 'alas! an unlucky parcipleplivia-
plemontis seizes my imagination'; and describing his friend John
Ireland as an 'eccentric phizpoop'.[79] Sancho clearly wanted to
impress upon his correspondents his facility in the English language, something his vocal malady prevented him from doing on
the stage. Born into slavery, he wished to slough off all vestiges
of social and intellectual passivity by becoming a creator, an independent manufacturer of new words and concepts.

The Shandean echoes in Sancho's letters weren't solely verbal.
He used asterisks when writing flirtatiously about rich farmers'
daughters. And in a letter to the First Clerk in the Board of
Control, John Meheux, he wrote:

> I hope confound the ink! – what a blot! Now don't you dare
> suppose I was in fault – No Sir, the pen was diabled – the paper
> worse, – there was a concatenation of ill-sorted chances – all –
> all – coincided to contribute to that fatal blot – which has so
> disarranged my ideas, that I must perforce finish before I had
> half disburthened my head and heart.[80]

At this point, the original edition reproduced a black blot.

Sancho – like Sterne – loved puns. They represented fun, randomness, peculiar verbal couplings. The scholar Walter Redfern
has claimed that puns are 'bastards, immigrants, barbarians, extra-
terrestrials: they intrude, they infiltrate'.[81] *Tristram Shandy* is a
celebration of such whimsical contingency. No wonder that
Walter, forever obsessed with daft intellectual ideas (names

determine success, noses determine greatness, the need to compile a 'Tristrapaedia' that contains all human knowledge), hates puns. He feels threatened by the disorderliness and unpredictability they represent. That said, Sancho's puns are almost uniformly excruciating. He wrote to one correspondent, after receiving a gift of fawn meat, 'Some odd folks would think it would have been but good manners to have thank'd you for the fawn – but then, says the punster, that would have been so like fawn-ing.'[82]

The most obvious sign of Sterne's influence on the *Letters* is found in Sancho's punctuation. Full stops, commas and semicolons have been largely replaced by dashes which resemble splinters strewn across a broken page. The effect is to hobble the reader who must pay particular scrutiny to each fragment of prose contained between the dashes. Instead of hurtling through each letter we're constantly being forced to slow down, to accustom ourselves to the different, more leisurely time-scale of the writer.

These stylistic borrowings from Sterne were anathema to contemporary critics. In *Notes on the State of Virginia* (1782), his unflattering account of the mental and moral faculties of negroes, Thomas Jefferson, the future American president, denounced Sancho for affecting 'a Shandean fabrication of words [...] his imagination is wild and extravagant, escapes incessantly from every restraint of reason and taste, and in the course of its vagaries, leaves a tract of thought as incoherent and eccentric, as is the course of a meteor through the sky'.[83] And in its otherwise complimentary notice of the *Letters*, *The Monthly Review* bemoaned Sterne's and Sancho's 'wild, indiscriminate use' of dashes which were 'a most vicious practice; especially injurious to all good writing, and good reading too'.[84]

Sancho used dashes for three reasons. First, as a means of sardonically critiquing contemporary racialist theory. One of the recurring themes of pro-slavery doctrine during the 1770s and

1780s was the inability of negroes to perform linear functions. Edward Long's notoriously poisonous *History of Jamaica* (1774) included a discussion of common African attributes:

> their corporeal sensations are in general of the grossest frame; their sight is acute, but not correct; they will rarely miss a standing object, but they have no notion of shooting birds on the wing, nor can they project a straight line, nor lay any substance square with another.[85]

So common was the stress on lineality in anti-Abolition literature that William Dickson felt compelled to challenge it in his *Letters On Slavery* (1789):

> The streets of many towns in this kingdom, and even of this metropolis, are crooked. If our ancestors, who laid out those streets were to be half as much calumniated as the negroes have been, it would probably be asserted, that they could not draw a straight line, between two given points, in the same plane.[86]

The likes of Edward Long and Samuel Estwick regarded lineality as a metonym for the ability to think straight, to rationalize. Ratiocination being the mark of humanity, Africans couldn't be human. Long, in his extended discussion of the physical and intellectual similarity between negroes and orang-utans, seems to have come very near to believing this.

Sancho was well aware that Africans were meant to be innately unlinear and irrational. One of his letters begins with the kind of ironic, grandiloquent agglomeration of a sentence that's also found in Salman Rushdie's descriptions of London in *The Satanic Verses* (1988): 'You have here a kind of medley, a hetrogeneous ill-spelt hetroclite, (worse) eccentric sort of a – a –; in short, it is a true Negroe calibash of ill-sorted, undigested chaotic matter.'[87] Breezily dismissive, Sancho sprays his sentences with dots and dashes to mock the idea that humanity and intelligence are dependent on smooth prosody.

Secondly, the dashes embodied the flurry and chaos Sancho faced in running an urban grocery. Neither the literary allusions nor the discussions of contemporary culture with which his *Letters* are studded should blind readers to the fact that he spent the last seven years of his life trying to raise a large family whilst warding off poverty. Corresponding with his friends usually required Sancho to snatch spare moments in between serving customers at the counter: 'I have a horrid story to tell you about the – Zounds! I am interrupted. – Adieu! God keep you!'[88] In an earlier letter to Meheux, he noted: 'Look'ye Sir I write to the ringing of the shop-door bell – I write – betwixt serving – gossiping – and lying. Alas! what cramps to poor genius!'[89]

The tone of this last remark is comic, but it also shows Sancho to be aware that both his presence among polite company and his aspirations towards becoming a belle-lettrist were regarded as anomalous. In a letter to one of his artist friends he cried, 'For God's sake! what has a poor starving Negroe, with six children, to do with kings and heroes, and armies and politics? – aye, or poets and painters? – or artists – of any sort?'[90] There's a palpable pride here; the contrast between the 'starving Negroe' and 'kings and heroes' is a touch overdone and wilfully self-dramatizing. And yet the letter bristles with a genuine anxiety that also emerged less hysterically in an earlier note to the same correspondent; it began with quotations from Young and Shakespeare before lapsing into self-severity: 'but why should I pester you with quotations? – to shew you the depths of my erudition, and strut like the fabled bird in his borrowed plumage'.[91] The dashes jolt and discombobulate. There's a stutter here, a nervous tic. Is it appropriate, Sancho seems to be asking, for a mere grocer ever to aspire to join the republic of letters?

Sancho's life lacked inevitability. His parents could hardly have expected that either they or their son would be sold into captivity. Nor was it probable that he would elude a life of hard labour under the noonday Caribbean sun by being shipped to England. Few imported slaves had the luck to encounter cicerones such as the Duke of Montagu. Fewer still ended their lives circulating among actors, writers and art connoisseurs while owning property a five-minute walk away from the Houses of Parliament. What's more, at Montagu House in Greenwich, Sancho spent much of his day working in the servant quarters at the bottom corner of the front courtyard; in Westminster his shop was located on the corner between Charles Street and Crown Court. The dashes embody these discontinuities. In geographic as well as in racial and biographical terms, Sancho always occupied an edgy, recessive status.

Finally, Sancho, like Sterne, chose to use dashes extensively 'to mock assumptions about the elegant measured unity of Enlightened discourse'.[92] Parentheses were condemned by eighteenth-century linguistic theorists for signalling mental incoherence and anti-authoritarianism. The menial status of dashes – they were often used for page numbers – was precisely why Sterne and Sancho, two writers who believed fervently in the importance of helping the stray, the dispossessed and the routinely scorned, were so keen to stud their texts with them. By wedging dashes into almost every line, right at the centre of their prose, they were trying to illustrate their belief that over-polished and over-polite sentence structures reflected an excessively linear, solipsistic way of thinking that not only glossed over quotidian happenstance, but also, at worst, led to the abduction and enslavement of peoples who didn't conform to such self-designatedly rational structures of thought. Irony, contingency, solidarity – these were the values they preferred to champion.

In his antepenultimate letter, written a fortnight before his death, when asthma had almost snatched away his last remaining breath and his body was swollen by gout, Sancho asked Spink to forgive 'the galloping of my pen' and thanked him for the kindness he'd shown 'like the Samaritan's' over the years: 'Indulge me, my noble friend, I have seen the priest, and the Levite, *after many years' knowledge*, snatch a hasty look, then with averted face pursue their different routes.'[93] Here, at the end of his life, when Sancho knew that he was dying, we find him brooding on a parable that he was familiar with from his own study of the Bible as well as the sermons of his beloved Sterne. He compares himself to the helpless roadside victim whose appeals for help were ignored by those travellers racing along the straight highway of self-interest. Only when the Good Samaritan slows down, looks sideways and steps off the beaten track, can he be saved. The dash-strewn, non-linear aesthetic that Sancho lifts from Sterne was similarly designed to stop his correspondent skating too swiftly, too insouciantly over the sentences, and to draw attention to the utterances, the needy existence of the narrator between the clauses.

Sancho was the first black writer to think of himself as metropolitan. He saw the city not just as a place to live in or to make money, but as a set of values, a tone of voice. At its best it was a form of conversation – learned, sophisticated, playful – in which he felt sufficiently confident to take part. His letters narrate both daily events in the capital (gobbets about trade, politics, entertainment), and, in their different registers (from coquettish gossip and news-chronicling to anomie-wearied *cri de coeur*), the very sound of the city. Long before George Lamming or V.S. Naipaul, and against the least congenial racial and political backdrop imaginable, Sancho saw London as a cultural centre, one that was the obvious place to be if one were – as he liked to think of himself – a man of letters.

Someone like Equiano thought of his work in terms of the good it could do; it might raise money and create publicity for the Abolitionist cause. He wrote with a very specific audience in mind. Sancho, though, wrote with few thoughts of publication. He merely sought a brief respite from the routine stresses of running a grocery. This doesn't mean that his letters weren't crammed with details of his quotidian, retail existence. They were. But, at the same time, he rejoiced in stylistic reverie to such an extent that we feel it's only in his letters that he could fully vent his imagination. He was interested in language, in metaphor (his wife 'groans with the rheumatism – and I grunt with the gout – a pretty concert!'[94]), in literary play. He experimented and fidgeted with grammar and layout. He concocted neologisms. One can feel the delight he felt in both writing and reading his own letters. He himself was aware of this and ended one note, 'Is not that – *a good one*?'[95] Brimming with energy and brio, they often begin with top-of-the-morning exhilaration – 'Alive! Alive ho!', 'Go to!', 'Bravo!' At his best, Sancho is an imp, a freestyler who's constantly jamming and improvising. He showed that black literature about the city needn't always be a species of protest literature, that it could be more than a crudely utilitarian discourse that exalts 'relevance' or 'resistance' at the expense of charm or aesthetics.

He was known to display such breezy confidence in real life too. A friend, William Stevenson, wrote:

When Mr Sancho lived with the Duke of Montagu, he was sent to ask the character of a cook who lived with a native West Indian Planter then residing in London. Upon his delivering the message verbally, the haughty Creole, eying him disdainfully from head to foot, exclaimed, 'What, Fellow! could not your Master write?' – My African Friend thus answered him, 'Sir, when an English Nobleman sends a servant out of livery to another Nobleman, he means to do him an honour. But, when he sends a servant out of livery to a Plebeian, he thinks he does him a greater honour; and the Duke of Montagu has sent me to do you that honour, Sir!'[96]

The language and imagery of the tradesman often spill over into Sancho's prose, resulting in the juxtaposition of moralizing abstraction and concrete retailing detail: 'man is an absurd animal – […] friendship without reason – hate without reflection – knowledge (like Ashley's punch in small quantities) without judgment'.[97] In one of his many excursions into literary criticism, Sancho regretted the commonplace insipidity of much of Voltaire's *Semiramis*, and added, 'From dress – scenery – action – and the rest of playhouse garniture – it may show well and go down – like insipid fish with good sauce.'[98]

The WISH

Standing at his shop counter every day, gossiping, joking, often griping about his ailing profits with customers for hours on end, Sancho's job supplied him with an unending stock of gags. Some were abysmal. He recounted one exasperating disagreement with a customer over the calendar: 'what? – what! – Dates! Dates! – Am not I a grocer? – pun the second.'[99] At other times, his tea-selling incited biting satire. Enthusing about the poetry of Phillis Wheatley, he wished

> that every member of each house of parliament had one of these books. – And if his Majesty perused one through before breakfast – though it might spoil his appetite – yet the conscious-ness of having it in his power to facilitate the great work – would give an additional sweetness to his tea.[100]

Humour is perhaps the dominant tone of these letters. Of course, debility, pensivity and gloom are never absent, either. But only through studied ebullience could Sancho hope to fend off depression. Much of this comedy was self-reflexive: 'The gout seized me yesterday morning [...] I looked rather black all day.'[101]

Such lines shouldn't be taken as self-loathing or a pitiable eager-ness to amuse his correspondents.[102] In a letter to Meheux, he observed that his pen

> sucks up more liquor than it can carry, and so of course disgorges it at random. – I will that ye observe the above simile to be a good one – not the cleanliest in nature, I own – but as pat to the purpose as dram-drinking to a bawd – or oaths to a sergeant of the guards – or – or – dulness to a Black-a-moor – Good – excessive good![103]

At one level, this passage demonstrates Sancho's love of literary play. The first half is playful, self-referential, and far removed from the straight-edge polemics of such black Abolitionists as

Ottobah Cugoano and John Henry Naimbanna; the second half, however, dispels any suspicion that Sancho is an apolitical Uncle Tom.[104] As in Sterne's work, the teasing and joking of this letter have a strong moral underpinning. Sancho stutters, he g(r)asps desperately for a third analogy to give balance to the sentence. The dashes and the repetition of 'or' show that time is running out. He'll cleave to a simile, *any* simile, that'll shore up this sentence in which he finds himself drowning. Which cliché does he use? That of blacks being stupid! Sancho frequently refuted similar non-senses in his letters and, here, implies that such noxious utterances can stem only from writers over-eager to lend their prose a polished sheen, a rhetorical (both in its literal and pejorative sense) sonority. It's a subtle and witty demolition of racist polemic.

Sancho's decision to couch political dissent in ironic and dep-recating modes emphasizes the fact that humour and conviviality are the abiding registers of the *Letters*. Such are their avuncularity and their jowly bonhomie that I'm inclined to agree with Lydia Leach, to whose letter of 14 December 1775 Sancho replied: 'There is something inexpressibly flattering in the notion of your being warmer – from the idea of your much obliged friend's caring for you.'[105]

One of the most unusual and appealing aspects of Sancho's letters are his vignettes of home life. Black people in the eighteenth century were often denied their privacy. Their physiological traits were itemized for auction purposes, their free time was dependent on their owners' whims. They were viewed as public performers, adorning the arms and advertising the wealth of aristocratic families. Black writers who appeared in print – Equiano, Cugoano, Naimbanna – all inhabited political roles: they assailed large audiences with accounts of the depredations wreaked on their countrymen. Their books were often exhortatory, redolent of the soapbox. Sancho himself wasn't averse to making loud proclamations on political or social issues. But there's another side to him. His letters show us a gentler, more intimate aspect of black London. In them he often speaks of his wife, his young children, leisurely family trips, a world that has nothing to do with the daily grad-grind of chopping sugar into lumps or scooping tea into containers.

The fact that Sancho had married a black woman was unusual in itself. Equally uncommonly, Anne Osborne was literate and often read the newspapers or the letters that her husband was busy scribbling. Her brother, John, lived with his own wife in Bond Street during the 1770s, and the two families got on well. In a bleak letter Sancho wrote after the death of his daughter Kitty, he announced, 'Tomorrow night I shall have a few friends to meet brother Osborne. We intend to be merry.'[106] At moments of the greatest distress, he found it comforting to drown his sorrows with people from a similar background.

Such bleakness was the exception rather than the rule. Anne brought her husband great joy. He referred to her jocularly as 'old Duchess' and 'hen', and to her and the children as 'Sanchonettas'.[107] He found being on his own in London very taxing, and missed Anne intensely whenever they were separated. In a letter from Richmond, Sancho wrote, 'I am heartily tired of the country; – the truth is – Mrs Sancho and the girls are in town; – I am not ashamed to own that I love my wife – I hope to see you married, and as foolish.'[108]

One might think these statements insignificant: they're the kind of soppy, affectionate words husbands are meant to say to their wives. Yet in over two hundred years of writing about London by African and South Asian writers, there are almost no accounts of quiet, domestic contentment. Home, all too often, is where the heartache is. This makes the Sanchos' married life in Westminster during the height of the Atlantic slave trade, and when slavery was still legal in England, all the more noteworthy. The fact that Ignatius led a public life – chatting with customers at the counter or the shop-door, discoursing about aesthetic theories or the latest West End show with artists, writing letters to newspapers – makes the unguarded, familial episodes in his letters all the more endearing. There's a dazed intoxication in the letter he writes to a female friend on the afternoon his wife had given birth: 'she has been very unwell for this month past – I feel myself a ton lighter: – In the morning I was crazy with apprehension – and now I talk nonsense thro' joy.'[109] Recounting his daughter Marianne's birthday, he observed – proudly, wistfully – how Mary was 'queen of the day, invited two or three young friends – her breast filled with delight unmixed with cares – her heart danced in her eyes – and she looked the happy mortal'.[110] Delighting in the progress of his only son, William, Sancho puts aside his usual verbal anticry and marvels that 'He is the type of his father – fat – heavy – sleepy'. Later he rejoices in Billy's teething and taking his first few steps.

But the joy is tempered with anxiety: Sancho is in his late forties and knows his health is deteriorating rapidly. He fears he won't be around much longer and becomes even more apprehensive about his children: 'The girls are rampant well – and Bill gains something every day. – The rogue is to excess fond of me – for which I pity him – and myself more.' In the earlier letter recounting Billy's first steps, Sancho wondered if he should 'live to see him at man's estate' and prayed that 'God's grace should [. . .] ably support him through the quick-sands, rocks, and shoals of life'.[111] His fears and fretting take on a special piquancy given the appalling circumstances of his parents' deaths: 'Say much for me to your good father and mother – in the article of respect thou canst not exaggerate – Excepting conjugal, there are no attentions so tenderly heart-soothing as the parental.'[112]

Most moving are Sancho's attempts to ignore the threat of racial contumely and to treat his children to the sights and smells of London. One evening 'three great girls – a boy – and a fat old fellow' eschew travelling over Westminster Bridge and, more excitingly, go by boat to New Spring Gardens, near Lambeth Palace. Temporarily liberated from the anxieties of commerce, far away from the stench, fogs and clatter of the capital's busy streets – which constituted the only metropolis most black Londoners would ever know – the Sanchos luxuriated in the August sunshine: '[they were] as happy and pleas'd as a fine evening – fine place – good songs – much company – and good music could make them. – Heaven and Earth! – how happy, how delighted were the girls!'[113]

They rarely enjoyed such simple pleasures as these. Unlike the legions of wealthy Europeans who toured England during the eighteenth century and visited such architectural and arboreal delights as Bath, Corpus Christi College, Oxford, and Blenheim Palace, Sancho's family could not afford regular excursions. Nor did they want to be objects of scrutiny for passers-by: the London mob looked 'on foreigners in general with contempt'.[114] A letter of Sancho's describes a day out at Vauxhall Gardens; as his family returned home, he says, they 'were gazed at – followed, &c. &c. – but not much abused'.[115] Eager not to bite back and create the kind of tension that might put his wife and children in danger, Sancho even refrained from the brusque wit that his friend William Stevenson later recalled him deploying on their ambles about the city:

We were walking through Spring-gardens-passage [near Charing Cross], when, a small distance from before us, a young Fashionable said to his companion, loud enough to be heard, 'Smoke Othello!' This did not escape my Friend Sancho; who, immediately placing himself across the path, before him, exclaimed with a thundering voice, and a countenance which awed the delinquent, 'Aye, Sir, such Othellos you meet with but once in a century,' clapping his hand upon his goodly round paunch. 'Such Iagos as you, we meet with in every dirty passage. Proceed, Sir!'[116]

The vague fear Sancho felt as he gazed at his children dangling at his knees and playing by his puffed-up ankles becomes more palpable when he talks of 'Dame' Anne: 'If a sigh escapes me, it is answered by a tear in her eye. – I oft assume a gaiety to illume her dear sensibility with a smile – which twenty years ago almost bewitched me.'[117] He sauced and flirted with his female correspondents, but his love for Anne never dwindled. It intensified in the face of his increasing enfeeblement. Caught up as we are in the gathering momentum of his death, the last few letters he wrote are impossibly moving:

> I am now (bating the swelling of my legs and ancles) much mended – air and exercise is all I want – but the fogs and damps are woefully against me. – Mrs Sancho [. . .] reads, weeps, and wonders, as the various passions impel.[118]

A week before his death, 'Mrs Sancho, who speaks by her tears, says what I will not pretend to decypher.'[119] It's an exhilarating moment in black English literature: here is a rare assertion of passion, mutual dependence and intimacy between a formerly enslaved husband and his wife. It's also a chastening moment: Sancho is about to die; the domestic joy these letters reveal would not be narrated again for over 150 years. The more one reads the *Letters*, the more one becomes aware of the existence of two Ignatius Sanchos. The first is a public man – he writes to the press, dines with leading artists of the day, discourses on cultural issues. The other Sancho is chafed by poverty and domestic grief, deems himself friendless, is confused and angered by the sense of a society spinning out of control.

It's the first Sancho who has attracted the attention, seized the imagination of historians and writers. This is hardly surprising. Who could resist the anomalous allure of a fleshy black Falstaff who was born aboard a slave ship but ended his life hobnobbing with the likes of Sterne and Garrick? Nor is this version of Sancho wholly wrong. After all, many of the letters show his keenness for staying abreast of topical affairs. He rejoiced in the acquittal of Jane Butterfield who had been charged with poisoning her benefactor. His politics – conservative by today's orthodoxies – shine through in his exultation that 'the Queen, God bless her! safe; – another Princess – Oh the cake and caudle! – Then the defeat of Washintub's army – and the capture of Arnold and Sulivan with seven thousand prisoners.'[120]

As well as reading and gossiping about the antics of rich and famous people, Sancho socialized with some of them. Gainsborough's friend, John Henderson, known as the 'Bath Roscius', pressed Sancho to see him perform in *Henry V*. Another friend bought him a box ticket so that they might see Henderson's *Richard III*; after the show they dined with Garrick, 'where goodnature and good-sense mixed itself with the most cheerful welcome'.[121] The composer and violinist, Felice Giardini, sent him tickets; he passed them on to a friend so that he might 'judge of fiddlers' taste and fiddlers' consequence in our grand metropolis'.[122] Such friendships often had financial benefits: George Cumberland was so pleased by Sancho's response to his 'Tale of Cambambo' that he told his brother, 'I shall like him as long as I live [. . .] In the mean time as he is a grocer I think it would be proper to buy all my Tea & Sugar of him.'[123] John Thomas Smith, later a Governor of the British Museum, recalled going with Joseph Nollekens to Charles Street to deliver a bust of Sterne.

He observed that Sancho 'spake well of art' and 'was extremely intimate' with the painter, Mortimer.[124]

However, there's another side to Sancho's account of life in the capital which is less grand. Though he never sank as low as Gronniosaw, he was by no means rich. Shops in Westminster were charged high rents compared to those in other parts of London. He couldn't always afford to keep his shop heated; the exodus of affluent Londoners to their country residences during the summer left trade alarmingly slack. He wrote once to Spink that

> I am at the present moment – thank fortune! not quite worth ten shillings – pity – cursed foolish pity – is, with as silly wishes, all I have to comfort you with. – Were I to throw out my whole thoughts upon paper, it would take a day's writing, and thou wouldst be a fool to read it.[125]

Finances were often so poor that he relied on his correspondents to send him old quills with which to pen his letters. In December 1779 he unsuccessfully applied to have his grocery act as a post office: 'it would emancipate me from the fear of serving the parish offices – for which I am utterly unqualified through infirmities – as well as complexion'.[126] The final dash gives this last sentence a quiet sting. Though Sancho couched his proposal in a tone of comic amiability – in doing so revealing a keen appreciation of how he was perceived by his fellow Londoners – there's no disguising his terror of having what few savings (and social status) he'd accumulated over the years suddenly wiped out:

> Figure to yourself, my dear Sir, a man of a convexity of belly exceeding Falstaff – and a black face into the bargain – waddling in the van of poor thieves and pennyless prostitutes – with all the supercilious mock dignity of little office – what a banquet for wicked jest and wanton wit.[127]

During these latter years of economic insecurity, Sancho felt London was becoming ever crueller and more amoral: 'Trade is duller than ever I knew it – and money scarcer; – foppery runs higher – and vanity stronger; – extravagance is the adored idol of this sweet town.'[128] Through the course of the *Letters*, he gets increasingly crabby. The city, he feels, has gone to the dogs and he is revolted by the decline in spirituality. As a shopkeeper, Sancho had daily contact with many of the fops he later lambasted. In one of his bleakest and most condemnatory letters, Sancho's belief that 'Trade is at so low an ebb [. . .] we are a ruined people' drives him to an excoriating survey of metropolitan morality:

> The blessed Sabbath-day is used by the trader for country excursions – tavern dinners – rural walks [. . .] The poorer sort do any thing – but go to church – they take their dust in the field, and conclude the sacred evening with riots, drunkenness, and empty pockets: – The beau in upper life hires his whisky and beast for twelve shillings; his girl dressed en militaire for half-a-guinea, and spends his whole week's earnings to look and be thought quite the thing. – And for upper tiptop high life – cards and music are called in to dissipate the chagrin of a tiresome tedious Sunday's evening – The example spreads downwards from them to their domestics; – the laced valet and the livery beau either debauch the maids, or keep their girls – Thus profusion and cursed dissipation fill the prisons, and feed the gallows.[129]

Sancho's outburst seems almost premonitory given the mass chaos that erupted a fortnight later during the Gordon Riots of June 1780 in which around 850 people died. Christopher Hibbert has located the cause of these riots not so much in doctrinal or anti-Catholic sentiment as in a confluence of aristocratic laxity and welled-up plebeian suffering. Sancho was blunter and lashed out at 'the maddest people that the maddest times were ever plagued with'.[130]

His hatred of foppery was influenced by Methodism which enjoined a distrust of ornamentation and anything smacking of Baroque excess. Sancho had converted in 1769 and loved to attend Sunday sermons. He particularly admired Dr Dodd, the preacher at Charlotte Chapel, Pimlico, on whose behalf he appealed – fruitlessly – for clemency after he was sentenced to death for forgery. Such sermons bolstered Sancho's belief in the importance of good works. In a letter written one Sunday evening to John Meheux, he praised that morning's sermonist, Richard Harrison, whose 'whole drift was that we should live the life of angels here – in order to be so in reality hereafter'.[131]

Chaos was the central fact of London life in the eighteenth century. The shopkeeper's life was one of long hours, modest profits, and both short- and medium-term insecurity. Noisy vendors kept Sancho's family awake at night by shrilly advertising late editions of the *Gazette*. Westminster was full of courtyards and alleyways which became no-go zones after dark. Writing a letter late one evening, Sancho was interrupted by a furious knocking at his shop-door. The man responsible had been delivering trunks for a lady when, his attention diverted, a boy he had asked to guard the other trunks in his cart had run off with them.

As in most English households at the time, infant mortality and sudden bereavement frequently afflicted Sancho's family. Personal and political anguish often meshed:

> The republicans teem with abuse, and with King's friends are observed to have long faces – every body looks wiser than common – the cheating shop-counter is deserted, for the gossiping door-threshold – and every half hour has its fresh swarm of lies. – What's to become of us? We are ruined and sold, is the exclamation of every mouth – the moneyed man trembles

for the funds – the land-holder for his acres – the married men for their families, old maids – alas! and old fusty bachelors, for themselves.[132]

Sancho was an ardent royalist who mourned that 'it is too much the fashion to treat the Royal family with disrespect'.[133] He felt further beleaguered by the economic and territorial wars that were breaking out throughout the Empire during the second half of the 1770s. At such fluxy times, Sancho often took refuge in his blackness. Invoking his African birthright seemed to give him a kind of spiritual and intellectual space into which he could retreat from the awfulness of his surroundings:

> Ireland almost in as true a state of rebellion as America. – Admirals quarrelling in the West-Indies – and at home Admirals that do not choose to fight. – The British empire mouldering away in the West – annihilated in the North – Gibraltar going – and England fast asleep [. . .] For my part, it's nothing to me – as I am only a lodger – and hardly that.[134]

Sancho may claim he's only a lodger but the mass of political details he supplied in this letter reveals someone who kept scrupulously up-to-date with contemporary affairs. This isn't the blasé or casually ignorant response of the genuinely detached lodger. More likely, it's the exasperated outcry of one hungry for quietude. Sancho's life had rarely been free from disruption, upheaval, and enforced reversals of fortune. Now, spent and almost decrepit at the end of his life, all he wanted was to be able to look after his family and balance his grocery's books. If he could also indulge in gossiping, or browse through the *Gazette* whilst reclining in his easy chair, occasionally gazing fondly at his wife slicing vegetables at a table and his children playing near the fireplace, then that was as close to happiness as he could imagine.

There may be two Sanchos, but neither one is any less real than the other. An appreciation of either persona – urbanely self-assured, or nervous and indigent – sharpens our understanding of the other. The Sancho who was cultured, exulted in the company of other artists, and possessed sufficient personality to warrant a portrait by Gainsborough, becomes all the more admirable when we see how hard he had to struggle to pursue his artistic interests. He wasn't to the manor born, he never possessed great wealth, writing and composing music had to be subordinated to the demands of retailing. Equally, the quotidian struggles of the tobacconist and tradesman become more fascinating when contrasted with the refined face he exposed to posh society.

Perhaps the defining image of his life in London is to be found in one of the last letters he wrote, three months before his death in December 1780. He'd just attended hustings for the election of two Westminster MPs to the House of Commons where he would have heard speeches given by some of the greatest public figures of the day: Sir George Brydges Rodney, the heroic Rear Admiral of the relief of Gibraltar in 1780; the Honourable Charles James Fox, leader of the Opposition. The venue was packed; emotions and rhetoric ran wild; 'the glorious Fox' was 'the father and school of oratory himself'; proceedings stretched out for over four and a half hours.[135] Here sits Sancho, taking in all the excitement and drama. He was born on a slave ship. Now he holds the franchise – the only black man in the eighteenth century known to have done so. Born in transit thousands of miles away, apparently destined for a short and brutally functional life, he finds himself in Westminster, at the very heart of Empire. He has arrived. He is at the centre. He belongs.

And yet, as the hustings come to a close, and Sancho has voted for Rodney and Fox, he tells his correspondent of how he 'hobbled home full of pain and hunger'.[136] To an onlooker, the sight of a well-dressed, rotund negro limping away from

Westminster hustings, perhaps comparing notes with other members of the audience, perhaps on his own, cursing and wheezing, would have been incongruous and funny. It does have a comedic aspect. But there's also pathos and poignancy. Sancho participates and is present at the great events of his day. Yet it's a struggle – his family is poor; he is famished. His body is falling apart and, though his feet are swollen with gout, he can't afford a carriage in which to go home. He has travelled so far in his life, he can barely hobble any farther. He has trafficked between the worlds of the grocery and of high culture, an enslaved past and a liberated present, the slave ship and the metropolis. He can't stride much farther. Almost at the centre, but not quite, Sancho's experiences foreshadow those of many of the writers who follow him down the centuries.

CHAPTER TWO

Sheer Chandelier

WILLIAM SANCHO – 'Billy' in the *Letters* – was almost as successful as his father. During the 1790s he worked as the librarian of the distinguished botanist Joseph Banks, and in 1803 became the first black publisher in the Western world when he brought out the fifth edition of Ignatius' correspondence. Four years later he also published Voltaire's *La Henriade*.

Another black man to strike it rich was Cesar Picton. Inheriting a legacy of a hundred pounds from a former employer, he added this sum to his own not inconsiderable savings and in 1788 began operating as a coal merchant in Kingston upon Thames. By the time he died in 1836, he was sufficiently wealthy to bequeath a house with a wharf and shops attached, as well as another house with a garden, stables, coach house and two acres of land.[1]

Sancho and Picton are exceptional in two ways – their financial success, and the social distinction they achieved. Most of their fellow black Londoners enjoyed neither. After the spate of books by and about black people that spewed from the printing presses at the height of the Abolitionism debate in the 1780s, references and allusions to them become far less common. Fashions changed and the prosperous classes began to regard negro servants as passé. At Knole there had been a black page – invariably named 'John Morocco' – since the reign of James I; after a house steward had killed the latest John Morocco in a fight in Black Boy's Passage, Chinese replacements were used. The most famous of these was Hwang-a-Tung, renamed Warnoton, who was educated at the grammar school in Sevenoaks and appears in a Reynolds portrait of Knole.[2]

By 1800 there were almost no famous blacks left in London. Ignatius Sancho, Olaudah Equiano, Julius Soubise – all had died, the last ignominiously in a riding accident in Calcutta. Sensationalist accounts of the slave revolts in Haiti from 1791 onwards led to a resurgence in the belief that blacks were bloodthirsty savages. This made it less easy to sentimentalize and patronize them, even if the motives for doing so were humanitarian – as with Thomas Wedgwood's pro-Abolition medallion which showed a kneeling slave in chains with the slogan 'Am I not a man? And a brother?' But the chief reason for the lack of black celebrities was that the number of Africans in the city had begun to shrink. After Parliament abolished the slave trade in 1807, few new blacks were brought to the capital. Those Africans wrenched away to the West Indies to labour on plantation estates were now regarded as commodities far too valuable to be ferried over to England as decorative knick-knacks. Many of the black people who chose to stay in London died of poverty and ill-health. Some went to sea; others moved to different parts of Britain (Equiano was married near Ely in Cambridgeshire, the county where his eldest daughter, Anna Maria, died in 1797; Francis Barber set up home in Lichfield). Some blacks were transported to America or, far more commonly, to Australia. Widespread racial intermarriage led to the steady blanching of the black population. A member of the London City Mission claimed that it would surprise many people

to see how extensively these dark classes are tincturing the colour of the rising race of children in the lowest haunts of this locality: and many of the young fallen females have a visible infusion of Asiatic and African blood in their veins. They form a peculiar class, but mingle freely with the others. It is an instance of depraved taste, that many of our fallen ones prefer devoting themselves entirely to the dark race of men, and [. . .] have infants by them.[3]

Furthermore, the increasing reluctance to bestow upon slaves such demeaning names as Mungo or Pompey means that hundreds, if not thousands, of Africans and Asians still lie undetected in the dusty pages of parish registers.

A small but visible rump of black people did, remain in London. Among the most celebrated of these were the street beggars who attracted disproportionate alms and affection from contemporaries. They tended to be called Jumbo or, yet more commonly, Toby – after Mr Punch's dog. They liked to gather in Covent Garden and Angel-Gardens, though one beggar who stood by a tea warehouse near Finsbury Square in 1813 was reputed, according to a Parliamentary report on mendicity, to have returned to the West Indies with a fortune of about £1500.[4] Some blacks, not least those who played musical instruments or who pretended to be blind, were seen as charming; others less so:

There is one whose real name I do not know, but he goes by the name of Granne Manoo; he is a man who, I believe, is scarcely out of gaol three months in the year; for he is so abusive and vile a character, he is very frequently in gaol for his abuse and mendicity; he is young enough to have gone to sea, but I believe he has been ruptured, consequently they will not take him. I have seen him scratch his legs about his ancles, to make them bleed; and he never goes out with shoes. That is the man that collects the greatest quantity of shoes and other habiliments; for he goes literally so naked, that it is almost disgusting for any person to see him in that situation.[5]

The most famous mendicant was Billy Waters. Born in America, he lost his leg in a maritime accident, and was forced to take to the streets around Covent Garden to support himself and his family. Success was instant; sporting a ribbon-decked cocked hat and feathers, a smile rarely leaving his face, he would sing so mellifluously (signature tune 'Kitty will you marry me./Kitty will you cry') and clowned with such skill that he was known as the 'Ethiopian Grimaldi'. Sometimes he would jazz up his performances outside the Adelphi Theatre in the Strand by kicking away his wooden leg and dancing around on the spot. His fans were legion and he was featured in Pierce Egan's best-selling *Life in London*. For W.T. Moncrieff's stage adaptation of the book, Waters was asked to play himself – this time inside the Adelphi. He was elected King of the Beggars by his fellow blackbirds. He was also made into a Staffordshire pottery figure, as part of the 'English Characters' series. His celebrity outstripped his financial success. He liked his gin and died in the workhouse in 1823. Covent Garden was brought to a standstill the day his funeral cortège passed through. Mourners included his friend and stage opposite African Sal, a legless man on a wheeled trolley, and Billy's young son who knocked back one bottle of liquor after another. A broadsheet published after his death summarized his life:

> Billy endeavoured up to the period of his illness to obtain for a wife and two children what he termed an honest living by the scraping of cat-gut by which he amassed a considerable portion of browns (halfpence) at the West-end of the town, where his hat and feathers with his peculiar antics excited much mirth and attention. He was obliged prior to his death to part with his old friend, the fiddle, for a trifling sum at the pawnbrokers. His wooden pin had twice saved him from the Tread-Mill. He lost his leg in his Majesty's Service, for which he received a pension. Every child in London knew him.[6]

BILLY WATERS.

Another popular figure was Joseph Johnson. Injury had forced him to retire from his job as a merchant seaman but he was refused a pension or parish relief and was forced on to the streets. He cadged lifts to rural villages and to market towns such as Romford or St Albans where his tatty cloth cap was soon filled with pennies from farmers delighted by his renditions of such patriotic tunes as 'The British Seaman's Praise' or 'The Wooden Walls of Old England'. There, and at Tower Hill in East London, he drew on the repertoire of sea shanties he had sung below deck with his fellow sailors (now without a tankard of ale in hand to jolly up affairs). Johnson's particular genius was to come up with the idea of building a model of the ship *Nelson* which he fastened to the cap he wore. This allowed him, 'by a bow of thanks, or a supplicating inclination to a drawing-room window, [to] give the appearance of sea-motion'.[7] All who saw him giggled and were enchanted. They were also reminded of his itinerancy, of the fact that he was a stranger much of whose life had been spent in the 'grey vault' of the Atlantic where so many of his countrymen perished during the slave trade.

Black beggars, then, were entertainers of a sort. They turned the pathos of their skin and their poverty into a visual spectacle from which they could profit. Their popularity and the affection in which they were held encouraged many white Londoners to black up as minstrels to earn a penny. According to the chronicler of London's underclasses, Henry Mayhew, by the early 1850s no more than one in fifty of the black buskers singing in the city hailed from Africa or the Caribbean: they were white locals who had frizzed their hair and blacked up the better to win the attention of passers-by.'[8]

Other blacks in nineteenth-century London were performers of a more conventional type. Chief among them were the bare-knuckle boxers who trickled in from America. Perhaps the most famous of these was Bill Richmond. Born in New York in 1763, he was brought over to Yorkshire as a fourteen-year-old by General Earl Percy, later Duke of Northumberland. Here he trained as a cabinetmaker before coming to London as a journeyman. He also took up boxing. During the first decade of the nineteenth century he could regularly be seen fighting whipmakers and coachmen in Blackheath, Kilburn, Wimbledon and Golders Green.[9] His most celebrated bout was against Tom Cribb, later

Etch'd Published as the Act directs
December 31 1815
by John Thomas Smith, N.º 8 Chandos Street Covent Garden

the champion of England. He lacked stamina and was beaten in a fight that lasted ninety minutes. Later, with the help of his wife's savings, he became landlord of the Horse and Dolphin pub near Leicester Square. He also exhibited his fistic skills at the Olympic Pavilion and Regency Theatres, and ran a boxing academy at which one of his pupils was William Hazlitt.[10] He died near the Haymarket in 1829.

Blacks could also be found tumbling and gyrating at circuses across the city, where they performed as acrobats, dancing girls and French-horn players. Here they contributed to the spectacle of novelty and exotic glamour, to the feeling that for one exhilarating evening the world was turned upside down – racially as well as gymnastically. Did dazzled audiences conflate these exuberant negroes with those beasts alongside whom they starred? Harriet Ritvo has argued that the representation of black people and zoo animals (a growing number of whom were being shipped to London) was remarkably similar:

> Zoo pets represented not Britain, but their native territories, which were invariably British colonies in Africa and Asia, and never colonies which, like Canada and Australia, had signified European populations. It is probably no accident that they were often accompanied by exotic human attendants who [. . .] were presented in the press as equally curious if not equally lovable.[11]

The exhibited creatures were often likened to human beings. Bartholomew Fair posters trumpeted orang-utans as 'Ethiopian Savages' or 'Negro Men of the Woods'.[12]

One of the most famous black performers was Pablo Fanque (1796–1871). Born William Darby in Norwich, he went on to become an equestrian, acrobat, rope-walker, and later a circus proprietor. He toured extensively in northern England, where stories about his achievements were passed down from generation to generation. The Beatles allude to him in 'Being for the Benefit of Mr Kite!' on *Sgt. Pepper's Lonely Hearts Club Band* (1967):

> There will be a show tonight on trampoline
> The Hendersons will all be there
> Late of Pablo Fanque's Fair – what a scene
> Over men and horses hoops and garters
> Lastly through a hogshead of real fire!

Fanque appeared at Astley's Amphitheatre in February 1847 where his talent was widely plaudited. 'Mr Pablo Fanque is an artiste of colour' stated the *Illustrated London News*, 'and his steed [. . .] we have not only never seen surpassed, but never equalled.'[13]

There were other black circus performers of note: Alexander William Beaumont, known as 'The African Lion King', wore a coat made from leopard skin and died at the age of twenty-seven in 1895 after being mauled by his favourite lion 'Hannibal', at the Agricultural Hall in Islington; George Christopher, whose father used to balance cartwheels on the streets of London, christened himself 'Herr Christoff', and became one of the finest ropedancers in the world.

Celebrity did not guarantee financial security. Performers grew frail and ended up destitute. Tightrope-walker Carlos Trower, also known as 'The African Blondin', died at the age of forty in 1889. Two months earlier his wife wrote to *The Era* appealing for help:

My husband has been ill for some time and three weeks ago went quite out of his mind. There are no hopes for his recovery, and he has been removed to Grove Hall Asylum, Bow. I am left with three children unprovided for. If you will mention this I am sure there will be a few friends that will help me.[14]

Not all black people in nineteenth-century London performed freely. There was a longstanding tradition of putting Africans and West Indians on display for the delight and wonder of citydwellers: Amelia Lewsam, 'the White Negro Woman' was exhibited in 1755 at Charing Cross, as was Primrose, the 'Celebrated PIEBALD BOY' at Haymarket in 1789.[15] In 1810 Saartjie Baartman was brought over to England by her Boer keeper. Promising her that she would make a fortune and be allowed to return home after two years, he renamed her the 'Hottentot Venus' and charged visitors two shillings to see her standing in a cage at 225 Piccadilly (where, reputedly, Eros stands today).

Baartman soon became widely known and featured in street ballads and political cartoons. Many of the spectators who flocked to see her noticed that she looked tearful and depressed as she was shunted to and fro across the cage for their benefit. One visitor 'found her surrounded by many persons, some *females*! One pinched her, another walked round her; one gentleman *poked* her with his cane; and one *lady* employed her parasol to ascertain that all was, as she called it, "*nattral*".[16] Baartman's humiliations never ceased. She was later displayed in Paris where, upon her death in 1815, not only was her body dissected, but plaster casts and wax moulds were made of her genitals and anus. Replicas of these moulds were presented to the Royal Academy of Medicine. Baartman's skeleton and brain were also preserved and, until the decision in early 2002 by the French senate to return her remains to South Africa, could be seen together with a plaster cast of her body at the Musée de L'Homme in Paris.[17]

In such cases two ideas about the nature of black people were crucial. First, the assumption that Africans were simply not human, which legitimized their ill-treatment as well as their enslavement. Secondly, the fact that blacks were not regarded as 'one of us' permitted them to be seen as mute and passive vehicles for the diversion and delectation of white Londoners. Blacks who, it was thought, lacked the powers of rationality, computation or, indeed, agency, were reduced to the status of spectacles. They became living, breathing, and, in Baartman's case, steatopygous incarnations of the cabinets of curiosities so popular during the eighteenth and nineteenth centuries.

Black people, whether descendants of those who had come to London during the eighteenth century or themselves recent arrivals from Central Africa and the Caribbean, could also be found living in the portside communities at Shadwell, Limehouse and Poplar. They worked on boats, lifting crates and bales, clearing decks, rolling casks, arranging ropes and sails. Those without regular employment could be found at West India Docks at six in the morning queuing up with hundreds of other men – ex-clerks, discharged sailors, Irish immigrants – for the chance to lug boxes of tea from wharf to warehouse. This state of affairs angered some. A dock-labourer's wife interviewed in John Law's *Out of Work* (1888) cried out, ' "Why should they come here, I'd like to know? London ain't what it used to be; it's just like a foreign city. The food ain't English; the talk ain't English. Why should all of them foreigners come here to take food out of our mouths, and live on victuals we wouldn't give to pigs?" '[18]

Not all blacks found jobs. Those who didn't were likely to be sent to workhouses, the raw and unsentimental nature of whose inhabitants is ably captured by Henry Mayhew and John Binny:

their behaviour was very noisy and disorderly, coarse and ribald jokes were freely cracked, exciting general bursts of laughter; while howls, cat-calls, and all manner of unearthly and indescribable yĕlls threatened for a time to render all attempts at order utterly abortive. At one moment, a lad would imitate the bray of the jackass, and immediately the whole hundred and fifty would fall to braying like him. Then some ragged urchin would crow like a cock; whereupon the place would echo with a hundred and fifty cock-crows! Next, as a negro-boy entered the room, one of the young vagabonds would shout out swe-ee-p; this would be received with peals of laughter, and followed by a general repetition of the same cry. Presently a hundred and fifty cat-calls, of the shrillest possible description, would almost split the ears.[19]

The East End in which blacks lived became synonymous in Victorian times with spiritual degradation. It was a man-trap, a Satanic stronghold, a dumping ground for human flotsam. It wasn't just that the area was blighted by poverty; the colour of its inhabitants encouraged reactionaries to see it as a place of contamination, of moral canker. The problem was one of poor (racial) hygiene. In sensationalist newspaper reports as well as in the accounts of social workers, it was seen as a dark zone which needed Christian reclamation just as urgently as those heathen lands thousands of miles away which were being penetrated by explorers and missionaries. General Booth, the founder of the Salvation Army, wrote a tract about London entitled *In Darkest England* (1890) that portrayed the East End as a 'lost continent', and argued that, 'The foul and fetid breath of our slums is almost as poisonous as that of the African swamp'.[20] Jack London claimed that, 'No more dreary spectacle can be found on this earth than the whole of the "awful East", with its Whitechapel, Hoxton, Spitalfields, Bethnal Green, and Wapping to the East India Docks. The colour of life is grey

and drab. Everything is helpless, hopeless, unrelieved, and dirty.'[21]
James Greenwood described the area as a 'modern Babylon' and
in *The Wilds of London* (1874) wrote of how

> Everybody addicted to the perusal of police reports, as faithfully
> chronicled by the daily press, has read of Tiger bay, and of the
> horrors perpetrated there – of unwary mariners betrayed to
> that craggy and hideous shore by means of false beacons, and
> mercilessly wrecked and stripped and plundered – of the sangui-
> nary fights of white men and plug-lipped Malays and ear-ringed
> Africans, with the tigresses who swam in the 'bay,' giving it a
> name. 'God bless my soul!' remarks the sitting magistrate.[22]

It wasn't only East End blacks who attracted press attention. The
spotlight fell on lascars too. These were sailors – Bengalis,
Muslims, Malays, Chinese – who sailed to England aboard trading
merchant vessels. Many thousands arrived each year in London
and in other port cities such as Greenock, Hull and Liverpool.
Their voyages had been taxing: poor ventilation and nutrition led
to high mortality rates. Dead lascars were often thrown overboard
in the English Channel.

Upon disembarking, lascars would go looking for somewhere
to lodge until they could find a ship that was heading back to
where they came from. They settled near to the docks in Shadwell,
an area commonly referred to as 'Tiger Bay' or the 'Black Hole
of East London'. Here they lived in dreadful accommodation in
dark alleys, narrow streets and blind courts, areas that were considered off-limits to many of the locals. As many as fifty lascars
could be found sleeping on the floor of a damp and fever-fogged
room. Some slept in tar-boiling sheds in the East India Docks.
The floors were hard, the windows unglazed. One eyewitness
spoke of how he had reeled from the stench and at the appalling
sound of so many ragged-trousered Indians crying out to him for
'blanket', 'more blanket'.[23]

Lascars were sitting targets for opportunistic criminals. Often these criminals were themselves Indians or Chinamen who lured them to their lodging houses with the promise of cheap rents and ethnic camaraderie. The day-to-day running of these houses was left to the proprietors' English mistresses. Here and in nearby tap-houses, much to the chagrin of city missionaries, the lascars would sing, drink, smoke opium, dance and jollify with women. They'd also while away their time listening to native fiddlers and musicians. They wanted a bit of fun as well as forgetfulness. A description of Indians in the Royal Sovereign public-house off Shadwell High Street evokes this well:

> Here they squatted on straw, passed round a hookah and listened to a turbaned musician play the sitar: He sometimes appeared to work himself up to such a pitch of excitement as to seem about to spring on some one, when he would suddenly relax into comparative quietness, to go through the same again. The song recited the adventures of a rajah's son who had been carried away to fairyland, and his unhappy father sent messengers everywhere to find him, but without success, till the jins and fairies, after he had married one of them, escorted him back to his father's house.[24]

If contemporary accounts are to be believed, landlords were simply buttering up their lascar clientele in order to fleece them. Within a short time they were encouraging their guests to run up huge gambling debts and fobbing snide currency upon them. Sooner or later the guileless lascars would end up in Horsemonger-lane Gaol or City Prison, Holloway, among a motley assortment of maimers, larcenists, brothel-keepers, dog-stealers, bestialists, embezzlers, fortune-tellers and pornographic print sellers. The fate of those who avoided jail was hardly much better. Some ended up in workhouses, others in hospital. These, though, were the lucky ones, for, as Joseph Salter put it:

The captain sails off to another land, and the lascar sinks into the stream of human life, and is noticed no more till he is seen shivering in rags, crouched in the angle of the street, and soliciting, in broken English, the beggar's pence, or is found dead by some night policeman in Shadwell.[25]

Small wonder that lascars became a *cause célèbre* in some philanthropic circles. Reverend James Peggs contrasted the public's indifference to their plight to the largesse directed towards black slaves during the Abolitionist campaigns of the previous century. 'Has the Asiatic less claim upon our sympathy, than the Negro?' he asked, before adding, 'we want, for Britain to be loved, and her benevolence to flow "*through every vein of all her empire*." But should it not be most powerful in *the heart of her empire*, the seat of her commerce, and the altars of her metropolitan devotion?'[26] The eventual establishment in 1846 of the Strangers' Home For Asiatics went some way, though by no means all, to alleviating the worst distress.

Some Indians did manage to muster a living of sorts – even if only through begging; a gentleman named Kareem was widely known for the diverting spectacle he made by standing under a railway arch in Westminster with his four young children all of whom were dressed in white garments. It was a fleeting vision of purity in a landscape of blackened murk. Indians were most commonly found peddling scarves and foodstuffs in Petticoat Lane, as well as at St Giles and Whitechapel where they performed as contortionists and tumblers for rapt audiences, swept crossings, vended curry-powder, played 'tum-tum' while spinning round and round, and sold Christian tracts from boards suspended in front of them. An 1848 issue of *Punch* depicted one sweeper at St Paul's churchyard who allegedly demanded a toll for crossing the street. Such contributions to the daily economic life of the city and to the cosmopolitan crosstown traffic were not confined to South

HINDOO TRACT-SELLER.

[*From a Daguerreotype by* BEARD.]

Asians. Reflecting on the changing face of the metropolis during Queen Victoria's reign, one popular historian claimed that many people 'would not like to lose the courteous negro omnibus conductor nor the picturesque black shop porters who now and again help us to realize that London is the capital of an empire which includes many different races of people'.[27]

Grim and inglorious as London was for very many blacks and South Asians during the nineteenth century, it seemed like heaven to black people on the other side of the Atlantic. For those toiling as slaves or indentured labourers in the States and the Caribbean, the English metropolis was but a vague and impossible dream. To be poor and vagrant was a small price to pay for individual liberty. It was a place of escape and comfort, just as Paris was to be for novelists such as Chester Himes, Richard Wright and James Baldwin a century later.

Such sentiments are expressed, albeit fleetingly, in the autobiographies of black American fugitive slaves such as Frederick Douglass's *My Bondage and My Freedom* (1855) and Harriet Jacobs's *Incidents In The Life Of A Slave Girl* (1861). Memoirs like these rarely deal with life in England for more than a few pages at best. They were published to abet American Abolitionism and, consequently, focused on the physical and moral savagery inflicted by Southern plantation owners, as well as on the terrors and hazards slaves faced during their bids for liberty. London, inasmuch as it cropped up at all in the autobiographies of slaves such as Moses Roper or William and Ellen Craft, was a place whose value lay in what it wasn't (Carolina, say, or Virginia) rather than what it was. London was not a city they fled *to*; rather, it was a city *away from* their real homes. If any place was to be romanticized or celebrated, it was the former slave port of Liverpool which was the English city where most fugitive slaves arrived. William Farmer, agent of the Massachusetts Anti-Slavery Society, claimed in his preface to William Wells Brown's memoirs that Liverpool was 'to the hunted negro the Plymouth Rock of Old England'.[28]

Not all writers, however, were insensitive to the freedoms and advantages that metropolitan life offered. Having travelled via Liverpool from New York to London, Harriet Jacobs booked into her lodgings at the Adelaide Hotel and reflected that

> for the first time in my life I was in a place where I was treated according to my deportment, without reference to my complexion. I felt as if a great millstone had been lifted from my breast. Ensconced in a pleasant room, with my dear little charge, I laid my head on my pillow, for the first time, with the delightful consciousness of pure, unadulterated freedom.[29]

William Wells Brown marvelled in his autobiography at the capital's teeming excitement: 'If one wished to get jammed and pushed about, he need go no farther than Cheapside. But every thing of the kind is done with a degree of propriety in London, that would put the New Yorkers to blush.'[30]

Brown, like Douglass and Jacobs, encountered little colour prejudice in London. Sent here because American Abolitionists thought it expedient for the English to meet 'some talented man of colour who should be a living lie to the doctrine of the inferiority of the African race', he was given an enthusiastic reception at The Music Hall in Stone Street and was also elected – 'as a mark of respect to his character' – an honorary member of The Whittington Club whose other members included Charles Dickens and Douglas Jerrold.[31] Brown was buoyed by such friendliness. It freed his tongue and made him more brash. Whilst visiting the Great Exhibition in the Crystal Palace in Hyde Park in 1851, he had an opportunity to compare English and American racial attitudes.

I was pleased to see such a goodly sprinkling of my own countrymen in the Exhibition – I mean coloured men and women – well-dressed, and moving about with their fairer brethren. This, some of our pro-slavery Americans did not seem to relish very well. There was no help for it. As I walked through the American part of the Crystal Palace, some of our Virginian neighbours eyed me closely and with jealous looks, especially as an English lady was leaning on my arm. But their sneering looks did not disturb me in the least. I remained the longer in their department, and criticized the bad appearance of their goods the more.[32]

One of Brown's proudest moments in the capital was on the evening in 1851 when he joined runaway slaves, MPs and Anti-Slavery activists from both sides of the Atlantic to address a packed Hall of Commerce in the City of London where his call for Abolition in the US was greeted with deafening applause.[33] Following the instant success of *Uncle Tom's Cabin*, chapters from which had been published in serial form throughout the summer and autumn of 1851, black speakers were even more of a prize draw on the capital's lecture circuit. At Exeter Hall, in particular, they would recount their life experiences and display the scars and welts from slaveholder lashings before packed houses. Some were advised to tell their stories as simply as possible for fear that excessive eloquence would detract from their 'authenticity'. Indeed, black speakers were often sandwiched between white orators who supplied what were purported to be more sophisticated political and theoretical perspectives.[34]

In the metropolis black people could also see in person those grand and penetrating thinkers who blithely dismissed them in print as savage and degenerate niggers. Returning from the Crystal Palace by bus, Brown caught sight of Thomas Carlyle who wore upon his countenance a forbidding and disdainful form, that seemed to tell one that he thought himself better than those about him. His dress did not indicate a man of high rank; and had we been in America, I would have taken him for a Ohio farmer. [. . .] As a writer, Mr Carlyle is often monotonous and extravagant. He does not exhibit a new view of nature, or raise insignificant objects into importance, but generally takes commonplace thoughts and events, and tries to express them in stronger and statelier language than others.[35]

Though his resources were limited, Brown managed to range across more of the capital than most of the black seamen, students and musicians who flitted through London during the nineteenth century. He spent ten days sight-seeing in September 1850, with two of those days at the British Museum alone. He embraced both high and low culture – visiting the National Gallery and the Tower of London as well as applauding the Punch and Judy show in Exeter Street off the Strand. 'No metropolis in the world presents such facilities as London for the reception of the Great Exhibition,' he gushed. 'Every one seems to feel that this great Capital of the world, is the fittest place whenever they might offer homage to the dignity of toil.'[36]

Wells Brown wasn't the only black writer in the Victorian era to attack the ignorant prejudices of leading public figures. Perhaps the most heroic counterblast, almost completely unknown today, came from the pen of J.J. Thomas in his acid polemic *Froudacity* (1889). The target of his derision was the famous historian James Anthony Froude. A brilliant speaker whose lecture tours attracted huge audiences, a prolific journalist and a writer whose books, like those of his friend Thomas Carlyle, sold tens of thousands of copies, Froude rose to become Regius Professor of Modern History at Oxford in 1892.

His work celebrated the buccaneering hardiness of English mariners and eulogized the Elizabethan age's commercial entrepreneurialism, its pioneering individualism. His upbeat rhetoric struck a chord with Victorian audiences basking in the knowledge that maps were painted ever pinker; that with every passing decade the Empire was growing bigger, broader, faster. Froude also produced accounts of his voyages including, in 1888, a typically forthright volume entitled *The English in the West Indies*, which expressed his disgust about the islands becoming 'nigger warrens' and lapsing into barbarism.[37]

Out in Trinidad the book was read by a local schoolmaster called John Jacob Thomas. Born in 1840, he had spent most of his life in rickety classrooms trying to teach restless agricultural workers in return for little glory or pay. Along the way he had taught himself Greek, Latin, French and Spanish. More unusually, and without linguistic training, he learned Creole and in 1869 produced a groundbreaking book on the language, *The Theory and Practice of Creole Grammar*. It won him, in 1873, election to the Philological Society.

Now, twenty years later, bedridden by rheumatism, with no institutional support and precious few resources, he wrote a devastating critique of the professor's scholarship. He labelled Froude a 'negrophobic political hobgoblin' and accused him of methodological slackness (conversing chiefly with the Anglo-West Indian communities, from whose balcony windows he would gaze down on the sable throngs), lechery (lionizing black women, while claiming black men were truculent layabouts), and gross political naivety (he ridiculed Froude's assertion that West Indian negroes enjoyed 'no distinction of colour' under British rule).[38] In 1888 Thomas came to London to study at the British Museum. He was short of money and his health was still poor. A previous visit had had to be abandoned because of sickness. He lived in Guildford Street, off Russell Square, near enough to the library to be able to visit it each day in order to examine etymological texts unavailable in the Caribbean. He also polished his book on Froude only to discover that publishers feared it lacked commercial appeal and wanted him to raise his own subscription list. This he did. Shortly afterwards, in September 1889, he died of tuberculosis at King's College Hospital.

Froudacity attracted scant attention when it first came out. It did little to topple the Oxford historian off his self-constructed pedestal. In that sense, but only in that sense, it was a failure. Now it reads as a heroic but doomed effort, well in advance of twentieth-century anti-colonialist historiography, to retard the flow of metropolitan propaganda about non-white people. That it was written by one enfeebled, impecunious Trinidadian without the kind of research budgets or institutional backing that many academics today enjoy, makes it yet more admirable. Its wit, lucidity and venom have not been surpassed.

Published a few decades earlier, the autobiography of another West Indian, Mary Prince, had more success than Thomas's history book. Prince was born around 1788 at Brackish-Pond in Bermuda on the farm where her mother was a household slave. They were sold together and for the next twelve years Mary lived a blissful life, partly because her new owner's daughter treated her as a pet, leading 'me about by the hand, and [calling] me her little nigger', and partly because 'I was too young to understand rightly my condition as a slave'.[39] Her happiness was soon cut short. Around 1800 she was sold again, this time to a couple who regularly abused her and flogged her with cowskins. Such mistreatment continued for many years, even after she had been bought by a new owner who took her to the Turks Islands. By 1814 she was a washerwoman for the Wood family in Antigua: during the day she was underfed and overworked so ferociously that she developed rheumatism and became lame; by night she was forced to sleep in a bug-infested and verminous outhouse. The floggings and lashings didn't abate for years. Nonetheless, this was the period in which she began to attend the Moravian Church, members of whose congregation taught her to read; she also met her husband, a carpenter named Daniel James; and, when her master and mistress were away, sold provisions to ship captains in order to save up enough money to buy her freedom.

In 1828 the Woods came to England and brought Prince along with them to look after their son who was to be educated here. Prince was delighted. She, like later writers such as V.S. Naipaul and Fred D'Aguiar, saw the metropolis as a healing zone, a place where the torments of Caribbean servitude would cease. The capital offered the possibility of both psychological and physical release: not only had she heard that her master might free her after their ship had docked, but she also hoped to have her rheumatism cured.

Predictably no medicine was forthcoming. Instead,

the rheumatism seized all my limbs worse than ever, and my body was dreadfully swelled. When we landed at the Tower, I shewed my flesh to my mistress, but she took no great notice of it [. . .] I grew worse, and could not stand to wash. I was then forced to sit down with the tub before me, and often through pain and weakness was reduced to kneel or to sit down on the floor, to finish my task.[40]

Prince's rheumatism hampered her mobility. The plenitudes and freedoms of London suddenly receded from view. It wasn't only her aching limbs that prevented her from roustabouting through the city: Mrs Wood forced her to clean piles of clothes so mountainous that even her English colleagues complained on her behalf. Prince's health grew worse, yet her mistress continued to scream and bawl. She was constantly threatened with expulsion from Leigh Street, but 'I was a stranger, and did not know one door in the street from another, and was unwilling to go away'.[41] After repeated humiliations she decided to leave and, with the help of Moravian missionaries based in Hatton Garden, was taken in by the family of Mr Mash, the Woods' shoe-blacker. After a bitter winter during which her rheumatism became more acute, Prince's fortunes improved. Charitable Quakers offered her money and warm clothing. She became a charwoman to a Mrs Forsyth who had spent time in the West Indies and was fond of blacks. Finally, following overtures to one of London's Anti-Slavery offices, she joined the household of the Pringles, a God-fearing couple who accompanied her to church and were happy to help when she suggested that her life story should be published.

Prince, like the first black English male writer Gronniosaw, required an amanuensis to take down her autobiography. Like him, and also Equiano, most of her narrative deals with her vicissitudinal life and the assaults she suffered on foreign islands. Yet Prince's limited record of her experiences in London also foreshadows many of the accounts written by black women over the ensuing 150 years. There are few references to specific districts or landmarks within London – the key site for Prince is domestic, that of the Wood household. Staying out of trouble there takes up most of her time. She has little energy for flexing her topographical imagination; escaping her Leigh Street imprisonment is her only goal. Her interest in geography is confined to the question of whether she is better off behind or beyond the threshold of her master's home. Mrs Wood exploits Prince's lack of metropolitan street wisdom in an effort to stop her leaving: if she were to go out, the story went, the people would rob her, and then turn her adrift. Prince leaves the house as an act of desperation: she does not cruise down the Thames, go sharking for men in taverns or alleyways, or savour London's pleasure gardens. Having to make her own way through the capital's open spaces is, for her, a source of shame. Even leaving her wicked owners she deems a kind of social failure. This is compounded by her reliance on the charity and generosity of other Londoners such as Mash, the Quakers and the Anti-Slavery Society.

Prince's autobiography was mired in controversy almost as soon as it was published in 1831. The Methodist Thomas Pringle assured his readers that the book was not only true but that it was 'essentially her own, without any material alteration farther than was requisite to exclude redundancies and gross grammatical errors'.[42] Yet the text's hints regarding the sexual harassment Prince's master may have meted out to her are so coyly brief that it's difficult not to believe that, at the very least, religious prudishness may have induced a degree of self-censorship.

The autobiography was successful and two further editions appeared within a year: the postscript to the first of these referred to Prince's growing blindness as a way of inducing 'the friends of humanity to promote the more zealously the sale of this publication'; an appendix to the final edition included a letter from Mrs Pringle to the Secretary of the Birmingham Ladies' Society for Relief of Negro Slaves which confirmed that the floggings Prince had suffered as a slave had left her body scarred and lacerated.[43]

In November 1831 James McQueen, a prominent defender of the West India interest and editor of the *Glasgow Courier*, wrote an article for *Blackwood's Magazine* in which he defended the Wood family whom, he claimed, had treated Prince as 'a confidential and favourite servant'. Only when the 'prowling anti-colonial fry in London quickly got about her', he alleged, had she started to malign her beneficent owners.[44] McQueen's plantocratic sympathies are evidenced by his assertion that if Pringle were proved to have libelled the Woods, then the Government 'must tell the country that the West India colonists are no longer to be persecuted as they have been by ignorance, and by zeal without knowledge'.

Pringle successfully sued the publisher of *Blackwood's* for libel in February 1832. He in turn was sued a year later by Prince's former owner, John Wood, who claimed that accounts of his cruelty had been fabricated. Pringle was unable to produce witnesses to back up his claims and Wood won the case by default. At this latter trial Prince herself was briefly called as a witness. A report described her as 'a negress of very ordinary features' who 'appears to be about thirty-five years of age'.[45] After this sighting, however, she disappears from view altogether.

Mary Seacole – arguably the most famous black woman in Britain before Winifred Atwell and Shirley Bassey – was also forced to rely on handouts and *noblesse oblige* on a number of occasions during her life. Seacole, often referred to as the black Florence Nightingale, was born around 1805 in Kingston, Jamaica. Like Robert Wedderburn, with whom in other respects she had almost nothing socially or politically in common, she had 'good Scotch blood coursing' in her veins and was proud to call herself a Creole.[46] Her father was a soldier; her mother kept a boarding house and was 'an admirable doctress'.[47] Seacole herself soon developed an interest in nursing and in 1851 helped her brother Edward open a hotel in Panama. Returning to Jamaica two years later she tended victims of yellow fever before deciding to head for the Crimea where she hoped to help the beleaguered British army.

Rebuffed by the military and medical authorities in London, she went out on her own accord as a sutler and set up a British Hotel between Balaklava and Sebastopol where she cared for sick and maimed troops. Her bravery and devotion were enskied by W.H. Russell in a despatch to *The Times* dated 14 September 1855, and he later contributed a preface to her 1857 autobiography, the first to be wholly authored by a black woman in England (Prince's had been transcribed by the minor poet Susanna Strickland). It was published to raise funds following her bankruptcy at the end of the Crimean War.

If the financial dependency into which Seacole sank following her return from the Crimea aligns her with Mary Prince and the hapless anonyms who comprised the black female population in London up until the second half of the twentieth century, there are, equally, other features which make her stand out. The most obvious is her nursing prowess. Seacole came to London to get governmental permission to heal rather than to be healed. Literate, proud of her mixed blood, and coming from a financially stable background, she didn't suffer from cultural cringe and didn't think of London as a sanatorium to lint and bandage her contused colonial psyche. Nor did she view it as a place to start her life afresh, a city in which she could satisfy those emotional and intellectual desires which a repressive and brutalized colonial adolescence had prevented her from fulfilling. Seacole claimed to have a 'roving inclination' and had already travelled widely before she arrived in England.[48] She possessed medical skills and was confident in them. By coming to London she was not gingering up to the starting line of a new and more meaningful life. For her, the city's value was largely functional. It would facilitate and rubberstamp her desire to help those British troops in whose well-being she took as great an interest as her 'patriotic lady' of a sister who, according to Trollope, wouldn't 'abandon the idea that beefsteaks and onions, and bread and cheese and beer [were] the only diet proper for an Englishman'.[49]

Almost nothing is known about the final two decades of Seacole's life other than that she left over £2500 when she died in 1881. Even this biographical shard is very revealing. For though Seacole returned from the Crimea financially ruined, it was only a temporary setback. In 1856 *The Times* printed several letters from potential benefactors who wished to pay off her debts. In July 1857 a four-night Grand Military Festival was held at the Royal Surrey Gardens for her benefit. She was awarded four Government medals and a bust of her was carved by Queen Victoria's nephew, Count Gleichen. She lived for long stretches in the affluent West End and told a friend that when she visited the Princess of Wales whose masseuse she was, 'I go up to her private sitting room and we sit and talk like the old friends we are.'[50]

Unlike Mary Prince and most of the black women in London during the eighteenth and nineteenth centuries, Seacole's lapses into penury were short-lived and remediable. Like Sancho, whose amplitude of girth she shared, Seacole had the kind of access to the upper strata of metropolitan society normally closed to the washed up (and washing up) working classes such as Prince. Her autobiography was not composed for polemical purposes, unlike those of Gronniosaw, Equiano and Prince. This accounts in large part for the absence of hectoring diatribes in her book. She shared with Sancho a strident patriotism which may strike modern readers as assimilationist:

> I think, if I have a little prejudice against our cousins across the Atlantic – and I do confess to a little – it is not unreasonable. I have a few shades of deeper brown upon my skin which shows me related – and I am proud of the relationship – to those poor mortals whom you once held enslaved, and whose bodies

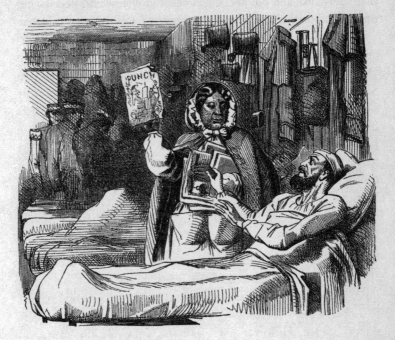

America still owns. And having this bond, and knowing what slavery is; having seen with my eyes and heard with my ears proof positive enough of its horrors – let others affect to doubt them if they will – is it surprising that I should be somewhat impatient of the airs of superiority which many Americans have endeavoured to assume over me?[51]

Yet there were times in London when Seacole feared attitudes towards black people were beginning to resemble those of the Americans. One of the most memorable passages in her autobiography concerns her disappointment upon learning that despite visiting not only Elizabeth Herbert, the Secretary of War's wife, at Belgrave Square, but also many other Government officials, her offer to go to the Crimea as a nursing recruit had been rejected:

> one cold evening I stood in the twilight, which was fast deepening into wintry night, and looked back upon the ruins of my last castle in the air. [. . .] Was it possible that American prejudices against colour had some root here? Did these ladies shrink from accepting my aid because my blood flowed beneath a somewhat duskier skin than theirs? Tears streamed down my foolish cheeks, as I stood in the fast thinning streets; tears of grief that any should doubt my motives – that Heaven should deny me the opportunity that I sought. Then I stood still, and looking upward through and through the dark clouds that shadowed London, prayed aloud for help.[52]

The passage heaves with melodrama. While Seacole's memoirs are normally terse and emotionally brisk, here she wallows in her misery. Yet the extract is a useful reminder that all colonial visitors to London need to recognize the possibility that they are there under licence. However enjoyable and equitable the treatment they receive, they always fear that under the froth of social acceptance bubbles a simmering hatred which at any minute might boil over. Writing about her very first visit to London many years before, Seacole recalled

> the efforts of the London street-boys to poke fun at my and my companion's complexion. I am only a little brown – a few shades duskier than the brunettes whom you all admire so much; but my companion was very dark, and a fair (if I can apply the term to her) subject for their rude wit. She was hot-tempered, poor thing! and as there were no policemen to awe the boys and turn our servants' heads in those days, our progress through the London streets was sometimes a rather chequered one.[53]

Both of these incidents, pivoting as they do on Seacole's colour, took place some years before she was lionized by *Punch* and consorted with members of the Royal Family. Without the fame and goodwill that her Crimean War exploits elicited, in the eyes of the London public Seacole was just one more derisible 'fuzzy wuzzy'. Lauded by *The Times* and by thousands of ex-servicemen, Seacole records no slights or slurs after her return from the Crimea. It's her (social) capital that makes the difference – not only in terms of where she can go and live, but also in how people respond to her, how the city, its corridors and drawing rooms of power and prestige, open up to her.

Seacole's autobiography shows how black women didn't all inhabit identical Londons. It might be expected that in the nineteenth century all black women's lives would have been equally miserable. Yet Seacole, unlike Prince or the Hottentot Venus, eventually attained both fame and wealth. She mingled in rarefied social circles. Although she also experienced a degree of privation and some racial distress, unlike many of her 'sisters' she overcame these hurdles to produce a narrative that's often humorous, relatively bereft of polemic and, on occasions such as the one quoted above, literary. She wrote a book the style and subject matter of which fly in the face of the generally accepted picture of what it was possible for a black woman to achieve in early nineteenth-century Britain.

As far back as 1798 the philanthropist Zachary Macaulay had brought around forty children from Sierra Leone to Clapham to be educated. Throughout the nineteenth century philanthropists and missionaries had brought young Africans to the University of London, medical schools in the capital and the Inns of Court. Their goal was to produce a cadre of learned blacks who would return home and devote their lives to converting their countrymen into civilized Christians. The numbers involved surprised William Wells Brown who noted that, 'In an hour's walk through the Strand, Regent, or Piccadilly Streets in London, one may meet half a dozen coloured young men, who are inmates of the various Colleges in the metropolis.'[54] By the 1860s, however, the efficacy of such schemes was being questioned. According to the historian Douglas Lorimer:

> The British rarely found that their schemes for black advancement fulfilled their exaggerated expectations and, rather than question their own vision, they revived the question of the Negro's racial inheritance and often found it wanting. [...] When this association between African descent and lowly social status became more firmly fixed, and was added to the latest suspicions and aversions produced by xenophobia and ethnocentrism, racial attitudes became more rigid and emotive in character, and a new inflexibility and contempt characterized English attitudes to the Negro.[55]

Few black students left accounts of their time in London. Indian students, however, did. Many of them came to the capital hungry with ambition and hoping to attain the qualifications required to join the Indian Civil Service or, indeed, any other serious profession. They studied medicine and engineering, but particularly law. As late as 1907 an India Office study estimated that 380 of the 700 Indian students in Britain resided in London and that 320 of these were based at the Inns of Court.[56] They did not come just to pore over books. They had the scent of power in their nostrils. 'As colonials living on the periphery of the empire Indians are naturally attracted to the metropolis,' one student wrote. 'The English are the ruling people in India and naturally ambitious Indian youth want to come to the centre of the life of these people, just as they used to go to Delhi in olden days.'[57] Their behaviour attracted much adverse comment back home in India and helped to create a largely negative image of metropolitan culture. S. Satthianadhan claimed that

> it is most imprudent to send young Indian lads to live in that great metropolis without proper friends to take care of them. I have known young men who have been leading the most reckless lives, squandering their money, and giving in easily to all the debasing temptations of the place, instead of making the best use of the opportunities as students.[58]

According to Behramji Malabari, the average Indian student in London 'learns to smoke, drink, gamble, to bet, and to squander his substance in worse ways. The life "in apartments," that he has often to accept, does not offer any relief from this round of vulgar dissipation.'[59] In partial confirmation of this point, Mohandas Gandhi recounted in his *Autobiography* (1927) how he strove to become a gentleman while studying for the Bar between 1888 and 1891. He frittered away his money on expensive chimney hats and Bond Street evening suits as well as lessons in dancing and French.[60] A fellow Indian who met him in Piccadilly Circus during this period dismissed him as 'a nut, a masher, a blood – a student more interested in fashion and frivolities than in his studies'.[61] Some English commentators, too, weren't enamoured of Indians in London. C. Hamilton McGuiness barked: 'It is positively nauseating to see them on the tops of buses, in the streets, at the theatres and almost everywhere one goes – coloured men and white women. These women have not the slightest idea of what grave risks they are running.'[62] Elsewhere, landlords and housekeepers were routinely portrayed as grasping and exploitative whilst life in lodgings was held to be solitary and secluded.[63]

Such rhetoric contrasts sharply with that of Harriet Jacobs and William Wells Brown. They saw London as a uniquely moral and civilized city, a joyous corrective to the unremitting degradation they faced back home. Black English writers of the eighteenth century also envisioned London as a giant pillar of virtue. In contrast, a number of Indian travelogues reveal that it wasn't only students who risked soul-pollution by living in London – even the most respectable gentlemen who journeyed there were thought to be vulnerable.

The first major travelogue was written by the Lucknow-born Mirza Abu Taleb Khan. He stayed in London during 1800 and 1801 during which time he was known as 'The Persian Prince'. His book, published in 1814, began a tradition of wealthy or well-connected subcontinentals describing at considerable length their stays in the imperial metropolis. Their accounts varied in length: from the hundred pages of T.B. Pandian's *England To An Indian Eye* (1897) to Khan's three-volume opus. Some – such as Behramji Malabari's *The Indian Eye On English Life* (1893) – focused almost exclusively on London. More commonly, as in T.N. Mukharji's *A Visit To Europe* (1889), portraits of France, Germany and Italy were also included; these visits were the Indian equivalent of the eighteenth-century Grand Tour. Publication in diary form was common – Jehangeer Nowrojee and Hirjeebhoy Merwanjee's *Journal of a Residence of Two Years and A Half In Great Britain* (1841) and K.C. Sen's *Diary In England* (1894) are examples. Romesh Chunder Dutt's *Three Years In Europe* (1896) was crammed with extracts from some of the many letters he'd sent to friends in India from England, whilst Malabari's book was as much waspish social commentary as it was travelogue. Taken collectively their accounts challenge the widespread view that travel writing is synonymous with whiteness – echoed below by the Indian critic and novelist Pankaj Mishra.

It is worth remembering here that very few writers from India or the Caribbean have published travel books. This is probably so because while a novel can be written anywhere, the modern travel book is a primarily metropolitan genre: part of the knowledge that a powerful culture accumulates about its less privileged others or adversaries in the world. It is usually difficult to write one without the support of a trade publisher and there is also the problem of tone and perspective. The exuberant persona of, say, Bruce Chatwin is not easily worn by a writer from the colonies, no matter how anglicized he is; the certainties of the great power and the wealth of the West that protected Chatwin on his adventures are not available to him.[64]

The authors in this chapter were, to say the least, 'respectable'. The Rajah of Kolhapoor was a descendant of Sivajee, founder of the Mahratta Empire; Bhagvat Sinh Jee was Thakore Saheb of Gondal; Bhawani Singh was Raj Rana Bahadur of Jhalawar; Malabari edited the *Indian Spectator*; Jhinda Ram was Pleader at the Chief Court of the Punjab; even the students Nowrojee and Merwanjee were, respectively, son and nephew of the master builder of the Honourable East India Company's dockyard in Bombay. Such social standing distinguishes these writers from those discussed earlier. They weren't dragged to London against their wishes; they didn't flee there to escape slavery; unlike Wells Brown, they weren't even required to tour the nation delivering Abolitionist broadsides. Nor did they require scholarships or subsidies: they paid for themselves and came here out of curiosity and in pursuit of pleasure.

Though they may not have encountered quite as much resistance back home as the students, still the impression abided: London was a moral abattoir. Gandhi's family told him that the food was terrible there, that he was bound to turn to meat, cigars, drink and shameless dress.[65] Ramakrishna delayed coming for forty years after his mother lamented that he would become 'a "walking corpse", a living dead body, a being socially and religiously lost to her, to our family and clan'.[66] Crossing the *Kâlâpani* (the black waters) was thought to breed discontent. It also implied a rejection of caste, an embarrassment at one's birthright. Some authors shared this fear that things would never be the same after leaving for England: T.N. Mukharji worried that, 'The elders of the family on whose bosom I prattled in my infancy will shun me as an unclean thing'.[67]

This anxiety about London spoliating its visitors stems from the puritanical rigidity that characterizes the upper ranks of the Indian caste system where all interaction with outsiders is viewed with suspicion. Indians who came to London in the nineteenth century were less inclined to revere the metropolis than subsequent writers such as Mulk Raj Anand, V.S. Naipaul and Dom Moraes. Those three, along with the Caribbean novelist George Lamming, were to a greater or lesser extent disappointed, but, unlike Mukharji or Ramakrishna, they did at least arrive in London eager to believe that the city embodied cultural virtue and purity.

Some Indian authors of the Victorian period claimed their travels were pedagogically or philanthropically motivated. Bhawani Singh wrote his book 'primarily for the benefit of my people in Jhalawar, whose ideas of European civilization were of the vaguest'.[68] Chunder Dutt wanted his to 'serve as a guide-book to Indian youths intending to visit Europe'.[69] Mukharji's preface-writer, N.N. Ghose, bluntly stated that the

book inculcates the principle of change in the direction of progress, he and others like him are among the main solvent influ-

ences acting upon a hardened social regime. No nation, left to itself, has improved to any great extent, and whatever tends to bring Indian life and ideas into contact with English, is desirable even more in the interests of India than of England.[70]

Others, meanwhile, wished to be thought of as cultural ambassadors: Nowrojee and Merwanjee hoped 'our humble efforts promote and increase the existing kindly feeling towards the natives of the East in the breast of the British public', whilst Ramakrishna intended to 'promote a sympathetic understanding' between Great Britain and India.[71]

The latter author also claimed that, 'To visit England was the dream of my life', and this trope reappears in Malabari's rhapsody on the 'Land of Freedom, the land of my youthful dreams, which holds so much that is precious to me personally, and so much more that is of greater value to the land of my birth'.[72] Earlier he'd admitted that, 'A trip to London has been my dream for years, a hope long deferred. More, indeed, than wish or hope, it has been a faith with me, to be rewarded in the fulness of time.'[73]

Malabari's dreams, like those of Ramakrishna and nearly all of the Indian students, princes and visitors who came to London throughout the nineteenth century, were realized to glittering effect. These men experienced few hardships or privations. They weren't forced to seek out cheap, dingy lodgings; nor were they shackled by overweening owners. Upon arrival K.C. Sen could afford to move into very expensive rooms in Norfolk Street, Strand. Jhinda Ram did the same, whilst Bhagvat Sinh Jee stayed at the Great Western Hotel. Even those few Indians who switched to insalubrious quarters weren't ostracized by polite society: Mirza Khan lived in Rathbone Place, half of whose inhabitants were courtesans, yet 'my friends had the condescension and goodness to overlook this indiscretion; and not only was I visited there by the first characters in London, but even ladies of rank, who had never in their lives before passed through this street, used to call in their carriages at my door'.[74]

Such 'condescension' is unsurprising. Indians were rare birds of passage: socially lofty, exotically dressed with fancy headwear, foreign-tongued and adhering to impressively ancient religious codes, they didn't have much in common with those filthy and downwardly mobile lascars who were the only other Asiatics most Londoners might previously have come across. According to his biographer, K.C. Sen was 'lionized' by London female society during his stay in the capital during 1870. Lionizing, she argues, was 'a recognized pastime of middle-aged women to take up con-

troversial figures and show them off as their own pet discoveries'.[75]
Similarly, Mirza Khan claimed that

> the Nobility vied with each other in their attention to me.
> Hospitality is one of the most esteemed virtues of the English;
> and I experienced it to such a degree, that I was seldom disen-
> gaged. In these parties I enjoyed every luxury my heart could
> desire.[76]

'Hospitality' and 'luxury' aren't words that crop up too often in
this book. Nineteenth-century Indian travellers spent most of their
stays in London being generously pampered. They had no financial problems, and could afford to circulate through the city by
coach, hansom cabs or, in Bhawani Singh's case, by motor car.
Not only did they make regular trips outside the capital – Brighton, Oxford, Manchester, Liverpool and Scotland were common
destinations – but they also ranged freely across London itself.
Each day brought new encounters, fresh vistas, a seemingly endless
conveyor belt of diversions and entertainments. A typical sojourn
in London would include, at the very least, visits to Madame
Tussaud's, St Paul's Cathedral, Hampton Court, the Crystal
Palace, the Houses of Parliament, the Zoological Gardens, the
British Museum, the National Gallery and Westminster Abbey.
Sporting events such as the annual Eton versus Harrow cricket
match at Lord's and the Henley Regatta were savoured as were
theatrical performances: Chunder Dutt acclaimed *The Mikado* the
'finest thing on the stage in London', whilst Bhawani Singh regularly attended the Apollo and Royal Court Theatres.[77] Many books
celebrated the greenery of Regent's Park, St James's Park and
Hyde Park. Nor were the worlds of science and commerce
neglected: Nowrojee and his cousin attended Royal Institution
lectures on Daguerreotype and the Gallery of Practical Science
in Lowther Arcade near Charing Cross, as well as the Poly-

technic Institution, Woolwich Dockyard, Custom House and St Katharine's Docks. In short, London was, as Syed A.M. Shah claimed, 'a place (if not *the* place) of wonders and curiosities, and it is *impossible* to see everything of note in London'.[78] For many of these Indian travellers, the metropolis was a massive fruit bowl which they eyed lasciviously, plucking from it the tastiest, the most succulent fancies. It wasn't the harsh, abysmal hole portrayed by Mayhew, Booth or even Dickens. London wasn't a city they really lived in – it wasn't a place where they worked, scraped, or tussled for bricks and money. Instead they skittered through its most celebrated chambers and drawing rooms, stopping only to sign the visitors' books of royalty, and chatter superficially with other social adepts, before moving on to the next engagement in their crowded itineraries. Their lives, mobile but depthless, busy and unaffiliated, in some ways prefigure those of Kureishi's flexi-sexual metro-bohemians.

Indian travellers were honoured and cherished newcomers to London. Both the black population of the eighteenth century and those lascars who cramped into the East End in the nineteenth century led anonymous and rather fugitive lives. Prisoners of their own misfortunes, they rarely had the money or need to shuffle out of their own smoggy enclaves. Apart from the colour of their skins they had almost nothing in common with someone like Bhawani Singh who could inform his readers that, 'When an Indian Chief visits London he has to call upon the Secretary of State for India. I therefore called on Mr Brodrick in my Indian costume. A red cloth was spread from the carriage to the house; this is a mark of honour paid to Indian princes.'[79] Meanwhile, the Rajah of Kolhapoor recounted in his diary how he had been greeted by the Political Secretary of the India Office at Charing Cross; Sen met Lord Shaftesbury and Benjamin Jowett, lunched with the Dean of Westminster who introduced him to Max Müller, and breakfasted with Gladstone; not only did Mirza Khan frequently attend the King and Queen's drawing room, but he was also invited to dinner by Alderman Combe who had just been elected Mayor of London. Allocated a seat at the same table as Lord Nelson, he was amused to find that his foreign garb and apparent air of superiority led many parties to come over throughout the evening, bend their knees and stoop their heads – to Lord Nelson for his victory on the Nile, 'and to me, *for my supposed high rank*'.[80]

This is a far cry from the altercations lascars had with washerwomen, crimps and prostitutes. Few Indians had the time or inclination to attend to the grimmer, ungilded parts of town. Bhawani sombrely visited the East End one afternoon, only to spend the evening gadding about at a State Ball held at Buckingham Palace. And although some Indian travellers did notice and speak to the city's destitutes, the registers with which they describe these encounters are frequently patronizing ('Oh the street arabs of London! Dirty, unkempt little urchins, out at elbow, often out at knee too, if I may use the phrase; lean and hungry as a rule, yet full of life, and always amusing'[81]), pompous ('London appears to a stranger the richest, most prosperous, and happiest city on the face of the earth. But stop for one moment. While you enjoy the magnificence and splendour of the Great Metropolis, do not fail to see the misery and wretchedness in its streets'[82]), or sanctimonious:

> we also think that much of the dissipation, and many of the robberies committed by young men, may be traced to an intimacy with improper females, which commenced within the saloon of a theatre. The saloons of those theatres that are allowed to be infested with such characters, are, instead of being an accommodation to the public, harbours of vice, at which a virtuous man frowns with disgust.[83]

Far more to the liking of the Indian travellers was the opportunity London gave them to inspect for the first time aspects of their own culture. Here they could see some of the ivory, manuscripts and gold pieces that had been seized from their country. It wasn't so very surprising that they had to travel to London to see their own arts and achievements displayed. After all, London was the capital of India. Imperial centre, the largest city on earth – it was from there that the treaties, curricula and legislative frameworks which shaped their lives were established. Political and economic issues pertaining to India were frequently discussed: J.S. Mill asked Sen about education, income tax, and the administration of justice in India; the Rajah of Kolhapoor attended an East India Association meeting at the Society of Arts to hear a Paper on Cotton.

London was also the place in which to see the sinews and arteries of Empire: Nadkarni went to the Bank of England to see Indian currency being printed; Sinh Jee walked along the Thames Embankment to the General Post Office to watch Indian mail sorted; Jhinda Ram marvelled at Tippu Sultan's girdle and helmet at the Tower of London. Some, like the Rajah of Kolhapoor, were 'quite surprised to see such a large collection of Indian things'.[84] Others, like T.N. Mukharji, were less enthralled. He inspected South Kensington Museum's extensive collection of Indian art-ware and also attended the Indian Bazaar at the 1886 Colonial and Indian Exhibition.

> A dense crowd always stood there, looking at our men as they wore the gold brocade, sang the patterns of the carpet and printed the calico with the hand. They were much astonished to see the Indians produce works of art with the aid of rude apparatus they themselves had discarded long ago.[85]

This response rankled him. After visiting other shows and galleries, he complained that:

The Museums in Europe, where ethnographical specimens from all parts of the world have been collected, bring to the mind of an Indian a feeling of humiliation and sorrow. There he finds himself ranked among barbarian tribes with their cannibalism, human-sacrifice, tattooing and all sorts of cruel and curious customs that denote a savage life.[86]

On the whole, though, Indian travellers enjoyed flitting through the city and taking in as many sites and sights as possible. Some, like Bhawani Singh, were lucky enough to stay at the Alexandra Hotel in luxurious rooms overlooking Hyde Park. Others climbed the steps to the top of St Paul's Cathedral where, unlike eighteenth-century black writers who only experienced the city at ground level, they viewed London from above. These perspectives allowed them to 'look down' on the capital, something that they, patrician and Olympian in mien, were not averse to doing.

Nineteenth-century Indian writers also grabbed the opportunity to drift through the city imbibing quotidian experiences. Malabari often slipped into the present tense to convey his sense of awe at London's whirr and whirl: near Regent Street, 'I stand breathless of an evening, watching what goes on before my eyes'; squeezing into an omnibus, 'I am between two of the prettiest and quietest, feeling a strange discomfort. As the 'bus hobbles along, I feel my fair neighbours knocking against me every moment.'[87]

Visitors were most dazed by the clattering locomotion and velocity of the world's most populous city. Noise and tumult assaulted them as soon as they alighted at Victoria Station. London seemed insomniac, so thronged and labyrinthine as to be utterly unknowable. And no matter how lofty their social station, irrespective of how long they resided in the metropolis, they never quite lost that initial disorientation. Pandian linked this surging energy to the city's capacity for hyper-manufacturing both ideas and commercial produce, while Mukharji speculated that Londoners, accustomed to confronting a thousand terrors and cacophonies every day of their working lives, had become so immune that they weren't 'even afraid of ghosts now-a-days, nor of witches, imps or fairies'.[88] Speech became comically deformed with bus conductors referring to such places as Chring Cruss, Stren, Oxf Strit, Pidly, Toria, Roloke. Friendship was almost impossible for 'The Englishman in London seems to have no time to dive after a drowning friend'.[89] All this led Malabari to observe caustically that:

> People live in a whirlwind of excitement, making and unmaking their idols almost every day. They seem to be consumed by a mania for novelty; everything new serves to keep up the fever of excitement. To-day they will set up a fetish, anything absurd, fantastic, grotesque, and worship it with breathless enthusiasm.[90]

Indian visitors marvelled at the most unexceptional features. Jhinda Ram and T.N. Mukharji were both entertained by the advertisements they came across in the press, on the streets, and upon looking up from the books they read on bus journeys. Both were diverted by the techniques used by Pears to sell soap to the public – Mukharji remarking drily that, 'The black races need no longer have the fear of being eaten up by white men for the sake of their complexion, for a single application of Mr Pears' Soap will whiten the blackest of black faces.'[91]

Even light became a source of joy. Many of the travellers attended expensive firework-shows which lit up the night sky above places such as Vauxhall Gardens. Nowrojee and his cousin cruised around the capital on the evening of Queen Victoria's marriage to Albert in 1840 ogling the specially illuminated street-scapes. The hidden subtext to this focus on light (so vastly superior, according to Mirza Khan, to that in Paris![92]) is made transparent in T.B. Pandian's florid encomium:

Old King Gas still holds his old sway as a lamp-lighter, but his throne totters, as his light itself pales before the more potent effulgence of the coming Raj – the Imperial brilliance of the electric light in perfected power and majesty.[93]

London's lighting is being praised here not just as a technological feat of the highest order, but as concrete proof that the country of which London is the administrative capital is a superior political overlord. The quote makes clear what many of the Indian travellers in this chapter had already suspected – that London was not only 'a pinnacle of magnificence and luxury' whose 'beauty and grandeur' led it to outshine any other city they had previously visited,[94] but that it was the most blessed, the most radiant

Mecca for the traveller in search of truth, a Medina of rest for the persecuted or the perplexed in spirit. Though centre of perpetual motion, it is still the Persepolis of human grandeur in repose. To the searcher after enlightenment it is a Budh-Gaya; a Benares for the sinner in search of emancipation. Damp, dirty, noisy London, thou art verily a Jerusalem for the weary soldier of faith.[95]

Mukharji contrasted favourably the 'soft subdued and mellowed shine' of the sun in London to that of India which 'rides roughshod over our head burning and parching everything with incessant darts of liquid fire'.[96] Even the artificial lighting found in the capital's streets and alleyways symbolized how majestically London rose above the rest of the world which was, if not swamp-like, certainly ancillary, definitely not as resplendent as the imperial metropolis. London was a beacon calling out across the oceans, a lighthouse summoning people from the dangers of backwardness. It was a chandelier of near-blinding loveliness.

Meanwhile, Nadkarni and Malabari praised the metropolitan constabulary for being consistently cheerful and helpful; the latter contrasting 'Dear old Bobby' to 'the stupid, peevish, insolent

Patawala in India!'[97] Cabmen, equally, were seen as 'very clever and civil people' who not only knew the capital's streets backwards but were very personable to their passengers.[98] What a difference a century makes. The Stephen Lawrence débâcle illustrates the difficulty faced by London's police force in countering the wide-spread perception that they are racists; the xenophobic loquacity of city cabbies is a staple butt of many stand-up performers stepping on to the boards at Leicester Square comedy clubs. Yet before 1900 both professions were felt to symbolize a security and ease that Indians lacked. Malabari articulated this belief, later revived by Tambimuttu and Naipaul, when he claimed that his countrymen lacked European people's 'order, discipline, presence of mind'.[99]

Unlike many of the black writers in this book, Indian travellers were spectators as much as they were recipients of attention.[100] They came to London on short-stay visits with the specific inten-tion of viewing as many famous people and edifices as possible. Brimming with the confidence that their wealthy backgrounds had granted them, they didn't instinctively avert their gazes when Londoners stared at them. Unlike Mary Prince and Una Marson, nineteenth-century Indians weren't haunted by the fear that they were somehow illegitimate, that their presence in the capital was unlicensed or likely to be penalized. They did, nonetheless, undergo the experience of being scrutinized. Local Londoners routinely flocked round freshly disembarked travellers to gawp at their tawny flesh, their Parsee costumes, and their accompanying coteries. Nowrojee and Merwanjee found themselves surrounded by a mob almost a thousand strong and struggled to reach their waiting carriage.[101] Public response was largely benign: Ramak-rishna announced with relief that, 'My oriental dress wherever I went, in the buses, in the underground railway carriages, in the London streets and in public places of resort, secured for me every attention and respect'.[102] Unlike Prince – unlike Sancho even – Ramakrishna didn't feel threatened by people gazing at him or commenting on his outfits. Nor did Mukharji, who was cannily waspish in his analysis of the public attitude to travellers like himself. Attending a colonial exhibition, he noticed a group of women staring at him, one of whom, after a long while, plucked up the courage to approach him, at which point she

> expressed her astonishment at my knowledge of English, and complimented me for the performance of the band brought from *my country*, *vis.*, the West Indian band composed of Negroes and Mulattos, which compliment made me wince a little, but nevertheless I went on chattering for a quarter of an hour and furnishing her with sufficient means to annihilate her friend Minnie, Jane or Lizzy or whoever she might be, and to brag among her less fortunate relations for six months to come of her having actually seen and talked to a genuine 'Blackie.'[103]

Following the Great Exhibition – held at the Crystal Palace in Hyde Park during 1851, and visited by six and a half million people – London regularly staged huge colonial exhibitions. In 1876 a number of snake-charmers, nautch-girls, jugglers and artisans were brought to the city to perform at the 'Indian Villages in London' show at Royal Albert Palace, Battersea. The later Ceylonese Exhibition at Agricultural Hall, Islington, required over eighty performers to be shipped in from Ceylon and Madras together with elephants and tigers. Such events were a curious mixture of conference, trade fair, and museum show. Shawls, sculptures, even reconstructions of foreign streets could all be seen here. Between 1883 and 1886 four exhibitions were held in South Kensington – on Fisheries, Health, Inventions, and Colonial and Indian produce – with the last, which T.N. Mukharji had been deputed to attend by the Indian Government, by far the most popular. The sequence of these exhibitions revealed, according to the historian Paul Greenhalgh, 'a good deal about British attitudes to empire; it was variously considered as a resource, as a commodity, as something the British had created, as an abstract concept; it could be many things in fact, except people with lives and traditions of their own'.[104]

To the extent that this is true – and it's always difficult to gauge what the public 'feels' about any issue as vast as the Empire – it may be the case that the whispering and finger-pointing that Indian travellers in the nineteenth century attracted arose precisely because they were non-abstract, people whose vocabularies and dress codes gave evidence of the fact that they possessed lives and traditions of their own. Staring didn't objectify or dehumanize them. Rather, Londoners squinted at them because they were palpably *not* objects, *all too* human. That Malabari, Ramakrishna, Nadkarni and Mukharji never complained about being stared at, whilst writers such as Mirza Khan and K.C. Sen were lionized, confirms this point. They didn't feel intimidated by the white gaze as black women writers such as Buchi Emecheta and Una Marson later did. Nor were they angered by the suspicion that they were under constant surveillance as do the characters in Linton Kwesi Johnson's poetry and in Caryl Phillips's plays.

Two Indian authors did complain vociferously about their treatment by Londoners. Could it be that they were, simply, pompous stick-in-the-muds? Jhinda Ram, who worked in a Punjabi court, where deference and hushed respect were compulsory, sounds positively Pooterish when he balks at the cheekily demotic village boys in Battersea Park who gathered round and gave him gyp:

> with as much indifference as if I were a stuffed figure. I never gained so much uncompromising information about my colour, nose, teeth, &c. as on that occasion. I need hardly tell you, that

those remarks were disagreeable to me, and leaving the bench
I walked out of the Park.[105]

It's difficult to sympathize with Nowrojee and Merwanjee when
they complain about the behaviour of the capital's theatre audiences. These authors, whose book groans with lengthy accounts of
the technical specificities of London dockyards, lash the 'smirking,
priggish-looking' Jews, gripe about Hackney coach drivers, and
weary us with their Puritan condemnations of the dissipated young
men and improper young females they see hanging around
theatres.[106] Always sit in the boxes rather than in the pit or gallery,
they instruct their readers, because these latter places are

> resorted to by the humbler classes, as well as by rogues, thieves,
> and pick-pockets, and should a stranger happen to be there, he
> is often teased and insulted with grogs and abusive language by
> these fellows, besides he could not see much of the perform-
> ances; we state this from the treatment we once experienced at
> Astley's Amphitheatre, but on our discovering the error, we
> immediately left the place.
>
> And here we would inform our countrymen that the majority
> of the lower orders in England are very rude in their manners
> and behaviour towards strangers, whom they do not like to see
> in their own country.[107]

Although the grousings of Nowrojee and his cousin were unusually
severe, they weren't the only Indian travellers to criticize London
life. As with Sancho, much of this condemnation was levelled at
metropolitan amorality. The speed and intensity with which life
seemed to be lived in the city, whilst thrilling, convinced Nadkarni
that Londoners were fixated on instant gratification rather than anything more spiritually deep-rooted.[108] Pandian hated to see 'Christians wildly careering about the thoroughfares of a great Christian
city on Sundays above all other days of the week'.[109] Malabari

glossed over the poverty and lack of education that disabled millions of Londoners from pursuing happiness when he casually remarked that, 'the back parts of not a few streets seem to have been given up to a Godless population, foreign and English'.[110]

Malabari, like many Indian authors, was appalled by family life in the capital. He could scarcely believe that mothers and nurses let their babies inhale the city's fetid air, and was shocked by the number of unmarried young men and women – particularly women – who in their 'scramble after happiness' filled 'the streets of London with all that is repulsive in life, and much that is subversive of the welfare of society'.[111] Mukharji, meanwhile, was aggrieved by the number of children who fled their family homes at the first opportunity, whilst Gandhi was disturbed by the excessive liberalism of those parents who allowed their daughters to flirt with visiting Indian students.

Many writers inveighed against the dangers of alcohol which, according to Malabari, debased and brutalized even more men and women in London than it did in Paris. Mirza Khan, Nadkarni and Pandian all believed drink was this country's besetting weakness, driving weak-willed members of the working classes to crime and ruination. The latter's hatred of alcohol was matched only by his hatred of gambling and smoking; 'As for the immorality associated with the British stage,' he wrote, 'I do not care to say much.'[112] His evangelistic fervour extended to his dislike of the nudes at Hampton Court and was rivalled only by Jhinda Ram who claimed that the sight of couples kissing under their umbrellas on Hyde Park benches was 'astonishing and shocking to my mind'.[113] Although Ram doesn't mention drama specifically, it seems unlikely that he would have thought any more highly of London's theatres than Pandian or Nowrojee and Merwanjee who all regarded them as breeding grounds for vice and impropriety.

Some Indian criticism did address slightly more serious issues than Malabari's outburst against English food which he felt lacked variety and seasoning.[114] Mukharji, in particular, was disappointed by his visit to the House of Commons: he sat in the Gallery eagerly hoping to hear the powerful rhetoric of those charismatic performers he'd read so much about in India. Instead, he felt mortified by the 'fact that the words that fell there decided the destiny of nations. It looked so like a debating club of old boys!'[115] Over a decade earlier in the summer of 1870, the Brahmin reformer Keshub Chunder Sen had sat in the same seats bemused by the absence of women from the Visitors' Gallery: 'Why this meaningless exclusion in this land of female liberty?'[116]

A suspicion that England was not quite as splendid and all-knowing as he'd been led to believe also underlies Mirza Khan's claim that vanity was one of the commonest English faults. He argued that they wrote and circulated books on the basis of the most wafer-thin insights on scientific subjects or on foreign languages, and went on to question 'the transcendent abilities and angelic character of Sir William Jones', whose Persian Grammar he regarded as defective.[117] Other writers also bemoaned the fact that many of the people they had met in London 'knew nothing else of India except the mutiny', and had the impression that it was 'steeped in ignorance and barbarism'.[118]

But although their parents and friends had fed them doomy reports about metropolitan decadence, and they were occasionally surprised by the poverty, materialism and ignorance about Indian affairs they found in London, all the travellers who published accounts of their stays left the city with nothing but the fondest affection. Many of them had also visited other leading European capitals such as Paris and Rome but, dizzying, dirty and Godless as it often seemed, London was adjudged to be superior. Whereas a century later authors such as Andrew Salkey and Linton Kwesi Johnson would chart the contempt that was meted out to Caribbean immigrants by white Londoners, Jhinda Ram, Nadkarni and Pandian singled out their friendliness and 'Christ-like magnanimity' towards foreign visitors.[119] Equally, in a passage which anticipates one of the key themes of *The Satanic Verses*, T.N. Mukharji wrote:

> England is not so much the home of Englishmen, as it is the home of imperialism, liberalism and human freedom. It is practically the home of all races, as any one can testify who has seen the large number of foreigners marrying and intermarrying there – the pigtailed Chinese, the dark lascars, the woolly-bearded Africans, the straight-nosed Jews, not to say of Germans, French, Italians and other people of Europe. [...] Why should we not accept that little strip of land as the great metropolis and common property of the empire of which our continent of India is an important part, and take pride in it just as we take pride in Calcutta, and help always to keep it in the vanguard of human progress?[120]

Bhagvat Sinh Jee, unwittingly recycling the language of Malabari and Ramakrishna, felt that his voyages had 'passed like a felicitous dream', while, according to his editor, the Rajah of Kolhapoor wrote a letter to a friend in India in which he claimed that his experiences in London had taught him 'what a very insignificant person [he] was out of his own territory'.[121] For Jhinda Ram, London was not only the centre of commerce and wealth but of intellectual and moral life.[122] Pandian went further and called it 'by a long way the most remarkable city on the face of the globe'.[123] But perhaps it was Malabari who caught the right tone – one that combined scepticism, bitter-sweet comedy and, most of all, head-spinning euphoria:

> And now farewell to London! Dirty little pool of life, that has grown and expanded into an ocean – the biggest, the muddiest, and yet the healthiest of this iron age. Great in varieties, great

in contrarieties; unequalled in the power of contrasts and in
the wealth of extremes; I sit entranced, watching the divergent
forces.[124]

Malabari is perhaps the author considered in this chapter whose
work affords the most literary pleasure. He's often sarcastic and
grouchy as well as funny and perceptive. Although he attended
nearly as many upper-class parties and receptions as some of the
rajahs, his journalistic instincts also encouraged him to follow
those city routes largely ignored by other writers. Malabari made
certain that his socially stratified itinerary didn't limit the range
and fervour of his ramblings. He is also exceptional in trying to
transcribe the speech patterns of the street arabs who accost him:
'"Jim, look at 'is 'at; look at 'is 'at, Jim"'; 'Of all the expletives I
have heard in London streets this "bloody" seems to be the commonest – bloody cheek, bloody hard, bloody fat, bloody fool,
bloody flower.'[125]

Most of the other authors only wrote one book. The likes of
Nadkarni and Pandian were writing in the golden age of Empire,
that period when scholars, adventurers and traders trotted round
the globe looking for terrain to master both intellectually and
economically. Their accounts – fetching huge prices at auctions
today – are often censured for effacing native voices. They're
commonly adjudged to gloss over important geopolitical issues.
Apparently they import their own concerns and prejudices and
judge the natives harshly for not living up to those standards. But
Indian writers do precisely the same when they lambast Londoners
for drinking, for being promiscuous and impious. Their books
can be read as early manifestations of the Empire writing back
but if this is true, their authors objectify and palsy their subjects
just as much (or just as little) as their European counterparts did
when cartographizing Asia and Africa. It may just be that travel

writing – always prone through limited pagination and the need for authors constantly to keep on the move – must always skim the surfaces of the cultures and histories which it intends to illuminate. As a genre, it has always been grossly deficient in being able to relay the myriad plenitudes and fascinating contradictions of individual societies.

But it's not only in its contribution to debates about the nature of colonial discourse that nineteenth-century Indian travel writing is interesting. The authors' eagerness to savour all the cultural possibilities that London has to offer anticipates Kureishi's lust for lapping up the capital's creative and sensory delights. The Indians in this chapter had the time, the contacts and the money to do so, and this not only distinguishes them from most of the other writers in this book, but also helps to scupper any theory about the relationship between colonials and the metropolis which assumes pre-twentieth-century contact was all as disastrous as that of Gronniosaw and Mary Prince. Their stays in what many of them felt was the centre of the earth were overwhelmingly joyful.

CHAPTER THREE

Coasting a Lime on the Serpentine

ELDERLY JAMAICANS, still trim, their trousers shiny-kneed but meticulously creased, smile spryly and recount with courteous diction their memories of treading down a former German warship's gangplank on to a grey, galey motherland. As they narrate their word-perfect anecdotes, a series of familiar archive images floods the screen: broad-brimmed, broad-smiled West Indians with their natty suits and meagre luggage; a scrum of cameramen snapping away at this strange and freshly-docked cargo; calypsonian Lord Kitchener acceding to a Pathé newsman's request and breaking into a reedy 'London Is The Place For Me'. Suddenly, according to most history books, a marvellous postcolonial transformation is about to be wrought on a monochrome, war-weary nation.

Actually the docking of the SS *Empire Windrush* at Tilbury Docks in 1948 did not herald the beginning of multi-racial Britain, a foundation myth which became entrenched in the wake of 1998's fiftieth anniversary celebrations. Long-established communities existed in Liverpool, Manchester, Cardiff, South Shields and Glasgow. In London, too, black and Asian people had continued arriving in the slipstream of Empire since the nineteenth century. Jack London, for once averting his horrified gaze from the East End, described the coronation in 1901 with celebratory relish:

But here they come, in all the pomp and certitude of power, and still they come, these men of steel, these war lords and world harnessers. [. . .] Up the street come troops of the auxiliaries, black Africans and yellow Asiatics, beturbaned and befezed, and coolies swinging along with machine guns and mountain batteries on their heads, and the bare feet of all, in quick rhythm, going *slish*, *slish*, *slish* through the pavement mud. The public-houses empty by magic, and the swarthy allegiants are cheered by their British brothers, who return at once to the carouse.[1]

In the foreign potentates marched, from India and Nigeria, Uganda, Sudan and Zambia, elaborate retinues trailing behind them, nodding appreciatively at the zoo exhibits, theatrical shows and gallery collections to which they were taken. Colour was not a hindrance; their elevated rank ensured that they obtained the same respect as any white monarch.[2] The same could not be said for those black men and women who appeared at exhibition villages across the capital. Most were from Africa – Senegal, South Africa. A large group of Somalis performed at the Coronation Exhibition in 1911. Three years earlier a number of Mandingo children from the Toy City and Fun Fair at Earls Court, still wearing the grass skirts and blankets donned for the benefit of metropolitan audiences, had made a public visit to John Burns, the first working-class man to become a Cabinet minister.[3]

Africans performed in a number of shows and assumed a range of ethnic identities. Many black Londoners of this period chose to become actors. Some did so illegally, sprucing themselves up to look like dandies or exotically-plumed royalty so that they could stay in large hotels and hire expensive cars in the West End. Others performed in more conventional venues – in minstrel shows and music hall – where they featured as coon acts, dancing boys, variety turns, and in choral groups and theatrical troupes.

African Pygmies in London

J. Benjamin Stone
Aug 9th 1905

They were so popular that critics complained about how the cake-walk dance they had introduced into England during the 1890s had begun to displace more traditional forms of dance.

A large part of London's colonial population was made up of men who had been seamen. Although the 'lascar problem' had subsided by the twentieth century, thousands of blacks and Asians continued to arrive in London having worked as ship firemen, chefs and stewards. A number were also stowaways who had smuggled themselves here in the pursuit of riches and adventure. Those who were prepared to take the underworld route of making money from prostitution and gambling often fared better than those who sought legal employment and, failing, were forced to pawn their belongings and rely on parish handouts and the

of compatriots to ward off starvation. Governmental
_ties were not always sympathetic to their plight. One par-
ti__rly severe worker at the Colonial Office's West African
Department claimed in 1910 that Africans who called there for
help were 'generally wasters', 'probably people who would not
stay in the workhouse, but simply go out into the streets to sponge
upon anything they can [...] It might be a useful thing to have
some compulsory power of repatriating people like that.'[4]

Many seamen did return home after a few years of trying their
luck in London. One man who didn't was twenty-seven-year-old
James Lockhard. He had been staying at the Wesleyan Seaman's
Mission in Poplar while waiting for a berth back to St Vincent in
the Caribbean. He was passed fit by the doctor to step aboard
the steamship lying in the West India Docks but, shortly after
performing a few menial cleaning duties, collapsed and died. The
official verdict was rupture of the aortic valve. According to a
doctor in attendance, 'The deceased had every appearance of being
a strong, healthy man.' Added the coroner, 'No doubt he got into
such a state of excitement that his nervous system was upset.'

After 1914 colonial subjects in London were viewed somewhat
more favourably. Their work was seen as crucial to the war effort.
They laboured in munitions factories and, now that white seamen
were needed by the Navy, sailed with the merchant service. Millions of Indians fought on the battlefields of Europe and, in due
course, came to London to be decorated for their gallantry by the
King or to receive specialized hospital treatment for their injuries.
Their brave contribution, and that of African soldiers, was celebrated in *The Black Man's Part in the War* (1917), a book by Sir
Harry Johnston, a friend of Cecil Rhodes and Henry Stanley.

African and West Indian troops were often demobilized in England. Many ended up in London where they found themselves
edged out of the job market. Factory production had subsided and

shipping companies gave priority to white foreign seamen rather than black seamen from Britain's colonies. Discontent grew. Seafaring blacks were a hardy lot – proud, savvy, quick with their fists. They did not care for the hostile reception they were getting. Rather than averting their gazes or looking bashful, they gave back – verbally, physically – as good as they got. It was inevitable that sooner or later there was going to be big trouble. During the summer of 1919 rioting broke out across Tyneside, Liverpool and Cardiff.

London was not exempted from that year's wave of racial violence. The catalyst was normally sex. White locals, many of them unemployed, took umbrage at 'their' women consorting with black men. In April a group of them, including some soldiers, entered a coffeeshop on Cable Street that they knew had a large black clientele. Words were exchanged, then blows, and soon gunshots. Locals tried to set fire to the building on the same road where in 1936 socialists and East End Jews fought a famous battle against Oswald Mosley's fascists. Peace was restored but only temporarily.[5] Barely a month later, the café was attacked again. Police who tried to protect the premises and its owners were booed. 'Lynch them!' was the cry. One newspaper claimed: 'There appears to be an organized attempt to inflame the East End white community not only against the Negroes, but against other coloured men.'[6]

Tension lay heavy across the East End all that summer. Black men out on the streets risked being set upon by packs of local toughs who, incited by press hysteria, were always spoiling for a fight. Those implicated were not only London's blacks but the 'chinks' inhabiting Chinatown in Limehouse. The toughs were joined by 'outside forces': thugs from Hoxton, infamous at that time for its marauding young gangs, liked to come along for the vicious ride.

A particular danger zone was the Limehouse end of Commercial Road between Limehouse Church and Jack's Place, the headquarters of the British and Foreign Seamen's Mission. Many black South Africans lived there while waiting for boats to take them back home. According to one paper: 'Local residents felt they "decoyed" young girls and lavished money on them.' One night

a couple of white girls who were being escorted by black men
to a tramcar were shouted at and pulled away. In the ensuing fight
a white man was stabbed. The following night a mob of over 5000
gathered outside Jack's Place and before long a full-scale riot had
blown up.[7]

Good came from bad. During these bitter days black people in
London clung together for safety and protection. They realized,
with fresh intensity, that their interests were not necessarily
the same as those of the white working classes. Yet the riots of
1919 helped to criminalize them in the eyes of many Londoners.
Special policemen were posted to dock areas where they looked
out for swarthy types who might be trying to smuggle drugs into
the capital. Black men were no longer seen as helpless indigents
who required handouts to rescue them from starvation; now they
were viewed as lazy, vicious cocksmen out to corrupt English
femininity. Newspapers and scandal sheets published stories of
'respectable' women who had been 'degraded' – or had degraded
themselves – through intercourse with blacks. 'Infatuation' was
the term commonly used. It implied mesmerism or a derangement
of the senses. Not the kind of thing 'decent' women would ever
permit.

Such sensationalized accounts were becoming common partly
because increasing numbers of black and Indian people were
moving to the centre of London where they were more visible
than they had been when they dwelled in no-go areas in Stepney
and Poplar. They tended to live in the Tottenham Court Road
and Bloomsbury area where they established cafés and clubs of
their own. The most infamous was 'The Black Man's Café' on
White Lion Street, Seven Dials, which was reputed to attract the
lowest type of people in the West End – that is, women of a
certain class keen on ne'er-do-well blacks who idled and gambled
the day away. Meanwhile, Rajani Mazundar owned the Caledonian

Hotel in Harpur Street which he allowed to be used as a brothel. There was also a black-run gambling basement in Bloomsbury High Street, a café on Denmark Street, and a restaurant and after-hours drinking joint called The Erskine Club on Whitfield Street. A few doors down was a club run by Sam Minto and Edward Felix, both black, the latter Secretary of the British Colonial Club. According to a police spokesman, it was 'one of the most disgraceful places in the West End. The inspector tells me it is frequented by persons of notorious character, bullies, cocaine traffickers, and the worst class of black men.'[8]

Little is known of these men other than through the unreliable pages of the contemporary press. *The Illustrated Police News*, a sensationalist rag with a penchant for bathetic headlines ('Another Terrible Crime Near Crowborough'; 'Footballer's Threat To Wife Of A "Clip Under The Chin"'; 'Artist, While Absorbed In Painting, Attacked By A Huge Octopus. Saved By A Sailor'), often carried stories about boxer-pimps and razor altercations between black men. Occasionally, though, it reported inadvertently evocative stories. One concerned Laurie French who ran out of his house on Little Russell Street completely naked just after midnight shouting: 'I was white in the war, and now I'm a nigger. Where is she?' before sinking his teeth into the arm of a policeman who tried to arrest him.[9]

Another involved Ben Simmonds, a black singer from the Gold Coast who was living in distressed circumstances in Lambeth. Given a saxophone to sell by a tobacconist, he pawned the instrument for four pounds and kept the money for himself. He duly appeared in court where it was noted that during the war he had served as a corporal in a white regiment:

'Then they say it isn't a free country!' exclaimed the magistrate. 'That couldn't have happened in America.'

Commenting on the registration of aliens, Mr Pope said this was 'the most free and go-as-you-please country in the world.' He sentenced prisoner to three months' hard labour and made an order for deportation.

'Newcastle, Glasgow, or Aberdeen are places I would suggest!' he added.[10]

The most notorious criminal of the period was Edgar Manning. During a decade full of drug scandals and mass panics about the rise in public immorality, he was dubbed 'The Dope King of London' and 'the worst man in London'. Born in Jamaica in 1888, Manning came to England during the war and worked in a munitions factory. After illness forced him to quit in 1918, he joined a touring theatre company before going on to play drums in a jazz band at Ciro's, a smart London nightclub. Anything went in this world, not only in terms of dance styles and dress codes, but also underhand transactions in drugs and women. Manning soon got in on the act and became a dealer using squads of prostitutes to do the dirty work for him. He rarely went anywhere without a loaded Colt revolver. It came in handy during a face-off with fellow gangsters near Shaftesbury Avenue in September 1920 that ended with him shooting and wounding all three of them in broad daylight. He was jailed but released the following summer.

Manning quickly became well-known, not least to the police who shadowed him for years. Many popular novels of the period featured evil black characters based on him; in Carlyle Maynard's *East and West of Soho* (1932) Black Eddie is a 'coon [who] was a pretty mean sort of a skunk; that followed naturally from his profession. In spite of his European garments, Roy recalled him as a leering Satan, a cloven-hoofed satyr tempting man with the emasculating viciousness of the potent drug.'[11] Black Eddie is rarely seen without an expensive Havana cigar and was a dandy, 'a striking figure in the flowered silk dressing-gown which covered his ordinary clothes and lent him an Oriental, almost mystic, appearance'.[12]

Manning's name kept popping up during investigations into drugs-related deaths. As a precautionary act he went into partnership with Zenovia Iassonides, owner of the Montmartre Café in Soho. They moved their headquarters to Regent's Park Road, a more discreet neighbourhood than the West End, and from there they started up a wholesale operation. When the police eventually busted the place in 1922, they found what one historian has called 'a complete kit of vice villainy: a bottle of cocaine, opium utensils, a syringe case and hypodermic needles, a pornographic book and photos, a revolver, and thirteen ounces of opium'.[13] Manning was jailed for six months, only to carry on where he had left off after being released. He was caught again and, this time, sentenced to three years' penal servitude in Parkhurst. Back on Civvy Street, the rest of his short life was spent ducking in and out of trouble. He opened Eddy's Bar, a gangster hangout, in a Soho back street, and moved in with a Russian prostitute called Dora Lippack. In 1928 they were caught in possession of goods stolen from Lady Diana Cooper; Dora was deported and he was imprisoned once more. He died in 1931.

A profession to which many Indians and black people turned was fortune-telling. It attracted both sharp-eyed crooks and individuals hoping to augment the meagre salaries they earned as teachers or cooks. Fortune-telling had become increasingly popular since the war when anxious mothers and wives had sought reassurance about the fate of their loved ones who were missing in action. They would do anything to hear good news. Taking advantage of their status as exotic mysterios who had ready access to occult, non-Christian ways of thinking, black people soon cornered the market. Often they would dress up in brightly coloured robes, choosing exotic pseudonyms such as 'Prince of Darkness'. They attracted huge crowds of shoppers who were seduced not only by their spectacular brand of public entertainment but by the nagging suspicion that, beneath the peculiar accents and even more peculiar headgear, might lurk discomfiting truths. 'Beware of a dark person. Beware of a poor person' read the piece of paper Joseph Phillips handed to a client who had spotted his sign which read: 'Indian, Hindu, Gypsy. Hand and face reading. Love, marriage and business.' 'That is rather alarming to beware of humanity at large,' commented the judge drily before fining Phillips a sum of seven pounds.[14] Abdul Khan, meanwhile, told a lady on Petticoat Lane whose hand he had just read, 'You are in some way connected with a blue uniform!' Alas, he was right. His client was a plain-clothes officer who later testified against him.[15]

Pretending to know the truth about the afterlife was just one of the many fictions spun. Few white Londoners knew very much about the countries from which they came; schoolchildren believed that seeing a black man would bring them good luck. Such ignorance was a boon to the wily trickster. Depending on his audience, he could claim to be a Bengali lancer, or a holidaying maharajah, or a tribal chief, or a wandering sage from tropical climes still undiscovered by the West. Shapeshifting was a fact of life: even law-abiding blacks often had many careers – as colonial runaways, film extras at Denham and Pinewood, restaurant staff, strolling players.[16] Their peripatetic lives helped them to see the repertoire of different roles available to them. In 1908 Mahatma Agamya Guru, the self-styled 'Holy Man of the East', and reputed (though mainly by himself) to be 'the strongest and happiest man in the world', was brought before the courts. Nearly seventy years old and living in West Hampstead, he brought a couple of young girls home on the pretext of requiring their secretarial help. When one of them, Maud Andrews, asked him what kind of shorthand

and typing duties she was expected to perform, Guru replied, 'All that you have to do is worship me all day long, and to be happy with the other five disciples who are in the house. I love them all very much indeed, and shall love you the same.'[17] Then he tried to grope her. He was sentenced to four months in prison with hard labour.

To dwell on the criminal activities of black and Asian people in this period, while a necessary corrective to those who would portray immigrants as perennially innocent victims of police and judicial prejudice, is to ignore the central, if less salacious, truth that their individual lives, then as now, were for the most part spent trying to make an honest living, and looking for some companionship. They worked as bookmakers, travel agents, domestic helps, restaurant waitresses. Some were apprentice mechanics. They toiled hard and, when they got off work, they liked to do the same kinds of things as the white working classes – go to the dogs at White City, see a picture, have a twirl at a dance hall. This side of black London – quotidian, intimate, undramatic – rarely finds expression in literature of the period.

It's particularly pleasing, then, to read an article entitled 'Coloured Children's Outing to Epsom' in *The Keys*, a progressive black magazine published before the war.[18] It describes a day-trip made in July 1933 by 195 children aged between five and fifteen. They had been picked up from seven different points – Shoreditch Town Hall, Commercial Road for Stepney; Spurgeon's Tabernacle for south-east London; The Tidal Basin, Docks; Poplar Town Hall; Friend's House for King's Cross; Tottenham Court Road and Hyde Park for West London – which represented the key residential areas of London's black population. The coaches all met together at Clapham Common and proceeded together to Surrey where during the afternoon the children went on walks, rode on donkeys, played on the swings. Funded by the Epsom

Brotherhood, they had the kind of fun that their parents could not normally afford for them. The photographs of them are startling: rarely, if ever, does one see so many black people together before the late 1940s and certainly not black children. Their faces are beaming, querulous, eager – like those of any youngsters placed in front of a camera.

Another group of "Youngsters" off to Epsom.
The Epsom Outing, Friday, July 14th.

Another aspect of life in London that gets written out of conventional immigrant narratives is the search for love. Few contemporary novels or newspapers during the early twentieth century say much about the topic. Black people are seen as hungry for sex rather than for love. They are libidinous rather than courtly. The exceptions to this rule are stories about love spurned. Grace

Stevenson, for instance, was a thirty-eight-year-old servant from Jamaica working in Ealing who gassed herself while wearing a bridal dress and jewels. She had wanted to join her lover back in Jamaica and he had promised to send her money for the voyage. But the money never arrived and she had been left to put up with tradesmen and women taunting her about her colour. In her suicide note she wrote:

> I am black, but I didn't make myself, but people look at me and think I have no feeling. I cannot bear it any longer. I am a lonely, broken-hearted girl, and I have no one in England. I tried to go home, but cannot do so; I have not enough money . . . I cannot face the world any longer; it is too hard. I have no strength left in me. God knows.[19]

A press report from a few years earlier tells the brief but poignant story of Marcus Clarke, a pensioned Custom House official from the Gold Coast. He had been living on Paddington Street at the time he was accused of assaulting a thirty-one-year-old nurse called Elsinore Jemmott. They had met abroad and had known each other for nearly a decade. On the day of the attack they had bumped into each other in the street and Clarke had pleaded with her to talk to him. 'Suppose I shoot you?' he said after she repeatedly refused. He slapped her and hit her across the face with his stick. Disgusted by what he had just done, he broke the stick across railings and threw it away.

> I did assault her and I didn't. I was not responsible at the time. I am very sorry to put Miss Jemmott to all this trouble. What would you do if you loved a lady for nine years? [. . .] Some uncontrollable spirit deprived me of my reason, sanity, and manhood. Loving this lady for nine years, finding her discarding me, and meeting her with a ring on her hand, all my reason

fled. I am guilty, and I shall prefer to go to prison to expiate my offence.[20]

When questioned by the magistrate, Jemmott denied that she had encouraged her suitor in any way. At this point, Clarke, who had sobbed throughout most of the proceedings, turned to her and asked:

> 'Don't you think you encouraged me when I went down with you three Christmases ago to Margate?' – No answer.
> 'You told me if I left another girl you would leave all the world and come to me. And haven't you written me 300 or 400 letters?' – No answer.
> 'And didn't you say you loved me?' – No answer.
> 'And didn't you offer me encouragement when I have kissed you thousands and thousands of times?' – No answer.
> 'And don't you think you encouraged me when you told me you would love me with the last breath in your body?' – No answer.
> 'And don't you think you have encouraged me in innumerable ways in your life?'[21]

Still getting no answer, Clarke announced that he would plead guilty and expiate his offence in prison. He was fined a hundred pounds and ordered to keep the peace.

The Londons inhabited by Edgar Manning and by Grace Stevenson and Marcus Clarke both find expression in the work of Jean Rhys. Long seen as a postcolonial writer or as a feminist Modernist, she is perhaps better read as one of the twentieth century's most affecting urban chroniclers of the demi-monde metropolis. Although she was born in Dominica she wasn't black and nor were most of the women she wrote about. Nonetheless, in her fiction, her letters and her memoirs, she talked of the Caribbean with longing and nostalgia. Rhys claimed in her autobiography *Smile Please* (1979) that she 'used to long so fiercely to be black'.[22] In *Voyage In The Dark*, Anna's dramatic friends call her a Hottentot. She herself claims, 'I wanted to be black, I always wanted to be black'; she tells her lover that she's a 'real West Indian [. . .] I'm the fifth generation on my mother's side'; her stepmother Hester refers to, 'That awful sing-song voice you had! Exactly like a nigger you talked – and still do.'[23] Her racial background and her identification with black women make it appropriate to incorporate her in this study.

Rhys arrived in London for the first time in 1907. She was seventeen and en route to the Perse School in Cambridge which she attended briefly before joining the Academy of Dramatic Art in London the following year. She later worked as a chorus girl, a film extra and a volunteer cook before – partly as a result of the encouragement of Ford Madox Ford, one of her many lovers – she published her first collection of short stories, *The Left Bank* (1927). Both this volume and her subsequent work draw heavily on the time Rhys spent living in the West End. Here she encountered glamour and its bleak flipside: fake impresarios, cynical casting directors, petty criminals and dope peddlers. Here pretty young girls, fresh from the provinces or working in suburban shoe stores, eager to see their names in lights or to be swept off their feet by handsome men, soon found themselves rubbing shoulders with ladies of easy virtue in the bars and restaurants around Piccadilly Circus and Shaftesbury Avenue. If they couldn't find wealthy suitors to keep them in nice clothes and good wines between acting engagements they might resort to a spot of prostitution themselves. The difference between actress, chorus girl, flapper and 'women of the unfortunate class' was never very clear in the public mind.

Almost without exception Rhys's novels portray young women

flitting between lovers and suitors in London and Paris. Cut off (or having cut themselves off) from the security of their families, they lack resources of their own, and are forced to rely on the generosity and handouts of ardent men they meet in clubs, restaurants and railway carriages. Anna Morgan in *Voyage In The Dark* (1934), Julia Martin in *After Leaving Mr Mackenzie* (1931), Audrey in 'The Insect World' (1976) and many other female characters all live in shabby bed-sits from whose endungeoning clutches they flee, wraithing and skittering from one dalliance to another, from one glitzy club to the next, always looking for Mr Goodbar. These are shallow, messy encounters, but at least they serve as a release from daytime London's choking psyche-lock.

Even as she travels down to the capital, Anna Morgan feels her heart sink:

> smaller meaner everything is never mind   this is London hundreds thousands of white people white people rushing along and the   dark houses all alike frowning down one after the other all alike all stuck together   the streets like smooth shut-in-ravines and the dark-houses-frowning-down.[24]

It's a passage that crystallizes many of Rhys's deepest anxieties about city life. Like Sancho, she plays with typography, keeping words away from each other, putting extra white space between them. These extended gaps reflect Anna's belief that the capital, despite the clamour, despite the skelter, is full of people who feel divorced and cut off from themselves as much as from their neighbours and the city around them. Tawny Anna also balks at London's lack of colour. Her outburst isn't just about race; she's terrified by the metropolis itself, how it sucks beauty and vitality from the people who live in it. Elsewhere in the novel she ponders on 'how parts of London are as empty as if they were dead. There was no sun, but there was a glare on everything like a brass band playing', and 'Looking out at the street was like looking at stagnant water'.[25] Similarly, in *After Leaving Mr Mackenzie*, Julia believes that, 'It was the darkness that got you. It was heavy darkness, greasy and compelling. It made walls round you, and shut you in so that you felt you could not breathe. You wanted to beat at the darkness and shriek to be let out. And after a while you got used to it. Of course. And then you stopped believing that there was anything else anywhere.'[26]

Julia's sense of imminent asphyxiation recalls Anna's description of the streets looking like 'shut-in ravines'. From the first time she came to Bloomsbury Rhys had regarded London as a penal colony which went out of its way to regulate and curtail pleasure. In her memoirs she describes her shock at being lambasted by both her aunt and the landlady of their boarding house in Upper Bedford Place for daring to fill her bath half full of hot water. In London, it seemed to Rhys, basic natural resources like water and sunshine were routinely rationed. The city was a necropolis.

Anna talks of its 'dead smell' and, upon moving into a new room in Adelaide Road near Chalk Farm Tube station, finds a poem left behind by the previous tenant which mourns, 'Loathsome London, vile and stinking hole . . .'[27] One of her previous bedsits in Judd Street 'had a cold, close smell. It was like being in a small, dark box.'[28] The short story 'Rapunzel, Rapunzel' is set in a convalescent home outside which even the trees droop 'in a heavy, melancholy way'.[29] The blinds are often drawn giving the room the appearance of a crematorium furnace. London's sluggishness makes its inhabitants both sour and prematurely senescent. The lead character in 'Till September Petronella' recalls going for

> long walks, zigzag, along the same way – Euston Road, Hampstead Road, Camden Town – though I hated those streets, which were like a grey nightmare in the sun. You saw so many old women, or women who seemed old, peering at the vegetables

in the Camden Town market, looking at you with hatred, or blankly, as though they had forgotten your language, and talked another one. 'My God,' I would think, 'I hope I never live to be old.'[30]

London hobbles and desiccates its population, draining it of all life: in 'The Insect World', Audrey is on the escalator in King's Cross Underground station when she suddenly becomes obsessed by the idea of jiggers – harvest bugs commonly found in the Caribbean – which could get in 'under your skin when you didn't know it and laid eggs inside you. Just walking along, as you might be walking along the street to a Tube station, you caught a jigger as easily as you bought a newspaper or turned on the radio. And there you were – infected – and not knowing a thing about it.'[31]

London, far from being curative, is transformed into a sick zone. Julia's mother, like Leila's in Caryl Phillips's *The Final Passage* (1986), is an 'invalid, paralysed, dead to all intents and purposes'.[32] In *Voyage In The Dark*, Anna Morgan has an abortion that severs her last remaining link to her lover Walter Jeffries and snuffs out any hope of regeneration and futurity. Soon all of London appears to want to injure and violate Anna who becomes

afraid to cross the street and then I was afraid because the slanting houses might fall on me or the pavement rise up and hit me. But most of all I was afraid of the people passing because I was dying; and, just because I was dying, any one of them, any minute, might stop and approach me and knock me down.[33]

Rhys's characters feel condensed by the city – it strains and squeezes the life out of them. And though they are almost exclusively white, this sense of physical incarceration, that London is draining away all personal vitality, is a response common to many women who came to the capital from the (former) colonies.

Particularly in the post-war period, Asian and Caribbean women were led to regard London not so much as an arena for sensory opportunity and acceleration, but as a place in which all their worries about poor finances and burdensome in-laws would soon cease. London, these immigrants hoped, would trigger an absence of anxiety and an end to strife, rather than a fusillade of high-speed adventures. They were encouraged to believe this by their husbands who had sent them photographs in which they posed, suited and booted, in studios the cameramen had carefully decorated with key signifiers of Western social success – leather briefcases, radiograms, televisions. Little wonder that these women, like most utopian-minded immigrants, viewed England and London as oases of luxury and creature-comforts. At last! they anticipated – an end to days spent crouching over tiny stoves, fingers getting charred and joints becoming arthritic. No more endless hours scrubbing cotton cloth. No more back-breaking work milking cows and scooping up their shit. No more constantly being at the beck and call of mean-minded relatives or prey to the gossiping and rumour-mongering of envious neighbours. From all these manifold tediums and toils London was expected to be a liberation.

Such hopes were rapidly dashed. Many Caribbean and Asian women arrived in London only to realize that their husbands had concocted romanticized pictures of life in the capital. They had done so to conceal from themselves how degraded their lives had become, in order not to lose face among the villagers back home, and also because they did not want to disillusion their wives and children from the outset. Those wives were forced to squeeze into tiny, squalid households in broken streets in rundown areas of the capital. Rooms were small, heat and lighting limited, the air a fetid combination of paraffin-heater fumes and damp clothing that hung in every inch of space.

Unlike the rogues who populate the work of Sam Selvon, these women rarely permitted themselves the time or the irresponsibility

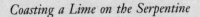

to go boulevarding along Bayswater Road or gallivanting in Leicester Square on a Saturday night. They were too busy trying to control family budgets and bring up their infant children in a foreign country. Often they found themselves being forced to work as hard as in the villages they had left behind. The only difference was that their living conditions were often far worse in

London: cut off from grass or sea, with even the capital's snivelly light often failing to penetrate the discoloured net curtains of their Harrow Road living quarters, it's no surprise that many black women regarded their homes as little better than cattle pens. They were confined. London, that epic arena for social admixture and advancement, shrivelled into a space that encompassed a distance barely further than that between their festering household and the local fruit market or their children's school.

Rhys's characters may share with many first-generation black female immigrants the view that life in London too often moved at the pace of a funeral cortège, but there's at least one important factor that makes their experiences distinct. None of Rhys's women are tied down by family commitments. They each have the time and freedom, if not always the inclination, to go out and about on the town. Yet Anna Morgan, Julia Martin, Petronella Gray – they all lack absolute choice and opportunity because of their poverty: they may have unshackled themselves of familial ties but, as a result, they've also been stripped of the (financial) support systems which could have smoothed their passages through the capital. These women have merely delivered themselves into another form of servitude, one that involves constantly cosying up to affluent, eligible men who can shower them with meals, gifts and prolonged glimpses of the high life. Living in London becomes for them a ceaseless ricochet through restaurants and hotel bars, primping and flirting with men whom they simultaneously despise and depend upon, trying not to feel defensive about their relative intellectual and cultural uncouthness. Petronella tells a likely young man that she's a member of the Apple Tree club: 'I had touched the right spring – even the feeling of his hand on my arm had changed. *Always the same spring to touch before the sneering expression will go out of their eyes and the sneering sound out of their voices.*'[34] Petronella here gauges precisely the hollow and functional essence of these encounters – snare a man, arouse his interest, build up his fascination or ardour so that he'll be prepared to offload lots of money for the foreseeable future.

Guileful and creative as such tappings can be, they're also reductive and dully formal. Rhys's women not only become commodities, but they commodify themselves. Display and get paid is the creed they follow. From an irritation born of acute self-recognition, Anna tells her friend Maudie to shut up after she announces that, 'People are much cheaper than things'.[35] But Maudie's right. Things, especially clothes, are very expensive. They're also essential for maintaining self-confidence and modernity in a city which jades and ages so many of its inhabitants. Buying clothes, however clichéd they may be as objects of fascination for women, represents a desire and ability to keep on top of the city, to move with the times rather than to be left behind by them. Rhys's women, like the author herself, are obsessed with clothes not only as instruments for winning the attention of men, but also as items which lend their lives – checkered and seemingly insubstantial – a degree of materiality. They buy them to alleviate loneliness. They're a form of self-pampering, a way to make themselves feel special. Anna, unable to afford new clothes, is filled with fear and desperation. She thinks people 'jaw, jaw and sneer, sneer all the time' at her, and even imagines that she repels the city itself: 'You look at the skirt of your costume, all crumpled at the back. And your hideous underclothes. You look at your hideous underclothes and you think, "All right, I'll do anything for good clothes. Anything – anything for clothes."'[36]

A manic insecurity underlies Anna's outburst. She really seeks to be draped and girdled by human warmth. 'Say it again,' she feels like shouting when her lover Walter Jeffries is about to leave their room, 'Say "darling" again like that. Say it again.'[37] In *After*

Leaving Mr Mackenzie, Julia makes herself up 'elaborately and carefully; yet it was clear that what she was doing had long ceased to be a labour of love and had become partly a mechanical process, partly a substitute for the mask she would have liked to wear'.[38] These women long to tattoo themselves on the city, to allay their feelings of endless drift and non-localizable pain. Audrey, in 'The Insect World', 'always wrote her name on the fly-leaf [of books] and tried to blot out any signs of previous ownership.'[39] But Rhys's women never can stand tall or independent. Their property is never their own – their homes are bed-sits, rented rooms; their books are second-hand; their dresses and jewellery bought by suitors. They cannot erase the fact of their utter dependence. Julia visits a former lover to borrow money off him: 'Because he has money he's a kind of God. Because I have none I'm a kind of worm. A worm because I've failed and I have no money. A worm because I'm not even sure if I hate you.'[40]

As in Prince's and Seacole's autobiographies, poverty and financial dependence play a large part in Rhys's descriptions of life in London. Like those two writers, Rhys's characters often feel isolated and bereft in a city that is cold, callous, and funereal. Yet there's an important difference. Topographical references are scarce in Prince and Seacole: the former lacked the money or the confidence to roam about the city and her arthritis also limited her mobility; The latter's *Wonderful Adventures* are chiefly concerned with her exploits in the Caribbean and the Crimea. Rhys's characters, in contrast, experience far more of the city's horrors and delights. Petronella takes long, circuitous walks through Euston Road, Hampstead Road, Camden Town. She talks of her love for Hyde Park. Like Anna Morgan and Julia Martin, she taxis to and fro between clubs and hotels in the capital, variously rebounding to and recoiling from the arms of moneyed suitors. Less glamorously, these women are often shown lugging their possessions between hostels and bed-sits in Chalk Farm, Notting Hill and the back of Selfridges off Oxford Street. Much of this movement is joyless: Anna and Julia may spin and kilter through the city but they lack security, love, and personal wealth. They get around but they get nowhere. Geographically their Londons may be more expansive than those of Prince and Seacole, but emotionally and psychically they are, at the very least, just as pinched.

One trope that recurs in many books set in London by Caribbean women is that of zoos. In *Smile Please*, Rhys recalls how, 'As for the zoo, I simply hated it. We saw the lions first and I thought the majestic lion looked at me with such sad eyes, pacing, pacing up and down, never stopping. Then we made a special journey to see the Dominica parrot. The grey bird was hunched in on himself, the most surly, resentful parrot I had ever seen.'[41] Rhys, to some extent, is merely expressing the sentiments of many visitors to zoos. Yet the reference to the Dominican parrot also bears a personal inflection. The animals in the zoo offer up a taste of the exotic, of far-away tropicality. They exhibit colour and wonder to Londoners starved of those qualities. But shipped over here, often having been ripped away from their families and the land they know best, confined to tiny cages and pens while still expected to behave gaily and frenetically for the benefit of gawping visitors, they regress into sullen depression. The parallels between the immigrant in the metropolis and animals in zoos are obvious.

Many black authors, writing autobiographically as well as fictionally, have noted how their colour and lowly social status attracted the attention of Londoners. Returning from a family outing to Vauxhall Gardens, the Sanchos 'were gazed at – followed, &c. &c. – but not much abused'.[42] Disconsolate at being turned down for Crimean duties by Elizabeth Herbert at Belgrave Square, Mary Seacole wrote, 'I dare say that I was a strange sight to the few passers-by, who hastened homeward through the gloom and mist of that wintry night.'[43] 'Why do you start and wince,' Una Marson asked the 'little brown girl' in her poem of that name,

> When white folk stare at you?
> Don't you think they wonder
> Why a little brown girl
> Should roam about their city
> Their white, white city?[44]

Only after the first decade of mass post-war immigration did black people cease to be considered curious and novelties. Some of the men who settled in London during the 1950s recall having their trousers tweaked by children and cheeky women keen to see if they had tails. But the frequency with which women authors have written about being stared at indicates that they felt particularly threatened at being the objects of aggressive and sexualized gawping by Londoners. Black women have traditionally had far less access to money and power in the capital than African and Caribbean men. To compensate for this they have often had to package and prettify themselves for male consumption. The insidiousness of this process is best exposed in Jean Rhys's work, where the constant need of her female characters to doll themselves up to stoke the interest of wealthy suitors creates such insecurity and panic that Anna Morgan believes even 'the shop-windows [are] sneering and smiling' in her face.[45]

It's this constant awareness and fear of the male gaze that accounts for the frequent allusions to zoos in writing about the capital by black women. Taking a child to London Zoo, Buchi Emecheta tells him that, 'London is a jungle in a way. It has all those captured animals in an artificial jungle and not far from them is our concrete jungle. You are right. London is a jungle too.'[46] In *Black Teacher* (1976), Beryl Gilroy is disturbed by the reaction of one of her pupils after a class trip: 'The Zoo, to Samlal, meant the jungle from which a jackal had come, torn a hole through the fragile hut in which his grandmother lived, and bitten her in the neck as she'd lain asleep.'[47]

Neither of these two authors is specifically alluding to the condition of black women in the metropolis: Emecheta is playing on the idea of London as urban war zone; Gilroy merely recalls an occasion on which she discovered the psychological traumas that a particular student of hers had undergone. Yet, given the repeated attention women writers have paid to their role as over-scrutinized underlings in the city, the very fact that both Emecheta and Gilroy choose to record these two incidents is significant. In *Head Above Water* and *Black Teacher* the authors discuss at length the many privations and humiliations they faced after arriving in London. Both talk about the shock of leaving countries rich in space, wildlife and greenery for a city so dark and tight. This environmental diminution is embodied by zoos which constrict and delimit the creatures they house. They're meant to evoke the fecundity of foreign terrains, but often succeed only in jolting visitors into thinking about the loss and bereavement the animals might be feeling. Rightly associated with pleasure and spectacle, zoos are also where dumped lovers, recently sacked employees, and old men and women hollowed out by loneliness go in order to sit alone and sob. For the female immigrant, so often emotionally hobbled by poverty or uncaring lovers (Prince, Rhys, Emecheta), so often confused and disorientated by London's unforgiving velocity (Marson, Prince again), zoos are a perfect metonym both for the lives they lead and the kind of lives they don't.[48]

War brought black men – particularly American GIs and West Indians serving in the RAF – to London in large numbers. Soho was full of smoky, single-room clubs, many illicit, which became homes away from home for East End racketeers, West African stowaways and those affected by the colour bar practised at many pubs. Students went to them eager to while away some time with fellow countrymen. West End bandsmen sought refuge from haughty managers and the women they had been cheating on. They argued about politics, swapped bawdy tall tales, smoked marijuana and frittered away their earnings on gambling and drinking sessions. Yet, according to one reporter, 'it would be a mistake to regard them as one big, happy family. The Martiniquans regard themselves as the black princes of their race. They affect to despise the Senegalese or "jungle boys." Some of these "white Negroes," West Indians and mulattoes, even go to local barbers to have their hair de-kinked.'[49]

White people were allowed entry at most of these clubs. In flocked crooks doing deals, vicars keen on social outreach, prostitutes, hipsters eager to check out cool new jazz trios, public-school-educated men and women after a piece of rough trade. Soho was 'run on hedonism and fast turnover'. It was the 'nearest London could get to the twilight world of fringe life in Chicago and New York'.[50] Club owners, like many of their regulars, were seasoned veterans. Over the years they had travelled widely across Europe and the Americas. After the glamorous Frith Street club owned by Frisco, aka Joslin Augustus Bingham, was bombed, he didn't tarry long before setting up shop in Sackville Street. He spoke fluent Yiddish and was a friend of Ernest Hemingway. Hutch, Joe Louis and Jesse Owens were all regulars at his club. Ever ready to dispense good-time vibes and whip-smart wisecracks, offering a port of call to blacks seeking shelter from the hassles and hatreds in the streets outside, he, and other club owners like him, became confessor figures, cultural go-betweens.

Some of these scenesters took such a shine to London that

when the war had ended they sailed back home vowing to return again one day. The chance arose in 1947 when, completely unheralded, the SS *Almanzora* docked at Southampton with 150 Jamaicans aboard. The state did not succour them with handouts or cheap accommodation; they spent the weeks after disembarking trying to stave off the coldest winter of the last century by blowing into their palms and loitering for as long as possible in the warmth of the Underground and Lyons Corner Houses.

The *Windrush*, contrary to popular belief, did not trigger a massive influx of new immigrants to England. Only a few hundred drifted across the Atlantic each year over the next half-decade. Ambitious West Indians found it cheaper to sail to Panama, Costa Rica, and to the United States. Many headed for Florida where they farmed, picked citrus fruit, and worked in canning factories. America had been a popular destination since the nineteenth century: by the 1920s, the decade of its artistic and cultural renaissance, a quarter of Harlem's residents could claim Caribbean roots, while half of New York's black businesses were owned by West Indians. In 1952, however, Congress passed the McCarran Walter Act which restricted migration to America, and forced potential migrants to consider joining those of their countrymen already settled in the UK.

Officially 492 West Indians, the majority of them Jamaican men with an average age of twenty-four, were on board the *Windrush* when it sailed for England on Empire Day in May 1948. Paying twenty-eight pounds and ten shillings – the not inconsiderable equivalent of three cows – and armed with JP-signed affidavits testifying to their good characters, they, along with the stowaways, were a socially heterogeneous bunch. In addition to the journalists, students, clerks, boxers, mechanics and actors on board, around a third of them were on leave from the RAF or were returning after being demobbed. Although the hurricane which hit Jamaica

in 1944 had destroyed the island's coffee and banana crops and
provoked deep recession, the early settlers were not economic
migrants. Most of them possessed marketable skills and did not need
to come to England. Selfhood was the motivation: they were drawn
by the opportunity to escape domestic responsibilities and the cosseted predictability of island life – to surge towards the vastness and
freedom to self-fashion that England represented. Only by fleeing
Jamaica – however much they told themselves they would return
in five or ten years – could they begin truly to exist.

Nowhere do these migrants exist more vividly than in the work
of Samuel Selvon (1923–1994). Born in Trinidad of Indian parent-
age, he produced a series of books – *The Lonely Londoners* (1956),
Ways of Sunlight (1958), *The Housing Lark* (1965) are the best
of them – that combine bitter-sweet comedy with memorable
characters and stylistic and linguistic innovation, making him one
of the greatest post-war writers of any colour. Black novelists,
in particular, have sung his praises. They include Caryl Phillips,
Gbenga Agbenugba (whose 1991 novel *Another Lonely Londoner*
draws parallels between the experiences of Selvon's city-dwellers
and those of a second generation growing up in the 1980s), and
V.S. Naipaul. As early as 1958 he argued that, 'because Sam has
written so authentically he has made it easier for the rest of us
who want to make people talk the way they do. Sam was the first
man, and I think we ought to give him credit for this, who made
it possible.'[51] And in a poem entitled 'Letter To Selvon' (1958)
Barnabas J. Ramon Fortune wrote:

> News I have heard of you
> Through miles of atmosphere
> And from the lips of friends;
> News of the music you
> Have strummed from English words,
> Like plumaged, tropic birds

Singing in brighter suns
Over the English fog.

And I have thought of you
As a discoverer
Who sets at nought the fear
Of those who stay at home
Fashioning failures for
Minds that are braver.[52]

Floridly expressed though they may be, Fortune's thoughts seem in retrospect to be very perspicacious. 'Discoverer' evokes the pulsing, concealed cartographies of London that Selvon was the first colonial writer to uncover. The allusion to the 'music' that he 'strummed from English words' reminds us that Selvon was also the first Caribbean author to create a London patois, to invoke not only the social and psychological changes that immigrants undergo when they encounter the metropolis for the first time, but the linguistic changes too.

Selvon travelled to London in mid-April 1950 aboard the same ship as the Barbadian novelist George Lamming with whom he initially stayed at the Balmoral Hotel in Queen's Gate Gardens, South Kensington, a hostel that was routinely recommended as a first port of call for colonial students. 'I came to London', Selvon later claimed, 'as any other immigrant. I had no high ideas that I was going to be a writer.'[53] After a spell in hospital with tuberculosis, he spent much of the 1950s moving from one poor, rundown house in West London to another. He couldn't afford to devote himself to full-time writing and took whatever work he could get. He served as a clerk at the Indian High Commission and cleaned bars and hotel kitchens around Bayswater.[54] Many years later he recalled how, after the publication of *Turn Again Tiger* in 1958, 'I was swabbing out the shithouse at a small private club owned by an affluent Irishman in Paddington who said, "I saw your picture in *The Observer* yesterday, I didn't know you were a writer." '[55]

Selvon, then, lived and worked with many of the people who populate his London fictions. He shared their hopes and scrapes and aspirations. He wanted to give voice to them, to show that they were so much more than the sociological problems they were painted as by the popular press. His journalistic background also disposed him to gravitate towards this social underclass. From 1946 to 1950 he edited the literary section of the *Sunday Guardian Weekly*, a supplement to the *Trinidad Guardian*. A typically plodding, respectable colonial organ dealing with the grey and the good, the paper had been transformed by the arrival in 1929 of a bullish American, Gault MacGowan. The new editor urged his reporters to be more aggressive, to scour and snout for stories in neglected parts of the island, and to celebrate quotidian diversity. These were also the qualities Selvon displayed in his work for the *Guardian*'s afternoon tabloid, the *Evening News*. His articles anticipated Tom Wolfe's 'new' journalism. Kenneth Ramchand has argued that Selvon's early writings offer:

> glimpses of the novelist-to-be steeping himself in place, and in the spirit of places. He walks the streets by night ('Nocturnal Ramblings') or during the normal waking hours ('The Life of a Day'), ostensibly on the lookout for some event or person to fit into a 'Now It Can Be Told' column. He becomes engrossed in the behaviour of his fellow Trinidadians in crowds ('I See People Watch a Fire').[56]

Seepersaud Naipaul also wrote for the *Trinidad Guardian*, where, according to his son Vidia, he learned that, 'literary talent doesn't exist by itself; it feeds on a society and depends for its development on the nature of that society'.[57] Selvon held similar views: he praised a poem by Barnabas J. Ramon Fortune because it

> glorified the commonplace and captured the essential quality of the ordinary. '. . . a heap of wares in the sink to be washed . . .' '. . . Making the insufficient money I give her do . . .' How reflective of a life we are all accustomed to, and yet fail to see any beauty in![58]

This determination not to overlook the seemingly mundane, to render the burr and plod of the lives of unexalted peoples, courses through all of Selvon's work. It was through his linguistic innovation that he made the quotidian vivid. No Caribbean writer before Selvon had narrated a novel using local idioms or speech patterns. Even the socialist realist fictions of C.L.R. James and Alfred Mendes published in the 1930s confined Creole usage to the dialogue. The end results often read like paternalistic, neo-anthropological documentaries about endangered tribes: the chasm between the narrators who speak in cool Standard English and the clamorous energy of their subjects is too great.

The Lonely Londoners was the first Caribbean novel to be written totally in dialect, or at least a version of it. Oddly, Selvon used this technique only for those of his works set in England. He explained his decision in a radio interview with Bernard Miles, claiming that he had become aware of the richness and diversity of Caribbean speech only after he had arrived in London. This is unsurprising. The islands of the West Indies are scattered far and wide: Trinidad and Grenada are a thousand miles apart, the same distance that lies between Berkshire and Warsaw. Living during an age with limited media outlets, and often in closeted peasant communities, few islanders had heard other West Indian accents or dialects:

It is only now, in the migration of people from all these islands
to Britain, that the opportunity occurs to get together and hear
one another talk. [...] And settling in this country has of
course given much opportunity for the invention of new phrases
or the novel usage of words.[59]

Selvon didn't try to reproduce all the different varieties of Caribbean English he encountered in London. Nonetheless, hearing so
many registers each day on the Tube, at street corners, and at
betting shops and local pubs, convinced him that to write a novel
about immigrants in London that failed to reproduce the exhilarat-
ingly 'new' English they used would be an act of treachery. A
short extract from 'Calypso in London' (1957) shows how Selvon's
use of dialect affects the reader's response to his characters:

[Mangohead] get turn away from the cigarette factory, and he
start to make a bee for the tailor shop, hoping to make a little
borrow from hotboy, something like ten shillings, or if not, five,
or if not, a two and six, or if not at least a cuppa, old man.[60]

Selvon begins with a plain report of Mangohead's journey to the
tailor's. The use of the present tense when describing past events
('get turn away', 'he start') is common among West Indians and
creates both flow and immediacy. Storytellers also routinely narrate historical tales in the present tense in order to mesmerize
their audiences, and Selvon's prose, similarly, evokes a persistent
nowness.

The narrator uses the kind of 'Creole' vernacular ('make a little
borrow') and truncated English slang ('make a bee') that Mango
himself would have spoken. These shared idioms assist the rapid,
almost imperceptible transition from impersonal report (Mango
can't get work at the factory) to laddish intimacy, concluding with
Selvon's near-verbatim transcription of Mango's cheeky request
for a loan. Because these final clauses ('something like ten shillings'

to 'old man') aren't shielded from the rest of the paragraph by the use of speech marks, the reader is almost led to believe that it's the narrator who's cadging off Hotboy. In effect, we've been teased into an empathy with Mango that, rationally, we know he scarcely deserves.

The language that Selvon's characters brought to London was a form of luggage, one considerably sturdier than the flimsy cases they hauled off the carriage racks at Paddington Station. Richly inventive, it also offered them a warm retreat from the arse-clenched frigidity they often came up against in daily life where they soon learned that locals sneered at their foreign accents and that such phrases as 'respectable tenants', 'experienced hands' and 'regular customers' were all but cant synonyms for 'white people'. Their language exuded motility, even if they felt their own lives were at a standstill. When we look back at Selvon's work today, and revel in the freshly-hatched rhythms, sentence structures and vocabularies it unleashes, it's hard not to feel that his fiction commemorates the moment at which 'Englishness' was being changed forever. The nation's accent – as well as its colour and racial composition – could less easily be taken for granted:

> Before Jamaicans start to invade Brit'n, it was a hell of a thing to pick up a piece of saltfish anywhere, or to get thing like pepper sauce or dasheen or even garlic. It had a continental shop in one of the back streets in Soho, and that was the only place in the whole of London that you could have pick up a piece of fish. But now, papa![61]

Selvon knows that language, as much as fashion styles, foodstuffs and an accelerated appetite for metropolitan living, is one of the key contributions his immigrants are making to London. At times he gets rather stroppy about this. In *The Housing Lark*, he uses the word 'buttards', about which he elaborates in parentheses:

That's a good word, but you won't find it in the dictionary. It mean like if you out of a game, for instance, and you want to come in, you have to buttards, that is, you pay a small fee and if the others agree, they allow you to join. It ain't have no word in the English language to mean that, so OUR PEOPLE make it up.[62]

Selvon's later work shows signs of linguistic disenchantment. Sarcasm and sour pastiche, rather than lyricism, predominate. By the mid-1970s Selvon's critical and commercial standing, like those of many Caribbean writers, had gone into sharp decline. African and Latin American novelists having supplanted them in literary fashion, they were also adjudged to be irrelevant to the concerns of second-generation immigrants in the UK. *Moses Ascending* (1975), a waspish satire of the Black Power movement, registers this disappointment, but is written in a mock-heroic style that is only sporadically engaging:

The alarms of all the black people in Brit'n are timed to ring before the rest of the population. It is their destiny to be up and about at the crack 'dawn. In these days of pollution and environment, he is very lucky, for he can breathe the freshest air of the new day before anybody else. He does not know how fortunate he is. He does not know how privileged he is to be in charge of the city whilst the rest of Brit'n is still abed. He strides the streets, he is Manager of all the offices in *Threadaneedle* street, he is Chief Executive of London Transport and British Railways, he is Superintendent of all the hospitals [. . .] he should look upon himself as a pioneer what preparing the way for the city's day, polishing the brass and chrome, washing the pots and pans. As he banishes the filth and litter, he could thunder out decrees in the Houses of Parliament and his voice would ring through the corridors and change the Immigration Act and the policies of the Racial Board.[63]

Selvon is at all times an ironic writer. This is not to suggest that he is cool or glib or disdainful or, indeed, that he embodies any of the negative values that the word 'irony' has come to connote in recent decades. Rather, it means that he has a tendency, one both melancholic and wise, and one that all those with an interest in the bumpy course of twentieth-century black politics are likely to share, to see the tragic undertow of human endeavours. Men are frail and foolish. Even the best intentions get scuppered. Knowing this makes it impossible for him to endorse the slogans and angry mantras that became the rage in the late 1960s. *Moses Ascending* mocks the pseudo-radicalism of black militants who champion ethnic separatism and 'brotherhood' but readily exploit or undermine those blacks who do not share their ideological or strategic fervour. They are passionate about 'unity' only when it suits them. Moses himself shies away at times from friends he believes are dragging him down to their underachieving level. He longs to escape his dull and derelict life in Shepherd's Bush and tells Galahad, 'When I leave here my past will be behind me, you inclusive.' His friend retorts, 'You can't erase me like that [. . .] I am part and parcel of your life.'[64]

Galahad's right. Moses can be a blustering and pretentious idiot, but he's never cruel or solipsistic. Though he cusses and grumbles, he can't shake off his concern for – and sense of obligation towards – the West Indians of London. He admits as much after bailing some of the Black Power activists arrested after the police raid a public meeting in North Kensington and indiscriminately grab members of the audience.

Actually Moses can't bear these hectoring ideologues. Nonetheless, 'I know all the failings and shortcomings of My People, their foibles and chicanery, their apathy and disunity, but I were less than a Pharisee to leave them by the wayside.'[65] Even his pompous solecism does not devalue the sentiment.

Many of Selvon's characters share this often equivocal but, ultimately, devoted attachment to the West Indian community. Moses
begins *The Lonely Londoners* in a sullen mood because he's been
called upon – yet again! – to meet a batch of newly-arrived immigrants at Waterloo Station. Though disgruntled, he's still prepared to take Galahad under his wing, to lend his camelhair coat
to the unreliable Cap, and to offer loans, advice and his company
to many of the disconnected, chaotic rascals who populate the
novel. He is a true Samaritan; a man who would rather risk being
a soft touch than allow himself to stand by and let his friends
and countrymen come to harm. His sense of obligation and his
willingness to look out for others are often abused. Yet Selvon
would far rather have his characters be exploited or labelled naïve
than have them enclosed in morally gated communities where
self-protection is the watchword.

Selvon loves his 'boys'. Errant and unreliable, hopeless and
harmless, they dream big but live small. Here they are in the city
whose towers and spires had soared so high in their childhood
imaginations, whose river winds its mesmerizing path through the
endless urban landscape, a city which appears bigger, vaster, taller
than anything they've ever seen on their own islands. And yet
now they've arrived, it seems squat and constricted. They lack the
money or contacts to be able to range far and wide across the
capital, zigzagging between landmarks and celebrities, breathless
through excess:

> The changing of the seasons, the cold slicing winds, the falling
> leaves, sunlight on green grass, snow on the land, London par-
> ticular. Oh what it is and where it is and why it is, no one
> knows, but to have said: 'I walked on Waterloo Bridge,' 'I
> rendezvoused at Charing Cross,' 'Piccadilly Circus is my play-
> ground,' to say these things, to have lived these things, to have
> lived in the great city of London, centre of the world. To

one day lean against the wind walking up the Bayswater Road (destination unknown), to see the leaves swirl and dance and spin on the pavement (sight unseeing), to write a casual letter home beginning: 'Last night, in Trafalgar Square . . .'[66]

Yet Selvon's characters reside in a London even more pinched and claustrophobic than that of Jean Rhys. Their terror of being paralysed in the metropolis leads to an obsession with mobility and kinesis. London, however, is faster, more aggressive than anything they have previously experienced. They know they can't afford to sit still and wait for better days ahead. Change is relentless – they have to keep on just to keep up. Even this proves difficult: in *Eldorado West One*, Galahad slips on an escalator and complains that 'In London you have to keep on the move all the time, you see. Even the steps keep moving.' In the story 'Come Back To Grenada' (1955), Fred has to stay on the run to elude those (friends) naïve enough to lend him money: 'One day you hear he living Notting Hill Gate, the next day you hear he move and gone Clapham, a week after that you might bounce him up in Highgate.'[67]

Life in London is composed of gerunds. Selvon's short stories have titles such as 'Finding Piccadilly Circus', 'Working the Transport', 'Waiting for Aunty to Cough'. His characters are always pursuing in vain: wandering the streets looking for a fiver they dropped weeks before, waiting for the day when they'll have a bed of their own to sleep in, searching for elderly passengers who got off the bus without taking all their belongings with them. The narrator of 'Calypso in London' will wait in vain for his friend to write the fantastic lyrics he's capable of. These stories are droll variations on a theme – the search for El Dorado. In *The Housing Lark*, Gallows treads Bayswater Road 'wondering if in truth the streets of London pave with gold'. 'If Winter Comes' (1957) shows Brakes scouring Soho 'his face rivet down to the ground'. In *Eldorado West One*, Moses tells a reporter, 'sometimes

in the night I see as if the Bayswater Road sparkling with dia-
monds. But then you look in truth you see is only stones and
gravel that mix-up with the asphalt.'[68] This motif serves as an
ironic, twentieth-century take on the imperial ravaging Spanish
and English conquistadors wreaked on the Caribbean in previous
centuries. It's also a modern version of one of London's own most
enduring myths – that of Dick Whittington coming to the capital
in the belief that its streets are paved with gold.

But if London's constriction foments a constant desire for
mobility, that very 'movement' – scouring, working, searching –
is largely in vain. It doesn't lead to social escalation or economic
ascendance. The characters don't, and couldn't afford to, move
to more prosperous parts of the capital. Small Change, the appositely-named indolent driver in 'Working the Transport',
embodies such stasis by contriving to reverse his bus into a wall.
At the end of *The Lonely Londoners*, Moses is convulsed by a fear
of urban paralysis: 'he could see a great aimlessness, a great restless,
swaying movement that leaving you standing in the same spot'.[69]

Selvon's West Indian arrivants aren't passively resigned to such
petrification. In *The Housing Lark* their refusal to allow London
to dwarf them is shown by how enthusiastically they clamour to
visit Hampton Court Palace. In Brixton, where they live, 'the most
you could do is cruise in the park or go to the cinema'.[70] Brackley's
friends also have limited geographic horizons: in 'Waiting for
Aunty to Cough' he tells them that his white girlfriend isn't local
– 'to the city boys, as soon as you start to hit Clapham Common
or Chiswick or Mile End or Highgate, that mean you living in
the country'.[71]

Selvon's female characters have even fewer opportunities for
going out and scanning the capital than their husbands and partners. Their enforced tunnel vision is best represented by Ma in
The Lonely Londoners, who cleans dishes at a Lyons Corner House

and is the only woman in the novel who is neither a cheap sex-object nor a bossy matriarch. Hour after hour, day after day, the only access she has to life in London comes via the 'wares [which] used to come from a square hole where the attendants push them. Only from the washing up Ma form an idea of the population of London.'[72] Writing about his experiences of working in a Lyons Corner House in the Strand during the late 1940s, E. Martin Noble has claimed that, 'A restaurant's dishwasher is the lowest in the order of staffing, and a black dishwasher the absolute bottom of the barrel'. A black *female* dishwasher probably represents a further rung down the social ladder.[73]

In contrast to the novels of George Lamming and V.S. Naipaul there are few middle- or upper-class people in Selvon's work. There aren't many white characters either. His immigrants lead

hermetic, enclosed lives. They don't, and perhaps couldn't, inter-
mingle with white people who, unless they're nice bits of skirt for
the boys to squabble over, are often portrayed as rather surly
potentates lurking behind the scenes: a London Transport inspector who fires Small Change for neglecting his duties; a malicious
coach driver who believes the excursionists should be returned to
Jamaica on a banana boat. At other times whites figure in rather
vague terms as part of a boss class whose eyes need to be opened
to the social realities charted in the novels:

> Them rich people who does live in Belgravia and Knightsbridge
> and up in Hampstead and them other plush places, they would
> never believe what it like in a grim place like Harrow Road or
> Notting Hill. Them people who have car, who going to theatre
> and ballet in the West End, who attending premiere with the
> royal family, they don't know nothing about hustling two pound
> of brussel sprout and half-pound potato, or queuing up for fish
> and chips in the smog.[74]

Occasionally Selvon's characters do get the chance to escape their
grim neighbourhoods and attend the key sites of what Rushdie
has called 'Proper London'[75]: Black Power demonstrators in *Moses
Ascending* gather triumphantly at Trafalgar Square; Caribbean
workers in the same novel are seen at the Bank of England's
headquarters; the narrator of 'Finding Piccadilly Circus' exults at
the prospect of seeing wild lions there. But all of these encounters
with the monuments and enduring landmarks of London are comically discomfiting. The rally in front of Nelson's Column descends
into mutually recriminatory squabbling; the Caribbean workers
don't discuss macroeconomic policy in the Bank of England's
boardrooms but, rather, polish the tables and clean the floors.

The bathos! After centuries of subservience and ontological
inferiority, London's blacks have become sufficiently free and

mobile to mark their presence on some of the capital's most famous sites and institutions. They needn't genuflect to an imperial past but can gleefully creolize these monuments. Actually, though, all these encounters do is bring into relief how very far Selvon's characters are from finding the centre, from belonging to – and feeling at ease with – the capital, its history, and the mooredness that these landmarks seem to symbolize. Names are routinely misspelt ('Threadaneedle Street', 'Hamdon Court'[76]); the narrator of 'Finding Piccadilly Circus' is puzzled that he can find neither real lions nor circuses there. Mere physical proximity to the heart of London doesn't guarantee the fulfilment of his dreams about the capital.

Language replicates this tense oscillation between hope and despair. The appositely-named character Big City keeps using,

unwittingly, a neologism – 'fusic' – instead of music.[77] Viewed positively, this sounds like 'fuse', a verb that implies addition and synthesis, qualities both linguistic and cultural that Big City and West Indians appeared to gift post-war Britain. Viewed negatively, however, such an inkhorn term denotes a slippage – a loss of control over correct language that mirrored the difficulty Caribbean immigrants during the 1940s and 1950s faced when trying to become true Londoners.

These bleak forebodings recur in *Moses Ascending*. Black separatists boom and bray with self-righteous indignation, but Moses sees that, 'On top of the column the one-eye sailor was looking over the Houses of Parliament, as if he didn't want to have nothing to do with these black reprobates slandering the fair country'.[78] Selvon feels there will always be an insurmountable gap between the immigrant and these concretizations of historical, 'proper' London. He's not satisfied with viewing the monuments as mere tourist diversions. Nor can he regard them – with a connoisseur's eye – as purely aesthetic entities. They represent a notion of power, belonging and permanence about which, as 'a poor coloured colonial from a backward island far across the world', he'd been instructed at school, and after which, as an impecunious, deracinated poet, he'd lusted.[79]

> My home says to me, slow down, old man, and make up your mind you aren't going anywhere. You haven't come all that far, and you're not going much farther.
>
> From the moment you arrive to the moment you die, you are always immigrating; always trying to find a good place, a good home, then a better one. It's sort of like you're on the run.[80]

The passengers aboard the SS *Empire Windrush* attracted a

cheerier response in London than they did in Jamaica, where *The Daily Gleaner* glumly spoke of 'New Life In Sombre Setting For W.I. Job-Seekers'. That paper's curmudgeonliness contrasted unfavourably with the *Daily Mail* which, in a spasm of magnanimity it would struggle to repeat over the following decades, announced 'Cheers for men from Jamaica'. More warmly still, the *Evening Standard* greeted the arrivants with the headline: 'WELCOME HOME'. It was a generous sentiment, one that recognized London's status as a maternal bosom for many colonial subjects. Over time, though, it might also have induced bitter cackles among many Caribbean immigrants. 'Home', as opposed to a mere house, connotes security, reassurance, the warmth and intimacy of the domestic realm. These were the very qualities often missing from the lives of West Indians in London during the 1950s.

Selvon had grown up knowing the importance of home ownership. Upheavals in the Trinidadian housing market following the Government's Slum Clearance Ordinance scheme of 1935 resulted in poor resettlement plans that forced many of the people now rendered homeless to construct their own jerry-built quarters. Later the arrival of American servicemen in the Caribbean during the Second World War triggered a huge urban influx as peasants left their villages in order to seek better-paid jobs near the US bases. Overcrowding and misery ensued. As a journalist during the late 1940s Selvon would have been more aware than most of these dismal events. In time, they formed the backdrop of his first novel, *A Brighter Sun* (1952), as indeed they did for Naipaul's *The Mimic Men* (1967).

Getting a roof above their heads wasn't easy for the West Indians who had migrated to London. Decent accommodation was scarce. Over 100,000 houses had been destroyed and half a million damaged during the war. The spurt in post-1945 birth rates, coupled with the large numbers of people returning from evacuation to the capital, meant that most London boroughs had long housing waiting lists. Immigrants were faced with the additional barrier of colour bars and colour taxes. Nearly half a century later, many of those interviewed in Mike and Trevor Phillips's oral history *Windrush* (1998) still appear shell-shocked by the icy responses they faced when they tried to find accommodation after disembarking from their trains at Waterloo and Paddington. Hour after hour, days crumbling into weeks, they filled out useless forms, pestered friends, scanned shop windows for accommodation ads free of the demand 'No Irish, No Blacks, No Dogs', only to trudge back to their hostel rooms most evenings cold, sodden and still smarting from the more-in-sorrow-than-in-anger weasel words of the latest slum landlord to close a door in their face. Animosity was not universal – an English woman travelling on the same London bus as Eric Huntley not only sheltered him from the rain with her umbrella but went so far as to escort him all the way to the Haroldstone Road house he was looking for.[81] Nonetheless, the cold responses they faced set the tone for their stays and became a standard trope for books and films about this period written by later generations. Indeed, as Andrew Salkey's Malcolm Heartland prepares to leave the capital after twenty years, he is suddenly seized by an epiphanic vision, one that he feels captures all that was most painful and enraging about West Indian life in London during the 1950s:

> He saw a large white door, at an angle of imminent collapse, with the small figure of a Black man, standing in front of it and knocking softly, as if the fist he raised were made of a dab of black cloud.[82]

Throughout his work, Selvon uses housing not only as a marker for how his characters are faring in the capital, but as a metaphor for their relationship to England and English culture. He identified closely with his characters' anxiety to obtain decent places to stay. A trawl through his radio contracts reveals that throughout the 1950s he was often on the move, changing addresses frequently. Mainly he lived on the same tumbledown streets in Bayswater and Notting Hill as his fictional creations. Other contemporary Caribbean writers such as George Lamming and Andrew Salkey lived in upmarket Hampstead which had comparatively small immigrant populations. Moses tells Bob in *Eldorado West One*, 'Hampstead is a posh area. It don't have many of US up there.'[83] Selvon's response to an interviewer's question about why so many of his characters were keen to acquire things – houses, beds – is stamped with bitter autobiography: 'Material things become very important when one gets out of one's land.'[84]

London's houses have an entombing effect upon the Caribbean

psyche. Selvon's characters feel submerged, buried away from the roaring hubbub of the metropolis. In 'Basement Lullaby' (1957), 'Even sounds in the house can't be heard: is as if down there the two boys cut away from life.'[85] Fred and Bar 20's room in Paddington is so dingy and depressing that it corrodes not only their friendship, but their ability to express themselves. The pianist is too weary to get 'the melody right' of the new calypso they've been playing at a club that night and, angered by Bar 20's chattering, he bashes away purposelessly at the piano in the corner of their room.[86]

These cramped quarters unleash no poetry or redemption. They offer no existential insights, no bohemian cred. *The Lonely Londoners* contrasts, with biting accuracy, Moses 'Lock up in that small room, with London and life on the outside'.[87] In *The Housing Lark*, Battersby, whose bed is jammed against the corner of a Brixton basement, thinks 'life was a dream', and wonders 'what London was like outside'.[88] Such sepulchritudinal rhetoric wasn't mere melodrama. Newspaper reports about West Indians dying, alone and prematurely, would have been read with silent dismay by immigrants during their lunch breaks at bus depots and postal sorting offices across the city. Dismal stories about isolation-induced madness would have been swapped and tut-tutted over in barber shops, public-houses and wherever West Indians assembled. Moses tells Galahad to 'look how people does dead and nobody don't know nothing until the milk bottles start to pile up in front of the door [...] That is a hell of a thing to think about.'[89]

These anxieties are captured most poignantly in *The Lonely Londoners* where the dissolute rogue, Cap, becomes so hungry that he resorts to luring seagulls into his room near Notting Hill Gate. His hunger, irritation, and his mounting panic as he tries to smother a gull flapping for dear life about his room, all conspire to make this one of the most memorable comic episodes in the entire novel. For seagulls, like Caribbean immigrants, are primarily creatures of the sea. When things are too hard for them by the sea, seagulls move to urban centres. Selvon describes them in terms similar to his accounts of the liming boys: you never know where you'll see them next; they 'hang out' by the Odeon in Marble Arch; sometimes you'll catch them at Trafalgar Square; they're scavengers and hustlers who can often be found near Notting Hill. Cap tempts the seagulls into his room with broken crusts just as West Indians were lured by crummy jobs and the promise of fiscal 'bread'. The seagull's neither stupid nor prepared to succumb without a fight – it hurtles around the room, desperate to stave off death. Similarly, Selvon's immigrants, such as Big City and Cap himself, show a trickster-like resilience in their ongoing battles to ward off indigence. Finally, however, the bird is trapped and suffocated – just like Moses' story of those West Indians who were gassed during their sleep.

The Jamaicans and Trinidadians who arrived in the capital during the 1950s came from islands that, for all their poverty, were blessed with clear skies, fresh air and low-rise housing. To their eyes, London's houses, row after grim, colourless row, looked like army barracks which rationed the individuality of their owners with a severity that outstarched all the other austerities of the period. To be chocked into cellars and basements below the city's surface was against nature. It was also psychologically debilitating, as can be seen from Nirad Chaudhuri's account of walking along Bayswater Road towards Hyde Park:

> The impression of solidity was so strong that if I had had a hammer in my hand I should have walked along unconsciously tapping the houses with it, and in a mood of impatience, which endless rows of bricks and stone often generate, I should have involuntarily thought of a battering-ram.[90]

The 'solidity' of the capital's topography which Chaudhuri finds so disturbing also reflects how concrete and insurmountable are the social barriers between West Indian and white Londoners: 'They tolerate you, yes, but you can't go in their house and eat or sit down and talk.'[91] Selvon's characters long to knock down and destroy the racist attitudes and the economic ceilings that hem them in. It is impossible. These houses come to determine their entire beings, to circumscribe their capacity for self-development: in *Moses Ascending*, the narrator confesses, 'I had the

feeling that if I didn't make the move now, I would be doomed to the basement brigade for the rest of my life.'[92]

Even as the characters hustle and lime, con and scrape, they must return – however late, however grudgingly – to their shabby rooms.[93] This is the one certainty in their otherwise random lives. In *The Lonely Londoners*, Galahad woos Daisy with words and gestures on a romantic date in the West End, but he 'feeling sort of shame' at taking her back to his pad which has the 'whiff of stale food and old clothes'.[94] In *Moses Ascending* the narrator speaks in a patrician, pseudo-aristocratic manner about his new home, referring to it as his 'penthouse' and 'my castle'. Not only does he designate himself 'Master of the house', but, revelling in the possibility of being eligible for jury service, indulges in monstrous delusions of power – 'You will go to jail, you worthless scamp, and await Her Majesty's Pleasure'.[95] Yet Moses knows full well that he's being hyperbolic, engaging in imaginative and verbal pyrotechnics. He actually lives in a 'derelict terrace house in Shepherd's Bush'.[96] Even the area's name makes it sound to him like a jungle. It hints at Moses' fear that, despite his bluster, his life is so shamefully primitive that, 'if I had Tarzan as a tenant it would of been ideal for him'.[97] There's a grim comic inevitability about the way he gets demoted from penthouse to basement *in his own home*, a demotion caused by his own fecklessness and intercrural twitchings.

Selvon's most thoughtful and prolonged exploration of the need for a home appears in *The Housing Lark*. This was his first novel about London to be published after the Notting Hill riots of 1958. The attitudes of London's immigrants towards everything in England – authority, politics, their neighbours – changed for the worse after that year. A West Indian who'd lived in Notting Hill since 1938 told the *Daily Mail*: 'This is the most disappointing thing that has ever happened to me. I am so hurt that I would like to rewrite the history books.' Baron Baker, another local resident, claimed that before the riots he was British, but that they had turned him 'into a staunch Jamaican. To think any other way would not have been kidding anyone else more than myself.'[98]

In *The Housing Lark* Selvon's immigrants have become sick of lying about who they are: Nobby has to pretend to be fond of dogs in order to ingratiate himself with his landlady; Sylvester is so desperate for accommodation that he resorts to approaching a landlord who will only take in 'real' (as opposed to West) Indians. Claiming to be called 'Ram Singh Ali Mohommed – Esquire', and reeling off as many Indian words as he can recall cropping up on his last vindaloo menu, he's finally exposed by a fellow conman – a big-bearded, turban-wearing Jamaican. 'I used to live in the East End,' Sylvester tells the landlord in desperation. 'That is not far enough East,' is the reply. 'Take a week's notice as from today.'[99]

Though comic, this last episode makes a serious point. Lying about oneself to obtain a room is demeaning. Any frisson or buzz Selvon's characters get from duping landlords is offset by their resentment at having to be so underhand. Insecurity about themselves and about the value of their lives in England sets in. They feel permanently panicked. Knowing that they might be rumbled and turfed out of their lodgings makes them feel vulnerable and rootless. They feel they're living double lives, tipping towards schizophrenia. In *The Housing Lark* Gallows believes that, 'if a man have a house he establish his right to live'.[100] Selvon's narrator empathizes with his characters' desire to move into proper homes and enjoins us to do so too: 'When Gallows left number 13A (let we number Battersby basement for him, he will feel good).'[101] Thirteen is an ominous number – it suggests that Bat's house-owning aspirations are probably doomed from the outset.

The centrepiece of *The Housing Lark* is the excursion made by the black Brixtonians to Hampton Court (this is Selvon's only novel set south of the Thames). The venue, so old and posh, seems far removed from the beat-up lives of these new immigrants. Its history reminds us that the Englishman, whose home is his castle, has long been inclined to keep black aliens as far at bay as possible. He has a fortress mentality. This knowledge makes the reader rather nervous about the proposed trip. We desperately want the families to have a good time. It's no ordinary day out; not a day out to *somewhere*, but *away from* the grey dolefulness of their normal lives. We want them to have fun, to believe that they can be gay and silly, and not furrow-browed or fretful. Please, we whisper to ourselves, don't let them make a hash of this day. They don't. They have a really good time. They make a real effort – plait their hair, wear their sharpest suits. They wander the Court with awed delight. Men and women, elders and kids alike, play and run about, take photos, laze on the riverbank, laugh skiff-skiff, talk the old-talk, gorge themselves on rice and peas, emit rummy belches. They feel themselves living again rather than merely existing. The day will live on in their memories, as it will in those of readers:

> You could imagine the old Henry standing up there by the window in the morning scratching his belly and looking out, after a night at the banqueting board and a tussle in bed with some fair English damsel. You could imagine the old bastard watching his chicks as they stroll about the gardens, studying which one to behead and which one to make a stroke with.[102]

There is, though, a brief altercation. A palace servant chides Teena for arguing too loudly with Fitz about aspects of Henry VIII's reign. It seems for a moment that not only is the right of West Indians to inhabit the aristocratic English home being queried, but also the likelihood of them ever taking part in 'proper' English history. Things soon pick up. In spite of the superciliousness of the jobsworths who patrol Hampton Court and the bilious bus driver who calls for the day-trippers to be repatriated, everyone goes home to Brixton exhausted and happy. They may not have bought their own homes yet – nobody in Selvon's work ever does own a nice one – but, vividly and unsentimentally, they have been shown to possess a resilience and joy unexpected in those who live in such poverty. They may have nothing in their bank balances, but London would be a vastly poorer place without them.

George Lamming once claimed that Selvon was essentially a 'peasant' writer: 'The peasant tongue has its own rhythms [. . .] and no artifice of technique, no sophisticated gimmicks leading to the mutilation of form, can achieve the specific taste and sound of Selvon's prose.'[103] Over the years this line of thinking has become a critical orthodoxy. Yet Selvon never did just reproduce the language of peasants; he invented, with considerable skill, a composite form of dialect, one that no West Indian immigrant actually spoke but which, nevertheless, conveys the tang of authentic speech. To 'invent' requires technique, something that all good authors need to master in order to distinguish themselves from journalists or anthropologists. The great bane of black artists, both today and historically, is that they have been prized for their capacity to 'tell it like it is' rather than for their powers of imagination or craftsmanship. Yet sophisticated literary technique, far from betraying working-class culture, might be its ally in that it is better able to evoke its rich complexities than the bluntness of socialist realism.

    In many ways Selvon is a strikingly Modernist writer. His subject is the city and he makes London his, just as Baudelaire did Paris and Joyce Dublin. Estrangement is the dominant emotion. Even the elements keep themselves to themselves; the sun in the sky emits no heat, but 'it just there in the sky like a force-ripe orange. When he look up, the colour of the sky so desolate it make him more frighten. It has a kind of melancholy aspect about the morning that making him shiver.'[104] Discontent and anomie riddle his solitary characters who wander the streets looking for some grand design that would help them to make sense of their confusion. Sex is automatic and ungallant; at one point Galahad talks of 'meeting a new piece of skin'.[105] And as much as his characters may feel detached from the people around them, they are also alienated from their own bodies on account of their skin colour. Galahad, upset by having kids point at him and recoil from his touch, and weary of two-faced workmates who claim to be his friend but curse other 'black bastards', lifts up his hands and starts to reproach it:

> Colour, is you that causing all this, you know. Why the hell you can't be blue, or red or green, if you can't be white? You know is you that cause a lot of misery in the world. Is not me, you know, is you! I ain't do anything to infuriate the people and them, is you! Look at you, you so black and innocent, and this time so you causing misery all over the world![106]

Selvon's Modernism extends to the form of his books. *The Lonely Londoners* has no plot as such; it's a series of loosely related sketches of metropolitan life. To read it is to undergo a series of jolts and tumbles as characters flit in and out of view; comic vignette rubs up against mordant reportage. The effect is rather akin to that of a whitewashed wall that, over time, has become a messy riot of colour as fly-posters, graffiti art and community news-sheets vie with each other to adorn it with newer and ever louder information.

One of the most unforgettable passages in *The Lonely Londoners* is a stream of consciousness effusion about love in the city. All one sentence, it goes on for ten pages without a single comma or colon. Beginning 'Oh what a time it is when summer comes to the city and all them girls throw away heavy winter coat', it skips on to rhapsodize about the joy and horrors of courting.[107] It details unnerving encounters in beat-up flats between Jamaican men and hysterical au pairs; the wretched prostitutes, their arms scored with needle marks from shooting up heroin, writhing beneath the shrubbery in Hyde Park; the casual deceit and violence that women put up with from the men in their lives. All humanity is here and on the hunt. From out-of-work immigrants to company bosses, voyeurs and well-spoken 'pansies' to idle toffs, everyone cruises through the greenery as if enacting a devolved version of Sunday afternoon at Vauxhall Gardens during the eighteenth century.* Days turn into months. Summer arrives and 'sun burn away all the tightness and strain;'[108] soon though the trees are naked and winter has descended. The quest for contact is desperate and damaging. It's both exciting and sad. His 'sophisticated gimmick' evokes a London in which it seems that most people might forever run on empty:

* Clubs like The Roaring Twenties on Carnaby Street were also places where white people of all classes could get to know West Indian immigrants. Stories circulated in the 1950s and early 1960s of the pleasure some aristocrats took in sexual slumming. Alfred Harvey came to London from Jamaica in 1954 as a stowaway. He soon acquired the name of 'King Dick': 'I've seen some things that you wouldn't believe it [. . .] Like walking down Bayswater Road, Sunday evening, you're nice, and you just see a big car pull up beside and, "Are you busy?" "No." And next thing you know, they take you to some posh house and you going to have sex with some posh white woman. One told me, "When you see me on the street, don't you talk to me." That's true. See her one day in Oxford Circus, and when she saw me she recognized me all right. And that's all I got. Didn't talk to her [. . .]

'Another one was Sarah Churchill. Yeah. I don't know, probably she was a nymph. She never satisfied one man – two – three. She come to the gambling house, and her chauffeur would be out there with his cap over his face fast asleep and she's in there gallivanting herself. So, it's somebody who I knew. She took three of us one night. She was living in Maida Vale, Carlton Vale or one of those Carlton, and she had some jewellery on mantelpiece, and one man start to pinch the jewellery. But then one was getting ready to go and having sex with her, and when she look at his underpants she said, "Get out. Get out." And she ran us out.'[109]

oh Lord Galahad say when the sweetness of summer get in him
he say he would never leave the old Brit'n as long as he live
and Moses sigh a long sigh like a man who live life and see
nothing at all in it and who frighten as the years go by wondering
what it is all about.[110]

It's in Selvon's obsession with speech and the difficulty of communication that he really comes into his own as a black Modernist.
For a writer often seen as artless and journalistic many of his
writings are highly self-conscious and self-critical. An early poem
'Modern Art . . .' (1948) satirized avant-gardists who sought novelty of expression rather than fidelity to human experience.[111] In
an essay, 'Little Drops of Water' (1967), he talked of wrestling
to freeze the moment and to reveal 'a full awareness [of] consciousness'.[112] His novels and short stories often contain key characters
who are desperate to put pen to paper, to compose calypsos and
stories that might structure and make tolerable their shoddy
environments.

Speaking is the dominant theme of Selvon's first novel, *A
Brighter Sun*. Its hero, Tiger, is obsessed with becoming a man.
He marries young, is sexually naïve, and feels ignorant about
everything: 'Unknowingness folded about him so he couldn't
breathe.'[113] His fellow villagers may be 'wise', but they're unedu-
cated; Tiger, though, wants to better himself, desires the paper
qualifications that he believes will enable him to become a fuller
human being. On a rare trip to the island's capital city, Port of
Spain, he finds himself travelling past a college in Maraval Road;
in another life he might have been educated there and been primed
for success. Suddenly he realizes 'what I want to find out most is
about things in general, about people, and how I does feel funny
sometimes. Man, if I tell you bout things I want to find out!'[114]
Seeing that illiteracy equals passivity and social impotence, Tiger

begins to study in his spare time. He rises to become a surveyor for an American company. His social cachet improves. At the end of the novel he's still waiting to hear whether his short story about a local highway has won the *Trinidad Guardian* literary competition. He may have been keen to speak, but would the world have been interested? Earlier, his wife had upbraided him for trying to impress her by using phrases such as 'small cylinders of narcotic rolled in paper' instead of 'cigarette'.[115] Would his short story have been a similar squawk of polysyllabic parrotings? If so, how could he hope to represent the lives of the people he wanted to write about?

Foster, the lead character in Selvon's next novel, *An Island Is A World*, draws up a literary manifesto. In it he rejects the theoretical and the abstract in favour of the 'actuality of life'.[116] Whereas Tiger saw writing as a way to distance himself from the vapidity of rural existence, middle-class Foster insists that artists shouldn't divorce themselves from their social roots: 'you've been taught from ever since that people who write and paint and compose music are little gods above you'. Instead, he plans to write a book called 'Ha-ha', 'Skiff-skiff' or 'Hello How Are You This Morning' about which 'The greatest compliment would be to hear someone say, "Ah, that's life for you".'[117] Yet here, as in *Turn Again Tiger* (1958), where the main character burns all his books because he feels they represent 'the top of the mountain while his feet were trapped in the canefields', and in *Those Who Eat The Cascadura* (1972), where an English travel writer abandons his attempt to write about local lore after he's sucked into a romance with a local Indian girl, no literature emerges.[118] Foster never writes his novel. Caribbean culture, it seems, evades all attempts to describe it.

This sorry track record of thwarted eloquence gets exported to England. In 'Calypso in London' Mangohead has the gift of the gab and a love of calypso. In response to his friend's admonition that

'This is London, man, this is London. The people want calypso on topical subject', he pens a few verses about Nasser and Eden, 'and how he will give them the dope – the best thing is to pass the ships round the Cape of Good Hope'.[119] Instead of capitalizing on this rare burst of inspiration he uses the temporary good favour in which he's held by his friends to tap them for loans. The calypso goes unrecorded. In *Moses Ascending*, meanwhile, the narrator's attempts at sophistication ('coop de grace', 'parabox') are mere linguistic inflation.[120] His poor spelling exposes the disjunction between his lofty rhetoric and the grotty reality that surrounds him.

One of the most memorable scenes in *The Lonely Londoners* takes place at Speaker's Corner, a spot much in favour with immigrants during the 1950s. In Andrew Salkey's *Escape To An Autumn Pavement* (1960) a white barmaid chides Johnny, the Jamaican lead character, for being brusque: 'You West Indians do have a lot of Hyde Park in you, haven't you?'[121] They saw the monument as a kind of English Statue of Liberty, a rare public platform for the disenfranchised, the unlettered and the unhinged. Selvon's rogues and toilers may have been men and women of immense charm and wit, but they didn't possess the social or cultural standing that enabled them to broadcast their own views.[122] Yet they had to put up with a good deal of uninformed public debate about them, much of it centring on their dirtiness, their obsession with women, and their general undesirability. And so, whilst West Indians were constantly being discussed and agonized over, they themselves were kept silent. As soon as Tolroy's family arrive at Waterloo they are greeted by a reporter from the *Echo*, a paper which later abuses Tanty's amiable garrulity by maliciously captioning its photo 'Now, Jamaican Families Come to Britain'.[123] Big City claims attendance at a star-studded party which is reported by the *Evening Standard* the next day, but 'they wouldn't put my name'.[124] The narrator of the short story, 'Poem in London' (1951), accurately contrasts the quiet 'ceiling-gazing' of immigrants who shiver in their bed-sits 'while London existed loudly'.[125]

Tired of such media black-outs, Moses and Big City goad Galahad to mount the soapbox at Speaker's Corner to contribute to a debate on the colour problem. It's a dramatic moment: here, at last, one of the brothers has come forward to speak on behalf of his people, to expose the privation, calumny and injustice his fellow immigrants face daily in the capital. A blast of his righteous verbals and, surely, walls will come tumbling down. What happens? Galahad becomes afraid. He feels foolish, his articulacy wanes, he's angered by Big City's efforts to help him. The audience begins to laugh. Galahad gets mad and climbs off the podium to attack Big City who he feels has upstaged his bid for oratorical renown.

It's an all too typical débâcle. Speaker's Corner is located at the top of Bayswater Road, the avenue along which the boys spend all their free time cruising. This proximity highlights the fact that Selvon's male characters would almost always go out flesh-hunting rather than get together to try to do something as worthwhile as shouting out against the poverty and discrimination they suffer. Given the habitual loucheness of his mates, Galahad's risible performance at Speaker's Corner seems in retrospect to have been sadly inevitable.

'Sometimes the words freeze and you have to melt it to hear the talk.'[126] Selvon has always been fascinated by the power of words – whether written or spoken – to allow low-caste peoples to find some purpose in their lives, to break free of their social and psychological shackles. The Speaker's Corner incident reinforces one of Selvon's key contentions about the extent to which black people were ignored and overlooked in the capital. Few Londoners, it seems, were prepared to hear, or 'melt', the words of the migrant. In his study of the official response to the behaviour of West Indian spectators at English Test matches in the early 1950s, John Figueroa argues:

> One felt that the 'noisy spectators' were trying to say something. They wish 'to be looked upon'; amidst their uncertainty and the threats of 'repatriation', they want to be associated with style, with verve, with success, with something literally 'to shout about'.[127]

In Selvon's work neither that success, nor the successful utterance, ever do materialize. Even in his final novel, Moses laments that 'I did never plant a flag, nor write my name on a wall, when I first came [. . .] To have spent all those years toiling [. . .] and just vanish without a ripple or a blink!'[128]

The redemptive irony is that by pointing to Galahad's failure to join the rhetorical pantheon of Cicero, Demosthenes and Burke, Mango's preference for cadging a shilling in place of penning a calypso, and by mocking Moses' overwrought windbaggery, Selvon merely draws the reader's attention to his own success in giving voice to his lowly characters. They may have failed through idiocy or misfortune to strike literary gold, but, through Selvon's gift for warmth and comic pathos, they now exist as loudly and memorably as the London that almost muffled them.

> Rain could have caused my beginning too, which fell sometimes on a nasty blue evening watching London coming to drown me if it found room.[129]

At the close of *The Lonely Londoners*, Moses briefly leaves his crumbling rented room for the banks of the Thames where he can escape the boys' company and spend some time alone mulling things over. He has been feeling black and blue for some time. Now he just wants to get away for a bit. It's a finale that may strike some readers as surprisingly sober. After all, despite its sensitivity to the poverty and borderline insanity of many of its characters, the novel is never less than comically affirming. Actually, those are the two reasons why the Thames was the most apt location Selvon could have chosen for this pivotal scene.

Water engenders dread in much of Selvon's neglected early prose and his work for BBC Radio's *Caribbean Voices*. His first story, 'The Sea' (1948), dealt with the six shipwrecked survivors of the *Ocean Pearl* who drifted for days on an open raft. Madness soon began to surface, rivalry developed, some were thrown overboard. Eventually, the whole raft sank to the bottom.[130] In 'Tropic (An Excerpt)' (1949), the poem's narrator goes to the harbour's edge late in the evening. Suddenly he feels morose and dwarfed, a 'little Trinidadian'. Looking out over the water, he realizes how absurd it is for a colonial like himself to dream of metropolitan culture. He tries to convince himself that he should restrict himself to West Indianisms and not 'Aspire to globe-girdling ideas/Symphonic music or epics'.[131] From the very outset of Selvon's literary career, then, water is closely associated with danger, sobriety, self-abasement, even mortality.

His books about London are equally awash with aquatic metaphors and imagery. In *The Housing Lark*, Harry Banjo likes to 'cruise around by the theatres' and 'float up to town'.[132] In *The Lonely Londoners*, Galahad 'drift down to Whiteleys'; Cap likes to 'coast a lime by the Serpentine'; unemployed men are compared to 'fish out of water gasping for breath'.[133] And while Selvon is hardly alone in using naval imagery to describe survival in London – in Jean Rhys's *Voyage In The Dark* Anna Morgan constantly dreams that she's at sea, unable to swim, drowning – his work is permeated more than most by maritime language. These verbs – coasting, cruising, floating – all possess a breezy fluidity; they connote the possibility of a liberating alternative to the endungeoning lowgrade housing in which his characters live. The peeling, pinched world of London's basements doesn't wholly determine their behaviour, and these water words conjure up the freedom which the likes of Cap and Galahad still lust after. They also evoke the pleasures and comparative carefreeness of the island life that they surrendered on leaving Trinidad. This gives a snatched, needy frisson to such apparently ordinary events as the night Fitz and Teena go 'coasting around Piccadilly Circus, holding hands!'[134]

Returning to the end of *The Lonely Londoners*, then, it's no surprise that Selvon, suffused by love for London, chooses to use the Thames as the physical embodiment of the fluidity and mobility to which his cooped-up characters aspire. There Moses seeks release from the drabness of his daily routine. He'd recently been 'thinking how to stop all of this crap, how to put a spoke in the wheel', and regretting that he 'get so accustom to the pattern that he can't do anything about it'.[135] As a Hindu, albeit not a very devout one, Selvon was also aware of the role that rivers play in washing away the stain of drear earthiness to allow the soul to proceed unencumbered towards *moksha*.

In the preceding few pages Selvon had sought to portray Moses as the embodiment of black Londoners' collective consciousness. As winter starts to bite, the boys seek refuge in Moses' room 'like if they going to church', 'like if is confession'.[136] Their anecdotes, questions and comments are unattributed and create a choral effect. Moses lives up to the Biblicality of his name and, in a characteristic act of burden-carrying, looks at the boys and 'feel a great compassion for every one of them, as if he live each of their lives, one by one, and all the strain and stress come to rest on his own shoulders'.[137]

So there is 'The old Moses, standing on the banks of the Thames'. And, as in 'Tropic', the place provokes 'some sort of profound realization in his life'. Moses becomes morbidly conscious of the aimlessness he and his friends inhabit. His language becomes apocalyptic: 'As if a forlorn shadow of doom fall on all the spades in this country.' He even feels he can see 'faces bobbing up and down in the millions of white, strained faces [. . .] on the surface things don't look so bad, but when you go down a little'.[138] His fear of submersion and drowning recalls Equiano's account of how he nearly died at the foot of Westminster Bridge. It anticipates the scene in *Moses Ascending* in which the narrator is arrested during a mêlée at Trafalgar Square and hurled into a police van:

> Like we was in the world of a slave ship. I remember them stories I used to read, how the innocent starboy get condemned to the galleys. Next thing you see him in chains [. . .] Any minute now the timekeeper was going to crack a whip in the Black Maria. I wonder if I play dead if they would jettison me in the Thames as we passing, and I could make my escape.[139]

As Moses stands near Chelsea Embankment he gazes down at the river. The chop and chunder of the waves makes him see how tedious and repetitive his life has become. The years are going by and London isn't getting any easier. He sees all too acutely that the hustling and 'swaying movement' of his fellow immigrants isn't taking them anywhere: it just left them 'standing in the same spot'.[140] The Thames's effect upon Moses, like his friends' experiences at Speaker's Corner, Piccadilly Circus and Nelson's Column, is chastening.

This scene is also a subtle reworking of a poem by the writer who most influenced Selvon's work: 'Ironically, perhaps, the poet I admired most was T.S. Eliot', he once told an interviewer.[141] The chief source of inspiration is 'The Burial of the Dead', the first section of *The Waste Land*. Eliot wrote:

Unreal City,
Under the brown fog of a winter dawn,
A crowd flowed over London Bridge, so many,
I had not thought death had undone so many.
Sighs, short and infrequent, were exhaled,
And each man fixed his eyes before his feet.[142]

Near the end of *The Lonely Londoners*, Selvon talks about 'the grimness of the winter, with your hand plying space like a blind man's stick in the yellow fog'.[143] Five pages later, Moses sees 'the black faces bobbing up and down in the millions of white, strained faces, everybody hustling along the Strand, the spades jostling in the crowd, bewildered, hopeless'.

The parallels between the scenarios painted by Eliot and Selvon are too numerous to be coincidental: winter, coloured fog, the crowds described in terms of liquidity ('flowed', 'bobbed'), the pessimism, the sense of a city not being quite there ('unreal', space being carved out by a blind man). Eliot, like Selvon, was a foreigner: in his description of a crowd he initially casts them as homogeneous and mono-dimensional, before introducing an American outsider, Stetson. Selvon also shows us the mass of woeful, swaying white faces before reminding us of the Caribbean immigrants in their midst.

This passage from *The Lonely Londoners* stems from the author's own experiences of walking and standing alongside the banks of the Thames. Similarly, footnoting line 68 in which Saint Mary Woolnoth is said to make a 'dead sound on the final stroke of nine', Eliot claimed autobiographical inspiration. This, he said, was 'A phenomenon which I have often noticed'.[144] Eliot was an office worker at Lloyds Bank during the period in which he wrote *The Waste Land* and line 68 is surely rooted in his experiences of commuting to the City. Selvon's vision of black London is also inspired by his daily traipse into town with his fellow immigrant labourers.

Revealing differences, however, exist between what the two authors are attempting. Moses was explicitly concerned with the plight of the 'spades'. While they, like Stetson, are outsiders, the colour of their skin affects them socially and economically to an extent that white Americans can scarcely imagine. Eliot's commuters may be spiritually torpid, but they at least have the luxury of the sort of white-collar respectability and financial security Selvon's characters can only dream about. These West Indians are both psychologically fragile ('they only laughing because to think so much about everything would be a big calamity'[145]) and, because of the petty discriminations they face all the time, forced to trudge around London seeking to make ends meet.

Selvon compels our empathy for the discrimination and daily struggle that his characters have to endure. In contrast, Eliot's 'Unreal city' passage lacks warmth or concern. There's a sardonic emotional gulf between the narrator of this section and his subject matter. Later, in 'What the Thunder Said', the capital is incorporated into a historical and apocalyptic framework ('Falling towers/ Jerusalem Athens Alexandria/Vienna London/ Unreal'[146]). Selvon's narrator is equally bleak, but is more concerned with the possibility of the immediate and very real psychic breakdown of his fellow immigrants than with making chiliastic pronouncements on the collapse of civilization.

Neither here, nor in another Thames scene that crops up in *The Housing Lark*, does Selvon plunge into drop-jawed metrophilia or abandon his concern for the West Indians who now stand at its banks. The river is a place for human fun, or at least for worrying about fun. Selvon never views the Thames aesthetically or as an impersonal entity: a river, just like any landscape, is nothing without its human dimension. In his work he tries hard to lever Caribbean immigrants into the imaginative topography of a river whose wealth and renown black people had for centuries been unwillingly instrumental in creating.

'Only in London did my life find its purpose' Selvon once told an interviewer.[147] The same might be said for the characters in his novels and short stories who have lived in London for so long and have become so used to its clutter and cacophony that they couldn't possibly live anywhere else. They're proud of this, and see themselves as cultural custodians. In *The Lonely Londoners*, Moses is described as 'a man about London', a 'veteran', 'mister London'.[148] The narrator of *Moses Ascending* proclaims with charming pomposity that

> I have weathered many a storm in Brit'n, and men will tell you that in my own way I am as much a part of the London landscape as little Eros with his bow and arrow in Piccadilly, or one-eye Nelson with his column in Trafalgar Square, not counting colour. I have been mentor and mediator, antagonist and protagonist, father and mother too, a man for all seasons and reasons.[149]

Selvon's characters, more than those of any other colonial writer of this period, are not ashamed to speak of their deep-rooted, sorely-taxed but, in the final run, unceasing love for London. They're often slighted or bad-mouthed, yet they never grow so disenchanted that they abandon the capital. Even the eponymous hero of *Moses Migrating* who has retired to Trinidad returns once more to London at the end of the novel. Selvon's characters are often jobless, fleeing from debtors, living on grisly corridors. Their run-ins with officials and their relationships with London's obelisks are vexed and uncomfortable. And yet, as the narrator of 'My Girl and the City' blurts, 'I loved London'.[150] It's this blunt

admission that sets Selvon apart: Nirad Chaudhuri may be awed, the Indian poet Dom Moraes thrilled, but only Selvon loves London with all the recognition and toleration of its faults that the word 'love' implies.

And faults there are in abundance. Selvon's London is not a pretty place. It's a city still struggling to get back on its feet after the war. Joy itself seems rationed. The city is blinded by peasoupers, and reeks of pigeon feed, paraffin fumes, week-old hair oil, drip-drying workers' overalls. There are sweatshops, immigrant hovels, junk-littered yards behind railway lines, the welfare office 'where hate and disgust and avarice and malice and sympathy and sorrow and pity all mix up'.[151] Ex-servicemen wander the streets confused: 'A lot of the men get kill in war and leave widow behind, and it have bags of these old geezers who does be pottering about the Harrow Road like if they lost, a look in their eye as if the war happen unexpected and they still can't realize what happen to the old Brit'n.'[152] West Indians, invited to rubble-strewn London to help the capital build itself up again, were all too often regarded as if they were part of that dereliction, the problem rather than the solution. Yet Selvon evokes pain, not in the cold and pickled voice of the sociologist, but as folk lament, pub sigh, the sweet-voiced threnody of the street-balladeer.

This voice is Selvon's most important legacy to the literature of London. He writes a form of pavement poetry. The city is seen from the point of view of those blowing into their palms on their way to an early shift, or tramping up to the dole office, or having just done a runner from a nasty hostel when they can't pay the rent. It's through their eyes that we gaze longingly at pretty young secretaries leaving their offices on summer evenings, at the friezes hanging from below the cornices of aged buildings, at the sheer dizzying pandemonium of the metropolis. And it's their voices we hear – slangy, vulgar, railing, sing-song, tender. It's the language, not of tradesmen or of churchmen or of rajahs, but of ordinary working-class people excitedly getting on with trying to make sense of their new city and the new people they've become. It's a great language full of warmth and humour and hard-earned wisdom. We want to speak it just as we wish to share their company. Selvon tries less to educate us or solve social problems than simply to convey joy.

His characters come to London neither in chains nor to negotiate treaties with politicians nor to inspect paintings in aristocratic art collections. They come to live, to become something different to what they already are. They're soon taught the benefits of worldliness, of keeping an eye out for con artists. Many of them become wily sharks themselves. Yet, for all the disappointments and sharp lessons they learn about mother London, they never quite lose their innocence. They're not cordoned off from the city; they're tentatively open to it all – and are enraptured as a result. And get hurt, too – but getting hurt is surely preferable to numbness or self-anaesthetizing. Does this make them 'comic caricatures or sentimentalized victims' as Mike Phillips has argued?[153] No, it just means that Selvon prefers to reveal them in all their foolishness, their venality, fear, aspiration, confusion, passion, rather than have them stand tall and man the barricades in the war for racial liberation. He is sensitive to how people are, rather than how they should be.

A final image: the new arrivals from the Caribbean jitter through the capital, checking for friends, checking for entertainment. 'They does treat Piccadilly Circus like Green Corner,' says Selvon, 'and walked down Oxford Street is if they breezing down Frederick Street, and if they meet you in the road or in a bus or in the tube, is a big shout, "What happening there, papa?"'[154] What's happening is that London is changing, becoming creolized. And it's Selvon who helps us to see that through his capacity for joyous wonder.

CHAPTER FOUR

Cultural Capital

THE DECISION TO PACK ONE'S BAGS, abandon relatives and birthright, and head across the oceans for London hasn't always been motivated by dreams of making one's fortune. The lure of culture has also been a magnet throughout the centuries. London offered a passport to sophistication, learning and self-improvement. Even at the height of the slave trade Ignatius Sancho could speak proudly of 'our grand metropolis', a verdict surely coloured by the capital's abundance of dramatists, sculptors and fine artists in whose company he delighted.[1] It's easy to dismiss Sancho as, in V.S. Naipaul's phrase, a 'mimic man', and to regard his views as colonial lackeyism. Other eighteenth-century writers, however, shared a similar response. Olaudah Equiano, often held up as the strident and self-possessed antithesis to Sancho's Sambo, claimed in his autobiography:

> I could now speak English tolerably well, and I perfectly understood every thing that was said. I now not only felt myself quite easy with these new countrymen, but relished their society and manners. I no longer looked upon [the English] as spirits, but as men superior to us; and therefore I had the stronger desire to resemble them; to imbibe their spirit, and imitate their manners; I therefore embraced every occasion of improvement; and every new thing that I observed I treasured up in my

memory. I had long wished to be able to read and write; and for this purpose I took every opportunity to gain instruction, but had made as yet very little progress. However, when I went to London with my master, I had soon an opportunity of improving myself, which I gladly embraced.[2]

Slaves in London were spared most of the cruel excesses that occurred daily on Caribbean and American plantations. Many of them served purely decorative functions in aristocratic households, and even though they commonly fled their masters, their lives were comparatively easy. Some of those masters devoted time and money to educating their wards, partly out of idle amusement, and partly because they were keen to refute racial theorists who claimed slaves were hapless sub-humans. They sought to provide textual and artistic uplift. The life of Ignatius Sancho – and his present-day renown – shows that such idealism was not misplaced.

There existed for black men and women in London, then, the possibility of being allowed to read, to attend the sermons of those clergymen whose fame extended across the Atlantic, and, if they were lucky, to be set free by their owners. While no one should regard Equiano's life as wholly representative of the 10,000 Africans who flitted across London during the second half of the eighteenth century, his statement should not be dismissed as stemming from a desire to butter up the liberal constituency whose support he relied on to abet Abolitionism and to sell copies of his own book. After all, Equiano didn't stint from criticizing the values and habits of Londoners elsewhere in his memoirs.

Nonetheless, the sentiments of the passage just quoted, allied with the pride taken by many Englishmen in the nation's efforts to abolish the slave trade, helped to foster the notion that London was a moral citadel. The Reverend James Peggs, one of the many missionaries who worked in the East End during the nineteenth century, spent much of his life preaching compassion for the thousands of lascars who washed up destitute in his parish:

> What an immense chandelier is London, the light of the world in commerce and science, philanthropy and religion; but how much darkness is found in her shadow, her suburbs. Alas! that the poor Lascars of her eastern districts should have enjoyed so little of the splendour of her light.[3]

It's in the work of twentieth-century authors, particularly those from the Caribbean, that a detailed picture emerges of what images and values London conjured up to those living in colonial societies. Devon, one of Donald Hinds's Jamaican interviewees in *Journey To An Illusion* (1966), recalls the pivotal role education played in making him believe that London, though thousands of miles away, was more 'real' than the ports and villages that lay nearby: 'I could recite passages from John Evelyn's *Diary* of the Great Fire of London; I still can. "3 September, 1666 – I took coach with my wife and son as far as Cheapside . . . the conflagration was so universal . . ."'[4] The classic novels, history primers and geography texts placed on school syllabi presented a gallery of triumphalistic images – Big Ben, Nelson's Column, the Houses of Parliament – all monuments signalling a lofty and noble past, concrete reminders that England was a land fit for heroes, the home of democracy.

Ambitious young men keen to improve themselves became external students of the University of London. Many laboured prodigiously, working through the night and ruining their eyesight to obtain degrees from that University's Institute of Education. Ill-lit by lamplight, they became ghostly figures during those years they pored over their texts. Their examination papers were sent to England for marking, which helped to foster the idea that status could only be conferred – and quality and rank only assessed – by the English. This was hardly surprising – English people were white, the same colour as most of the doctors, judges, lawyers, and governing legislative councillors in the Caribbean.

Englishness was associated with a kind of stiffness, the pulling up of one's socks, a standing to order and attention. In the Cadet Corps, on school Speech Days, whenever the National Anthem was played, Englishness seemed to compel a tautening, a sense that one was on show, that one had constantly to be on best behaviour. It exacted a sartorial regime – starched collars, scrubbed elbows, polished shoes – that was at odds with the Caribbean environment. 'Negroes do not learn without blows' was the motto of one Trinidadian primary school, and everywhere else in the region too a strict version of Englishness was drummed into students. Invariably conflated with whiteness (despite the long-standing existence of a white West Indian community), this Englishness induced hushed voices, a certain deference, and the precise, unfair gradation of students into achievers and non-achievers. It represented inflexibility, something with pedigree and authority. To speak the Queen's English was to speak the language of discipline and correction:

> Our culture of Sundays, regular as our bowels on a first-Sunday; regimented as the dry-peas and rice and baked chicken, sweet potatoes, pear, lemonade and rum-punch, was Rediffusion's recorded church services of ponderous, sonorous sermons delivered by Inglish vicars whose language was not the language of our miseries, and could not determine nor define what was contained in our hearts. They did not even know our sins. Or it would be choirs from Westminster Abbey, with which we joined in, demonstrating our own arrogant belief that Barbadians sang Hymns Ancient and Modern better than anybody born.[5]

London and England became interchangeable. The former embodied and magnified the latter's virtues. It was the home of the

Queen (God save her!) whose stamp on mustard jars and Quink bottles confirmed that, even in the realm of consumer articles, England was not only an arbiter, but also a manufacturer of the highest quality. In *Growing Up Stupid Under The Union Jack* (1980), the Barbadian Austin Clarke recalls that, 'in the classes at Combermere we were taught that the best things were made by the English'.[6] These included clothes, books, pencils, book bags, tortoiseshell combs, medicines, neckties, perfume, and the 'Brilliantine which made our heads shine, slicked back, concealing the African kink in our hair'.[7]

Though it may have loomed large in their imaginations, very few people had any real sense of contemporary London. As described by Pepys, Shakespeare, Thackeray and Dickens, the capital appeared to be ancient and archival. It was held to be a place of order and stability rather than, as younger, home-grown authors such as Hanif Kureishi later envisaged, a city which could be bent and remade in one's own image. Occasionally a stray copy of *Punch* or *Reader's Digest* would find its way on to the islands. Movietone newsreels at the Empire Theatre offered a flicker of new information about the imperial citadel. Otherwise, before the proliferation of the telecommunications industry, a colonial villager would arrive at a composite picture of London assembled from English postage stamps, a regulated press, and the fruity-toned authority of Bush House broadcasters whose words – swooping and oscillating across variable short-wave signals – crackled through on purple Bakelite transistors.

> radio was always on in the tailor shop, always English news – 'This is London calling' – And you heard John Arlott and Rex Alston speaking from Lords ... and you hear Raymond Glendenning describing boxing and horse racing. And you heard ... the boat race ... these sort of commentators were household names ... you hear about Regent Street and Charing Cross,

those things you knew . . . I had a very good understanding of
England . . . every aspect of English life . . . the Festival of
Britain . . . the Coronation . . . Everest . . . he started with that,
he says, 'with the news that the British expedition have con-
quered Everest.'[8]

London was a sacred geography to many incoming West Indians.
It was the inner temple. Going there was like entering the labora-
tory against whose glass windows they had previously only been
able to press their noses. Imperialism had drilled into them the
romance of its streets and heritage. To say this is not to diminish
its allure or to suggest that their love for it was purely a function
of rote learning, a form of false consciousness. Their love was
real, tinged though it may have been with fantasy. England itself
was the mother country, the breast from which the colonial
peoples supped. It was a home away from home, their real home.
This conviction distinguishes them from black Americans whose
fractious relationship with white America is inextricably tied to
the fact that they lived in a country to which their enslaved ances-
tors had been transported against their wishes. The British did
haul countless Africans across the oceans to the Caribbean, but,
generally, not to England. This factor is not unimportant when
considering the comparatively relaxed and fluid relations between
black and white people on this island over the course of the last
three hundred years.

The decision to leave the West Indies wasn't just motivated by
dreams of homecoming. It was partly about selfhood. To go and
actually live at the source of much of their identity was a challenge
of *Mayflower*-like magnitude. In *Escape To An Autumn Pavement*, by
the Jamaica-born Andrew Salkey, a woman asks the main character,
'What are you going to do here that you couldn't do over there?'
'Live, I suppose.'[9] His response may sound rather tentative but it
tells a passionate truth. The Caribbean offered spiritual petrifi-

cation, England the potential for endless possibility. In George Lamming's novel *The Emigrants* (1954), Harris spies English soil for the first time from his ship's porthole and thinks to himself, 'There was life, life, life, and wherever there was life there had to be something other than no-THING which did not matter.'[10]

Emigration was fuelled by love too. Tens of thousands of West Indian conscripts had been prepared to die for England during World War Two. They had served as flight mechanics, skilled technicians and even, in some cases, as bomber pilots. Caribbean women signed up with the Auxiliary Territorial Service for jobs as radar and searchlight operators. In England they were often cold-shouldered and roughed up by American GIs who sought to re-enact the segregation and cultural apartheid that was rife back in the States. Meanwhile back in the Caribbean, their younger brothers and sisters busied themselves saving up halfpennies and farthings to drop into collecting tins at schools and knitting blankets and bootees as part of the war effort.

This 'way of seeing' London is also evident in the work of Mulk Raj Anand, Dom Moraes, Nirad Chaudhuri, George Lamming, and – my chief concern – V.S. Naipaul. London is depicted as a cultural lighthouse, a mighty beacon radiating strength and assurance. It's a city they come to, not as economic migrants or political refugees, but in order to be educated or to become writers. They are travelling to careers. And not ones that involve punching tickets for London Transport or heaving crankcases in provincial factories. They want to lead 'metropolitan' lives, to inhabit a city of the intellect and the imagination. Their contribution to London won't, they hope, be calculated in monetary terms, but by their eloquence and the acuity of their prose. Their goal is to look at – and not to be looked at by – London.

All accounts of the capital are determined to a greater or lesser degree by the place from which the author hails or has recently moved. Descriptions of London are relative: the place is raved about or rubbished in comparison to the remote glen, sheltered university town or loitering suburb from which the writer has just emerged. Colonial authors in London have to make a more difficult cultural transition than most, and as a result they're especially hungry to draw comparisons – good and bad – between different geographies. The narrator of a poem by Malawi-born Jack Mapanje claims that visiting London is akin to drinking water from its source. Eventually, however, 'We must turn back to the peripheral mosaics of home/Revealing the depth of their natural negatives.'[11] In precisely this fashion, writers who eulogize London's cultural plenitude, its history, or the entrepreneurial spirit it encourages, are invariably contrasting it to the artistic dearth, threadbare genealogies, and lack of economic opportunities in their own land.

Such dualisms are fundamental to V.S. Naipaul as to no other writer. Trinidad, the island he left for Oxford in 1950 at the age of eighteen, is constantly portrayed throughout his novels, journalism and travel writing as a place of chaos and negation. At best, it incubates a desire for escape. It is as raw rum to London's fine liqueur, frayed worsted to the smooth velvet of the metropolis. In *The Mimic Men* (1967), the political exile, Ralph Singh, asserts that on Isabella (a Caribbean island clearly based on Trinidad, but also typical of other colonial societies), 'We lack order. Above all, we lack power.'[12] This isn't just a statement of realpolitik fact, but a condition that Naipaul lived out as a young man:

> To see the possibility, the certainty, of ruin, even at the moment of creation: it was my temperament. Those nerves had been given me as a child in Trinidad partly by our family circumstances: the half-ruined or broken-down houses we lived in, our many moves, our general uncertainty. Possibly, too, this mode of feeling went deeper, and was an ancestral inheritance.[13]

This ancestral inheritance refers to the Hindu belief in the cyclicality and hollowness of earthly reality. Many Indians who came to the Caribbean as indentured labourers in the nineteenth and early twentieth centuries sought, like Naipaul's grandfather, to combat their loneliness and sense of deracination by regarding Trinidad as 'the interlude, the illusion'.[14]

The colonial education system intensified Naipaul's indifference towards his own country: 'The maps in our geography books, concentrating on British islands in the Caribbean, seemed to stress our smallness and isolation.'[15] The lack of relevant textbooks helped to foster a widespread ignorance about the island's own antiquity and made it possible to 'feel the truth of the other, aboriginal island' (that pre-colonial realm inhabited by Caribs and Arawaks) only by travelling thousands of miles away to the reading rooms of the British Museum and the Public Record Office. Art and culture were not seen as pivotal to Trinidadian well-being. As on other Caribbean islands, there were few libraries, museums or literary journals that idealistic young men and women could turn to. They usually had to content themselves with the emporia in Port of Spain's old colonial main square which 'sold school books and perhaps children's books and colouring books, and had perhaps as well a short shelf or two of Penguin books, a few copies of a few titles, and a few of the Collins Classics (looking like Bibles)'.[16]

London offered correctives to this catalogue of shortcomings. It seemed as embossed vellum to the flimsy paperback of colonial life, a stable for thoroughbreds rather than weakling colts. It was the set text, the standard primer, the root to which the Caribbean was forced to decline. In the size of its buildings, its population and the territory it covered, it clearly possessed a magnitude and significance that Trinidad lacked. And as the administrative centre of a colonial power that held jurisdiction over much of the Caribbean, it possessed a sway and authority that exposed the flimsy impotence of native institutions. Trinidadian schoolchildren were led to believe that they had no history of their own worth learning; in contrast, London abounded with tradition, pageants, fascinating and important figures. London's history had dates, was quantifiable. Indo-Trinidadian history was vague and imprecise, a series of often conflicting and bitter folkloric anecdotes passed down from generation to generation. The poet and editor Tambimuttu expressed similar beliefs in his poem 'Out Of This War' (c. 1940):

Here, Death is measured with Big Ben or theodolite;
The cerements of mansions, neat on the washing line.
Neatly brewed and bottled, the heady liquor,
Lies different on the tongue, to our simple wines.

Tapes and set-squares, cones, tangents,
The formal property of the cupboard brain;
Are projected into further lines, cones and tangents,
A nut too well precisioned for my head.'[17]

Tambimuttu is being rather trad and hagiographic here. He envisions London as a place of tabulation and notation. Time is regulated from Greenwich. Colonial governance is determined by Westminster. Cultural merit is assessed by committees at Burlington House. In prizing the capital's systematic qualities, his claim that its lines and tangents are 'too well precisioned for my head' recalls those clichés about the inability of swarthy people, specifically Africans, to compute and to rationalize which Sancho sought to refute in his correspondence.

For Naipaul, if Trinidad was all of a jumble, a chaotic and noisy squall that signified nothing, then London was structured, assured, presence rather than absence. In *Finding The Centre* (1984), he contrasts the 'municipal order of each day' in London favourably to life in Chaguanas.[18] Small wonder that he moved there. Anyone with literary aspirations was expected to; that 'was where the poets were. The poets were my people.'[19] The capital served as a mastertext, the standard work of reference. Explaining why so many of his fellow islanders had left the Caribbean during the 1950s, Lamming claimed that 'each exile has not only got to prove his worth to the other, he has to win the approval of Headquarters, meaning in the case of the West Indian writer, England'.[20] The ultimate test of his literary prowess, the day on which he finally enters the heart of culture, comes when he is called upon to recite his poem 'The Boy And The Sea' at the ICA on Pall Mall:

> The crowd down there may be placid, but the young poet up on that platform is in deep waters. If he really believes in the sanctity of the I.C.A.; if he trusts to the critical predictions which those great men present are capable of making; if he believes in all this, then that might can be his calvary; that solitary climb to his full standing height may be his first and only climb to the cross; and there simply is no resurrection for a young poet who is not Christ.[21]

London is where the writers and arbiters of cultural merit lived. Their books were published there, as were the journals which contained fierce aesthetic manifestos, internecine literary debates, and learned reviews of the kind rarely found in the Caribbean. It was from Bush House in the Strand that programmes such as *Caribbean Voices* were broadcast. Aspiring West Indian writers huddled by their radiograms thousands of miles away and listened to the likes of Roy Fuller and Arthur Calder-Marshall discussing the poems and short stories they had submitted. For these authors 'it was London, or nothing'[22] because back in the Caribbean the 'educated middle class' had 'no time for them'; and the 'dancing girls in the Diamond Horse Show simply didn't know what it was all about. In other words, it was not only the politics of sugar which was organized from London. It was language, too.'[23]

Naipaul came to the capital to find this language. In *A Way In The World* (1994) he claims, 'Everything depended on my writing – that was the whole point of my being in London, living that life'.[24] Only after completing his first book was he able to believe that, 'My life in London at last had purpose'.[25] Naipaul associates urbanity with literary sophistication – it signifies not only a certain body of knowledge, a canny insider-ness, but also the skill to hold a slyly aloof distance from that material:

Metropolitan – what did I mean by that? I had only a vague idea. I meant material which would enable me to compete with or match certain writers. And I also meant material that would enable me to display a particular kind of writing personality [. . .] Somerset Maugham, aloof everywhere, unsurprised, immensely knowing; Aldous Huxley, so full of all kinds of knowledge and also so sexually knowing; Evelyn Waugh, so elegant so naturally. Wishing to be that kind of writer, I didn't see material in the campers in the big Earls Court house.'[26]

This quotation, characteristically candid, highlights the gulf between Naipaul and his Caribbean contemporaries such as Sam Selvon. The latter arrived in London with only vague and ill-formed ideas of becoming a writer. Although he'd published poems, reviews and short stories back home in Trinidad, he lacked a clear-cut conception of what kind of author he wanted to be. Living for over a decade in rundown districts such as Notting Hill and Bayswater, ones with large black populations, helped to shape his notions of the kind of social classes and environments he should write about. Naipaul, in contrast, seems to have decided well in advance. His clarity of vision hindered him as much as it helped him; London appealed in direct proportion to how pre-scripted and textual it appeared. So, in *The Enigma of Arrival*, he is initially excited by eating breakfast in the basement dining room of a grotty lodging house because, 'I had read of basements in books; and this room with an electric light burning on a bright sunny day seemed to me romantic. I was like a man entering the world of a novel, a book; entering the real world.'[27] Later, though, he speaks of how much better he would have liked his life if he had read Patrick Hamilton's bed-sit classic *Hangover Square*, for it would have 'peopled the area and made it romantic and given me, always needing these proofs from books, some sharper sense of myself'.[28]

Too fervent a belief in the idea that London is a cultural citadel can be bad for an author's sanity. Life in the city can hardly fail to be a disappointment. Everything imperfect – from spilling tea over one's lap in a Kilburn cafe, being bumped into outside Marble Arch station, getting caught in an afternoon rain shower – tends to be read as a metaphor for metropolitan diminution. Even the quality of city light, something that the Reverend James Peggs and other nineteenth-century urban missionaries celebrated, becomes an issue of overwhelming symbolism. In *The Enigma of Arrival*, Naipaul expresses his desire to leave Trinidad in terms of lusting for the 'large world [which] had always existed outside my little island – like the sun above the clouds'.[29] And in *The Mimic Men*, Ralph Singh speaks of London as 'that city of the magical light in which I could walk without shadow'.[30]

London's light is doubly important to Naipaul because of the blackness from which he feels he has emerged: 'That marvel of light, soft, shadowless, always protective [. . .] It was a light which gave solidity to everything and drew colour out from the heart of objects.'[31] In *Finding The Centre* he talks of 'that darkness, that lack of knowledge' in which he'd grown up in Trinidad.[32] Critics have often complained that Naipaul believes those living in the colonies or the developing world lead ancillary, deformed lives. One of his earliest forays into travel writing, a book about India, was called *An Area of Darkness* (1964); in *The Mimic Men*, Ralph Singh contrasts 'London, the great city' with 'my past, my own darkness'.[33] The point of fleeing to the capital is to cure the psychological deformations that a colonial upbringing can wreak, to switch from ignorance to enlightenment: 'Coming to London, the great city, seeking order, seeking the flowering, the extension of myself that ought to have come in a city of such miraculous light.'[34] Becoming an author, a vocation enabled by living in London, is also a way of leaving night behind: 'To be a writer as O. Henry was, to die in mid-sentence, was to triumph over darkness.'[35]

How could the real London live up to such expectations? Naipaul came to it looking for freshness and airiness; instead he found a bomb-riddled shell of a city still struggling to get back on its feet after the war. Hoping to smell the scent of freedom in his nostrils, he merely inhaled the fug of rough tobacco, sticky hair oil and boot dubbin. Disappointed, he spent the next fifty years depicting the metropolis as an area of murkiness. Even Nirad Chaudhuri, not always the most generous of souls when assessing the merits of other cultures, was able to talk about metropolitan light without damning London:

> To me it always seemed to be dawn there, and I often asked myself, 'Is the sun never going to rise high in this country?' I found it quite impossible to guess where it was in the sky from the condition of the light, which was not only unnaturally low, but also shot through and through with an all-pervasive grey [...] This light contributes to the sense of unreality. It also creates a mood of pensive wonder, so that a man from the tropics finds it impossible to be gay or blithe in England, although he may be very happy and even achingly joyous.[36]

Writers such as Lamming, Naipaul, Salkey and Selvon flocked to the BBC in whose hospitable environs they served their literary apprenticeships. Ralph Singh, narrator of *The Mimic Men*, recalls the glee he initially felt at taking his white girlfriend Sandra to eat at Bush House in

> the canteen of a radio service which, when picked up in remote countries, was the very voice of metropolitan authority and romance, bringing to mind images, from the cinema and magazines, of canyons of concrete, brick and glass, motorcars in

streams, lines of lights, busyness, crowded theatre foyers, the world where everything was possible.[37]

Now this same institution offered them employment – often irregular and certainly not lucrative – in the fields of acting, script-writing and radio-announcing. With the benefit of hindsight the comings and goings at the Colonial Service during the 1950s represent a golden dawn for Caribbean literature. Writers who had previously been divided by poor inter-island communication networks were able to meet each other regularly. Hearing different dialects on a daily basis, at the BBC as well as on the streets outside, they came to appreciate the richness and pliability of Caribbean languages. In addition to those authors already mentioned, the likes of John Figueroa, Jan Carew, Sylvia Winter and Edgar Mittelholzer all took part in important debates and productions. For the first time in Caribbean history there came into existence a strong, self-reflective and high-quality literary culture. Ideas were exchanged, intellectual alliances brokered, tastes and distastes formed. Over the airwaves Caribbean writers debated whether they should use 'nation' language, the obligations artists bore to the communities from which they had sprung, and the extent to which they should allow themselves to be influenced by Western authors and poetics. Few of these writers thought of themselves as pioneers at the time. Like most people who have worked for the BBC over the last seventy years, they were too busy bitching about office conditions and the derisory freelance wages they felt they were earning. Grumbling dissatisfaction was the norm. Naipaul was especially upset. He had come to the capital seeking security and strength; instead, he spent much of his time mithering and sweating for inspiration in the Caribbean Service's freelance room that was located opposite Broadcasting House, on the second floor of what had formerly been – and is now again –

the Langham Hotel. In *Finding The Centre* he recalls that 'free-lance' was 'not a word suggesting freedom and valour, but suggesting only people on the fringe of a mighty enterprise, a depressed and suppliant class'.[38]

Short-term, fixed contract, part-time – all these phrases so commonly bandied about in contemporary economic debate create a feeling of temporality and insecurity that can cause trauma and panic. In London, as in other big cities jammed with millions of commuters, this terror is compounded by the belief that everybody else has direction and drive, place and position in the world. For Naipaul who equated 'metropolitan' with literary self-possession and self-assuredness, and who has always aspired to a quality of stillness, working conditions at the BBC were a persistent psychological drain. Ralph Singh may have been giddy with excitement at the idea of lunching at Bush House but the actual experience was a letdown: 'there now, at the heart of that metropolis, we sat, at a plastic-topped table, before thick cups of cooling tea and plates with yellow crumbs, each drawing out the frenzy from the other'.[39]

Other Caribbean writers were no less disappointed. Lamming claims to have been shocked to learn that authors were paid according to the length of their contributions. He'd expected that literary London remunerated authors on other criteria – quality or genre perhaps: 'It is impossible for a poet to evoke sympathy from people who use words as a way of measuring time; and time as the measure of how much money. This attitude comes to its full obscenity in the Colonial Section which is seen – when it is seen at all – as the arse-hole of the Corporation.'[40]

The real problem here is one of power. The colonial author tends to know a lot about metropolitan history and culture. Throughout his childhood he has lapped up scraps of knowledge, read as many canonical texts as he can get hold of, and has studied hard – often in the face of familial and local scepticism. However advanced his critical faculties, he will tend to be rather awestruck and reverential about London. After all, it was such ardour that sustained him during those dark days when he despaired of ever being able to leave his home village or country, when the sneers and indifference of his local community became too painful. His admiration for the imperial centre is so great that, believing it to be a cultural fount – amply resourced, secure, effortlessly and historically masterful – he assumes his knowledge about it will be reciprocated. When he finally learns that artists and thinkers in the capital know or care little about the civilization from which he hails the fall-out can be severe.

This process is memorably described by the Indian writer Mulk Raj Anand in *Conversations in Bloomsbury* (1981). Much of this autobiography replays his encounters with some of the great and good literary figures in London during the middle of the 1920s. He frequents Harold Monro's Poetry Bookshop, visits T.S. Eliot in his Faber offices, and meets Aldous Huxley, Bonamy Dobrée and D.H. Lawrence. A conscientious student at the University of

London, Anand is understandably thrilled, but also nervous about mingling with such luminaries. Yet the more he talks to them the greater is his awareness that his idols are flawed. Their knowledge of Indian culture and politics turns out to be rather shallower than he had imagined:

> I was too overwhelmed by the presence of these legendary literary men. I felt that they did not know very much about my country, and what they knew was through Kipling or through superficial impressions [. . . most] seemed to believe, more or less, in the 'Empire on which the sun never sets'. I, who had been to jail in the Gandhi movement, was fuming inside. I had left home because my pro-white-Sahib father had beaten my mother for my going to jail. And I had learnt to be a rebel. While I helped to clean the glasses, I realized that I had taken umbrage about wrong words said about India, and for being considered 'lesser breeds beyond the law'. The humiliation for being inferior seemed like a wound in my soul, which would never heal. The more I licked it the more it became tender. And I decided in my mind that I would fight for the freedom of my country forever, though I may admire these English writers for their literary skills.[41]

This isn't the only occasion on which Anand feels angered by the ignorance of his literary hosts. On meeting Virginia Woolf he tells her that while he was growing up he'd been a keen fan of – and greatly influenced by – George Reynolds, author of the twenty-volume 'Mysteries of London' series. He's confounded and appalled by the disdainful manner in which Woolf claims never to have heard of Reynolds. 'In the folly of low browness' Anand persists in questioning her about the likes of Rider Haggard and Marie Corelli. He does so 'because I felt that if I was honest about the bad taste of my youth, Virginia Woolf might also acknowledge some blunders she had committed. Actually, I wanted to dethrone her from the perch of the goddess to the common clay in which her husband had revealed himself under the chestnut tree in Tavistock Square.'[42]

The word 'goddess' here points to Woolf's exalted reputation at this stage in her writing career. It also implies that colonial criticism of metropolitan literary culture is a form of apostasy. Anand becomes angrier by the minute; he seeks to knock Woolf and all her other blithely ignorant peers off their pedestals. This act of sacrilege, hinging as it does on London's holy status for many of its colonial chroniclers, carries with it a violent rhetorical undertow that is also present in many of the works looked at in this book.

This sense of imminent violence is not confined to descriptions of the underclass. It's present in Nirad Chaudhuri's account of walking up Bayswater Road and finding that 'in a mood of impatience, which endless rows of bricks and stone often generate, I should have involuntarily thought of a battering ram'.[43] It's also found in Naipaul's *Mr Stone and the Knights Companion* (1963) where Stone ends the novel yomping across the city, feeling vacant and purposeless: 'As he walked up the [Brixton] street to his home with long, hard strides, he felt himself grow taller. He walked as the destroyer, as the man who carried the possibility of the earth's destruction within him.'[44]

A disgust at the cultural pretensions of white Londoners, combined with a desire to smack them in the face for their complacency, is expressed most powerfully in George Lamming's *The Emigrants*. Collis is invited to dinner by Pearson, a well-meaning British Council sort, whose brother-in-law is a welfare officer in Trinidad. The evening should be of great use to Collis: it's not long since he arrived in London, he's had little time to settle down or make himself secure. Pearson might offer him useful advice, might become a friendly face in a sea of white strangers. His house seems a model of assuredness: sherry flows in the neat and nicely decked-out room; conversation is structured and polite. Here is the absence of confusion or doubt for which the young Naipaul had pined. Collis notices that the behaviour of the Pearsons 'followed a certain order known only to them. When they were together they functioned like things which worked according to the laws of their environment. Their behaviour was a device. The pattern was fixed, and they entered it, assuming the roles to which such a marital relationship had assigned them.'[45]

Yet despite these twitchings of discomfort, Collis is slowly beginning to feel a bit more at ease – when the telephone rings. He overhears a colleague of Pearson complaining that a black man they're responsible for has been in trouble with the police. Pearson returns to the living room in a grouchy mood. Avoiding Collis's eye, he probes him on why so many West Indians are flocking to England in a manner that enrages him:

> There was a coarse certainty about Mr Pearson. He was one who quickly defined the other, calculated the responses which he should present and having done that, proceeded to make social intercourse an encounter between a definition and a response. Collis understood that he did not then exist for Mr Pearson, and he understood too that Mr Pearson didn't exist for himself.[46]

Lamming – characteristically explicatory rather than evocative – believes that this relationship between the two men, skewed from the outset by Collis's colour and background, is a negative template for all the cultural transactions that went on between black and white people in 1950s London. Looking around the living room Collis notices that the

> books had a decorative aspect like those rare commodities that are only meant to be looked at. He could barely read the titles at the top. *David Copperfield* and *The Pickwick Papers*, *The Works*

of Anthony Trollope, Pride and Prejudice. And the Bible. And at
the bottom, laid on their sides like weary performers, were two
bound collections of *Punch* [...] He would have liked to kick
him in the stomach, not in anger, but as a way of evoking some
genuine emotion. Only violence could make Mr Pearson feel.
He looked at the photograph and clenched his fist against it as
though he were going to wipe out the nose.[47]

Collis wants to counter indifference and social blindness with
violence. This urge to leave some mark or trace – brutal or otherwise – on a city that seems so impervious to its inhabitants is not
confined to people from foreign countries. And yet it's striking
that over the centuries so many writers of Asian and African origin,
often from very different classes too, have all lapsed into pugilistic
rhetoric when depicting social and intellectual interactions between new and settled Londoners.

What's equally interesting in the passage just quoted are
Lamming's literary references. Dickens and Austen were two of
the most well-known English writers in the Caribbean. Insti-
tutionalized by school curricula, they came to stand for all that
was most valuable about metropolitan culture and, by association,
the metropolis itself. Part of the discomfort Collis feels hinges on
his realization that even though men like Pearson are wealthy
enough to buy canonical literary texts, they don't necessarily read
or appreciate them. Literature in the metropolis is not a sacred
activity. It's not about 'great books'. Rather, it's something far
cosier, a type of superior furnishing. For Collis this insight tar-
nishes not only Pearson, but the books themselves. Culture's halo
has slipped.

Cultural considerations alone do not explain metropolitan
ennui. Accommodation also fuels bitter dissatisfaction. Naipaul
came to the city seeking largeness and solidity. Instead, for the
few months before he moved on to University College in Oxford,

he found himself living in Earls Court, described by Jonathan Raban as 'a place to disappear into'.[48] It's long been a district with little sense of permanence or community. Congested with hotels and boarding houses, people forever coming and going, tourists and backpackers staying for short periods, where anonymity is the rule rather than the exception, Earls Court is a stopping-off point, a lay-by on the route to somewhere else. Such transience and constant upheaval were precisely what Naipaul came to London to escape. Instead, he finds himself in a lodging house full of Asiatics, North Africans, men and women from the English provinces. They are outsiders, misfits, temporaries. They are too much like Naipaul himself for him to be comfortable with them. One of the early tell-tale signs that Mr Stone's hopes of finding purpose in his life will be dashed is that the false-toothed Mrs Springer whom he later marries lives in a private hotel in a crescent off Earls Court Road.

A horror of short-stay, fly-by-night boarding culture – the residential equivalent of the short-contract, part-time work that Naipaul was forced to do to eke out a living – emerges in many of his novels. In *The Mimic Men*, Ralph Singh creeps into the bedroom of his landlord who has recently died. The sashes are crooked, the paint peeling, and from the dirty window all he can see are grey sky, roofs and bombsites: 'looking out from that empty room with the mattress on the floor, I felt all the magic of the city go away and had an intimation of the forlornness of the city and of the people who lived in it'.[49]

These grimy, shrivelled rooms are the negation of everything Naipaul (a writer for whom houses have always been an important symbol of stability and social security – most famously in his 1961 novel, *A House For Mr Biswas*) dreamt London would be like. Metropolitan light seems to be as rationed in these houses with their small windows and filthy curtains as the food and fabrics of recent post-war memory. Life in London feels like a subtraction, a slow and remorseless sinking. The personal cultivation and extension of self for which many writers came to the capital appears a distant dream as they pull on an extra sweater and huddle up tight in cramped and claustrophobic rooms. The world outside their windows seems too close, a cold and useless million miles away. Rather than meeting and mingling with new people in London's vast acreage, they feel cut-off and lonely as they while away the penniless hours staring at cracked ceilings, churned up with anguish, trying to muster up plans for the future.

This alienation is far more psychological, and far less economic, than that faced by the characters in Selvon's fiction. In fact, it can seem rather put on. Like the other writers in this chapter Naipaul didn't suffer excessive financial hardship. After he came down from Oxford he was able to lodge in a Paddington basement that was being rented by an older cousin who was in London studying law; later he lived in Kilburn in two rooms of a house belonging to a BBC commissionaire. The jobs he secured – presenting *Caribbean Voices*, reviewing new fiction for the *New Statesman* – were far more prestigious than, say, Selvon's succession of menial posts at sausage factories and London hospitals. Not one of the characters in Naipaul's London books ever treads the streets of Bayswater scouring for dropped coins as Gallows in *The Housing Lark* is forced to do. Yet Naipaul rarely takes pleasure in his media activities. Nor does he consider it a privilege to be paid to review other people's work or to be able to broadcast his thoughts and opinions and criticism to international audiences.

None of the Indian and Caribbean writers in this chapter found it easy to make lasting friends or find a fulfilling sense of community. They didn't always try very hard to keep in touch with people from their own backgrounds. Perhaps they thought they had nothing in common with them: Naipaul was a Brahmin; the highly educated Chaudhuri came from an upper-class East Bengali family, and was having his travel expenses paid for by the BBC. It speaks volumes about the circles in which Dom Moraes moved that he could be so shocked on arriving in London from Oxford to find a flat with a 'No Coloured' sign.

> [It] gave me a strange sensation: it had been years since I had thought of myself as being any particular colour. I had been taught not to, and the idea of a colour bar filled me with sudden rage and hatred. I tended always to be unaware of things until they affected me personally, and this seemed a personal affront. To reassert myself, I raised my price range, and soon found a very expensive flat in Chelsea.[50]

Moraes, whose father edited the *Times of India*, may have had his ego bruised during his discovery of the colour bar, but at least he's rich enough to be able to buy himself security – a luxury not available to most immigrants. But Moraes had little contact with them and describes them in the manner of a particularly gauche sociologist: 'Sometimes in the streets I have passed a haggard brown face amidst the white ones and felt a sudden terror of I'm not quite sure what – guilt? shock? There are beautiful women and handsome men in India and Pakistan, but the immigrants one sees in London have an ugly pinched look of deprivation, the joyless quality of the outcast.'[51]

The bewilderment that Moraes feels is preferable at least to the snobbery exhibited by James Meary Tambimuttu. A Hindu from Ceylon, he arrived in London in 1938 and often claimed to be a prince. He soon fell in with the Fitzrovia set that included Dylan Thomas, William Empson and Anthony Powell. Their work featured heavily in the pages of *Poetry London*, the famous if perpetually cash-strapped journal that 'Tambi' founded and edited. Surrounded by artists renowned for their love of drinking, he strove hard to cultivate a louche personality. He was shifty and unreliable, not just to his creditors (of which there were many), but to his female staff. According to Julian Maclaren-Ross he also held the working classes in low esteem. This condescension extended across race. One evening he was eating a curry at an Indian café near Oxford Circus where a group of East Indian sailors was also dining:

> Tambi for some reason loathed and despised lascars who, though all mankind was his country, did not to him belong to mankind, and it was not long before trouble arose.
>
> All went outside to settle matters, Stewart Scott a dauntless fellow of only apparently frail physique took on several lascars who luckily hadn't knives, but Tambi like President Wilson was too proud to fight: he stood by with folded arms and mesmeric stare fixed upon the fray, calling to Scott as his tongue flicked in and out: 'Don't sully yourself Stewart by fighting with this scum. Let me look at them with my eyes, and they will flee abashed'. And they would have, too, if Tambi could have only got his eyes on them.
>
> Which didn't prevent Scott from being thoroughly done-up and having to have stitches in where his head had been thumped against some railings.[52]

Naipaul, meanwhile, had very little time for people who shared a background similar to his own. They reminded him of his roots and stirred in him feelings of ancestral shame. Also, they were not 'metropolitan' enough. He claimed that 'racial diminution formed no part of the material of the kind of writer I was setting out to be'.[53] This is borne out by his rather sniffy account of some of the black people he used to see on the streets of London at the start of that decade:

> men in pin-stripe suits and bowlers, with absurd accents. Some-times they greeted me; they were prompted to do so by solitude,

but they also wished to find someone to boast to. One wet winter evening one of these men, met in a Regent Street bus queue, straight away took out his wallet and began to show me photographs of his house and his English wife. They were shipwrecked men. They had lost touch with themselves and now, near the end, were seeing the fantasies they had lived on washed away by the arrival of the new immigrants from Jamaica and the other islands.[54]

The writers in this chapter pay scant attention to any Asian or West Indian who is not interested in art or ideas. They dwell almost exclusively on the 'cultural capital', and balk at the idea of producing 'state of the immigrant nation' treatises. Anand's memoirs focus almost exclusively on his encounters with London's literati. When Moraes isn't dining with the Spenders in Hampstead, meeting Cyril Connolly and Raymond Chandler, or listening to *Dies Irae*, he's consorting with writers and painters such as Francis Bacon in bohemian Soho clubs. Chaudhuri, like nineteenth-century Indian travellers, spends his time in London looking for its beauty spots and sampling its 'historical monuments and scattered gems of architecture'.[55] He leaves the country able to say that he has seen 'more paintings, statues, and works of art in general, more plays, fine buildings, gardens, and beautiful landscapes; heard more poetry and music; ate and drank better; and altogether had a more exciting and interesting time than in all the rest of my life'.[56] For all Lamming's growing scepticism about the cultural authority of organizations such as the BBC and the ICA and officials like Pearson, he recognizes that certain districts are almost unsurpassable in their artistic vitality. He described Hampstead where he lives as 'the home of both foreign and native intellectuals. From street to street, the sound of typewriters, in the early hours of the morning, is as frequent as rain.'[57]

Naipaul and Lamming may mingle with intellectuals, yet their

relationships with them are often just as thorny as those they have with fellow colonials. They certainly don't suck up to the metropolis; in fact, they often lash it. Even Chaudhuri, so often dismissed as an Anglophile toady, admitted that he was astonished by the 'wholly unstatesmanlike appearance and behaviour' of Churchill whom he went to hear speak at the House of Commons in 1955: 'He looked very much like his figure in a toby jug, but was much more rosy, white-haired, and childlike than I could have imagined him to be.'[58] It's this willingness to harbour heretical thoughts about the metropolis that distinguishes these authors from the rajahs and students who wrote about London at the end of the nineteenth century and whose criticisms were usually couched in embarrassed, conciliatory terms. The authors in this chapter grew up during the dying days of Empire, when mocking the 'immense chandelier' that London was once held to be by Victorian evangelists (and these writers themselves as they grew up in the colonies) was far more politically acceptable than it had been before. Words no longer had to be honeyed. Bowing and scraping were no longer necessary.

And yet, these authors were all writing in a pre-pop era, that still-thriving epoch in cultural politics during which the likes of Rushdie, Linton Kwesi Johnson, Hanif Kureishi and Victor Headley have all fed off and lionized the fissiparous energies and intensities of the capital. These latter authors, many of them brought up in post-imperial England, don't prize order and stillness to anything like the extent their literary forebears did. They don't conceive of London as the heart of lightness. Writing about Brick Lane, Railton Road in Brixton, the badlands of Tottenham and Hackney, their characters lack cultural capital or contacts. They're forced to become gatecrashers, scamsters.

The likes of Anand and Moraes may be blessed with self-possession and the knowledge that they can savour the highest culture the metropolis has to offer, yet there lurks in their work a nagging suspicion that black and white people can only circle around or toy with each other, never truly connect. Even Naipaul – so often seen as self-sufficient and aloof – wrote in 'London' (1957) that, 'The privacy of the big city depresses me. There are no communal pleasures in London [. . .] I do not sign petitions. I do not vote. I do not march. And I never cease to feel that this lack of interest is all wrong. I want to be involved, to be touched even by some of the prevailing anger.'[59] It's easy to see Ralph Singh's decision to collect 'trophies' such as stockings or pairs of shoes from the bedrooms of the women he's slept with as – in part – a deluded way of convincing himself that his enjoyable but trivial one-night stands give his life in London some kind of substance, that his relationships with other people in the capital carry weight.

It wasn't only personal affairs that disappointed. Some writers felt that the much-vaunted topography and landmarks of London were a let-down. In Naipaul's *The Enigma of Arrival*, the seemingly autobiographical narrator recalls arriving in the capital after the war and embarking upon tourist excursions to look

> for size. It was one of the things I had travelled to find, coming from my small island. I found size, power, in the area around Holborn Viaduct, the Embankment, Trafalgar Square. And after this grandeur there was the boarding house in Earls Court. So I grew to feel that the grandeur belonged to the past; that I had come to England at the wrong time; that I had come too late to find the England, the heart of empire, which (like a provincial, from a far corner of the empire) I had created in my fantasy.[60]

A touch melodramatic, maybe, but this admission pinpoints the moment in Naipaul's life when he realized that geography in itself isn't a solution to anything. To move to a different city, country, or continent does not guarantee that personal traumas will suddenly disappear. In his essay 'London', he claims to like the city and admits that it's the best place for him in which to write. Nonetheless, by 1957, the year in which he wrote the article, he knew that London was never going to be a balm for his bruised self.

In *The Mimic Men*, Ralph Singh tries to codify the various stages in the rise and fall of the average colonial would-be radical: 'For those who lose [political struggles], and nearly everyone in the end loses, there is only one course: flight. Flight to the greater disorder, the final emptiness: London and the home counties.'[61] Later in the same novel he talks about what he calls his 'London fear'. This amounts to a sickening 'fear of the unreality around me; it was the fear of the man who feels the veils coming down one by one, muffling his deepest responses, and panics at not being able to tear down the unreality about him to get at the hard, the concrete, where everything becomes simple and ordinary and easy to seize'.[62]

Perhaps, as the critic P.S. Chauhan has claimed, Naipaul's concern with change and transience stems from the Hindu belief in perpetual rebirth and cyclicality.[63] In *The Enigma of Arrival* Naipaul argues that these attitudes had been drummed into him as a child in Trinidad where he'd become chastened by 'the half-ruined or broken-down houses we lived in, our many moves, our general uncertainty'.[64] Even the white protagonist in *Mr Stone and the Knights Companion* shares such anxieties. Towards the end of that novel he walks along the Embankment feeling numb and empty: 'He stripped the city of all that was enduring and saw that all that was not flesh was of no importance to man. All that mattered was man's own frailty and corruptibility. The order of the universe, to which he had sought to ally himself, was not his order.'[65]

This insight perks him up rather. It gives him a fleeting jolt of certainty and vigour. Yet it is also expressed condescendingly. Stone believes, mistakenly, that he is superior to his fellow Londoners whose Pooterish habits mirror his own:

Taller and taller he grew, firmer and firmer he walked, past the petty gardens of petty houses where people sought to accommodate themselves to life, past the blank, perceptive faces of cats, past the 'To Let' and 'For Sale' signs, and all the transient handiwork of Eddie and Charley.[66]

This is similar to a passage in *The Mimic Men* where Ralph Singh discovers the hollowness of all that he'd previously held to be solid:

> Here was the city, the world. I waited for the flowering to come to me. The trams on the Embankment sparked blue. The river was edged and pierced with reflections of light, blue and red and yellow. Excitement! Its heart must have lain somewhere. But the god of the city was elusive. The tram was filled with individuals, each man returning to his own cell. The factories and warehouses, whose exterior lights decorated the river, were empty and fraudulent. I would play with famous names as I walked empty streets and stood on bridges. But the magic of names soon faded. Here was the river, here the bridge, there that famous building. But the god was veiled. My incantation of names remained unanswered. In the great city so solid in its light, which gave colour even to unrendered concrete – to me as colourless as rotting wooden fences and new corrugated-iron roofs – in this solid city life was two-dimensional.[67]

The scene depicts – with sadness but also a savage relish – the undermining of all the hopes and dreams that he (and Naipaul) had held about London as a youth. The landmarks about which he'd read so much in colonial schoolbooks fail to leap out at him or to respond to his desire for them to talk back. The fact that he worked so hard to get to London means nothing to the metropolis. Singh has quickly discovered that which the tourist rarely does, and that which takes the disaffected provincial or utopian romantic a long time to do: abandoning one's background does not guarantee that one will find a sense of belonging elsewhere. Although the city seems to brim with energy, Singh detects the solitariness that underlies it all ('each man returning to his own cell'). He understands that too often the manic pursuit of buzz, of kicks, is a forlorn effort to stave off loneliness, the personal and familial darkness that he and others will always carry with them wherever they flee to. A new landscape can't ease this persistent ache – even the factories and warehouses whose lights shimmer at night were 'empty and fraudulent'. The light may be solid in this 'great city', but life is still two-dimensional. This disparity between surface sheen and sullied reality is also ironically highlighted in Jack Mapanje's 'Travelling In London Tubes' where the London-intoxicated narrator rhapsodizes that

> here, even the dust is subtle
> the way it blows
> with the seemingly fresh breeze [...]
> it is not until your sudden
> aitchoo!
> that you begin to see how much
> charcoal was in your nose
> eyes lungs
> travelling in those lovely tubes[68]

Ralph Singh's realization that for too long he has been chasing an impossible dream is one that is shared by Johnny Sobert, the lippy anti-hero of Andrew Salkey's *Escape To An Autumn Pavement*. He wanders through the novel in a constant state of sarcastic irritation, lashing out randomly at everyone around him.

'Listen to me, I walk around London and I see statues of this one and the other . . . I see litters of paintings in your museums and galleries. St Paul's. The Tower. All of them. There's even Stonehenge! And d'you know how I feel deep down? [...] I feel nothing. I feel nothing at all! And yet, I want to feel just a little something.'
'But why?'
'Why? Because Africa doesn't belong to me! There's no feeling

there. No bond. We've been fed on the Mother Country myth. Its language. Its history. Its literature. Its Civics. We feel chunks of it rubbing off on us. We believe in it. We trust it. Openly, we admit we're a part of it. But are we? Where's the real link?'[69]

Later on he bemoans how pointless and wasted his life seems. He realizes, he says, 'that I was headed nowhere like a hundred million others: I had escaped a malformed Jamaican middle class; I had attained my autumn pavement; I had done more than my fair share of hurting, rejecting, and condemning; and I had created another kind of failure, and this time, in another country.'[70] The sentiments in these last two outbursts are bleak indeed. Yet they are voiced with such fieriness that they create an energy that is the very opposite of doleful inertia. Johnny's capacity to be enraged – by London, by himself – suggests that the life hasn't been fully squeezed out of him yet.

The same cannot really be said of V.S. Naipaul. His accounts of London, fictional and essayistic, from *The Mimic Men* in 1967 to *Half A Life*, published in 2001, are all variations of the one sad theme: the world begins and ends in loss. Naipaul's dirge-like threnodies typically involve a young man, not so dissimilar to himself, who has fled the backwardness of life in India or the Caribbean to start anew in the metropolis. The young man is usually a student, and would like to become a writer. He wants to join the club, feel on the inside. But he jangles with nerves, is edgy and tense and red-raw. He craves calm, sedation, silence. London offers none of those things. Quite the reverse; it is full of hucksters and mayhem and dinning noise. So Naipaul's characters never quite fit, and they take out their discomfort on the city itself, claiming it is raddled and hollow. It exacerbates the sense of loss they had felt when first they arrived from the colonies. London leaves them feeling even less anchored in the world.

This response is based to a large extent on his own experiences of the city. As early as 1950 he wrote a letter to his parents (which he decided not to send), comparing Christmas in Trinidad to the one he was currently enjoying in Earls Court:

> We were always on the outside of a vague feeling of joy. The same feeling is here with me in London. Yet there is so much more romance here. It gets dark at half past three and all the lights go on. The shops are bright, the streets are well lit and the streets are full of people. I walk through the streets, yet am so much alone, so much on the outside of this great festive feeling.[71]

It's easy to believe that Naipaul's writings on London have a tremendous grandeur. They all have sweep, a sense of the epic. They narrate one of the grand stories of our time: the flight of dispossessed people from the Third to the First World in pursuit of new and better lives. And they do so without dwelling on 'trivia' – workplace prejudice, inclement weather, paraffin dramas. They probe more deeply into emotional and psychological substrata than most 'immigrant novels'. Even the pessimism they express – and engender – seems to possess the force of a great truth. They mine a seam of urban melancholy that most of us have felt at some point in our lives, but prefer not to dwell on – or in – for very long. Naipaul mainlines that emotion to produce fictions that linger and resonate in the imagination for a long time.

And yet. One of the reasons they linger is because they're so deeply irritating. Naipaul's London story, the journey to disillusion that, sadistically, he forces all his characters to endure, quickly stales through repetition. We recoil from this part of his oeuvre in the same way that we abandon the company of a pub bore endlessly and bitterly narrating anecdotes about the days when he could've been a contender. The tales he tells us are coercively downbeat. They dare the reader into disagreeing with

their bleak prognoses for life in the capital. In *Half A Life* Willie
Chandran despises his father, a Brahminical clerk who married a
low-caste woman for political reasons back in the 1930s; at the
first opportunity he leaves India to enrol at a college of education
in London. He arrives in 1957 to find that the city is different to
how he had imagined it:

> He was disappointed by Buckingham Palace. He thought the
> maharaja's palace in his own state was far grander, more like a
> palace, and this made him feel, in a small part of his heart, that
> the kings and queens of England were imposters, and the
> country a little bit of a sham. His disappointment turned to
> something like shame – at himself, for his gullibility – when he
> went to Speakers' Corner. [...] He expected big, radical,
> shouting crowds, like those his mother's uncle, the firebrand of
> the backwards, used to address. He didn't expect to see an idle
> scatter of people around a half-dozen talkers, with the big buses
> and the cars rolling indifferently by all the time.[72]

It's a passage that is remarkable for the brutal and totalizing vision
of the city it reveals. Chandran takes a minor incident, a tourist
site being a bit of a let-down, and transforms this commonplace
event into a disaster of almost cosmic proportions. The damage
it wreaks on him is both interior and exterior. He not only damns
himself for ever believing that Buckingham Palace could amount
to much, but also loses faith in other Londoners, in their political
convictions, in the monarchy, in the nation. His reaction is so
excessive it becomes funny. Chandran is risible in many ways. But
I don't think we're intended to laugh at his sentiments here.
Rather, we're supposed to share in his sense of disillusion, to see
the tragedy. That is hard to do. If we can't laugh, then at least
we must scoff at the pomposity of a young man who dares to
inflate his own feelings of disappointment into a treatise on the
worthlessness of the nation he inhabits.

This is, of course, what Naipaul has been doing since the 1960s in much of his writing about non-Western countries. Critics of a certain age, usually veering towards right- rather than left-wing political beliefs, have long commended him for the honesty of his vision. He is praised for being caustic and clear-sighted, for 'telling it like it is'. His inability to say anything too generous or hopeful about developing nations is seen as a mark of his independence, as his admirable distaste for sentimentality. Yet few critics applaud his books about London. They are discussed infrequently and never read as authoritative field reports 'explaining' the metropolis. Unsurprisingly so: we all have some knowledge about London, its good and its bad sides, and we know that Naipaul's vision of it is, at best, a partial one. That much is evident from a quick comparison of his description of Piccadilly Circus with that of his fellow Indo-Trinidadian Sam Selvon. In *The Lonely Londoners* there is a scene in which he describes how his boys like to get spivved up and go out on the town. Life at work is hard for them, and life in general no less tough, but come the evenings they set aside their greasy overalls and battered work boots in order to tog themselves up so fancily that, money or no money in their pockets, they feel like kings. Galahad is especially happy to head into town:

> Always, from the first time he went there to see Eros and the lights, that circus have a magnet for him, that circus represent life, that circus is the beginning and the ending of the world. Every time he go there, he have the same feeling like when he see it the first night, drink coca-cola, any time is guiness time, Bovril and the fireworks, a million flashing lights, gay laughter, the wide doors of theatres, the huge posters, everready batteries, rich people going into tall hotels, people going to the theatre, people sitting and standing and walking and talking and laughing and buses and cars and Galahad Esquire, in all this, standing there in the big city, in London. Oh Lord.[73]

In *Half A Life* Naipaul also wrote about Piccadilly Circus.

> [Willie] went very late that evening to Piccadilly Circus. He
> walked around the streets, hardly daring to look at the aggressive,
> dangerous-looking streetwalkers. He walked until he was tired.
> At about midnight he went into a bright café. It was full of prosti-
> tutes, hard, foolish-looking, not attractive, most of them drinking
> tea and smoking, some of them eating soft white cheese rolls.[74]

Naipaul's Piccadilly is devoid of any joy or romance, merely
shabby and threatening. For a writer who is often credited as
plain-speaking, he uses a lot of adjectives, most of them expressing
disquiet and disgust. They don't, however, succeed in conveying
a very precise sense of place. By contrast, Selvon's description,
almost toppling with dizzy wonder, is as happy as a balloon. He
captures its rampant commercialism and the gladsomeness of the
people who flock to it; conveys its accelerated atmosphere in his
sentence structure; even recycles advertising slogans without lapsing into cliché. Galahad is poor and much put-upon, yet that does
not diminish his capacity for loving London. An enduring and
redemptive brio pulses through Selvon's writing. Chandran, however, like many of Naipaul's characters, seems incapable of deriv-
ing any pleasure from the capital; he shuffles through its streets
weighed down by fear, ennui and surly contempt for its inhabitants. He forecloses the possibility of happiness; to admit it would
be to expose oneself as deluded and second-rate. Perhaps
Chandran is merely exposing a part of his personality he had
spotted in himself even when he was living in India: 'I began –
though it might seem strange to say so – to take refuge in my
melancholy. Courted it, and lost myself in it. Melancholy became
so much part of my character that for long periods I could forget
the cause.'[75]

What is most absent in Naipaul's writings about London is

transformation. Writers from Sancho onwards have celebrated the capital's ability to effect changes – both good and bad – in newcomers, to draw out and magnify aspects of their selves, to confound their expectations, to dazzle with the promise that they can reinvent themselves. None of those things happens in Naipaul's work. The city confirms and deepens the dolefulness they harboured back in the colonies. Nothing seems to happen by chance in his books; a pall of predestined ruination hangs over his chapters. Perhaps that's not surprising. In a letter to his sister Kamla, written in 1949 when he was seventeen years old, he claimed: 'My thesis is that the world is dying – Asia today is only a primitive manifestation of a long-dead culture; Europe is battered into a primitivism by material circumstances; America is an abortion.'[76] Indeed, his stories and essays read like autopsies. They are cold, impersonal (even when narrated in the first person), and odourless. The metropolis is viewed in drizzly twilight. His characters barely ever show rage or passion. They lack the lust for life or the monumental ire that animates those in Rushdie's work. London shrivels under their jaundiced gazes.

It takes a particular kind of talent to be drawn towards decrepitude with the relentlessness that Naipaul displays. Where other writers narrate the joys and sensualities of metropolitan life, celebrating the energy surges and emotional intensities it induces, Naipaul always sees the skull beneath the comely face. Boredom, disillusion and futility are always in the air, waiting to poke out like a ribcage. In itself that's no crime. After all, Jean Rhys's novels are hardly mirthful. At least, though, they are distinguished by a mirrorball prose style that combines glinting hardness with elliptical poignancy. Equally, in Selvon's fiction, the penny-pinched characters use a creolized form of English, one whose language and grammar feels simultaneously new and as traditional as the coney-catching Elizabethanisms of Thomas Nashe.

Naipaul's prose, so often praised by writers and critics, is crucial to understanding how narrow is his vision of London. He eschews embellished sentences, seeing in them evidence of mendacity and obfuscation. He prefers his sentences scalped and peeled. They are shorn of excess, of anything that might be considered 'fine writing'. As a result each page resembles a barren landscape, an emotional tundra. His paragraphs, weighted and measured, never arc or spin or fizz out of control. They are as heavy as breeze blocks – and about as aesthetically pleasing. They do not generate new rhythms. Nor do they experiment with syntax, just as none of his characters dares to embrace the sprawl and chaos of the city, but step back prudishly, sipping without gulping. In his books London is sapped of its vitality. His writing, then, may be graceful, but it is metropolitan rather than urban. It lacks the vulgarity, the quickstep neologisms, the amped-up fidgetiness of the best London literature.

It's striking that none of the writers looked at in this chapter produced a book about London that might remotely be considered a classic. Doubly so as most of them have produced some of the most enduring works of the twentieth century: Mulk Raj Anand's De Sica-like account of a day in the life of a young Dalit, *Untouchable* (1936), has attained Penguin Classic status; Nirad Chaudhuri's *The Autobiography of an Unknown Indian* (1951) is one of the finest memoirs ever written; Naipaul, whose *A House For Mr Biswas* is as inexhaustible and indispensable now as it was in 1961 when it was first published, was awarded the Nobel Prize for Literature in 2001. Their books about London, as well as those by George Lamming, are, in comparison, minor works. Could it be that these writers' erudition and their longstanding interest in high culture is to blame? A desire to locate and lavish praise on establishment London is, I think, likely to hamper the production of truly great metropolitan fictions. It's in new neighbourhoods, communities and social milieux that vitality lies. The huckster, the conman, the migrant – these are the people who most fiercely grab hold of the economic opportunities that the city offers. They're on the make with nothing to lose. It's London or bust.

It may just be that a classic London novel can never be set at the BBC or at the ICA. The superior eloquence of those institutions, and that of the elevated worlds depicted or pursued by the authors looked at in this chapter, is too dusty and rarefied. The city really needs a literature more devolved, something more mischievous and dirty.

CHAPTER FIVE

Pop Goes the Centre

Pop Art is:
Popular (designed for a mass audience)
Transient (short-term solution)
Expendable (easily forgotten)
Low cost
Mass produced
Young (aimed at youth)
Witty
Sexy
Gimmicky
Glamorous
Big business
(Richard Hamilton manifesto, 1957)[1]

DO ASIANS BELONG IN LONDON? On the face of it this may seem an odd question. After all, as earlier chapters of this book showed, at any time in the city's history over the last three hundred years there have been hundreds, if not thousands, of Asian men and women living in the city. From ragged lascars tramping the streets of Shadwell to bedizened princes holding court in Mayfair, from elderly ayahs clicking their knitting needles in Hackney to the firebrand students plotting revolution in Gray's Inn library – those born in the subcontinent have long lived here, both floundering and flourishing. Yet their stories are relatively unknown. It is the lives and escapades of black people – of Olaudah Equiano and Ignatius Sancho, of Mary Prince and Mary Seacole – that have been celebrated of late. Slavery, dedicated to the erosion of human dignity, also magnifies and brings it into relief. Stories about ex-slaves in London are accorded a weight and a significance, moral as well as historiographical, far in excess of those about deracinated Hindus. Even the phrase 'post-war immigration' tends to evoke images not of Asians, but of the thousands of Caribbean islanders who arrived in London during the 1950s. It's their calypsos, wafer-thin suits and tiny suitcases that nestle in the imagination.

Yet a limited number of Asians – chiefly professionals from the educated classes such as doctors, teachers and ex-Indian army personnel – did also live in the capital during that decade.[2] There were a few gurudveras and temples at which they could worship, and a few curry houses where they could eat and natter, but there was no geographically specific community to which they could go for sustenance. They lived scattered and largely respectable lives. Few boarding-house keepers pinned up signs to warn them off; some landlords actively distinguished between Indians (good) and West Indians (bad). On the whole they were left to their own devices. They were demonized far less than Caribbean immigrants, who were routinely depicted as drains on the taxpayer's coffers, as red-blooded menaces to society.

On 1 July 1962 the Commonwealth Immigrants Act came into force, restricting entry to the United Kingdom to those men and women who carried work vouchers issued by the Ministry of Labour. The Asians who now arrived in England tended to come from farming backgrounds and had received only basic schooling. They soon learned that British agricultural production no longer relied on intensive labour. Their poor spoken English meant that few of them, unlike Jamaican and Barbadian immigrants, could get work in public transport or in nursing. Following the post-war decline in London's manufacturing base even unskilled industrial jobs were at a premium. A large number of Sikhs settled in Southall where they worked at Woolf's rubber factory or at the recently built Heathrow Airport. Most Asian men, though, were forced to flee the bright lights of Piccadilly Circus that so tantalized Caribbean settlers and head for drab, grey cities such as Bradford, Leicester and Birmingham whose foundries, steel mills and textile factories offered them ready, if menial, employment and where rent and travelling expenses were enticingly low. By 1966 only thirty per cent of Asians lived in the Greater London area, as compared to sixty per cent of West Indians.[3] Even by 1982, the figures were thirty-four and forty-nine per cent respectively.[4]

Across the industrial heartlands of England, in the back-to-back terraced houses in which they lodged and which they later bought, Asian men ground out the lifestyles that were to characterize Asian life in England for the following decades. They worked all the double shifts and overtime slots they could grab. Their homes were no more than dormitories. They penny-pinched and hoarded. Rarely did they go out after work – they were too tight, too tired. Their main goal was to save enough money to bring over the wives and children that they had left behind in Indian and Pakistani villages. Pleasure was renounced. Rarely did they have the energy or inclination to go out to pubs or cinemas during the evenings. Their lack of fluency in English discouraged them from mingling with the wider white community. Such routines, which all immigrants tend to slide into, became ingrained. The virtues of austerity – both financial and behavioural – were drummed into their children. Canny observers such as Ray Gosling picked up on this. Writing about life in Rochdale he admitted:

I thought the immigrants would bring calypso bands and colour and freedom and life to our drab industrial towns. It hasn't happened like that in Rochdale. As the native English Nonconformist has faded away, these new arrivals have come along and, particularly the Muslim immigrants, have brought it all back. The spirit of my father. The spirit of hard work, abstemiousness and self-sufficiency. Don't drink. Don't smoke. Don't kiss in the street. Don't marry unless your father approves.[5]

Asian men's remorseless work ethic intensified, rather than lapsed, after their families joined them in England. They prized money, not culture. This led to the accurate perception that most Asian parents would never be happy unless their children became doctors, lawyers or accountants. They were seen as dour and insular: there was no Asian comedy – no Lenny Henry or Kenny Lynch. In programmes like *It Ain't Half Hot Mum* (1974–1979) and *Mind Your Language* (1977–1979) Asians wore comical headwear, swung unpredictably from hand-clasping obsequiousness to eye-rolling outrage, and were at all times the butts rather than the tellers of jokes. From Peter Sellers singing 'Goodness Gracious Me' to the Carry On team running amok in the Khyber Pass, it was mainly Asians in Asia, however, who were being lampooned. End-of-pier comedians and working-class comics preferred to get laughs by cracking jokes about darkies and sambos. Pakis were unknown material, off the cultural radar.

Public service broadcasting fared a little better. The BBC transmitted native-tongued series such as *Nai Zindagi Naya Jeevan* on Sunday mornings. Asian families across the nation would stumble out of bed early to eat their porridgey breakfasts more quickly than normal so as to be ready and waiting in their sitting rooms when the programme, a mixture of news, religious homily and music, and whose title translates as 'New Life, New Times', began at nine o'clock. The programme was a lifeline, a fleeting opportunity for isolated families and communities to feel less alone, to have their existences endorsed. It was well-intentioned but rather sombre. That was fine for mothers and fathers, but their children were sometimes a little less enthralled. They found it hard to believe that the classical musicians wailing ghazals or beating out tabla mantras were in tune with their new lives. Such disconnection was accentuated by mainstream news and current affairs coverage which, apart from the occasional exposé of the barbarism of arranged marriages or footage of disputes involving Leicester textile workers, tended to be negligible.

Young Asians had no cultural ambassadors or role models. They lacked sporting heroes such as Cyrille Regis, Brendan Batson and Laurie Cunningham, West Bromwich Albion's Three Degrees. Even more importantly, they lacked an indigenous youth culture. They forged no musical alliances such as those between rude boy ska and skinhead stomp at the end of the 1960s, or 1976's reggae-punk axis. It was these marriages encompassing fashion, music, sex and shared attitudes that helped to create the open-minded, pick'n'mix, urban British youth culture which flourishes to this day and which, through such style-magazine-designated epiphenomena as 'new Asian kool', 'bhangramuffin' and 'the future soundz of India', Asians have only recently entered.[6] Even back in the 1960s, hippies may have loved the East, but they didn't have much interest in those whose parents actually came from there. English Asians were bereft of sonorous accents, sexy garments, mystical unguents. They were dour and provincial. They were English. Metropolitan life was increasingly coming to be associated with the bubbliness and buzziness of pop culture. How could Asians be seen as part of it? With their timid gaits, their outdated fashions and their love of work rather than play, they seemed to belong more to the world of soot and terraces. They hosted no shebeens, no backroom joints at which any hipsters would want to slum. They spent more time reciting theological scripts at after-school temples than hanging round street corners or piling in at the rucks that blew up every Saturday afternoon when the local footie team clashed with away supporters.

That proportionately few Asians lived in the capital wasn't the only reason they were never thought of as urban; it was because they weren't urban in disposition. They lacked 'attitude' and street-cred. They worked too hard. Throughout its history toil had been an integral part of London: from the navvies queuing up each morning at the docks ready for a day of baling to the Jewish tanners and saddlers in the old East End, the capital was seen as a place of drudgery and work. But Asians had arrived at a time when labouring London was in decline. The service sector was beginning to take over and immigrants who sweated from dusk till dawn in factories and foundries outside the capital were deemed anachronistic. They were seen as dull and rather back-wards-looking. Their lack of interest in pop culture suggested premature middle age. The twin imperatives of religion and family conspired to limit women's autonomy and ensured that the vast majority of second-generation children knew, and dared not exceed, their allotted social roles. Living way out west or up north, far from the prying cameras and busy notepads of a metro-centric media, they were to all intents and purposes an invisible community.

If there is one figure who is responsible for dragging Asians in England into the spotlight it is Hanif Kureishi. Through a series of plays, films and novels – from the end of the 1970s to the present day – he has presented their lives to mainstream audiences with unrivalled wit and candour. Not only did he show that their lives were worthy of public attention, but he did so in a manner that eschewed worthiness. He managed to leapfrog that turgid stage so familiar to students of minority literatures in which ethnic writers spend years churning out angry, joyless polemics which counter-productively enjoin 'society' to respect and reimburse the communities they oppress.

Ribaldry and bawdiness were more to Kureishi's liking. He produced entertainments which showed everyone – including Asians themselves – that they were far more varied, messy and interesting than they were commonly assumed to be. His work featured drug pushers, tyrannical ex-Foreign Ministers, bogus mystics, brutalizing landlords, togged-up likely lads, sex-hungry cripples. They duped and slagged off one another. They argued constantly. They were also not to be taken at face value: in *My Beautiful Laundrette* Omar is sent to a flash new hotel where he is due to pick up an unspecified consignment on behalf of his business associate Salim. The hotel-room door is opened to reveal an elderly-looking Pakistani whose sprawling white beard makes him resemble a devout mullah. Suddenly, to Omar's astonishment, the 'mullah' peels off his beard, which, it turns out, he uses for smuggling sachets of heroin. It's a shocking scene not only for its sudden exposé of criminality but, more importantly, because it shows how Asian elders needn't always be respected or deferred to, and that they are often just as corrupt as the world against which they inveigh. By secularizing the old order in this fashion, Kureishi inspired second-generation Asians to look at the world anew: they could and should try to make their own ways in life without feeling familial and religious nooses around their necks.

Kureishi was the first major Asian or Caribbean writer to have been born in England. His father Rafiushan had arrived in London in 1947 to study law, but never completed his course. He did, however, marry an Englishwoman, Audrey Buss, and, after partition, began working at the Pakistani Embassy in London. He also dabbled in freelance journalism and wrote novels, all of which were rejected by publishers.[7]

Kureishi was born in Bromley, Kent, in 1954. The only Asian pupil at a high school whose alumni included H.G. Wells and David Bowie, he has often stressed in interviews how miserable his childhood was: he was spat at and racially abused every day between the ages of four and sixteen; one of his teachers insisted on calling him 'Pakistani Pete'; his friends' idea of a good night out was to go Paki-bashing. He transferred to technical college rather than stay on at school, and later read philosophy at King's College, London. By this time he was already sitting in on rehearsals at the Royal Court Theatre to which he'd sent one of his early plays. After university he continued to work for the Royal Court, the Joint Stock Company and at Riverside Studios. He also supplemented his income by writing for a porn magazine called *Game*. A number of his plays were produced during this period, including *Mother Country* (1980), *Outskirts* (1981) and *Birds of Passage* (1983), and he also received commissions to adapt Kafka's *The Trial* for Radio 4 in 1982 and Brecht's *Mother Courage* for the Royal Shakespeare Company in 1984.

It was *My Beautiful Laundrette*, however, that made Kureishi's name. His first screenplay, it told the story of Omar (played by Gordon Warnecke) who, tired of being patronized and bullied by his extended Pakistani family, decides to get ahead in society by opening a gleaming new launderette in South London. Having acquired the necessary start-up cash by conning a family friend in a drug deal, he employs as his partner a former schoolfriend, Johnny (Daniel Day-Lewis), from whom he had drifted apart after his pal had joined a gang of skinhead racists. While they busy themselves falling in love, all around them is chaos – Omar's uncle's mistress is poisoned by his wife; Johnny's abandoned cronies go ballistic.

Comic and knowing, socially engaged without lapsing into earnestness, the film (directed by Stephen Frears) was a great success on its release in late 1985. It was seen as a welcome riposte to the heritage cinema of *Chariots of Fire* (1981) and *A Passage to India* (1984). An ironic critique of the entrepreneurialism and individualism paeaned by Thatcher, it also seemed to open up the possibility of a popular and oppositional British film culture. Balking at the film's cast of gays, blacks and young people, Norman Stone, then Oxford Professor of Modern History, bemoaned 'the overall feeling of disgust and decay' it conveyed, complaining that Kureishi, together with other film-makers such as Derek Jarman and Ron Peck, was inciting a 'sleazy, sick hedonism'.[8] Audiences disagreed. They loved its liveliness and wit. Costing £600,000 to make, the film grossed $15,000,000, and earned Kureishi an Oscar nomination for best screenplay. Numerous critics and fellow artists have praised it for its vision of a contemporary England in which race, sexuality and, most of all, urban culture are portrayed with a rare pungency and wit. This sort of city life – young, polyracial, politically dissident – had only rarely received literary attention before Kureishi's emergence. Nearly all of his work has been set in and around London, a city whose energies, clamours and dangers he has been inventorizing for the last twenty years.

Kureishi's passion for the metropolis, like that of many people over the years, is intensified by the fact that he did not grow up there. Much to his later chagrin he was brought up in Bromley, a place that inspired a vitriol fantastic to read. A borough ten miles south of London Bridge, and a twenty-minute train journey from Victoria, Bromley has long been seen as quintessentially suburban. Neither truly urban nor rural, it is, for its critics, marooned somewhere in-between, a lingering and painful half-life. Hardly surprising, really, given that the suburbs have long been dismissed as monotonous shrines to 'golf, God and gardening'.[9] They've been condemned for generating traffic jams, for repudiating the vitality of the inner city, and as representing the triumph of individual expression over communality.[10] As far back as 1933 the International Congress of Modern Architecture described them as 'a kind of scum, churning against the walls of the city' and 'one of the greatest evils of the century'.[11]

Artists who loathe suburbia do so not for its aesthetic or architectural shortcomings, but on social and ethical grounds. Ever since 1893 when George and Weedon Grossmith published the diary of the inept Pooter, the Holloway clerk who liked nothing better than a bit of obsessive tin-tacking or blinds-straightening, the suburbs – and those who live in them – have been lampooned in literature (for J.G. Ballard they represent 'the death of the soul'), cinema (Mike Leigh's eviscerating *Abigail's Party*) and in TV sitcoms such as *Keeping Up Appearances* where status-fixated Hyacinth Bucket insists that her name be pronounced 'Bouquet'. Following the rural exoduses and slum clearances of the first few decades of the last century over half the English population now lives in suburbia. Yet for many artists, most famously John Betjeman, only bombs could make these places palatable. In *The Buddha of Suburbia*, Karim, the novel's ambitious narrator, lashes the dull materialism of suburban life: the people of Chislehurst 'would exchange their legs for velvet curtains, stereos, Martinis, electric lawnmowers'.[12] Indeed, 'it was said that when people drowned they saw not their lives but their double-glazing flashing before them'.[13]

Kureishi believes that suburbanites value education purely for its social cachet. They decry forms of culture that challenge or disrupt, that seek to extend – rather than merely confirm – established modes of thought or structures of feeling. In *The Black Album*, Shahid leaves Sevenoaks because the people there aren't interested in culture, 'but only gardening guides, atlases, Reader's Digests'.[14] In *Buddha*, Karim envies those who can 'talk of art, theatre, architecture, travel; the languages, the vocabulary, knowing the way round a whole culture – it was invaluable and irreplaceable capital'.[15] Such capital abounds in the capital. London alone can challenge Karim intellectually and spiritually. The scorn with which, in *The Black Album*, Shahid's father and brother regard his plans to become a writer suggests that cultural myopia isn't the exclusive preserve of white suburbanites.

In *Nattering in Paradise* (1988), an oral study of suburban life conducted by Daniel Meadows, the residents of Beckenham, less than two miles from Bromley, and the home of Eva Kay, Haroon's mistress in *Buddha*, talk about themselves with a mixture of sadness and complacency that suggests the two values they most cherish are compromise and convenience. Their abiding concerns are personal and financial security. A sardonic estate agent from the area claims that his clients put tree maintenance, clear footpaths and public golf course upkeep at the top of their list of ontological priorities.[16] Similarly, Karim asserts that 'In the suburbs people rarely dreamed of striking out for happiness. It was all familiarity and endurance: security and safety were the reward of dullness.'[17] One is reminded of the speech made in 1993 by John Major in which he spelled out his less than compelling vision of what it meant to be English: 'long shadows on county grounds, warm beer, invincible green suburbs, dog-lovers and pools-fillers'.

Kureishi's white suburbanites instinctively shudder at the idea of sharing the same environment with people of different races. In *Borderline* (1981), Del and Bob attack a passing Asian man. In *Birds of Passage*, Eva prepares a plate of sandwiches for the lodger Asif, and asks 'Corned beef's all right for Pakis, isn't it?'[18] Her husband Ted always turns off the TV at the first sight of black faces. As such he seems to confirm the assessment made in 1909 by the black travel writer A.B.C. Merriman-Labor:

> In the low class suburbs a black man stands the chance of being laughed to scorn until he takes to his heels. And, in such low quarters, until the Diamond Jubilee of the late Queen Victoria which by bringing hundreds of black soldiers and others into Britain made black faces somewhat familiar, bad boys will not hesitate to shower stones or rotten eggs on any passing black man, however high he may be in his own estimation.[19]

Does a deep-seated xenophobia underwrite all of suburbia? Surely not. Yet every one of the adolescent and idealistic Asians Kureishi creates comes to learn that they must move away or, inevitably, be fucked over. Literally so. Karim, in *Buddha*, goes to visit his girlfriend Helen, but is repelled by her father who proudly announces, 'We're with Enoch'[20] Karim turns to leave but, before he can do so, is trapped against the garden fence by the family's Great Dane who clambers up high and shoots a load of canine spunk over him. What a fate! What an epiphany! Buggered by a (racist) Englishman's best friend, his dog, in those suburbs which, according to Eva in *Birds of Passage* – 'if you want to see what England's really like, come out to Chislehurst sometime' – embody all that's best about this country.[21] Karim flees to London with all the desperation of the political refugee.

It's not only such treatment by white people (and their dogs) that makes Kureishi's characters want to move away. Anti-suburbanism has a special resonance for young Asians. Their parents have traditionally seen the suburbs as a promised land, light at the end of the industrial tunnel. It is a reward for decades of economic frugality, an escape from the sound and mental fury of frontline living. Their children, brought up cushioned and cosseted, often view things differently: in *Borderline*, set in Ealing, an area with a high concentration of Asians, Haroon becomes tired of the constant appeal by ethnic elders to tradition, family, and religious morality: 'This place and the past, it's like an octopus.'[22] Later, he complains to his girlfriend Amina: 'All of us. Shut in for safety. Strong and solid now. But stifled here together. Here my brain feels like a tight ball.'[23] It's a passage that pre-echoes a scene in Meera Syal's *Life Isn't All Ha Ha Hee Hee* (2000) in which Tania feels like screaming as she listens to the conservative, small-minded gossip of the middle-aged guests at an Indian wedding:

> She suddenly remembered why she had stopped attending community events, cultural evenings, bring-a-Tupperware parties,

all the engagements, weddings and funerals that marked out their borrowed time here. She could not take the proximity of everything any more. The endless questions of who what why she was, to whom she belonged (father/husband/workplace), why her life wasn't following the ordained patterns for a woman of her age, religion, height and income bracket. The sheer physical effrontery of her people, wanting to be inside her head, to own her, claim her, preserve her. Her people.[24]

Kureishi has written at length about how important pop music was to him as he grew up and how the excitement it engendered in him not only shaped his ideas about which subjects literature should cover, but also the effect it should have on its readers.[25] Much of that music was shot through with a disdain for suburbia. 'The Wanderer', 'Born To Be Wild', 'Born To Run', 'Live Forever' – the urge to be free, mobile, and to escape from the shackles of domesticity have long been central motifs of pop music.[26] More specifically, many of the groups who were most successful as Kureishi was growing up scorned suburbia as that deadening zone where, as the Bonzo Dog Doo-Dah Band sniggered, 'My pink side of the drainpipe keeps me away from you'.[27] Siouxsie Sioux, of Siouxsie and the Banshees, was one of a group of friends, nicknamed the Bromley contingent, who were punk's most visible acolytes in its early days: 'The only thing that was looked down on was suburbia. I hated Bromley: I thought it was small and narrow-minded.'[28]

Lower-middle-class teenagers such as Mick Jagger, Ray Davies and David Bowie also felt that questions of race, sexuality and self-identity could all be explored more easily and creatively by moving to London. Jagger, brought up in Wilmington, on the outskirts of London, met a black cook at a nearby US base who played rhythm and blues to him.[29] It was a revelation. Soon, singing and dancing in a heavily negro-inspired style, name-checking the incarcerated black activist Angela Davis, dining with Cabinet ministers and sleeping with glam models, Jagger came to epitomize 'Swinging London'. This was a place, a state of mind, as well as a cultural and historical period where the objective was 'the avoidance of dull, boring, conventional reality'.[30] That was precisely what Lennon and McCartney did; they went instead to parties hosted by Harold Pinter, met Bertrand Russell, became entranced by Indian transcendentalism after attending lectures by the Maharishi Mahesh Yogi, and dined and fraternized with pop artists such as Peter Blake and Richard Hamilton.[31]

David Bowie, or David Jones as he was then known, moved from Brixton to Plaistow Grove in Bromley at an early age. He went to the same school as Karim who observed that 'Boys were often to be found on their knees before this icon, praying to be made into pop stars and for release from a lifetime as a motor-mechanic'.[32] The occasion on which Bowie took home 'some pretty boy in class' and 'fucked [him] on my bed upstairs' in Bromley seems to have been the inspiration for Kureishi's description of the epiphanic handjob that Karim gives Charlie in *Buddha*.[33]

Bowie wrote the music for the television adaptation of *The Buddha of Suburbia* (1993). He also sang the theme music for *Absolute Beginners* (1986), the film version of Colin MacInnes's 1959 novel that, in its focus on youth, its celebration of speed and sex, its transcription and its creation of teenage argots, its sophisticated portrayal of multi-racial London, and its riotous dénouement, anticipates Kureishi's own work. Bowie's escape from suburbia, and 'from class, from sex, from personality, from obvious commitment', into London's realm of free play, make-believe and self-gratification, is a trajectory that resembles the odysseys undertaken by Kureishi's characters.[34] It's for freedom that Shahid comes to London, so he's particularly annoyed when his relatives try to drag 'him back into an earlier self and life, one he had gratefully sloughed off'.[35] Suburbia's only function is to serve as 'a leaving place'.[36] The cruellest insult Nina can hurl at Nadia as the latter steps off a plane in 'With Your Tongue Down My Throat' (1987) is 'you look as if you live in Enfield'.[37]

The most comically poignant scenes in *The Buddha of Suburbia* come when the twin worlds of suburbia and metropolitan pop collide. Charlie's manager turns up in a flash pink Vauxhall Viva outside the school gates to pick up his youthful protégé. They roar off into the distance – '"Wanker," boys said despondently, devastated by the beauty of the event. "Fucking wanker." We were going home to our mothers, to our rissoles and chips and tomato sauce, to learn French words, to pack our football gear for tomorrow. But Charlie would be with musicians. He'd go to clubs at one in the morning. He'd meet Andrew Loog Oldham.'[38]

'There is no such word as "home" in our language,' wrote the Nawab Mehdi Hasan Khan in 1890, 'I had heard the word so often that I was anxious to see an English house and real home life.'[39] In the books of Asian writers before Kureishi – and also of Caribbean writers such as Selvon, Lamming, Salkey – the idea of London is inseparable from the idea of it as their spiritual (as well as their geo-colonial) home. That they often end up living in dingy bed-sits and chilly boarding houses in dismal parts of town is said to signpost their status as degraded, second-class citizens. What they crave, more than anything, is nice wallpaper, the sense of legitimacy that decent residential quarters would afford. A proper home is a metaphor for 'proper London'. It proves that the immigrant's long voyage across the ocean was not in vain. Owning one means there is no need to worry about being in thrall to eccentric patrons and erratic charitable handouts, or about being kicked out of lodgings in midwinter by curmudgeonly West-bourne Grove landlords, or about having to trudge dispiritedly from one flea-infested hostel to another.

Kureishi's characters grew up plumped by domestic comforts and securities. They took them for granted and are now hungry to lap up the disorderly and heterotopian possibilities of metro-politan life. Domesticity and the familial realm are prized only by Kureishi's less appealing fictional creations. In *Birds of Passage*, the vacuous Eva boasts of her house: its lawn, flowers and 'honeysuckle along the back wall'.[40] Her husband Ted runs a central-heating firm whose profits are used to finance Eva's constant redecorating. David remarks of their house that 'Every time you visited, the walls were in a different place. Or they were extending the extension.'[41] In *London Kills Me*, Lily, wife of the gun-toting, Elvis-obsessed pornographer Stone, is embarrassingly proud of how her house, one without books, has been 'done up'.[42]

During the course of *The Buddha of Suburbia*, Eva becomes a successful interior designer. One could view this job positively: it symbolizes our desire and our need to refashion and transform ourselves. On the other hand, it's a job that panders to the belief that a new wall-unit or colour combination amounts to a meaning-ful improvement in the quality of one's life. Interior designers are actually obsessed with the exteriority of human lives – the cosmetic as opposed to the ethical. *Buddha*, which ends on the night of the 1979 General Election, maps in advance the new contours that Conservatism would assume so successfully in the 1980s. By making Eva a designer, Kureishi is able to isolate one of the key arenas in which the battle between Left and Right was fought during that decade – the housing market.

London saw a much-heralded rise in luxury developments. Gentrification led to moneyed professionals moving into pre-viously unfashionable areas such as Clapham and Notting Hill.

At the same time, working-class people were told that the right to buy their council houses was a substantive step towards empowerment and social enfranchisement. There was a housing boom: at one point in 1985, the value of a three-bedroomed suburban cottage in Beckenham increased by £1000 a week.[43]

But there was also a darker side to the capital's housing market. Analysts have highlighted the under-investment in new buildings and a decline in private rented accommodation which led to a huge rise in the number of people sleeping rough under the Embankment, in the doorways of Covent Garden restaurants, and huddled amidst the dustbins behind Irish pubs in Camden.[44] These changes repelled Kureishi. In 'Finishing The Job', a 1988 essay on that year's Conservative Party Conference, he notes with palpable distaste:

> Walking past the houses of my childhood I noticed how, in an orgy of alteration they had been 'done up' [. . .] It was DIY they loved in Thatcherland, not self-improvement or culture or food, but prosperity, bigger and better homes complete with every mod-con – the concrete display of hard-earned cash. Display was the game.[45]

Do It Yourself soon degenerates into Do It (Only For) Yourself. It's a celebration of self over society, the latter being something whose existence was famously questioned by Margaret Thatcher. Kureishi is worried that buildings, in particular their value, are beginning to be seen as more important than the people who live in them. Eviction, one symptom of this kind of mentality, features heavily in his work. In *Birds of Passage*, Asif, who had come to lodge with David and Audrey, ousts them when they fall into financial straits and converts their house into lucrative student flats; *My Beautiful Laundrette* begins with Salim throwing Johnny out of his squat; Danny's caravan under a motorway arch is bulldozed at the end of *Sammy and Rosie Get Laid*; the posse whose exploits comprise *London Kills Me* have their belongings hurled into the street by a gang of toughs. Kureishi allies his hatred of suburbia and home in a scene in *Sammy*, when Rosie reveals that her 'crude, vicious, racist and ignorant' father was not only the Mayor of Bromley, but – shame! – ran a furniture store.[46]

Conservative ideology in the 1980s also supplies a crucial context for Kureishi's repeated depictions of metropolitan housing. The right to buy, to 'do up' one's house with furniture bought from Habitat became an extension of the traditional Tory belief in the sacred importance of property, the idea of an Englishman's home being his castle. Such a metaphor, with its implicit suggestion of the house as a fortress and defence against intruders, was concretized and racialized in *The Buddha of Suburbia*'s 'dog-fuck' scene.

Houses are also of huge symbolic importance to first-generation Asian immigrants. Since the 1960s they have achieved high levels of home ownership. They also have the most inhabitants per household of any ethnic group.[47] The need to save enough money to bring over their dependants made male settlers reluctant to go out socializing. Such attitudes, combined with religious codes restricting their children's freedom – especially that of their daughters – meant that the domestic sphere took on a highly privileged place within Asian cultural life. If many parents were beset by a limited grasp of the English language, and shied away through suspicion and timidity from the exigencies of social life, then at least they knew that upon returning home they were entering a controlled, less complicated zone where they could impress upon their children the religious, matrimonial and educational imperatives they held so dear.

Many of these values were bound to be tested over the years. In *Borderline*, teenage Amina's increasing Westernization is seen in spatial terms: 'She has moved far from us.'[48] Believing that an interest in English values inevitably amounts to a rejection of 'home', her father Amjad tries to arrange her marriage. In *My Beautiful Laundrette*, Omar's mother leaps in front of a train and his cousin Tania runs away, having warned him that her family will 'swallow you up like a little kebab'.[49] Almost inevitably, it's London that offers these women, and many of Kureishi's male characters, a refuge in which to escape from the conformity, the suffocating orderliness of the family household.

None of Kureishi's more lovable or deserving characters lives in a wholly tidy, respectable or 'hygienic' house. In *Laundrette*, Omar's alcoholic father, who had been a famous radical journalist in Pakistan, has a 'small, damp and dirty' flat in South London which 'hasn't been decorated for years'.[50] Johnny used to be a squatter before he moved into a noisy, rundown house full of endlessly partying Pakistani students. In *Buddha*, Jamila leaves her family home to enter a commune full of rotting tarpaulins and leaking pipes, one which is inhabited by radical lawyers, intellectual lesbians and jazz-lovers. Here, ties of blood matter less than collective goodwill and mutual commitment. In *London Kills Me*, Clint's posse occupy a flat in Whitehall Gardens which, for all its problems, seems far more desirable than his mum's fraught and niggly set-up with Stone. In *The Black Album*, the liberated and liberating college lecturer Deedee lives in an unkempt house full of crumpled magazines, old bikes, yellowing papers and Malcolm X posters. Shahid himself has a raucous, dilapidated bed-sit in Kilburn where cooking smells, loud music, the whiff of drugs, foreign students shouting in dozens of languages and near-fatal gas leaks all combine to make daily life less than tranquil.

No one who lives in a conventional or plush manner is depicted positively. In *Buddha*, Karim takes part in an orgy in the four-storeyed, Indian-friezed, and excruciatingly elegant St John's

Wood mansion of the theatre director Matthew Pyke, who's a repellent and manipulative control freak. Karim's girlfriend Eleanor, meanwhile, has a lovely pad in Notting Hill, a wealthy family, important and powerful connections, but she's still emotionally scarred by the suicide of her black boyfriend Gene, and by the tedious class-guilt posh people so often love to indulge in. In *London Kills Me*, college professor Headley, despite her arty and tasteful flat, is cold and self-obsessed.

Kureishi rejects the idea that having a stable, well-decked-out house is an important signifier of a person's value. Bricks and mortar may supply a degree of rootedness, but they can't guarantee happiness. It may be that the Londoners Kureishi shows opting out of this system are rather privileged. To some extent their degentrification is a lifestyle choice, the traditional messiness that is the luxury of well-connected dropouts and would-be bohos. Still, by depicting – with sympathy and approval – crumbling households, unorthodox communities and designs for living that are contingent and slung together, Kureishi offers a vision of domesticity hateful to both Thatcherite and traditional Asian notions of propriety.

This interest in brokenness, the disreputable and chaotic aspects of London recurs throughout Kureishi's work. In *Buddha*, Karim recalls the train journeys from Bromley he used to take as a youth with his Uncle Ted to watch Chelsea play at Stamford Bridge:

> Before crossing the river we passed over the slums of Herne Hill and Brixton, places so compelling and unlike anything I was used to seeing that I jumped up, jammed down the window and gazed out at the rows of disintegrating Victorian houses. The gardens were full of rusting junk and sodden overcoats; lines of washing criss-crossed over the debris.[51]

The sensation of speed, the novelty of these environments, and the fact that these are lawnmower-free zones all magnetize the adolescent Karim. Similarly, in *The Black Album*, we're told that 'Before Shahid came to the city, [he] sat in the Kent countryside dreaming of how rough and mixed London would be, his brother Chili had loaned him *Mean Streets* and *Taxi Driver* as preparation'.[52] Even after they've arrived in the capital, Kureishi's characters still get a buzz out of living amidst ruins. The directions to *My Beautiful Laundrette* order Omar to walk 'along a South London street, towards NASSER'S garage. It's a rough area, beautiful in its own falling-down way.'[53]

Passages like these show a manifest commitment to the cultural vitality of the inner city, no matter how rundown or neglected it may have become, that is deeply political. Following the abolition of the Greater London Council in 1986, the capital lacked its own democratically elected governing body for the first time since the London City Corporation was established in 1888. No central planning or administrative body existed to tackle the growing problems of social polarization, unemployment, and an emergent underclass. It seemed to many, including the directors of such films as *Empire State* (1986) and *Close My Eyes* (1991), that rentiers, unelected city quangos and foreign capital had taken control of the city. At the close of *Sammy and Rosie Get Laid*, the ramshackle homes of the community forged by junkies, beggars and homeless people under a motorway bridge are bulldozed whilst a property developer announces, 'I'm proud to say – [we're] making London a cleaner and safer place.'[54]

There's a subtle ellipsis here. What the developer is saying, of course, is 'a cleaner and safer place *for people like us*'. This is the totalitarian language of social hygiene. Glossy, streamlined, showpiece – all yuppie adjectives. Kureishi believes in urban messthetics – the idea that dirt, confusion and contamination

define urban life. People move to cities to be nearer ideas, fashions, strangers. A tremendous turnover and wastage is involved in this process: cities are environmentally unsound places. Yet there's also an exhilarating friction at play here – as people of extraordinarily different tastes and backgrounds jostle against each other. This is the source of the energy of metropolitan culture. To deny this – or to seek to minimize this – is a form of extremism. There's a parallel between the property developer's attitude towards London and that held by Riaz, the Islamic fundamentalist, in *The Black Album*. Early in this novel, Riaz is shown walking the streets 'rapidly in a straight line. To keep up, and to avoid charging into the Irishmen who gathered outside the pubs, Shahid had to jig on and off the pavement.'[55] The property developer wants to clean up London in order to allow the swifter flow and accumulation of capital by multinational corporations. Riaz wants to clean up London –

and Western society – by diverting people from the path of rampant secularization and by leading them to Allah. Both projects, for Kureishi, are brutal and inhuman; driven by ideology, they hold scant regard for human individuality, for the lives of the six million people who pour through the streets of London each day.

In an essay entitled 'Some Time With Stephen' (1986), Kureishi describes businessmen as 'semi-criminals' and admits that he still thinks 'in terms of the "straight" world and the rest'.[56] Straightness, of course, means 'square', 'unsussed', not alert to fashion or the sly paths, intersections and underpasses of contemporary culture. It means bourgeois, suburban, conformist. It also refers to the teleological and linear approach to life in London taken by Riaz and the developer.

'Straightness' is as bad as the cult of 'home': they both imply permanence, an intolerance of deviation, a resistance to change, something fixed and unbending. Kureishi, by contrast, tries to permeate his accounts of London with fluidity and flow. His two most common symbols for such relentless momentum are bicycles and shoes.

In *My Beautiful Laundrette*, Tania's need to fly from her suburban home is shown in the scene where she disgraces herself in front of her relatives by wildly riding around on a bike in her parents' back garden. Karim's similar desire to escape the slow-moving, atrophied world of Bromley is captured in his account of how he used to cycle intoxicatedly through South London, 'nipping through traffic, sometimes mounting the pavement, up one-way streets, breaking [sic] suddenly, accelerating by standing up on the pedals, exhilarated by thought and motion'.[57] Throughout *London Kills Me*, an Asian called Bike pedals about, cutely mute, but, like an all-seeing narrator, constantly circling the other protagonists, his friends. Movement is everything for Kureishi's characters: they fear stasis more than death.

Meanwhile, the browbeaten unhappiness of the mothers of both Bob in *Outskirts* and Karim in *Buddha* is evidenced by their jobs as shoeshop assistants. In *Borderline*, Amjad's growing inability to lord it over his family is embodied by his swollen legs. Omar, in *My Beautiful Laundrette*, is caught between the immoral monetarism of the drug-dealing Salim and his own father's embattled idealism. His need to break free from both modes of entrapment is visualized in two consecutive scenes: the first shows a brutish Salim treading on his nose; in the second, immediately after, a badly bruised Omar can be found sitting on the end of his father's bed cutting Papa's filthy nails.[58] The entire plot of *London Kills Me* revolves around Clint's efforts to get hold of a decent pair of shoes which will enable him to start work as a restaurant waiter and leave his penniless days behind.

These examples show that, at some time or another, most of Kureishi's characters feel the need for change, to break out of the ruts they find themselves in. Mobility, transformation, shapeshifting – cities permit and encourage these activities. Freed from family, from community, from the slower timeframes of suburban and provincial life, the city pell-mells with traffic, randomness, neon brightness and multiplicity. That's what, in *The Black Album*, Shahid and his tutor both love about London: Deedee enjoyed the feeling of 'speeding – towards what she had no idea. Nothing would hold her; velocity was all.'[59] During one of their arguments Shahid consoles himself by thinking 'at least he was in a London taxi . . . [he] had no idea where they were going. You could drive for two or three hours through this limitless city which had no shape, and not come out the other side.'[60] In *Sammy and Rosie Get Laid*, Danny and Rafi walk down a Tube tunnel; Kureishi writes in the directions: 'As an expert, I suggest the tunnel that connects the Piccadilly with the Victoria Line at Green Park – a superb sensation you get here of endless walking in both directions.'[61]

Kureishi's archetypal London landscape is populated by young people who have abandoned their scabby rooms to cruise through the streets, past myriads of multi-ethnic shops, restaurants and diversions; they'll smile, laugh, absorb both high and low culture, usually to the accompaniment of pumping dance music which captures the skelter and dense medley of young London. In *The Black Album* Shahid and Deedee giggle their way through Islington; they kiss, wander past the shops selling Indian-print scarves or punk bootlegs, buy Greil Marcus and Flannery O'Connor books, visit pubs. 'It was rare to see anyone over forty, as if there were a curfew for older people.'[62] This, for Shahid, is the life – the clamour and congestion for which an Asian upbringing had left him gasping. It's with this aspect alone of London society – deregulated, energized, pop – that Kureishi's characters identify. They relate to the city not in terms of particular places – Selvon's Bayswater Road or Kwesi Johnson's Brixton street corners – but as a mood, an attitude of openness and brio. More than just a space, London represents an ideal, that of change, the possible transformation of both self and society.[63] Perhaps the most charming scene Kureishi has ever written comes in *Sammy and Rosie Get Laid*, when Sammy enthuses to his baffled father about the joys of kissing and arguing on the Hammersmith tow-path, strolling through Hyde Park, watching alternative comedians in Earls Court abuse the Government, and attending semiotics seminars at the ICA where Colin MacCabe discusses 'the relation between a bag of crisps and the self-enclosed unity of the linguistic sign', before concluding, 'We love our city and we belong to it. Neither of us are English, we're Londoners you see.'[64]

This rhapsody came at a time when metrocentric lifestyles were not so routinely cannibalized by Lottery-funded film-makers and late-night TV schedulers as they are today. It anticipated – and is far superior to – the London-lite stories that appear in luridly packaged paperbacks with titles such as *Skunked* or *Shagging Darren*, full of tedious accounts of clubbing, copping off and charlie-snorting. It's also interesting because the sentiments it expresses are rarely articulated by the writers I am investigating.[65] For all the racial violence in Kureishi's books (the skinhead thugs in *Laundrette*; the pigs' heads hurled through the window of Anwar's South London grocery in *Buddha*; the daily attacks on Bengali estates in *The Black Album*), there exists, at least in his earlier works, an unquenchable optimism of spirit. Perhaps this is because it shows second-generation Asians who are fascinated by and embroiled in pop culture, that realm at the 'fringes of the respectable world [where there is] marijuana, generational conflict, clubs, parties, and [a] certain kind of guiltless, casual sex'.[66] English pop, never as racially segregated or monochromatic as in America, has always been one of the few areas where class, race and background become subordinated (though never entirely effaced) to the eternal 'now' that lies at the heart of pop music and where, as Rakim rapped, 'It ain't where you're from – it's where you're at'.[67] This is a dictum that appeals to many of Kureishi's Asians who do not wish to be defined by their parents' belief systems.

The importance of Sammy's assertion cannot be over-estimated. It talks of love, not hatred or ambivalence. It doesn't agonize over the issue of 'belonging'. It also makes clear that not only do young Asians like London more than they do England, but that they do so precisely because it isn't England. Kureishi sees the capital as being about *aggregation*, a happy realm where he can wear as many masks, create as many personae, explore as many new avenues as he wishes. *Place* is crucial in fomenting and facilitating such cross-cultural encounters. And *London* is the place. It throngs. It's multiplicitous. The freedom from homes, from families, from

'bourgeois' constraints allows Omar, Shahid and Karim a limitless palette of intellectual, social and sexual possibilities. Stepping out into West Kensington for the first time, the latter feels that 'being in a place so bright, fast and brilliant made you vertiginous with possibility'.[68] It's this potential for self-fashioning and the constant mutation and updating of the self that terrifies fundamentalists like Riaz. While under his charismatic spell, even Shahid begins to wonder if he's right to have 'plunged into a river of desire and excitement'. Should he renounce the filth of London and the Thames for the calmer waters that religious orthodoxy offers? Resolving to become more devout, he steps out of the mosque on to the London streets, only to be dazzled and seduced by 'the bustling diversity of the city'.[69]

The very title of *The Black Album*, as well as invoking the illicit, doomsday presence of Salman Rushdie's *The Satanic Verses* (1988) which shadows the novel's proceedings, is also the name of an album by Prince which went unreleased for many years. 'He's a river of talent,' says Shahid to Deedee at his college interview.[70] If so, he's a filthy and polluted river for, as Deedee points out, Prince smashes and grabs something from all musical styles – rock, disco, funk, rap. Like Kureishi's hero, David Bowie, nearly every album of his sees him assume a new persona. Prince is a satyr, an androgyne, a symbol – the latter, along with 'The Artist Formerly Known As Prince', being one of the numerous handles by which he has insisted on being catalogued. Polymorphous, perverse, self-transforming, limitless in ego and imagination (although increasingly limited in sales), Prince is a perfect embodiment of what London can mean and offer to a young (ethnic) newcomer to the metropolis.

Similarly, in *The Buddha of Suburbia*, Karim becomes an actor, a job which involves the repeated donning and casting aside of costumes and of personae. Attending the funeral of Anwar, his father's friend since boyhood, Karim begins to feel 'ashamed and incomplete' because he isn't sufficiently Indian.[71] He makes a resolution: 'If I wanted the additional personality bonus of an Indian past, I would have to create it.'[72] The key word here is 'create'. A sense of culture is no longer a curse, no longer a birthmark that must be carried all life long. Rather, it may be fashioned from nothing: it's a 'personality bonus' – words straight out of an Argos catalogue. And if Indianness is addable, it's also subtractable. Is this a loss? A tragedy? Many immigrant writers would think so. Kureishi, however, cherishes London for being a city that, though basted with history, doesn't enforce pastness on its inhabitants. Tradition is there only if you want it.

*　　*　　*

Kureishi's London young people are always on the move. They cruise through the streets, up the social ladder, jump from one bed to another. They hustle and circulate. On the Tube, at Islington parties and at art gallery private views, men and women of different races, classes and ages bump into each other, gossip, fight, and chat each other up. Such unexpected encounters are, of course, one of the defining features of metropolitan life: international financiers leaving expensive restaurants are touched for fivers by drink-sodden down and outs; impoverished students in East End cafés are startled to see that the oily meat dishes they've ordered are being served by ex-wives of Ugandan dictators; freshly uncloseted provincial boys from Loughborough stumble into the toilets of South London techno clubs where they come across Labour junior ministers being fellated by a 6'4" Canadian muscleman called Erik.

This cross-mingling is to the point. Privatization of space and experience is anathema to Kureishi. He has spoken of his revulsion against such systems of thought as psychology and sociology which, he feels, slot individuals into neat, discrete categories.[73] They most resemble the suburbia that his characters leave behind. Karim and Shahid are bored with the same-old same-old; they are hungry for contingency, culture-clash, unpredictability. In *The Buddha of Suburbia*, Charlie argues that people should be appointed jobs randomly: 'People in the street must be approached and told that they are now editor of *The Times* for a month.'[74]

Juxtaposition and collage, creative modes that are especially good at evoking the congestion and collision of metropolitan life, recur in different forms throughout Kureishi's work. Collage was a favourite medium for many English artists in the 1960s, including Gwyther Irwin and Stuart Brisley who believed that 'the illicit, violent and socially transgressive was bound up in the process of image scavenging'.[75] Peter Blake was the most famous deployer of collage and, with his then-wife, Jan Haworth, designed the cover of *Sgt. Pepper's Lonely Hearts Club Band* (1967). Kureishi, a life-long fan of The Beatles, personally asked Blake to design *The Buddha of Suburbia's* jacket. *Sgt. Pepper* shows J.H. Ross and Diana Dors, Karl Marx and Marilyn Monroe rubbing shoulders together; *Buddha* has Kureishi (with Carnaby Street faux-Indian garments pasted on to him) lurking inside a Richard Hamilton-style living room together with glossy actresses and an overfleshy swami.

Collage, as seen in the works of George Grosz or John Heartfield, is the most democratic of art forms. It's combative and impolite. Found images, tabloid pin-ups and pencil sketches are all flung together to fashion a rough-hewn newness. By juxtaposing figures of elevated social standing with pop icons and the urban underclass, collage creates a new imaginative space in which individuals can no longer guarantee that they'll be cordoned-off into privileged VIP zones or unpolluted spheres from which other races and classes are barred.[76] It's arguable that this merely reflects the quotidian exigencies of urban life: the homeless Clint will find himself stealing food at private views or flirting with actresses at upmarket diners; Charlie will end up in nightclubs vomiting into the lap of a famous footballer; Eleanor, the daughter of a close friend of the Queen Mother, will mingle with Rasta dope dealers every time she goes to the pub, and will sleep with a 'grossly fat and ugly sixteen-stone' Scottish roadsweeper.[77]

Juxtaposition, which lies at the heart of collage, often takes a linguistic form in Kureishi's work. In *My Beautiful Laundrette*, Omar, puffed-up and righteous, predicts great success for his business venture: 'It'll be going into profit any day now. Partly because I've hired a bloke of outstanding competence and strength of body and mind to look after it with me.'[78] These lines embody Kureishi's claim that, 'Irony is the modern mode, a way of commenting on bleakness and cruelty without falling into dourness and didacticism'.[79] Omar's greed is rendered both vacuous and horrid by the jargon he parrots, one that marries the rhetorics of corporate high finance and Hollywood biopic. The gulf between the grandiosity of his language and its material basis (a measly launderette) is exposed by the word 'bloke'; hyperbole rings hollow when all it endorses is this slangy monosyllable.

Kureishi is right to highlight the importance of irony. Through its deployment he shows Asian writers a route out of earnest, humourless literal-mindedness. His irony is not the same as that wan melancholy that shadows Selvon's fiction or the serrated omniscience that Naipaul's narrators employ. It is, rather, a whip-smart, deadpan way of speaking that seems both to ape and to mock 'straight discourse'. It's playful and casually knowing. *Daily Mail* op-ed arcadianism meets wideboy salacity when Rafi, the avuncular if murderous Third World tyrant in *Sammy and Rosie Get Laid*, opines that, 'For me England is hot buttered toast on a fork in front of an open fire. And cunty fingers.'[80] Kureishi's language is cocksure, aphoristic, suited-and-booted. It embodies the urban sass to which his characters aspire.

My Beautiful Laundrette is a particularly good example of how juxtaposition can be didactic as well as descriptive. Whereas cultural chauvinists believe that blackness and Britishness – or immigrants and the nation's economic well-being – are mutually opposed, Kureishi takes palpable delight in collapsing such polarities, in showing how London exists and thrives through the repeated jamming together of disparate groups. In this work, the author juxtaposes a rundown vestige of a decayed past – a launderette called Churchill's – with two social lepers who decide to refashion it. It's a startling act of transformation: Churchill stands for an older England – he represents stability, the luxury of historical continuity, nostalgia and a certain strain of imperial aristocracy.

His name was often invoked for nationalistic ends by Margaret Thatcher during the Falklands War. He was also trusted by that older generation of Asian settlers who, in Kureishi's work, often retard their children's drive towards independence. Amjad, who sought an arranged marriage for his daughter Amina in *Borderline*, confesses that 'the day Churchill died, that winter, the English neighbours in Ealing came to us. We watched his funeral. You see he was our man too. You trusted things here though they fell down sometimes.'[81]

But Amjad is speaking posthumously, via a journalist's cassette. His life ended in failure: he died without seeing his daughter get married. His wife has returned alone to Pakistan. Amjad and Churchill both represent a fading world order which is no more secure or ballast-supplying than the map of London which Danny draws for Rafi in *Sammy and Rosie Get Laid* but which the rain soon smudges and renders useless. The launderette represents the old England axed out of existence during Johnny's lusty refitting of Churchill's. Kureishi implies that if there's to be any English regeneration, any possibility of recapturing the kind of glory and national swagger many associate with pre-immigrant Britain, it will only come through the homosexual pairing of a gauche Paki and a fascist sympathizer who both reject their ethnic and subcultural obligations and, in doing so, provide an eyebrow-raising recipe for national rejuvenation: in short, through sodomy, miscegenation and financial acuity.

By bringing discrete and seemingly disconnected elements into close quarters, juxtaposition and collage often create a rather surreal effect. In Kureishi's work, the borders, hinterlands and loci that people maintain within the capital are knocked sideways, dissolved and transformed into something unreal. Taking his cue from the trippier aspects of 1960s' pop culture ('the first lesson of LSD was that reality was more evanescent and fugitive than most of us imagined for much of the time'[82]), Kureishi included many hallucinogenic scenes in *Sammy and Rosie Get Laid*. At one point, a bunch of straggly kids are seen on waste ground by a railway bridge playing chess with huge iron-sculpted pieces that they heave and drag across the equally large set. The ghosts of Dickens and Jacob Marley are evoked in a subsequent scene in which the Pakistani Government Minister Rafi is confronted by an Asian cab driver who has had his eye bandaged and part of his skull smashed in. He's a ghostly representative of all those who, like him, were tortured and murdered back in Pakistan on Rafi's orders. London may be an escape – from suburbia, from the retribution of the newly Islamicized masses on the subcontinent – but that doesn't mean the past will stay past, or even that it lacks threats, dangers and ghoulish encounters of its own.

Kureishi uses a form of surreal, psychedelic juxtaposition to more heartwarming and utopian effect in *My Beautiful Laundrette*. Here, the all-new 'Powders' is within minutes of opening its doors for the first time. The advance publicity has been so successful that customers line the streets outside. Some peer through the glass. What they see bewilders them: Nasser and his mistress Rachel waltz across the launderette floor, caught up in the Viennese classical music that's playing on the in-house system, love-giddy and utterly oblivious to those watching them. Nasser can't see, although the reader/viewer does, that all the time he's been dancing, Omar and Johnny have been '*making love vigorously, enjoying themselves thoroughly*' in the back room of the launderette.[83]

It's a bizarrely lyrical scene. Transgression has rarely appeared to be so courtly. Music, dancing and guiltless sex are all conjoined. Humour too. How nice these misfits are! And how thrilling when we spot Omar and Johnny again in *Sammy and Rosie Get Laid*

KITCHIN STUFF.

checking out the action at a party. Similarly, during one of their loved-up promenades in *The Black Album*, Shahid and Deedee find themselves in an Islington record shop poring over bootleg tapes of Charlie Hero, Karim's schoolfriend and idol in *The Buddha of Suburbia*. Clearly, just as Kureishi's characters can't be entirely confined to one particular text, his work illuminates one of the traditional features of London life – its ability to thrust people from different backgrounds and social spheres into sometimes fractious, sometimes harmonious co-existence. London isn't an organic community. On the contrary, it's a restless, clamorous agglomeration of exiles, migrants and refugees. And juxtaposition and collage are the ideal aesthetic modes for incarnating this higgledy-piggledy commotion of a metropolis.

A large part of London's appeal, like that of all major cities, is the promise it holds out for unfettered sexual activity. Young Ignatius Sancho, champing at the bit to leave the Montagu household for the highlife of the metropolis, would have agreed. So would the nineteenth-century Indian students scolded by the press back home for their gallivanting excesses. Memoirs and oral histories of Caribbean immigrants often mention how the prospect of rubbing up against lots of white female flesh in London was one of the reasons they came. They're right to link sex and the city: outsiders have long flocked to the capital because they want to do new things with new people without neighbours and families gossiping or moralizing. And while the sundering of old ties can lead to anomie and isolation – both Jean Rhys and Sam Selvon showed the anxieties that the weakening of community induces – freedom from constraint is a liberating and joyous thing.

Pop culture has always thrived on and celebrated these new licences. Rather than adopting a Dick Whittington attitude to London – one that dwells on the financial advantages of moving there – it cherishes the opportunity the city allows for sloughing off one's old, socially-constricted self. It doesn't care very much for office culture, the weekly wage or for the life of the commuter. It privileges randomness, appetency, and sexual hedonism. Many of the pop stars already discussed were well-fêted examples of incoming Londoners who chose to explore and indulge in the creative and sexual possibilities offered by the capital: it was at Indica Books and Gallery off Duke Street in London that John Lennon met Yoko Ono; it was in London that Mick Jagger bedded Marsha Hunt; and it was only in London that the young Jimi Hendrix could escape both the stylistic and the sexual segregation that American culture in the 1960s imposed upon him.

It was these artists who helped to rebrand the capital and make it attractive to a generation of suburban teenagers. For those adolescents born outside London in the 1960s who grew up listening to pop music on illicit pirate radio stations and sneaking in under-aged to their local cinemas to gawp at a naked Julie Christie or a blissed-out Mick Jagger, the city became, in their collective imagination, the only place where they could, as Karim says, 'live always this intensely: mysticism, alcohol, sexual promise, clever people and drugs'.[84] Kureishi has written that living in the suburbs triggered Gulf Syndrome, 'a dangerous psychological cocktail consisting of ambition, suppressed excitement, bitterness and sexual longing'.[85] Pop offered young people like Kureishi a vision of London similar (though more picaresque and less functional) to that outlined by Edmund White in his discussion of the special relationship between urban space and homosexual culture: 'The city is the human market-place that allows strange people to seek out those of fellow-feeling, it offers economic independence, the anonymity and randomness needed to sponsor original styles of life.'[86]

Kureishi does not sentimentalize sexual relations, as readers of *Intimacy* (1998) who recoil at the image of Jay masturbating over his wife's knickers will attest. Many of his characters have blotched, disfigured bodies: Rafi's stomach, chest and back have been criss-crossed with scars from innumerable operations – his body is a

'geography of suffering'.[87] Near the end of *My Beautiful Laundrette* Rachel reveals her 'blotched, marked' stomach to her lover, Nasser;[88] in *The Buddha of Suburbia*, Eva undergoes a mastectomy; in the same novel, Changez, Jamila's arranged husband, is obese and suffers from a withered arm; in *London Kills Me*, Clint's body is so cracked and eczematous that he never stops scratching.

These are characters of widely differing ages, genders and races. Their bodies may be ebbing and breaking down, but they're as eager as ever to get it up and get it on. Passion and desire have not declined. It's a similar situation with Kureishi's portrayal of London's wilting landscape: he homes in on the capital's underbelly, its squats, rundown pubs, dangerous Bengali estates and battered motorway arches, in order to show that economic disenfranchisement and low social standing don't preclude creativity, energy and newer, more contingent forms of urban community. Imperfection and deformity – somatic or metropolitan –

needn't restrict human sexuality. London's inner city may have been neglected during the 1980s, its social and economic fabric increasingly left to ruin, its inhabitants further disabled by the running down of local government; Kureishi, however, believes that its 'geography of suffering' is by no means fatal. The city is as resilient as the people who live in it.

Bodies aren't always associated with handicap or disfigurement in Kureishi's work. Often they're symbols for the multiplicitous pleasures and temptations which urban life offers. 'Karim,' Marlene commands in *The Buddha of Suburbia*, 'I want you to put some ice up my cunt.'[89] As well as being crammed with frozen water, the body becomes decorable (women in both *Outskirts* and *Sammy and Rosie Get Laid* have each buttock tattooed with the letter 'W' so that when they bend down their male partners see – and think! – WOW); the body is also a palette of exquisite pain (Charlie has hot wax dripped on his cock).

In the mid to late 1980s such joyfully explicit scenarios proved rather shocking to many people, not least Asian parents. They warned their children against indulging in the squalid, lascivious ways of English teenagers. All social interaction with whites outside of the classroom was dubious; it was bound to lead to all kinds of nastiness and, probably, pregnancy. It wasn't just yashmakked Muslim girls who needed to be veiled from society; all Asian kids had to avert their gazes. Sex didn't not exist: it was just furtive or coded. Teenagers lapped up coyly titillating cinemags studded with quote breaks from up-and-coming Hindi starlets who proclaim, 'I will show twenty per cent more than Rifi, but fifteen per cent less than Bobby.' And so, given that sex scenes, explicit language and nudity were largely circumscribed, Kureishi's accounts of Tania swishing her breasts before a startled Zaki in *My Beautiful Laundrette*, and Jamila's intercrural voracity in *The Buddha of Suburbia*, aren't merely descriptive, but provocative assaults on the sensibilities of his more delicate Asian audiences. They also show how Kureishi's women desire at least as much as they are desired. In many of his sex scenes – Eva on the garden bench in *The Buddha of Suburbia*, Rachel with Nasser in his garage, Anna at the beginning of *Sammy and Rosie Get Laid* – women are on top, the active partners, taking the lead role.

Tania's display is also one of many scenes in Kureishi's work involving exhibitionism and voyeurism. Omar eavesdrops on his uncle having sex in *My Beautiful Laundrette*; Karim watches his father and his future stepmother, Eva, make love in her garden near the start of *The Buddha of Suburbia*; Vivia and Rani, two growly punkettes, make sure that Rafi sees their aggressively self-conscious lesbian clinching in *Sammy and Rosie Get Laid*; Nina spies on Nadia and the Flounder as they pump away all night in 'With Your Tongue Down My Throat'. Karim justifies watching his friend Charlie being tortured by a New York prostitute on the following grounds: 'How educational it could be! What knowledge of caresses, positions, attitudes, could be gleaned from practical example!'[90]

The word 'educational' is well chosen. It bears exactly the right connotations of didacticism and of *épater les bourgeois*. During the second half of the 1980s Kureishi wrote against a background of what he felt was a Government-sponsored rise in narrow-minded homophobia and sexual repression: Thatcher's call for a return to Victorian values; the vilification of the Greater London Council by both the Conservative party and press for funding, in addition to other 'loony Left' organizations, various gay and lesbian groups; the introduction of Section 28 of the 1988 Local Government Act which forbade local authorities from promoting homosexuality. Asked why so many British films of the 1980s depicted homosexuality, Bruce Robinson, director of *Withnail and I* (1986), replied, 'Because we're living in more and more repressive times, and the people who make films are people who are anti the repression.'[91]

My Beautiful Laundrette makes this point bluntly in the scene in which 'Powders' is about to be opened to the public. The launderette, buffed and newly equipped, gleams splendidly. Even the piped music sounds tremendous. In the back room Johnny and Omar bask in the satisfaction of a job well done and the prospect of imminent success. As Johnny begins to massage Omar's shoulders it seems that nothing could sour the triumphal atmosphere. This is, after all, the apex of Omar's career so far, crowning proof that he isn't the loser that most of his relatives have always assumed him to be. He thinks of his father and is suddenly envenomed. 'Remember?' he asks his boyfriend, alluding to how Johnny had repaid Papa's kindness and hospitality towards him by becoming a fascist:

> He went out of his way with you. And with all my friends. He did, didn't he! [...] years later he saw the same boys [...] What were they doing on marches through Lewisham? It was bricks and bottles and Union Jacks. It was immigrants out. It was kill us. People we knew. And it was you. He saw you marching. You saw his face, watching you. Don't deny it. We were there when you went past. Papa hated himself and his job. He was afraid on the street for me. And he took it out on her. And she couldn't bear it. Oh, such failure, such emptiness.[92]

It's a fraught moment, the film's pivot. How heavy is history? Will the two men's racial pasts be too painful for them to be able to carry on with their affair? No. Johnny kisses Omar and, within moments, they start fucking. Sexual desire can be stronger than politics. Mutual physical dependence, not hectoring diatribes, will combat ethnic separatism. Director Stephen Frears illustrates this optimistic message a couple of minutes later by having Johnny's face on the outside of the back room and Omar's on the inside blended together by means of a two-way mirror. A colourless reciprocity has been attained.

This scene is counterpointed by one later in which a party is being held at the house of Omar's uncle. The setting is chintzy and self-congratulatory. Middle-class Pakistanis and Americans gurgle platitudes. Business ventures and profit margins are shuttled to and fro over the clink of wine glasses. Johnny and Tania, so bored they've decided to get drunk, have found a bicycle that they ride unsteadily round the garden. Omar, meanwhile, is being subjected to a patronizing homily by a yuppie thug called Salim: 'Don't in future bite the family hand when you can eat out of it.'[93] As the camera homes in on Omar's face, we see that the lighting has been rigged up so that the rain on the verandah windows is reflected on to his face making it appear gashed and riven. 'The family hand' is a claw. It scars all those it touches. Here, at his uncle's affluent house deep in the heart of the English countryside, Omar should feel nourished; this visual epiphany shows us that he finds more joy in his urban, trans-racial, homosexual, cross-class relationship with Johnny than in cleaving to those who are ostensibly closer to his 'own kind'.

London, as Lord Kitchener nearly sang, is the place to meet. It's a place of excess. An oasis of joy and gratuitous debauchery. Near the end of *Sammy and Rosie Get Laid* (originally titled 'The Fuck'), there is an extraordinary scene in which, at one and the same time, Danny and Rosie, Sammy and his girlfriend Anna, and Rafi and his colonial rose Alice are all shown fucking. The first pair are in Danny's caravan which sits on a stretch of waste land that's soon to be redeveloped; the second pair lie on the roof of Anna's arty studio; the third occupy a crumbling bedroom in an expensive North London mansion. Between them, these six people represent a wide social spectrum. Danny is an itinerant and hustler; Anna, a photographer; Sammy, a businessman; Rafi, a former Government Cabinet minister. They come from different generations – Danny could be Rafi's son. They have conflicting political views – Alice's old-fashioned Conservatism is at odds with Danny's street-sussed radicalism. The latter is black, Rafi and Sammy are Pakistani, and the others white. Collectively, they cover a cultural range the breadth of which can only ever be found in cities like London. And here they all are 'in energetic, tender and ecstatic climax', welded together by Kureishi in a 'COLLAGE OF COPULATION IMAGES'.[94]

One part of the sexual triptych involves Sammy and Anna making love on a roof that overlooks a London motorway while a helicopter whirrs over their heads. Similarly, as Jamila commits adultery with Karim in *The Buddha of Suburbia*, the windows in her flat are open, 'drenching the atmosphere in car fumes and the uproar of the unemployed arguing in the street'.[95] There's no double-glazing insulating the lovers from the outside world. No curtains are drawn, or indeed any of the other social screens that Kureishi associates with the suburbs. Sex is not a retreat from the world, nor an escape into a privatized realm of desire; it needn't entail individualism or a neglect of the real world. Rather, it's a dirty and impure celebration of chance, of difference – qualities that the metropolis itself represents.

London in Kureishi's work is both witness to, and an active fomentor of, mass sexual activity, whether heterosexual or homosexual, male-centred or female-slanted, onanistic or orgiastic. The city abounds with individuals who have arrived thirsting for novelty, excitement and new experiences; it's hardly surprising that it is sexualized. One of the most memorable passages in *The Black Album* involves Shahid travelling along the Northern Line and recalling a fantasy his girlfriend Deedee had masturbated to:

She would be walking around the city in high heels, lipstick and a transparent dress, her nipples and cunt visible, not being touched, but looked at. And as she walked she would watch men watching her; and as they masturbated she would stroke herself.[96]

The language and imagery may be lurid, but the fantasy itself is not so unusual. Deedee is turned on by the licence and liberty that she feels the city affords to newcomers like herself. She could never have been so exhibitionistic in buttoned-up Bromley. She's also putting herself, metaphorically speaking, in the hands of the city that she trusts, stripping away those layers of reserve that Kureishi believes are more present in those who live outside the capital. Deedee can't be harmed because bystanders may not touch her. It's an idealistic vision, as is perhaps borne out by Kureishi's comment that the sexed-up platform of Baker Street Station 'was Arcadia itself'.[97]

The men aren't distinguished or individuated. They stand for London itself. That they masturbate on seeing Deedee indicates how London has traditionally thrived on and been stimulated by each new wave of incomers. Its enduring vitality has always depended on the willingness of arrivants to use London as an arena for heightened commercial, creative and sexual energy. The sheer momentum and thrill of living in London inspires its peoples to hustle, dream and overcome the limitations of prejudice, penury and timidity. London is itself sustained and constituted by their energies. It's a reciprocal relationship.

One day, in *London Kills Me*, Clint's posse decide to leave the capital. They need a break, a day out. Clint has no job, no home, little money. He can't even steal the pair of shoes he needs to find paid work. And he's scared that the drug dealer Mr G is going to pay him back for the previous night's botched business deal. Time for a bit of a getaway: the posse set off for the countryside thinking they might drop by Clint's mother's house. They need to escape the noise, the fumes, the endless pressure of city life. They want some fresh air, and they want to be revivified. They fail, of course. As soon as they get off the bus and begin to walk down the country lane they are 'a little bewildered, looking lost'.[98] Clint's mum, Lily, isn't pleased to see them. Nor is her husband Stone who abuses them for being jobless 'slaves of sensation'.[99] An argument breaks out. Clint starts tussling with his stepfather.

The posse return home. It's been a miserable day. But it has allowed Clint to come to a mushroom-fuelled insight about the kind of life he truly values. And it isn't one he'll find in the country where 'the people are sly and cunning and ignorant [. . .] I know what I want to do. Get back to London and be with the only people for me, having adventures . . .'[100]

A telling quotation. Clint is hapless, dependent, just about as lowdown and slungout as he could be. In this sense, London is killing him, grinding him down. But, for all that, Clint finds life in the capital preferable to the corrosive mean-mindedness of the countryside. London, at least, is full of action, possibility, adrenalizing happenstance – like a good joke, it 'kills' him.

It's his toleration of – and even revelling in – the more fractured, fallen aspects of London life that distinguishes Kureishi from the other authors in this study. His characters skank and skelter their ways through the capital with stressed but striving abandon. They don't pine for the order and mature certainties that writers since Gronniosaw have sought. London for them is something of a spree, a passport to mobility, a chance to rid themselves of their cosseted suburban pasts. Consequently, they're not interested, as Naipaul was, in 'finding the centre'. That entire notion was more poignant for pre-Independence writers who'd grown up believing – and being taught – that they were on the outskirts, the margins of English culture. Kureishi was born into a relatively affluent family in snug

Bromley and didn't hanker after solidity or permanence. He values London not for the stability and assurances it offers, but for its power to disrupt. London is still a centre, for sure, but one, he hopes, where things fall apart, where the centre cannot hold.

Kureishi's work on London is also notable for its relaxed attitude to the way the capital changes people. The traditional Hindu concern for self-purity led many nineteenth- and early twentieth-century Indian writers to fear that London would muddy or canker their souls. T. Ramakrishna even delayed leaving for England because his mother feared he would become 'a "walking corpse", a living dead body, a being socially and religiously lost to her, to our family and clan'.[101] When he did finally arrive in London, he vowed to remain ' "untainted", as pure a Hindu as I was when I first saw the light of day'.[102] In *The Buddha of Suburbia*, Karim's father Haroon, although a Muslim, experiences on arriving in England in the 1950s a comic version of Ramakrishna's anxieties: 'no one had told him the English didn't wash regularly because the water was so cold'.[103] Kureishi, however, associates such talk of cleanliness with social and moral hygiene, with values Asian characters thought they had left behind when they came to London. They headed for the capital to pursue the skewing and pollution of identity.

Pollution, or 'messiness', is terribly important to Kureishi. The way the word 'messy' is used within club cultures (a certain frazzled, happily bewildered post-Ecstasy comedown) is useful here. Also, it suggests the recuperation of parts of the city that, especially in the 1980s, many people (especially those on the New Right) considered derelict and worthless. This has special emotional resonance for Asians who have long known that in some quarters they are seen as filthy, verminous, scorbutic – not just in actual terms, but also to the extent that their presence in England sullies the purity of the national heritage. Kureishi paved the way for other artists to celebrate ordure: in Rushdie's *The Satanic Verses*

Saladin Chamcha is transmogrified (to his chagrin) into a malodorous goat who defecates everywhere, only to become a hero to the Bangladeshi (and African-Caribbean) communities of East London; in *White Teeth* (2000), Zadie Smith uses excrement as a metaphor for the all-too-complicated, all-too-human traces left by history for present-day immigrants to deal with; Chris Ofili won the Turner Prize in 1999 for a series of elephant dung canvases. He was trying to do something that many artists have sought to do – transmute the squalor and dirt of daily life into something vivid and extraordinary. He also wanted to make viewers laugh. The riot of colour and multi-textured bricolages of his art stem in large part from his engagement with the King's Cross locale in which he works. This area – dirty and noisy and largely unloved – is one of London's major communication nodes; it's festooned with call cards, graffiti and fly-posters. It's rough and it's alive. Or at least it was: recent gentrification has led the crazies and crackheads to migrate west to Camden.

For these artists and for Kureishi metropolitan messiness isn't a sign that entropy imminent. Nor is it the kind of misanthropic excrementalism that's found in the cityscapes of Ben Jonson or Jonathan Swift. Rather, it's both mimetic (inasmuch as Asians often live in fairly down-at-heel areas), and also celebratory (in the sense that something creative and communal can be fashioned from unprepossessing circumstances). It was Kureishi, I feel, who anticipated and enabled this reverence for the fallen city. He helped to show that inner London was by no means the dismal, darkest Africa that sensationalistic Tory writers claimed. He also taught second-generation Asians who were ashamed at the crumbling environments in which they lived and who thought of their double or triple identities as a form of tragic schizophrenia a crucial lesson. That lesson was this: good can come of fracture and brokenness. By picking up and rearranging the shards – of history, of ethnicity, of locality – and by cut-and-pasting disparate cultural elements, a new and vital culture may slowly be nudged into being.

Kureishi, like Sam Selvon before him, has had a galvanizing effect on younger artists: Ayub Khan Din, who in 1988 played opposite Frances Barber in *Sammy and Rosie Get Laid*, went on to write the hit play *East Is East* (1997), the film version of which became the highest-grossing fully British-funded movie. Cornershop, whose single 'Brimful of Asha' (1997) is one of the best pop songs ever to reach the top of the charts, had a song called 'Hanif Kureishi Scene' on the B-side of their curry-coloured first single; Meera Syal, one of the sour-faced lesbians in *Sammy and Rosie Get Laid*, is well-known as an author, star of comedy series such as *Goodness Gracious Me* and *The Kumars At No. 42*, and writer of the book for Andrew Lloyd Webber's Bollywood musical *Bombay Dreams*.

Kureishi also made London a viable terrain for Asian and black writers to exploit. His influence on the wave of fictions by young women about the city that began to emerge during the 1990s is obvious. In the novels of Yvette Richards, Atima Srivastava, Andrea Levy and Shyama Perera London no longer seems as uniformly drab or hostile as it did in those by Jean Rhys or Buchi Emecheta. In Richards's *Single Black Female* (1994), an American-born Dee, thinks that, 'London sounded like a cool city with no guns and little violence, where people were polite to each other and there was much more history and culture than Chicago'; her friend Donna flees the West Country in the belief that 'Nobody's going to notice you in a small town like Bristol. You've got to go to where the action is – London.'[104]

Irony and sarcasm are second nature to these chick-lit writers. The humourlessness of much seventies and eighties immigrant writing has disappeared. They're flippant, not least about the rottenness of London boroughs. In Atima Srivastava's *Transmission*

(1992), Angie, a Hindu, refers to Stoke Newington as 'Stoke Trenchtown', while her Jamaican friend dubs it 'bushland'; Angie's uncle, meanwhile, labels Sikh-dominated Southall 'South hole Fraudway'.[105] In Andrea Levy's *Never Far From Nowhere* (1996), Olive claims her mother thought of Brixton as 'her Sodom and Gomorrah'.[106] In *Rude Girls* (1996), we realize what a phoney creep Maurice is when he moans that his girlfriend Janice was born in Hampstead Royal Free Hospital rather than somewhere more authentically African. Janice's friends distrust Maurice for many reasons, not least because he lives in a smart Chelsea bachelor pad and distances himself from the North London black community in which they were raised. In *Transmission*, a television producer comments on Angie's 'authentic' cockney accent only to be told, 'I grew up in North London. [White] Kathi's a cockney. She's from the East End.'[107] Earlier, Angie's brother Rax had spoken of going to Vauxhall Arts Centre – 'South London, I thought. Abroad.'[108]

The joy of mobility is another theme these writers share with Kureishi. Not for them the mechanical and joyless skittering around the capital to which Rhys subjected her characters. They love danger and velocity. In *Transmission*, Angie zips around London: 'Drinking and driving is not a good idea. I know it. I know all the speed traps, the slowest traffic lights, the shortest routes from Stoke Newington to Finchley.'[109] Elsewhere, she admits that, 'I was driving faster than normal but I liked driving fast.'[110] Paula, Janice and Shree, the black teenage heroines of Vanessa Walters's *Rude Girls*, all try to forget what great financial and family pressure they're under by glamming themselves up and attending musical all-dayers: 'Driving up the hill to Hackney Downs it seemed like they were part of a nationwide migration. Cars, cars, cars.'[111]

Rude Girls is a book about fun. So is *Single Black Female* in which London appears to be awash with brasseries, ragga nights, clubs, and wine bars at which socially mobile women like Dee can drink, schlep, and pick up men whenever they want. In *Transmission*, Angie thrives by day on the buzzing fast-forward, ideas-rich atmosphere of the TV production company in Soho she works for; during the evenings she smokes spliffs, drives dodgems with her boyfriend, and checks out slummy basement clubs full of pimps and dealers.

These women aren't adrift or isolated. They've built their own support networks. Their identity is a communal one. Dee, Donna and Carol, the three central characters in *Single Black Female*, get on brilliantly in their shared Wimbledon house despite coming from different classes and countries. They laugh, gee each other up, swap notes on how awful men are. Towards the novel's end, the heterosexual Dee even confesses to entertaining a lesbian fantasy:

> I dreamt that we were making love – me, Donna and Carol – and having toe-curling orgasms. We made love for hours and hours on the conservatory floor and then later because it was a summer's day moved out into the garden to lie in the sun in our bikinis [...] Before I knew it we were exploring each other's intimate parts again and then the orgasms came again, several of them. Donna and Carol both seemed to know exactly what to do to bring me to a climax.[112]

Fantasies, sexual or otherwise, are one of the hallmarks of Kureishi's writing. Previous black and Asian chroniclers of London were very much wedded to the idea of the real. Enraged by hearing their friends and communities maligned, they sought to produce corrective accounts. Black English literature came to be seen as almost exclusively protest-orientated. The street, that hallowed zone of gangsta rap today, was the source of authentic creativity. These elements are all present and correct in Kureishi's own work.

And yet, perhaps because his aesthetic is so shaped by the desires of pop culture, his London is less a bulletin from the frontline of ethnic subculture than a creative utopia, one that takes the most feisty and progressive aspects of 'the real' and alchemicalizes them into a design for future living. He suggests that black London is a place that needs to be imagined at least as much as it needs to be documented. This may mean that certain places end up traduced – most notably the suburbs which are far more complex and varied than he allows. That's a small price to pay for the sheer élan and bodyrocking brio of his early work.

Kureishi showed Asians in motion, on the make, dashing to places they don't yet know. Desiring transformation, they head to the one place where they think it is possible. London, random and debauched and unknowable, strikes them as a city of the future, where they can see and do and be things that their parents, wedded to the past, have spent their lives proscribing. And the future, worrisome and painful though its pursuit may be, is so sympathetically evoked by Kureishi that it's hard for his readers not to want to tag along. His role is that of a cultural Pied Piper. Catch us if you can, he and his characters seem to say. Flushed with joy and excitement we want to try, not least because his books have reprogrammed us, given us a new lexicon for seeing the relationship between second-generation immigrants and London: escape, not archaeology; discontinuity, not tradition; self-gratification and elective affinity instead of unthinking communalism. It's a lexicon that, as the next chapter will show, not every writer chooses to employ.

CHAPTER SIX

─◄O►─

Digging Our Scene

ALL CITIES ARE TEMPORARY PLACES. People, ideas, fashions, businesses, buildings come and go in the blink of an eye. Lose touch with a friend and it can be hard to make contact again: they will have moved on, perhaps a number of times. Romantic movies about cities often make play with the idea of serendipity, chance reunion in a packed café or on the noonday metro that leads to happy ever afters. They tend to be popular; unsurprisingly so, for they feed our desire to believe that urban life needn't be as emotionally amputating as, in our unhappier moments, we worry it is.

Is there a relationship between temporariness and neatness? To a greater extent than, for example, Paris or Rome, London is an untidy and inchoate geographic sprawl. This is what makes it so distinctive. Its borders and boundaries are ill-defined: few people know when London stops being London and becomes Greater London. Even its buildings seem to keep their distance; they do not tower against the skyline or loom large every time a corner is turned. As an ungridded city, one whose lanes and streets sprouted up contingently rather than through the design of urban planners, much of its beauty is tucked away. One cannot peer down century-long avenues or swoon from afar at majestic spires in adjacent boroughs. Even the construction of the city's architectural landmarks has been less dependent on government than on the whims and rivalries of speculators, unregulated financiers and narcissistic aristocrats. Perhaps this is why so many writers throughout the centuries have bemoaned London's apparent absence of ballast, certainty, and authority. Jonson, Pope and Eliot all lamented the capital's sheer disorder. Previously I have shown how their exasperation was shared by Nirad Chaudhuri and V.S. Naipaul. The paradox that confronted these two colonial authors was that London, an ancient city whose origins go back to pre-Roman times, and whose marmoreal structures are famous throughout the world (especially Britain's own colonies), never seemed to offer any reassurance or vertebrating sense of heritage to its own inhabitants. They would have demurred from the enthusiasm with which the distinguished architect Steen Eiler Rasmussen pointed out that, though historically old, London's capacity for self-regeneration makes it a uniquely youthful capital.[1]

London doesn't demand loyalty from its inhabitants. It doesn't bully newcomers into liking it. When quirky or oddball things happen there, no one pipes up 'Only in London'. Its hands-off quality, sometimes interpreted as aloofness by outsiders, lends it a neutrality that many find appealing. For the young, the migrant, the adventurer, London's lure has been that it serves as a new start, a blank page, a place of rebirth and fresh beginnings. In Romesh Gunesekara's *Reef* (1994), a young Sri Lankan called Triton accompanies his master, Salgado, into exile in London. Triton recounts how he went to classes and libraries constantly, 'broke all the old taboos and slowly freed myself from the demons of our past: what is over is over forever, I thought'. He asks Salgado why it is that they both find London less frightening than their native island. ' "It's your imagination," he said. "It is not yet poisoned in this place."'[2] Psychologically as well as physically, London is less totalitarian, less intrusive than many other major cities.

Yet such freedom from the past has consequences, not least the sense that perhaps there is no past, and that one may always be compelled to bob along on a sea of present-minded amnesia. Equally scary is the idea that the lives and achievements of most city dwellers are doomed to remain unrecorded and uncommemorated. Jonathan Raban has argued that a 'good working definition of metropolitan life would centre on its intrinsic intelligibility: most people are hidden most of the time, their appearances are brief and controlled, their movements secret, the outlines of their lives obscure'.[3] It's an accurate assessment, however bleak, and one that's especially pertinent to any putative historian of the lives of immigrants in London. Many of the books I have examined show how the dark-skinned newcomer – under-educated, insecurely employed, and living in dingy accommodation in poor neighbourhoods – often has only the most tenuous contact with other Londoners. In *Moses Ascending*, Sam Selvon's narrator asks: 'What is that heavy footfall on the cold damp pavement before the rest of the world is awake? What is that freezing figure fumbling through the fog, feeling its way to the bus stop, or clattering down the steps of the sleepy underground at this unearthly hour?'[4] The answer, of course, is 'the black man', and it's this economic and social invisibility that accounts for the ubiquity of the 'underground' motif in literature written by black writers.

The quest to make black Londoners more visible developed after World War Two. There had been some interesting work on the topic before then, most notably Aleyn Lyell Reade's 1912 biography of Dr Johnson's black manservant Francis Barber, and a monograph by Wylie Sypher on Abolitionist literature of the eighteenth century. Coincidentally, it was around the time that the SS *Empire Windrush* brought over part of the first wave of Caribbean settlers to post-war England that a number of sociological studies of East London appeared – by Michael Biddiss, Anthony Richmond, Kenneth Little and Michael Banton – all of which contained brief but invaluable passages about black and Asian people living in London since the sixteenth century.

In the wake of decolonization during the late 1950s and 1960s a number of academics started writing histories, compiling anthologies and republishing long-forgotten texts by African authors. These catered to the growing appetite for discovering black peoples' rich cultural and historical traditions, topics that colonial schoolmasters had been reluctant to broach. A number of the scholars were refugees from other disciplines: Paul Edwards, who produced landmark editions of Ignatius Sancho and Olaudah Equiano, was educated at Durham and Cambridge and began his career as an old Icelandic specialist.[5] He had also taught at African universities. Another distinguished academic, George Shepperson, had served with black soldiers during the war. Both had discovered at first hand the oversights and prejudices inherent in the historical syllabi they had been fed at school.

The 1960s and 1970s saw a huge growth in the history of minority groups. James Walvin, pioneering author of *Black and White. The Negro and English Society 1555–1945* (1973), has cited as an influence E.P. Thompson's work on formerly maligned plebeian groupings. Across the Atlantic, too, there was a growing appreciation that in order to go forward – towards equality and political freedom – it was necessary to be able to look back in time. America was convulsed by Civil Rights struggles and the emergence of Black Power, while students at Berkeley and elsewhere clamoured for more radical curricula which would enable them to explore pressing issues about personal identity and civil society. In the Caribbean, meanwhile, there was uproar after the

Guyanese historian Walter Rodney, who later wrote the liberation classic *How Europe Underdeveloped Africa* (1972), was banned from entering Jamaica on the grounds that his Afrocentric teachings would further incite an island already broiling with social unrest.

Small wonder that some English academics were worried. In *The Rise of Christian Europe* (1965), Hugh Trevor-Roper bemoaned the fact that undergraduates, 'seduced, as always, by the changing breath of journalistic fashion', were increasingly interested in the history of black Africa: 'Perhaps, in the future, there will be some African history to teach. But at present there is none, or very little.'[6] To think otherwise, he went on, was to indulge in a form of relativism that would eventually lead us to 'neglect our own history and amuse ourselves with the unrewarding gyrations of barbarous tribes in picturesque but irrelevant corners of the globe'.[7]

It was equally understandable that the idea of Africans in the United Kingdom, especially in historical periods popularly associated with starchy aristocrats and 'people like them', might appeal to second-generation immigrants, a disproportionate number of whom were being expelled from schools or being sent to ESN schools on the flimsiest of pretexts. They, like many millions of white viewers, were captivated by *Roots* (1977), the hugely popular international TV drama series, which charted the American author Alex Haley's (now largely-discredited) success in tracing his family line back to Gambia in 1767.

The most important spur the development and reception of black London history was the New Cross Fire. It erupted three months before the Brixton Riots flared up on 10 April 1981, and three years after Margaret Thatcher delivered a speech in which she appeared to empathize with people who felt the United Kingdom was being 'swamped by people with a different culture'.[8] On the night of 17 January 1981 thirteen young black men and women were killed in a blaze while attending a party at a West Indian family home at 439 New Cross Road, South London. The official verdict was arson, but to this day no one has ever been charged in connection with the fire. The minimal media coverage granted to the deaths seemed to imply that suffering and tragedy had become racially inflected, that black people's lives were less valuable than white ones. On 2 March 1981 nearly 20,000 people, ninety per cent of them West Indian, marched from New Cross, across Blackfriars Bridge into the City, down Fleet Street, through Regent and Oxford Streets, until, seven hours later, they finally reached Hyde Park. It was the largest demonstration by black people in British history. According to one of the organizers, the Trinidad-born poet and publisher John La Rose, the campaign of the New Cross Massacre Action Committee, under whose auspices the march took place, 'gave an enormous self-confidence to the black population in Britain – that has expressed itself politically, culturally, since 2nd March 1981'.[9]

The fire and its attendant lack of media coverage had two important long-term consequences. First, many black people began to feel that they should create their own channels of discourse rather than wait for white media organizations to give them a public platform. In February 1981 the Black Media Workers Association was set up; later the same year, the *Caribbean Times* was launched. The following year saw the emergence of *The Voice*, whose subtitle – 'of Black Britain' – made it the first black-run paper in British history aimed at a home-grown coloured audience, rather than the free-floating constituency of colonial lawyers, students and radicals to which previous journals had catered.[10]

Creative organizations also began to flourish. A set of Midlands-based art school graduates, including Eddie Chambers and Keith Piper, formed The Black Art Group in 1981 to help develop, in part, 'our sense of "somebodyness"'; 'we try,' they said, 'to avoid

blind mimicry.'[11] Black English film collectives such as Ceddo, Sankofa and Black Audio were also set up. The latter, founded in 1983, was particularly concerned with the 'politics of representation' and the critical exploration of how 'racist ideas and images of black people are structured and presented as self-evident truths in cinema'.[12] Their interest in narrative form as much as content mirrors that found in the work of many contemporary writers such as David Dabydeen, Caryl Phillips and Fred D'Aguiar.

The second by-product of the New Cross Fire was the critical rediscovery of London's black past. The capital was, after all, where the majority of Caribbean immigrants and their children lived. The fire seemed to awaken people to the fact that their grasp on the city where they had settled since the 1950s was perilous, and that their contribution to its sustenance and vitality had gone largely unrecognized. John La Rose claimed with pride that before the march to Hyde Park, 'Blackfriars Bridge had not been crossed by a major demonstration since the Chartists in the 1830s.'[13]

The project to assert black people's cultural and economic importance to metropolitan life was given further impetus and historical underpinning by the proliferation of studies which dealt with the black presence in Britain.[14] During 28–30 September 1981 the first International Conference on the History of Blacks in Britain was held at the University of London and had a catalysing effect. People were hungry for this kind of history. After the publication of *Staying Power* (1984), Peter Fryer gave over 200 talks and lectures at adult education centres, sixth-form colleges and public meetings across the country. Councils such as the GLC began to fund oral history workshops and the publication of ethnic local histories.[15] Black London historiography was espoused as an innately political cause, not least by some of the historians themselves. Fryer claimed that he wrote in order to expose not only 'the contribution made by black slavery to the rise of British capitalism', but also 'the effect English racism has had on the lives of black people living in this country'.[16]

Other historians, more modestly inclined, simply hoped to highlight an aspect of British history that had been forgotten – conveniently though not deliberately. Their success can be seen from the fact that Sancho, Cugoano, Equiano and Mary Prince have all been assigned Penguin Classic status; Equiano was featured in the 'Faith' Zone at the Millennium Dome during 2000; in 1997 the National Portrait Gallery put on a show about Ignatius Sancho, while both Leyton Orient and Charlton Athletic football clubs sponsored a CD of his music to accompany a weighty education pack about him that was distributed to schoolchildren in Greenwich. At a less institutional level, hip-hop magazines, websites, community walking tours and street-stall booksellers all contribute to the popularization of this once-marginal subject.

That such successful dissemination has not gone unnoticed is evident from a brief glance at Roy Kerridge's waspish *The Story of Black History* (1998). The book was published by The Claridge Press who also put out *The Salisbury Review*, a conservative journal most famous for printing the work of Ray Honeyford, the Bradford headmaster who was removed from his job after decrying anti-racist educational policies. Kerridge thinks that black history encourages young people to renounce the 'decent cosiness' of England in favour of Africa. It makes them cocky too: 'Black triumphalists wear expensive clothes, with lots of gold, and if female, lots of gaps between the clothing. They are not low-life, but high-life, for their loud-voiced super-confidence wins them both grants and bank loans (depending on whether they have Blackademe-type jobs or are company directors).'[17] In certain areas of London such as Hackney and Willesden Green (the latter the setting for much of Zadie Smith's *White Teeth*, a novel full of zesty counter-imperialisms), local people have too much self-esteem: 'While the link between Black History and Black Crime cannot be proved, the myth of the African Lost Paradise undeniably has helped in the creation of a brash new-rich Black British type of Black triumphalism. Scorning their humble, hard-working

West Indian immigrant parents, some rich "black conscious" Black Britons have "invented themselves" as a super-fashionable Master Race.'[18]

In their desire to learn as much as they can about London's pre-*Windrush* black history, second-generation immigrants distinguish themselves from their parents who focus on tomorrow rather than yesterday. Migrants always dream of the future, the day when they might attain economic security, that success and reward for which they laboured so conscientiously and in pursuit of which they travelled thousands of miles. If migrants do contemplate the past, it's the past of their parents and grandparents, of the colonial city or village from which they hail. This ancestral realm is alien to their children who don't share the same geographies, memories, or idiolects. What can second-generation migrants do to locate themselves? Where are the contours of their sense of self? They can derive only limited pleasure from reminiscing about mother countries they scarcely know.

Those who grew up in the 1980s hoping to assert their Englishness knew that, as far as Margaret Thatcher was concerned, they were a threat to national cohesion.[19] What was helpful about the emerging historiography of black London was that it offered a convincing counter-argument. Fryer and other historians told young blacks that they had not only a legal right to be here, but a historic one too. Such scholarship also served as an implicit critique of the burgeoning field of 'post-colonial' academic study which, largely in pawn to post-structuralism, glibly celebrated concepts such as instability, alterity, undecidability, and the impossibility and undesirability of genealogy or tradition. In contrast, the books that were now published, the seminars that were arranged, and the talks that were delivered told the second generation unequivocally that African and Asian people had lived, worked, married and died in the UK for hundreds of years. They could no longer be considered illegitimate. The sense of righteousness that this information gave them, as well as the ballast and belonging, informed the work of many young writers.

Bernardine Evaristo, for example, was first inspired to write her verse novel *The Emperor's Babe* (2001) by a small passage in *Staying Power* in which Peter Fryer refers to the three-year sojourn in Britain of the Libyan-born Roman Emperor Septimius Severus (AD 146–211). Though the Emperor spent most of his stay near Carlisle (he died in York), Evaristo's book is set in London and revolves around the adventures of Zuleika, the daughter of Sudanese immigrants who was married off at the age of eleven to a Roman senator three times her age. She's quite something, this 'Bella Negreeta', the It Girl of ancient Cheapside. She bounces round the town with her low-life friends, past the 'slums, swarming with immigrants', through the 'drizzle of this wild west town', often in the company of her friend Venus who runs a dodgy bar at the junction of Ludgate Hill and St Paul's Churchyard called Mount Venus.[20] Her London is as colourful and festooned as the city described by Richard of Devizes in the twelfth century: everywhere there are florists touting bouquets, ivory vendors selling Kenyan tusks, perfumed oils from Arabia and Ethiopia, goldsmiths, cloak- and cabinetmakers, money-changers, horn-tuners, coppersmiths, even a bow-legged mystic called Ganesh. As they pass by the spear-carrying guards the summer evening air has a smell of Thames-fresh trout and chamberpot turds that have been hurled from tenement buildings.

Zuleika's life soon gets complicated after she is spotted by Septimius at the theatre, and before she knows what's happening she has embarked upon an adulterous affair with him. Born of lower-class parents, she descends into a full-blown identity crisis:

> Am I the original Nubian princess
> From Mother Africa?
> Does the Nile run through my blood
> In this materfutuo urban jungle
> Called Londinium?
> Do I feel a sense of lack
> Because I am swarthy?
> Or am I just a groovy chick
> Living in the lap of luxury?
> Am I a slave or a slave owner?
> Am I a Londinio or Nubian?
> Will my children be Roman or Nubinettes?
> Were my parents vassals or pharaohs?
> And who gives a damn![21]

Yet *The Emperor's Babe* is hardly dark. The very language makes that impossible. The estuary English and 'Cerberus est canis' Latinisms are too swish, too bubbly. So the novel is best read as a romping, highly enjoyable, and surprisingly affecting piece of silliness, the literary equivalent of a seven-inch bootleg that slathers dance beats on to an old 78rpm tune.

Evaristo's Bridget Jones meets *Up Pompeii* levity is unusual. Black writing about London, especially that which alludes to older black accounts of the city, tends to be rather pensive in tone. Akin, the Anglo-Nigerian subject of Gbenga Agbenugba's *Another Lonely Londoner* (1991), comes across a novel that helps him to contextualize his black metropolitan self:

Although it was placed in another generation, Akin could still relate to the book, the cold, the harsh times for immigrants, the fun times, the overt racism, that had now become more subtle. It was all in there, the book was Sam Selvon's 'The Lonely Londoners'. Life in Britain '1990' had not changed much for Black folk since Sam Selvon's picture of immigrant community life during the late fifties and early sixties.[22]

Not all of the books to be looked at in this chapter are any cheerier. Perhaps that's because many of their authors – Phillips, Dabydeen, D'Aguiar – are also academics. Modern university departments are not usually mirthful places. Writer-teachers of whatever colour seem to find it hard to temper the urge towards pedagogy in their fictional works. It's the extent to which they do so and their ability to evoke the pungency and peculiarity of the past – something that poring over yellowing documents in research libraries does not in itself guarantee – that makes their work notable.

Caryl Phillips was born on the British colony of St Kitts in 1958; four months later, his parents moved to Leeds, taking him with them. His father, who worked as a manual labourer for British Rail, abandoned his wife and children when Phillips was around eight years old. In 1973 the family moved south to the more middle-class King's Norton area of Birmingham. He studied English at Oxford from 1976 to 1979 during which time he directed six plays and decided to become a full-time writer. In *The European Tribe* (1987) he claims that much of his undergraduate career was spent trying to escape the monochrome cossetedness of Oxford by going to London, where he loped around Ladbroke Grove, hung out in Brixton pubs and bookshops, attended gigs and films by black artists and generally tried 'to "plug into" black life'.[23]

'Plugging' suggests both a connection to something pulsing and electric, as well as an attempt to stop something from leaking or spilling away. Both senses of the verb inform Phillips's dramatic, fictional, and critical writings. Whether telling of an elegant eighteenth-century West Country lady who finds herself marooned on a desert island with a slave whom she despises but is wholly reliant upon, or of Martha Randolph who escapes her owners and heads into mid-nineteenth-century Dodge where she lives with a black gamer and gunslinger, or of a Yorkshire lass abandoning her husband during the Second World War in order to pursue an affair with a negro GI stationed in her village, Phillips has consistently tried to map the diverse and trajectories that black people have taken during the last two centuries.[24] Knowing that black and white audiences alike are unaware of much of this history and that the struggles of women like Martha might be overlooked or taken for granted spurs him on.

Implying that imaginative and economic poverty are closely linked, Phillips has argued that 'There is an underdeveloped sense of history in the Caribbean'.[25] This underdevelopment is particularly strong among immigrants who 'want to forget because they are so concerned with their kids becoming a part of the New World. They want them to become part of the new society, so they don't want them to remember where they came from. That's really what happened with me. My parents didn't talk about it, and it wasn't something that was taught in school.'[26] As a result 'I, and many other writers who are non-white, have [...] the need to work against an undertow of historical ignorance. Our history is also our bank balance. And we have a responsibility to the people who produced us.'[27]

'Ignorance' is a harsh word. Yet it's true that even post-war immigration is a largely unknown story. To this day a common perception exists that money alone lured Asians and West Indians to England. The story goes that colonial peasants, captivated by the overtures of various Colonial Secretaries and transfixed by posters or newspapers advertising cheap aeroplane and ocean-liner tickets, set aside their hoes and cooking pots, grabbed whatever savings they had, and flocked to the capital. This doesn't happen in Phillips's work; those of his characters who are motivated by money, such as Albert Williams in the play *Where There Is Darkness* (1982), are portrayed as vicious solipsists. He boasts to his son, 'Only reason I get your mother pregnant is because I know her father going give out the money for us all to come to England.'[28]

The heart, rather than the purse, is the main impulse behind immigration. Phillips's characters arrive in London as emotional refugees. In *The Final Passage* (1985), Leila boards the SS *Winston Churchill* hoping for 'a new start after the pain of the last year' in which her husband Michael has neglected their infant son, procured a mistress, and swaggered around their house lazy, drunken, and foul-mouthed. In *Higher Ground* (1989) Irena is the only member of her Jewish family who manages to escape to England her sister and parents. When the war ends she flees from Yorkshire to London after the double misfortune of losing her unborn child and discovering that her husband, formerly a rather lovable conscientious objector, has become a short-tempered beer monster.

This escape is short-lived too. Although Irena is far from both Nazi-overrun Poland and her violent husband, she can't escape her painful memories. She hurls herself under a train and is placed in a mental hospital. Similarly, in *The Final Passage*, Leila quickly learns that moving to London hasn't cured Michael of his macho surliness and his philandering. Irena's and Leila's lives, wretched as they are, are by no means untypical: their trajectories set the pattern for all of Phillips's work located in London. Characters go there hoping that their social and economic wounds may heal, only to be maimed again by the capital.

The weather doesn't help. An emotional and meteorological pall hangs over every work Phillips has written about London. It almost amounts to a pathetic fallacy. In his introduction to *Playing Away* (1987), a film about an inner-city cricket team which is invited to play against a village eleven, urban Britain is defined in

terms of 'traffic jams, fog, smog, pubs, and factory floors'.[29] At the end of the movie, the Conquistadors' team coach takes them back home to Brixton where they are 'caught in the slow moving inner city traffic. It is raining lightly, and the glare of the street lights and the traffic lights is reflected in the puddles. They have returned to a familiar urban gloom.'[30] In *Higher Ground* the grey climate jaundices Louis, who is living in a poky hostel: 'There was no vista to this landscape, no hills, and initially a slow persistent drizzle had cast a mournful aspect over his wanderings; then it had turned to snow, magical and welcome when it first arrived but now chilling him through to his bones.'[31]

Ice, fog, rain: they represent the hostility that Phillips's immigrants come up against, their lack of direction, the endless pressure from which they seek refuge. In *Where There Is Darkness*, Albert claims the weather has been made bad with the express aim of driving West Indians out of England. He warns his son Remi, 'You don't realize yet that the white man is like a storm of rain trying to wash us away. Piss on us at will'; in *The Final Passage*, as Leila 'got off the bus she looked up in momentary alarm. The sky hung so low it covered the street like a dark coffin lid.'[32] Hope and optimism are what are really being extinguished. The rain and mists seep into and rust the immigrant's soul. All dreams of distant horizons or gold-potted rainbows are washed away. In *The European Tribe*, Phillips returns to London after nine months of travelling on the continent: 'I found the capital stimulating but not sustaining. The days were short and dull, the weather a perpetual drizzle, the people slouched around the streets afraid of the "future".'[33]

The only bit of warmth in *The Final Passage* comes at the very end of the novel. Having concluded that her marriage to Michael is over and that any kind of friendship with her white neighbours in Florence Road is impossible, Leila decides to return to the Caribbean. Before doing this, she makes a bonfire of all 'the objects and garments that reminded her of her months in England. The room became warm and Leila began to laugh as she searched everywhere finding new things to drop in the now empty pillow-case. A bunch of plastic flowers, a shopping bag, a small vase, a set of ashtrays.'[34] It's a bleak irony that only burning those few items that she has managed to save up for during her brief stay in a grotty district of West London can rid Leila – however fleetingly – of the chill in her veins.

Phillips is the first black writer since Sancho to write at length about family life in London. But whereas Sancho loved domesticity, seeing it as a source of comfort and strength in the face of economic worries, for Phillips it offers no such refuge. All personal relationships – husbands and wives, fathers and sons – are scarred by jealousy, animosity, mistrust. Black men are especially selfish and culpable. In *The Final Passage*, Michael rarely humours or helps his pregnant wife for he has decided that 'How much he left [this country] with seemed to depend totally upon how much he wanted, and how hard he was prepared to try. This being the case Michael would sleep soundly and defend his mind against thoughts of Beverley or Leila or the children.'[35] In *Where There Is Darkness*, Albert abandons his wife Muriel with little explanation shortly after arriving in London; when his mistress Lynn falls pregnant she asks him for financial assistance only to be told, 'You just open your mouth again and the next time you do so going be in the dentist chair.'[36] He also spends most of the play arguing with his son Remi, whose pregnant black girlfriend he accuses of being a whorish gold-digger before telling her to 'fuck off, and take your ugly little foetus with you. I going get a drink.'[37]

No compensatory friendships with fellow arrivants are struck up. There is no brotherhood, just snobbery and one-upmanship. In *The Shelter*, Louis distances himself from the growing number of Africans – lawyers, doctors, students, stowaway waterfront boys – that came to London in the 1950s: 'I don't have anything to do with those people. I don't eat bananas on the top deck of a double-decker bus, and I don't walk around with my head in a damn book and tell all the girls my name is "Prince" this, or "Duke" the other.'[38] Another Louis, this time in *Higher Ground*, is depressed by the lack of camaraderie among London's black population. Trying to 'throw off the blanket of loneliness that was choking him', he asks a bullet-headed Dominican acquaintance the directions to a local club: 'Sonny Mac took away his finger, allowed his sunglasses to drop back on to the bridge of his nose, and walked away as though disappointed that he had been made to divulge the location of a place as well-known as the 62 Club. Louis realized that Sonny Mac now considered him ignorant beyond redemption.'[39]

Black Londoners fluff whatever chances arise to affirm their solidarity. In *Playing Away* the Conquistadors, though they ought to be drumming up team spirit, allow old grudges and disputes to mar their performance. Jeff, who's frowned upon by his team for marrying a white woman, confides to Viv, a lonely village wife, that the Conquistadors' unity is as illusory as that of the Sneddington team they're about to play – 'Sometimes we don't even have a team . . . People only turn out when they think there's something in it for them. Like this, a weekend away from London.'[40]

Such disunity is galling, not least because the Conquistadors have good relations with white Londoners to sustain them. New arrivals feel that they're forever being spied upon, scrutinized, assessed. They believe that white people – regardless of their social class – enjoy lording it over them. Sexual antagonism is rife: in *Higher Ground*, Louis and a Polish refugee go to see a film in Leicester Square: 'Afterwards they walked by the river and Irena thought that only the strongest men could survive the glares of disapproval that he pretended not to notice.'[41] Such staring, even if it's involuntary and non-aggressive, renders normal life impossible. In *The Shelter*, Louis complains to Irene that people have stared 'at us, for over a year now, like they're thinking they should be fucking, not out shopping for furniture, or at the pictures enjoying themselves, or on a bus going home [. . .] But don't you see how they look, hoping we won't do anything human like laugh, or cry, or kiss.'[42] Such surveillance inevitably deforms the domestic realm. In *The Final Passage*, Leila feels that, 'the eyes of the white people on the posters never left her no matter how quickly she glanced at them'.[43] Louis in *Higher Ground* starts to fear English women and, although feeling tenderness and affection for Irena, he knew that he must steel himself and step out into the crisp, sweatless, fresh, cold, white, snowy night and walk back down to the river so that he might witness the day break over this great city of London. Then at dawn he would return to the men's hostel and take his bag and leave. It was probable that this woman would extend and demand a severe loyalty that he could never reciprocate. Not now. Sorry.[44]

One of the most obvious features of Phillips's work is how commonly it hops and flits between different historical periods. In *Where There Is Darkness*, Albert, who has just held a leaving party at his London suburban home, is stricken as he recalls his life in the capital during the 1950s. In a series of increasingly distressing flashbacks the audience sees the newly-arrived Albert quickly learning about metropolitan prejudice and economic hardship, becoming more self-interested, conning his business partners, betraying his wife before abandoning her. In between these recollections, and back in the present tense, Albert is still a selfish and violent man whose poisonous misogyny drives his current wife to leave him and his prospective daughter-in-law to harbour serious doubts about marrying his son. By the end of the play, Albert himself can't distinguish between past and present – he takes off his clothes and waddles into the garden imagining that he's back picking mangoes in the Caribbean. In *The Final Passage*, meanwhile, Phillips rejects linear chronology in favour of zigzagging between different periods and islands. The novel begins with a section entitled 'The End' and Leila waiting at the harbour for the SS *Winston Churchill*; Phillips then backtracks to describe her prickly relationship with Michael, before lurching forward in time to chart Leila's miserable first few weeks in London. Only at this stage does Phillips provide an account of Leila's and Michael's voyage to England, before leaping forward six months to the point where the disillusioned Leila is about to take a 'final passage' home.

This jolting narrative technique allows the author to make telling comparisons between seemingly disconnected historical periods. The third section of *Higher Ground* details the loneliness and deracination in London felt by Polish refugee Irena, and draws subtle parallels with the novel's first section ('Heartland') which concerns the entrapment and theft of West Coast Africans in the eighteenth century. Both diasporic groups have shown resilience, an ability to survive in the midst of grotesque and penurious urban environments.

Many contemporary black writers feel that they have to destabilize narrative flow and use jarring juxtaposition in order to chart the fractious and schizophrenic relationship to England and Englishness held by many immigrants and their children.[45] New arrivals are routinely disorientated and unsettled (positively in Kureishi's case, negatively in Naipaul's) by the smells, noises, manners, accents and weather in London. Whatever they had read or heard about the city, nothing could have prepared them for the shock of arrival. Easy prey for sharks and hustlers (many of whom were their fellow immigrants), unmoored and discomfited, immigrants may begin to forget why they left home or where they thought they were travelling to. A linear narrative would be too tidy, making their journeys seem bogusly inevitable; in fact, their voyages were leaps into the unknown, anything but expected.

This has been one of the recurring themes of this book. As early as the 1770s Ignatius Sancho had identified the trope of unbroken linearity as the preserve of solipsists, pseudo-racial theorists, and non-Latitudinarians. Salman Rushdie is another writer influenced by Laurence Sterne and dismissive of linear narrative. He structures his novels to avoid what he describes as the 'narrow one-dimensionality of a straight line'.[46] Elsewhere Rushdie has approved Edward Said's view that the 'broken or discontinuous nature of Palestinian experience entails that classic rules about form or structure cannot be true to that experience; rather, it is necessary to work through a kind of chaos or unstable form that will accurately express its essential instability'.[47] David Dabydeen, a writer whose academic work on Hogarth and whose novels have dealt with black metropolitan life from the eighteenth to the twentieth century, has also refuted the notion that only linear narratives are capable of describing the world. In *Disappearance* (1993), a Guyanese engineer has his beliefs in planning and orderliness challenged by his worldly landlady, Mrs Rutherford, who advocates

> the sinuous, the curved, the circular, the zigzagged, the unpredictable, the zany, the transcendental and the invisibly buried. There are stories enough in the brick houses, crooked and abrupt stories that contradict their seamless straight line.[48]

Rejecting linearity needn't entail a celebration of skewedness. Rather, it should be seen as true to the imprecision and messiness of quotidian life. Fred D'Aguiar has argued this in his preface to *A Jamaican Airman Foresees His Death* (1991), in which he explains his play's complex dramatic structure:

> Part of this movement away from the straightforward linear-narrative way of looking back had to do with the thing under scrutiny. The Jamaica of World War Two was a colony that had emerged out of a slave society. This experience involved forced migration, settlement and resettlement, and government from abroad. A drama that sought to reflect this complex reality would at least have to find a form with a matching fluidity, with elements of fracture and artificial juxtapositions and impositions, if it was to make a serious claim to explore that past.[49]

Such 'migration, settlement and resettlement' – and the tangling of the Caribbean consciousness that ensues – apply not only to wartime Jamaican society but to immigrant life in London. Phillips has written that, 'Like a potter's wheel that has suddenly been jammed to a halt, West Indians have been flung out into history and tried to make good wherever they have landed'.[50] The disjointedness and lack of direction that result from being 'flung out' in this way colour Phillips's portrayals of black London past and present. The boys from Brixton in *Playing Away* couldn't read a map to save their lives.[51] 'Crooked' is one of the commonest adjectives in *The Final Passage*. It's used both to characterize the ramshackle and impoverished colonial island from which Leila and Michael hail, and to signify the disappointing rankness of 1950s London for many Caribbean immigrants. Aboard the SS *Winston Churchill* sailing to England, Leila sees an old man close to tears with 'his crooked elbow to his knee'; the young nurse who treats Leila's mother has 'sloppy hips and a crooked smile'; the estate agent's receptionist has teeth that are 'crooked and too big for her mouth'; in the shabby house that Leila finally buys 'Michael stood and looked at the crooked floor'.[52] Phillips' belief that the history of black people in London is essentially one of crookedness, a narrative in which the immigrant's expectations and his actual social circumstances fail to gel, and in which coloured arrivants are shunted aside and left beleaguered by white condescension and racism, leads him to employ a crooked, non-linear form.

Time and time again the London of Phillips's imagination is a dismal, funereal place. There's little laughter or joy. Newcomers who arrive looking to start afresh don't succeed. Constriction rather than liberation is the norm. Louis in *The Shelter* says he feels like a 'sparrow not an eagle'.[53] Not just the weather, but city dwellers too, are shown to be bleak and cold. White characters are portrayed with a casual savagery: in *The Final Passage* we're told that 'Across the aisle from [Michael] were two men, both of whom were as fat as armchairs and both of whom had veins and moles sketched on their faces in random patterns of ugliness'; in *The Shelter*, Louis describes going to a pub and finding 'dead people playing games on green tables, or drinking, or listening to greasy music'.[54] London itself functions as a largely uniform and dreary backdrop to the miseries that the immigrants undergo. The rivers that Leila's bus lurches over in *The Final Passage* 'were like dirty brown lines, full of empty bottles and cigarette ends, cardboard boxes and greying suds of pollution'[55]; *The Shelter* is set entirely in 'a grimy Ladbroke Grove pub'.[56]

Phillips is revisiting the London about which Sam Selvon wrote so memorably. He has described that author as one of his two biggest influences (the other is George Lamming).[57] Yet this debt is hard to discern – his is a more jaded, frost-bitten vision of the city. Selvon, after all, had a communal bent and focused on clusters of characters rather than solitary individuals; he was a master of the comic vignette; his characters, though they're often feckless and profligate, are never as brutal or thuggish as those in Phillips's work. Neither Michael in *The Final Passage* nor Albert in *Where There Is Darkness* would ever tolerate, as Moses' friends do, being called 'boys'. They would shy from any kind of gang loyalty, and also balk at the tiniest suggestion that they were anything other than men's men.

Selvon's boys are also less geographically boxed-in than Phillips's characters. They don't let their 'situations' stop them from having a good time. They 'con' and 'lime' around Bayswater Road and Hyde Park, go out combing the streets for gold or attractive girls, become giddy with excitement at the thought of venturing as far as Leicester Square. In contrast, Phillips often traps his characters in dingy pubs or in squabbling households. When they catch buses we never see which parts of the city they're passing through or heading towards. The capital is a greyscale void, drab and inclement, entirely bereft of delight. It's almost as if Phillips, who watched a lot of 1950s newsreel footage while researching *The Final Passage*, believed that the whole decade, the entire city even – rather than just the film reels – was lived out in scuffed black and white. Describing the house in Florence Road that Leila moves into, he focuses on how cold and filthy it is, before labelling the other homes in the area as 'small, clearly cramped and uncomfortable'.[58] Selvon also described slum districts: in *The Lonely Londoners*, Tolroy and his family live off the Harrow Road, 'where men know what it is to hustle a pound to pay the rent when Friday come. The houses around here old and grey and weatherbeaten, the walls cracking like the last days of Pompeii.'[59] Yet it's entirely typical of Selvon to wish to pinpoint spots of colour and optimism within this dereliction: first, by highlighting a wall on which someone has painted 'Vote Labour and Down With the Tories', he insinuates that Caribbean lives might be transformed by political means; secondly, by talking of how 'the poor people buy tulip and daffodil to put in the dingy room they living in', he implies that poverty needn't obliterate self-respect or a desire for beauty.[60]

The vision of London that percolates Phillips's fiction, drama and critical writings is best embodied in the 'England' section of *The Final Passage*. Here we learn that one of Leila's main reasons for leaving the Caribbean was to be with her mother in London. She arrives only to discover that Mrs Preston (her first name is never disclosed) is lying seriously ill in hospital (her ailment is never specified). Their relationship has never been as warm as Leila would have wished, and now she longs for 'something that would make her mother more like a friend. As it was they just sat there and stared at each other [. . .] nothing seemed to be able to bring them together and this first exchange had been more interview than conversation.'[61] Although Leila visits her mother another 105 times, every day except Sundays, their conversations are rarely any more intimate or rewarding. Every day Leila has

to travel by bus past the people who look 'sad and cold', past the dirty river, past the walls daubed with racist graffiti through to the 'etherized sterility of the hospital' where sloppy-hipped nurses march around completely unable to help her dying mother. These bus rides are the true final passage of the novel's title, and the daily journeys to the hospital are painfully ironic plays on the immigrant's notion of England as a mother country. The mother certainly exists, but she's sick and dying. She shows her daughter little emotion; almost her first words to her are 'Leila, child, London is not my home'.[62] Like so many of Phillips's characters, Leila's hopes of a fresh start and of remaking herself are dashed immediately. It's been a passage to nowhere, a journey to disappointment. Her mother's sickness is really that of the palsied London in which she finds herself hospitalized.

Phillips's inability to portray post-war London as anything other than a sickly doomscape was partly a function of the period in which he was writing. The first half of the 1980s was an altogether grim time for black people in the United Kingdom. Unemployment was high, police harassment common. Triumphs at school or in the workplace were rare. No discussion of inner-city life was possible without the words 'injustice' or 'discrimination' cropping up. The past, then, might have served Phillips as a safety buffer from the miseries of the present. By writing, as he often did, about life in the 1950s and 1960s, he might have offered audiences a picture of black London that was less apocalyptic than the one they saw through their windows and on their TV screens each night. But his past is just as bad as the present. History is neither uplift nor decline, just more of the enervating same. He told one interviewer that younger black people faced

> almost hostility distilled. There is no longer any curiosity about black or West Indian faces. I think part of the anger or hurt which may permeate my work comes from the fact that when I look at the life of my parents, and people of my parents' generation, I feel they have been given a terrible deal by Britain.[63]

Is it the case that dire social circumstances need always be written up gloomily? And can it possibly be true that life for black Londoners in the past, even the 1950s and 1960s, was so unremittingly bad? Phillips's early writing, scoured of frivolity or fancy language, as bare as a deserted office block, would suggest so. Kureishi, whose *My Beautiful Laundrette* came out in the same year as *The Final Passage* was published, took the view that in harsh times laughter was as important as outrage, satire as much as realism.

Phillips's own opinions on British race relations have become steadily less acerbic over recent years. It may be that the comparative perspective available to him through living and teaching in

America, a country where relations between black and white communities are far more volatile than in England, has forced him to lighten up. It may just be a case of an angry young man mellowing with age. Whatever the cause, Phillips's 1996 TV adaptation of *The Final Passage* has a considerably more upbeat ending than that of the original novel. In the screen version Leila opts to remain in England and bring up her son Calvin who becomes a besuited, VW-driving official at a London law centre. Calvin discovers that his father, ill and alone, is living in a bed-sit in the capital; he decides to visit him, and they achieve a belated reconciliation. The final scene of the screenplay finds a proud Leila declaring to her son that 'Whatever troubles I've had in England – and I've had plenty – England could never take you away from me [. . .] This England is your home. And as long as it's your home, it's my home too.'[64] Phillips explained to an interviewer that the film version of *The Final Passage* was 'more optimistic because it's 1996 now and I originally wrote it in 1985. Britain has changed dramatically. Of course there is a lot to be done, but our parents got through it. They survived. We survived. And young Black people are more confident.'[65]

That optimism is also present in S.I. Martin's *Incomparable World* (1996), a little-known novel, but probably the best evocation of historic black London to date. It's set in the district of Seven Dials (also known as St Giles), near Covent Garden, which in the eighteenth century was an area notorious as a breeding ground for career criminals. Law officers were scared to enter it. Beggars, thieves and whores were all to be found there, as were many blacks. So many in fact that they were labelled 'St Giles blackbirds', one of the most celebrated sub-castes of London's floating army of ragged mendicants. Those few lucky enough to have regular shelter lived in filthy tenements and diseased ruins called 'rookeries'. As an underworld stronghold, a last resort for the capital's outcasts and dogtribes, Seven Dials housed many of the black Londoners who have featured in this book. Lack of documentation has meant that historians have been unable to describe this milieu in any detail. Contemporary black writers are of little help: the St Giles blackbirds represent the rump, the base multitude that Sancho and Equiano sometimes sought to champion, though the nature of their books – domestic epistles and spiritual autobiography – meant that they incorporated little documentary material.

Against such absences, Martin's novel comes as a welcome repopulating. It begins in 1786 at the time that thousands of black Americans who had fought on the side of the English during the War of Independence were living in the capital. Buckram, the main character in the book, had been raised in the household of a Pennsylvania armourer, but had taken up arms against his rebel masters. A former groom and master horseman, he has just emerged from a stint in Bridewell Gaol where he was serving time for possessing a stolen prize-fighter cock. Prison was tolerable until he was forced to have sex with (white) women – whores, greyhound girls, young maidens – for the titillation of paying outsiders. As soon as he resisted, he was flung back in his cell and punished with 1500 lashes.

The novel covers a period of just a few months, from May to October 1786, with a brief coda in autumn 1787. We follow Buckram ducking and diving through the city, trying to make a living by selling *Aethiopian Secret Papers*, a pornographic pamphlet full of sketches of white men having sex with Angola Molly, a local black whore. He has a friend called William Supple who is eager to get back in touch with the wife and kids he has left behind in New York. Both of them are drawn into the orbit of Georgie

George, unscrupulous king of the local blackbirds, who hatches a plan to con a visiting planter from Virginia by dressing up as African chiefs and offering him slave-trading rights in an area of the Niger Delta for a fee of £12,000. Buckram, meanwhile, finds himself struggling to disguise his poverty after he falls in love with Charlotte Tell, a freeborn black who teaches maths and Latin at a local school.

The plot of *Incomparable World* is not unimportant, but the novel's real achievement lies in the fidelity with which it portrays subterranean London. The sheer mass of detail would, in a lesser writer, be mere antiquarianism; Martin, though, takes such relish in the very naming of things – places, objects, foodstuffs – that the city feels fingertip palpable: 'The cookhouse was a long wooden shed with a chain-strung counter giving onto the corner of Cross Lane and Castle Street. Trays of baked potatoes swimming in lard were displayed alongside suet pudding with lumps of fat as large as walnuts. Pea soup, hot eels and sheep's trotters were arranged on a hotplate to one side.'[66] Martin displays the tendency, shared by most great writers about London, to produce compound sentences. He likes lists and inventories. Boxers, whores, drunks, howling madmen; the Coach and Horses in Charles Street, the Pineapple in New Road, the Charioteer on Brydges Street; buglers, fife-tooters, drummers and triangle-ticklers. Such thick description – of down-at-heel wretches, down-at-heel taverns, musicians' jobs that will save wretches from being down-at-heel – makes the novel as heaped and congested as the rookeries with their overspill immigrants.

Such swarming and excess are crucial in convincing the reader of the largeness of this 'incomparable world', in impressing upon us the fact that vast areas of metropolitan history are missing from most literary guides to London. Martin's city is one whose culture, both high and low, uproarious and desperate, is evoked rather than invoked. Life, gross and stinking, is burped and vomited from each paragraph. We feel saturated and violated by this sensory overload. It's not an unpleasant feeling though – especially when it is accompanied by the author's marvellous characterization. The specificities of place and daily life render the city, even its horror or ennui, more vivid. It also makes the capital, as in the fictions of Kureishi and Selvon, more bearable than those accounts in which London is a vague and unlocalized wash of dejection.

Buckram's world may not be vast, but it is racially porous. Seven Dials was too small for ethnic enclaves to thrive. This is worth stressing as some academics in the past have spoken of the 'black community' in the eighteenth century as if it were a discrete, self-sufficient entity. That seems highly unlikely; black and white plebs had a good deal in common, not least their outlaw status and their hatred of the local constables who they regard as a 'Bunch of cutpurses, fucksters and drunks'.[67] Not having much in the way of material goods serves to bring them together:

> Every second step he would bump up against other pedestrians similarly charging through the gloom, but these incidents passed unchallenged in a parish inhabited almost exclusively by people who are stronger and stranger than anything you'd care to know. But Buckram felt safe. His ragged clothes betrayed no jingle of money or arms, he was a threat to no-one and his dark skin drew no second glances.[68]

Martin would appear to go along with the findings of labour historians Peter Linebaugh and Marcus Rediker who have argued that during the seventeenth and eighteenth centuries there existed a transatlantic class of people – motley in dress and ethnic composition, landless but mobile, dispossessed but endlessly resourceful and creative.[69] Present in attenuated form in London, they're more clearly visible at the end of the novel when William Supple and Georgie George, having fled England after their successful heist at the American embassy, find themselves in the Brazilian port of Recife, desperate for a refuge from the negrophobic soldiers who have been chasing them through the crowded streets. They're saved by a group of English sailors who push them into a tavern and take up arms against the soldiers. Says Georgie to the incredulous William:

> Like it or not, this is an English inn and we are English speakers. Until we blacks use our original African language, our lives are linked with these people and theirs with ours, even against our proper interests, with the best will in the world [. . .] To these drunken seafarers, it mattered less that we are black men than that we have a common tongue. Language fosters conspiracy.[70]

Nowhere is this kinship more evident than in the following scene, one of the funniest in the history of black and Asian writing about London. Buckram has just started his new job covertly selling porn on the streets. Unsure about whom to approach, he heads for a bawdy house on the corner of Russell Street. He spots a respectable-looking middle-aged man coming out of the front door and asks him, 'New in town? Seeking exotic delights?' The man is furious and barks, 'Distance yourself, nigger, lest I have you flogged for insolence.'

> But Buckram stood akimbo, blocking his path.
>   'Where do you hail from, slave-owner?'
>   The American drew his arm. Before the fist could fly Buckram had reached and grasped it with his own. The soft, rich man's rage had all the momentum and menace of a mechanical toy. Buckram twisted his wrist and slammed him against a pillar.

A gaggle of onlookers was gathering, so Buckram raised his voice and spoke London English for all to hear.

'I asked where you came from, rebel. Answer me!'

The man's nostrils flared. He looked to the crowd for support, but they were all passing fops and St Giles's toughs, non-partisan wastrels, eager for a fight to staunch their boredom.

'Are you going to let this nigger defy me? Will you allow him to besmirch the honour of the white . . . !'

Buckram cuffed him across the mouth; his knuckles felt teeth loosen in the gums.

'Dob 'im one on, blackie! Dob 'im one on for the lads!' came a plaintive voice from the crowd.

Buckram's ruse had worked. The crowd was siding with him. The American, realizing this, squealed like a Smithfield pig and sagged to his knees, cupping his bloody mouth with his hands.

'Where's home, rebel? Where's home?'

'Camden, Carolina.'

'Ah, Camden,' Buckram declared. 'Know it well. Spent a good time there during *your* war against *our* king.'

The market-folk warmed to this mention of shared sovereignty.

'Camden. Fine little town. Swived many a young lass there. Me and my fellow blacks. Mayhap your wife or daughter was one of their number.'

'Oooooooooh!?!' smarmed the Londoners.

The American gathered up the vestiges of his dignity and spat blood in the ex-slave's face.

Buckram grabbed him by the scruff of his neck and presented him to the crowd.

'You see these colonials. See them? This is the gratitude we get for trying to save their filthy hides from the folly of independence. This is how they repay us. Take that!'

He punched the planter in the stomach.

'That's for Boston!'

'Woooaaargh!' went the audience.

He clapped the man's left ear as hard as he could. He felt the impact resound through his tightened muscles. 'That's for Philadelphia!'

'We're with you, darkie!'[71]

The white plebs in Martin's London may be 'with' the darkies, but those darkies still value each other's company intensely. This book is about the dream of community. Having cut themselves off from their homes thousands of miles away, living in a cold and foreign city where the scream of cart-horses, wares-touting peddlers and atonal street chaunters deafen them from dawn until dusk, the black Americans pine for the kind of tenderness and silent intimacy of which they feel only people the same colour are capable. There's a real compassion to the scene in which Buckram is approached by a tongueless runaway slave whose neck is bruised with collar marks: 'He had no money to give the child and gestured as much. The beggar bowed and curtsied before spiralling away to his haunt at the tavern's dog porch.'[72] The muteness of both blacks, a condition inflicted on one by a vicious aristocrat, on the other by utter helplessness, is appallingly eloquent.

Wandering towards the Piccadilly end of Leicester Fields one day, William realizes that he's been following a black couple walking hand in hand: 'He wondered where they'd come from, where they dwelt. What wayward impulse to happiness had driven them to stroll with such calm confidence here in the heart of the white man's world?'[73] Buckram loves Charlotte for her status as much as her beauty and grace: she has the 'strident, over-confident sonority of a freeborn Black Briton'; he is bewitched by her kind-faced parents and almost paralysed when Mr Tell introduces himself – 'This was something he could never have imagined: seeing a black adult in the company of their parents. It was as much as he could do to gasp and take the older man's hand.'[74]

For all the pleasures of togetherness, it's the tensions and gossipy in-fighting of black Londoners, especially the more elevated ones, that make Martin's book so delightful. His attitude towards the past is less than reverential. Samuel Johnson's man-servant Francis Barber is shown as a nouveau-riche social climber, all faux-country-squire joshing, and eager to have minions attend to his whims and vanities. His ego is taken down a notch only when layabouts at Vauxhall Pleasure Gardens pelt him with soggy onions and horse shit. Meanwhile, Ignatius Sancho, another contemporary whose life has been gilded and heroicized of late, is discussed cattily. Charlotte invites Buckram to a dinner where one of the guests compares Sancho's work unfavourably with that of Gronniosaw – his prose is as 'stale and unappetizing as the almond custard his wife sells in that dreadful shop of hers'. To which Buckram replies, 'I am acquainted with the Sancho establishment and do not wish to speak ill of the dead. In his defence, however, it must be stated that his widow is a purveyor of the most exceptional apple dumplings.'[75]

The guest is Ottobah Cugoano, author of the Abolitionist polemic *Thoughts and Sentiments on the Evil and Wicked Traffic of the Slavery and Commerce of the Human Species* (1787). He's joined at Charlotte Tell's dining table by Thomas Hardy, founder of the radical London Corresponding Society, and by 'Ola' Equiano. The latter is shown as a serious and rather testy man who doesn't take kindly to having an uncouth, foul-smelling imposter in his presence. He insists that Buckram hand over a copy of the pamphlet that the blackbird has been distributing: ' "What form does it take: essays, criticism, perambulations, personal recollections? [. . .] *Aethiopian Secret Papers*!" he sneered. "I thought as much. You're nothing but a Piazza pimp, preying on the weakest daughters of Afric." '[76] Though Equiano's elitism is being teased here, the idea of literature certainly isn't. Books may be prized for the money they help rake in for their sellers, but they're also a route out of the spiritual ghetto. When William's lodgings burn down, it's his magazines and letters that he most misses. In paper he found a kind of 'sanctuary'; it was 'the one thing that kept him in touch with human life. Without it he was nothing, simply spinning idiotic fictions in voids of his own creation: like Buckram, illiterate, insolvent, invalid.'[77]

In the end, what's most valuable about *Incomparable World* is its lack of piety. It shows the black past as one that's full of rogues, tricksters, profiteers. The St Giles blackbirds are not portrayed as sodden victims of circumstance or frozen figures in a mural of atrocity. We're not invited to pity them. They're silly and greedy and vulnerable; the moment it appears that Buckram, despite his poor schooling and lack of social skills, might indeed be about to marry Charlotte, they come across a barefoot Northern lass, her face caked in dirt and her mouth toothless, who 'reeked of soused herring and wore a patched mob cap, a patched dress, and a patch over one eye'.[78] Running ahead of her is a malnourished, mixed-race girl – Buckram's daughter.

This is a sunken London, one populated by men and women felled by drink, illness, slavery. Yet for all the determination with which its inhabitants seek to move away – by means of gambling, fleecing frocks, marrying into the middle classes – Seven Dials isn't damned as a nihilistic zero-point, symbolizing the status of blacks throughout metropolitan history. Rotting away in Brazil while he awaits a passage to his family in New York, Supple drifts into a nostalgic reverie and recalls '*Back home*. Hot chestnuts and mulled wines – that's what they'd be selling in the Piazza right now. Logfires blazing a warm welcome from the windows of packed kens at every slushy corner of the Court End. Books, gambling parlours, high conversation, Stepney ale.'[79]

We shouldn't see this as mere sentimentality, the lazy conserva-

tism in which exiles are prone to indulge. For implanted in
Supple's dreamtalk is the potential, haltingly realized over the
subsequent two centuries, for black people and London to be seen,
not as warring and mutually antagonistic forces, but as intimates.
That intimacy, as evidenced in Martin's novel, will by no means
be cosy. The bare-knuckle hardness of the prose makes that very
clear. Indeed, he rides away from the capital at the end of the
book, though he will surely return again at some point. Yet for
all the wariness and fear with which Buckram imagines the future,
it is at least a future; life in the black metropolis of the 1780s
wasn't dire enough to snuff that out:

> Suddenly, he was seized by a delirious vision of this land, this
> London, in time to come, teeming with generation after genera-
> tion of his kinfolk, freedmen, English-born and bred; transform-
> ing this wet, cold island with African worship and celebration.
> Imperial orphans in communion with a fractured past – his
> present – leading Albion's hag-masses to a greater, more whole-
> some dance of life. And would they, like him, still be hovering
> by closed doors, waiting for scraps from the master's table? And
> would they, like him, still be able to rely on the kindness of
> curious suburban strangers? God willing, death would find him
> before either of those futures came to pass.[80]

A similar appreciation of – and pride in – the ways in which black
Londoners have managed to 'tough out' trying circumstances is
found in the work of Fred D'Aguiar who was born to Guyanese
parents in London in 1960. Given his fascination with the history
of the Thames, it's ironic that his father was a London Transport
bus driver and his mother a bus conductor. Poverty forced them
to send him to Guyana at the age of two where he was looked
after by his grandmother, but he returned to London in 1972 by
which time his mother had converted to Islam to please her new
husband, a Pakistani Muslim.

After he left school D'Aguiar trained and worked for three years as a psychiatric nurse at Maudsley Hospital in Camberwell and at Bethlem in Croydon. He also attended a series of writing workshops at Goldsmiths' College, later studying English Literature at the University of Kent and joining a black writers' workshop in Brixton called Black Ink. The group, which encouraged writers to incorporate oral and rhythmic elements into their work, had a big influence on him. Blurring the division between written and performance poetry, D'Aguiar later argued, was one of two major characteristics of black English poetry of the 1980s, the other being 'a sense of public address, though this may be mediated through an intensely private mask or persona'.[81] Similarly, in a signed editorial for *Artrage*, a black cultural magazine for which he wrote during that decade and two numbers of which he edited, D'Aguiar claimed that, 'artists who are seeking a synthesis between the various art forms have most to say to our society and times', before adding 'we can only understand what it means to be creative now if we have an understanding of what it was like for past writers. We also show that the past can still serve writers and artists today depending on their approach to it.'[82] Both these themes – the importance of form, and history viewed imaginatively as much as scholastically – inform *Sweet Thames*, a poem written for television as part of BBC2's *Words on Film* series. The thirty-minute programme was joint winner of the Commission for Racial Equality's 1992 Race In The Media current affairs/documentary award, and won its director, Mark Harrison, the British Film Institute's Award for Innovation the following year.[83]

The very fact that D'Aguiar chose the Thames as the focus of his contemplation of black metropolitan history shows the scope of his poetic ambitions. Previous chapters have touched on aspects of the river's imperial past: the merchandise (some times human) it carried; Olaudah Equiano who was nearly drowned near West-

minster Bridge; the misery of the nineteenth-century lascars await-
ing ships to transport them back to the continents from which
they first sailed. One contemporary writer who had visited the
East End slums where they lived observed that, 'Images of Vishnu,
Genesa, and other heathen gods, and curiosities of strange work-
manship, are in many windows, while the names and signs over
them show that the traders are from other lands'.[84] This kind of
enterprising industry, together with the fact that a number of
lascars married and settled in the area, suggests that commiseration
is not the only response we should feel when thinking about immigration and the Thames.

Small communities formed near the river in the first part of the
twentieth century. Many Africans arrived there as stowaways on
freight ships. The Sierra Leone-born Ernest Marke has recounted
how as an underage ship worker on the SS *Prashu* he disembarked
at Millwall Dock a couple of days before Christmas 1917. Having
straight away set off to see the 'Bloody Tower and all its trim-
mings', he only got as far as the West India Dock Road before
being pelted with snowballs by the local urchins.[85] He gave chase
but after 'sliding and twisting all over the street like a comedy
contortionist doing a star turn', decided to head back to his ber-
thed ship: 'How ironic it was that less than three weeks ago the
thought of London had made me as happy as a pauper turned
millionaire. And now – brrrhh!'[86]

During and after the Second World War increasing numbers
of stowaways and Nigerian waterfront boys sneaked into London
on ships.[87] They attracted the attention of pulp-fiction authors
such as Roland Vane who wrote that Cable Street, 'snakes its
sinister way from Stepney to Dock Street' like 'an ugly black
mamba', and was full of sharks, harpies and other menacing types:
'its environs form a Cosmopolitan and polyglot entity with a large
portion of its population changing constantly as ships come and

go from the near-at-hand London Docks'.[88] In 1968 dockers from Tilbury, the port to which the *Windrush* had sailed twenty years previously, along with Smithfield Market meat-traders, were among the most vociferous demonstrators to march to Westminster in support of Enoch Powell's 'Rivers of Blood' speech.

The Thames, then, has historically been both a point of arrival and departure – forced and voluntary – for black and Asian Londoners. Its ports and dockside communities have provided them with employment, however fitful or illegal. Tens of thousands have died beside it. And sometimes in it, as was shown by the appalling murder in October 1997 of Ricky Reel, the young Asian student whose body was found in the river following a racist attack in Kingston upon Thames. The story of the black Thames, as with the story of Seven Dials, revolves not just around suffering, but around resilience and hard-won happiness, too.

Perhaps stories would be more accurate. It's D'Aguiar's aim in *Sweet Thames* to spotlight some of them, and to reclaim the river

from those who would use it as a symbol of a nation being deluged by unwanted immigrants. Observing the Thames Barrier at Woolwich he notes that it seems to have a multiplicatory effect on the sun that shines down on it, and 'adds brothers/and sisters to that family of one'.[89] Such aggregation seems ironic for the Barrier is normally conceived of in terms of blocking (floods) and diminishing (tidal waves). Two ruminative stanzas on this topic are followed by three pieces of archive footage showing, successively, Enoch Powell, Margaret Thatcher and Harold Wilson all using river imagery to question the value of immigration to the United Kingdom. Powell's Rivers of Blood refers to how 'Father Tiber takes a drop too much, bursts his banks and floods the countryside for many miles around'; Thatcher strategically co-opts the rhetoric of the burgeoning National Front in 1978 to express her fear that the country is in danger of being swamped; Harold Wilson is shown fretting over influxes of foreigners in 1969.[90] Later, the bovine right-wing Conservative MP Terry Dicks asks: 'Why should this country pick up the flotsam and jetsam from all over the world?'[91]

Sweet Thames can be seen in environmental terms; D'Aguiar wants to filter out from the river the pollution of xenophobic invective. There's a bardic heroism to this goal; the poem is a last-gasp effort 'Before you/whiten the water', a phrase that recalls Moses' complaint in *The Lonely Londoners* that 'a lot of parasites muddy the water for the boys'.[92] D'Aguiar is not interested in the language of apocalypse, however: he prefers to go back in time, and to evoke the wonder and excitement felt by newcomers to London throughout the centuries. Three examples are offered – Olaudah Equiano, whose landmark autobiography was published in 1789, the 492 passengers on the *Windrush* in 1948, and Harry Surju, a nurse who came to England from Mauritius in 1972.

D'Aguiar begins with footage of the calypsonian Lord Kitchener disembarking from the *Windrush* and singing 'London Is The Place For Me'. Kitchener is diffident and clearly taken aback to be asked to break into song before he has even left the quayside. But he's also keen to show off his versifying talent. Falteringly at first – for he lacks a guitar or, indeed, any other instrument, and is unused to performing for cameras – but with mounting confidence, he sings a calypso of beguiling loveliness:

> London is the place for me.
> London, this lovely city.
> You can go to France or America,
> India, Asia or Africa,
> But you must come back to London city.
>
> Well, believe me as I am speaking broadmindedly,
> I am glad that I know my mother country,
> I've been travelling to countries years ago,
> But this the place I want to see
> London is the place for me.
>
> To live in London you're really comfortable,
> Because the English people are very sociable.
> They take you here, and they take you there,
> And they make you feel like a millionaire.
> London, that's the place for me.[93]

These are not uncommon sentiments: the notion of coming back or returning 'home' to England; the claim that London is preferable to all other places recalls those widely-travelled rajahs in the nineteenth century who saw the capital as the apex of their journeying; 'millionaire' evokes the writers of the 1950s who dreamed London's streets were paved with gold.

It's a delight to hear this calypso, and to see it being performed. It's also rather painful. To view it today – especially if one is the child of immigrants – induces conflicting emotions. One's tempted to feel pity for Kitchener and his fellow Jamaicans: were they not harbouring unrealistic hopes about what England might hold in store for them? Some might snigger nervously: how old-fashioned his clothes and his singing are! How retro-cute! Others might bridle at the fruity-toned self-assurance of the Pathé reporter. Is he not pandering to the complacency of his white audience by glossing over some of the social and economic reasons that brought West Indians here? Is it not belittling to present Jamaicans as all-singing, happy-go-lucky innocents who are pathetically grateful to be allowed into England? These are bitter thoughts coloured, understandably, by our knowledge of what the following decades held in store for these new arrivals.

But there's also a less bitter response that's difficult to put into words without appearing rather soppy but one, I think, that D'Aguiar is trying to foster. Kitchener looks so skinny and vulnerable. We imagine that our parents must have looked like that too when they first arrived and we want to hug him, hold his hand, tell him that everything will be all right, even if we have no idea if that's actually true. Given no advance warning, singing 'cold' and in a cold climate, without musical accompaniment, Kitchener's lyrics are deeply poignant. His voice too has a fragility, a tip-toe tentativeness that is very different from the tough-man flexing of so much 'urban' music today. It's a love song he's singing, but it's so frail and gauzy that it also sounds like an elegy. What D'Aguiar is doing is a form of 'sampling'; but the sample here is not used ironically, or as clever juxtaposition, or even poetic laziness, but as a kinship claim.

What's so moving is the way that D'Aguiar has isolated this fleeting moment before the idealism of Caribbean immigrants turned sour. Here are twitchings of giddy possibility, the utopianism many migrants feel when embarking upon new chapters of their lives. The optimism of Kitchener's calypso makes the viewer nostalgic for a time when black and Asian people genuinely believed their mother country was happy to see them, a time when they could anticipate the future with relish. Those imagined futures didn't always work out as well as they would have liked. Still, by showing his audience a pre-lapsarian past, D'Aguiar seeks to re-energize them, to encourage them to dream and plot and strive to create better futures for themselves. The poem tries to revivify those palsied forebears, those who became 'calcified in their spines' and reduced 'to a stoop' from the moment they disembarked.[94] Only when their stories and their hopes are recaptured can the poet hope 'to straighten History,/straightening into these lines'.[95]

The note of hopefulness that D'Aguiar sounds when mapping out this project is also heard in his meditation on the life and work of Olaudah Equiano. That the Thames is the site for this act of historical re-imagining may seem odd. After all, as Caryl Phillips says in *Crossing The River* (1993), 'There are no paths in water. No signposts. There is no return.'[96] David Dabydeen, in *A Harlot's Progress* (1999), a novel in which the main character, Mungo, is London's oldest black inhabitant (he is described as 'a ruined archive') goes further. He suggests that the few extant literary works by eighteenth-century ex-slaves shouldn't be seen as the unvarnished, uncomplicated truth; in fact, they're often fabricated and partial. Mungo tells his life-story to an Abolitionist ghost-writer for money, stuttering and rambling so that he'll pick up extra guineas:

> In Mr Pringle's society, expression is vaunted, and a book is deemed the highest achievement of man. But, for me, the book is no more than a splendidly adorned memorial and grave. To speak is to scoop out substance, to hollow out yourself, to make space within for your own burial, so I have kept in things as bulwarks against death.[97]

Imagination is as important as the archive when it comes to making history come alive. D'Aguiar claims to hear 'Voices made by water washing/itself' and 'the noise of a tide where/two tides meet'.[98] As he recalls Equiano sailing up the Thames for the first time at the end of the 1750s, a sculpted mask appears on the screen as if to underline his belief that any hope of recovering the 'real' Equiano is doomed. Yet the fact that unmediated, non-textual access to the past is impossible doesn't mean we will be forced to travel light forever, or that we are sentenced to the loneliness of those bereft of memory. Perhaps, D'Aguiar suggests, it might be possible to resurrect past lives by invoking their absence; perhaps a shadowy, ghost narrative might emerge. So vehemently does he

implore Equiano to 'give me your hand, extend it/from your sla-
ver's time to mine' that he seems to think historical black London
might be conjured up through force of desire alone.[99]

Soon the action moves from Tilbury to Westminster where

> We are beside the Palace,
>
> shouldering the bridge, where
> in 1760, you were
> pushed into the element
> you'd worked for years, but not
> learned to swim.[100]

'We' indicates D'Aguiar's belief in the essential unity that exists
– or should exist – between eighteenth- and twentieth-century
black Londoners. Meanwhile, 'shouldering', as in shouldering a
burden, has an almost mystical resonance. It implies that if young
people today were to learn about the likes of Equiano, and to
appreciate what hardships previous generations of black Londoners went through, those distresses might be exorcized. The
point is made more emphatically through footage of John, a black
pupil of London Nautical School, and fifteen years old – '(your
age then)' – diving into the Thames:

> When John surfaces, Equiano, you
> rise with him, from your time to
> ours, show the two times are one.[101]

At first the injunction to 'show the two times are one' seems very
bleak, almost suggesting that black metropolitan experiences have not
improved in the 230 years since Equiano was nearly drowned. More
positively, though, D'Aguiar is arguing for the possibility of historical
translation, and of individual lives, events and traumas maintaining
their affective resonance across the passing of centuries. He believes
it's possible, albeit with great strain and difficulty, for present gener-

ations to connect with the past, and to help bear its anguish and ecstasies. He places fictional words into Equiano's mouth:

> When those boys pushed me in
> it was for good or dead or both.
> That's why when the water
> quick time cover my head
> I summoned Legba, Dahomey,
>
> Shango and their God too
> customized into mine.
> With so many gods to my rescue
> I was laughing all the way
> to the bottom of the Thames. [...]
>
>   But I hugging
> water shaped like my embrace,
> a nought; I kicked off the bed
> laughing all the way back up.[102]

Like his literary role model, the Guyanese novelist Wilson Harris, D'Aguiar is arguing that an immersion in ancient hurt and pain – like Equiano's embrace of the water that nearly drowned him – is the first step towards transcending that tragedy. In much the way that Equiano, fixed at the bottom of the great chain of being, reduced by slavery to the status of a social zero, hurdled the barriers that should have consigned him to non-life, so D'Aguiar feels that contemporary black Londoners must overcome their bitterness and loss by staring the Thames Barrier (as well as other sites of exclusion and disenfranchisement) full in the face before moving on up.

This idea of confrontation is one of the key motifs of *Sweet Thames*. The poem begins with, and is regularly interrupted by, an immigration official asking, 'May I see your passport please sir?', 'How long do you intend to stay?', 'Where are you heading?'[103] He's a human version of the Thames Barrier and a bureaucratic enforcer of the entry regulations imposed by Wilson and Thatcher. Of course, black Londoners throughout history have been the interrogated rather than the interrogators. The notorious 'sus' laws of the early 1980s, the period in which D'Aguiar was formulating his aesthetics, are the clearest illustration of this: they empowered the Metropolitan Police to stop and question any pedestrian or motorist who they felt was behaving suspiciously. Resentment flared up when it became clear that a disproportionate number of black people were being stopped. The law was rescinded in the mid-1980s after considerable protest and a marked deterioration in community relations.

D'Aguiar feels it crucial to 'answer back', to question the questioner. That is readily apparent from the series of three stanzas that follows archival footage of Jamaicans arriving at Waterloo and Ugandan Asians stepping on to the Heathrow tarmac two decades later. A Super-16 camera transports the viewer to contemporary Tilbury where D'Aguiar ruminates on this 'floating, lopsided wharf' which, over forty years earlier, had been 'put in its place when dwarfed/by a liner':

> Dear Windrush,
> when your deep, wide berths
> closed round little old Tilbury,
>
> a forest of cranes stiffened
> in a tension held since then.
> Rust in their iron fretwork
> bled where there should be a heart.
> After waiting all night in the open,
>
> why did the cranes keep their hands
> from sight, their Mexican
> waves kept to themselves? Why no crush
> to unload your trunks?[104]

The dockside machinery and engineering equipment tauten and shudder from contact with the new arrivals in the same way that many English men and women balked at social interaction with Caribbean immigrants during the 1950s and 1960s. The port's physical landscape concretizes the icy receptions that many of the newly arrived West Indians faced when they went house-hunting in Paddington, out dancing in Aldwych, looking for jobs at the capital's labour exchanges. Tilbury's hostility pre-echoes that of the entire city. D'Aguiar, who has come to the Thames in deference to his forebears, can't understand this curmudgeonliness: 'why did the cranes keep their hands from sight' he asks, before adding, 'Why no crush/to unload your trunks?' There's an increasing aggression here – an anger and urgency similar to the lurching vigour of which the cranes themselves are capable. D'Aguiar spits out a final rhetorical question: 'What was/it about you that was so blinding?'[105]

The answer is, of course, the colour of their skin. Elsewhere in the poem, D'Aguiar's questioning is less charged. The third quarter of *Sweet Thames* consists of Harry Surju talking about how the Home Office tried to prevent him from bringing his wife Sheila to England from Mauritius. Although Harry lives in Handsworth, Birmingham, it's the idea of the hurdles or barriers (here imposed by Government legislation) placed before his family, that links him metaphorically to D'Aguiar's meditations on Woolwich Dockyard:

> Handsworth far from the Barrier?
> Not far enough. Its clutches
> reach all Britain's shores.[106]

Clearly, the Thames is being seen here – rightly or wrongly – not only as a symbol of black travails in London, but as the focus for an assessment of all of black English history. D'Aguiar is particularly interested in Harry's case because his job, like that of the poet during his teenage years, involves looking after mental patients. At one point the Mauritian is shown talking to an elderly female patient who claims not to have seen her sister for three years. 'Actually', says Harry, 'she came here. She came here a few months ago.'[107] The scene is intended as an oblique commentary on the tendency of whites (and also, it should be said, many blacks) to overlook the historical presence of African, Caribbean and Asian people in the United Kingdom. D'Aguiar goes on to question Sheila: 'Can you tell me how you feel now, what you're worried about, about the baby and all that. What do you feel?'[108] His circumspection compares favourably to the brusque questioning of the immigration official who crops up throughout the poem. D'Aguiar's enquiries are gentle, concerned with giving Sheila the opportunity to discuss her emotions, to speak for herself, just as he earlier enjoined Equiano to 'tell your story through your mask' and, before that, for the 'Sweet Thames' to 'run soft till I end my song' while standing on the South Bank opposite Westminster.[109]

Harry's and Sheila's story ends happily. They have a baby and, as the closing credits fade out, a twenty-second caption appears on the screen which tells us that Sheila's appeal to stay on in the country has been successful. This mood of optimism is perhaps the most striking aspect of *Sweet Thames*. D'Aguiar's poem is all about prising open the imagination, trying to create new ways of seeing London's black past as well as its future. By taking us back to three starting points in history, three beginnings spanning the centuries, D'Aguiar hopes to convince us that this poem itself amounts to a new beginning, a fresh start – that the conjunction of poetic memory and historicized urban imagination can liberate viewers from their contemporary impasses, helping them (in the words of Caryl Phillips's novel) to cross the river, to take them to the security and prosperity which Equiano, Kitchener, and Harry and Sheila Surju had found to be so elusive.

Crucial to this utopian project is the linking of white and black metropolitan experiences. Opposite Westminster, D'Aguiar observes how the Thames reflects 'bridge and Palace,/cardboard city's sprawling spaces'.[110] We're told that Equiano sailed from near Deptford's Queen Steps where Raleigh 'lay his cloak on a puddle/for Elizabeth I and Raleigh/got a notion that cost him/his versifying, scheming/head'.[111] Most poignantly, when a riverboat sails past Tower Bridge near the close of the poem, D'Aguiar points out that black people do not hold a monopoly on dark memories of the Thames:

> Our party steers a course
>
> shadowed by the Marchioness,
> let those 51 souls be at rest,
> as still as this river smoothed
> by the reflection erasing night
> and the promise all darkness keeps of light.[112]

That final line, with its Wilson Harris-like idea of redemption through suffering, is one more example of D'Aguiar's hope that poetry can be remedial, a source of healing. And, while there are certainly points in *Sweet Thames* when the poet's voice is harsh and declamatory, these are outweighed by D'Aguiar's conciliatoriness ('Dear Windrush/when your deep, wide berths/closed round little old Tilbury'; elsewhere he asks the river to 'mirror too my argument/without rancour and malice'[113]). The end of the poem sees D'Aguiar bidding a taxi driver to

> Drive me on hard water to where we
> can both be happy.
>
> Drive me as
> the water splinters in artificial light,
> not into black and white but all colours[114]

As these lines are delivered, the viewer sees young black people dancing on a river cruiser to 'One Love', Bob Marley's euphoric call for pan-racial harmony. The poem itself has plotted the transformation of the Thames from a site of drowning and pensiveness, to a place of pleasure and hedonism. Only after confronting the often-wretched history of black London, it seems, can second-generation immigrants hope to prosper and live fully. 'One Love' segues into Judy Garland singing 'Somewhere Over The Rainbow', a title that evokes both a promised land and multi-racial unity. Salman Rushdie claimed that the song

> is, or ought to be, the anthem of all the world's migrants, all those who go in search of the place where 'the dreams that you dare to dream really do come true'. It is a celebration of Escape, a grand paean to the Uprooted Self, a hymn – *the* hymn – to Elsewhere.[115]

Such utopianism is what distinguishes the poem from T.S. Eliot's *The Waste Land* whose section entitled 'The Fire Sermon' D'Aguiar is consciously evoking. Like Eliot, he uses a bricolage technique, grafting visual quotes (footage of Kitchener, disembarking immigrants, Thatcher and Wilson discoursing about the colour problem) on to the poem's structure. Again, like Eliot, D'Aguiar deploys a number of voices: they range from the vatic ('Make [my story] clear and give it style/like the sugar from Tate and Lyle'), to the fatherly ('Boys, you are all fluent/in water on Equiano's behalf'), right through to that of the community spokesman ('Despite/government pressure she has/given [Harry] a son, despite/all the ignorant legislation/against us in this land').[116] These voices are often those of real people: a black flood engineer, Kofi Armaning, is heard talking about the varieties of rubbish Londoners regularly hurl into the Thames (and, in doing so, makes a pointed commentary on the way politicians such as Terry Dicks or Enoch Powell despoil the river by using it to attack coloured immigrants); Bill Nelson, spokesman for Tate & Lyle, delivers an unintentionally tart account of the sugar-refining process which functions as a reminder of the river's economic importance down the centuries, and of the uneasy status of black people within the capital:

> And we also with those impurities, remove colour, the colour is in fact a manifestation if you like of the types of impurities in the sugar. And when we get to our products we end up with white sugar which is 99.95% sucrose or better.[117]

Like Eliot, whose vision of the Thames extended from Richmond to London Bridge to 'Greenwich reach/Past the Isle of Dogs'[118], D'Aguiar's poem has several riverside loci – Deptford, Thames Barrier, Tower Bridge and Westminster Bridge – which he describes at greater length and with more historical depth than writers such as Equiano or Selvon, both of whom wrote about isolated Thames locations. In summoning up the ghosts of the eighteenth century and of the *Windrush* generation – which, in turn, he hopes to transmute at the end of the poem ('We dance coloured by time./Now and for all our futures') – he wants to creolize Eliot's idea that 'Time present and time past/Are both perhaps present in time future/And time future contained in time past'.[119]

The critical difference between Eliot's and D'Aguiar's use of the Thames lies in the question of audience. Eliot's is a solitary voice charting the disintegration of a singular consciousness. D'Aguiar is more communal – he often speaks of 'we' or 'us'. By drawing on a community of texts, both literary (Equiano's autobiography) and visual (Pathé newsreels), he offers fresh genealogies and historiographies of the river. Plunging into its murky depths, he rescues for the public consciousness the memory of the thousands of black men and women who had arrived at, lived, worked and died by the Thames over the previous three centuries. He seeks to restore their voices, to repopulate the river. Eliot, on the other hand, is more preoccupied with a dried-up Thames, the evacuation of presence and meaning signalled, in part, by the departure of the nymphs and 'their friends, the loitering heirs of City directors'.[120] Against Eliot's forlorn and despairing attempt to shore up '[T]hese fragments [. . .] against my ruin', D'Aguiar's creative reassemblage of aspects of black metropolitan history offers a constructive and cheering vision of the river.[121]

It's tempting to end my exploration of black and Asian descriptions of London at this point. There's a certain roundedness and symmetry to closing with a chapter about the way in which contemporary authors such as Phillips and D'Aguiar have rediscovered and been energized by the metropolitan narratives of Equiano, Sancho and Selvon. These writers all share a dislike of the linear form which they believe is incapable of conveying the vagrant circuits of their far-travelled lives, or the messy congestion and density of metropolitan culture. Many of them fixate upon homes – both metaphoric and actual. With the possible exception of Sancho, the black communities they portray in their work are poor, long-suffering, and tend to be found in beleaguered enclaves in Bayswater and the East End. And yet, in spite of such thematic, formal and topographical similarities, to end on such a note would be to endorse a notion of historical and literary continuity that, although true to a surprisingly large extent, would also mean excluding a great many fascinating texts and cultural cross-currents.

D'Aguiar's identification of the Thames as the centre of black metropolitan history is itself an example of how such a project is flawed. *Sweet Thames* was broadcast in 1992, nearly three decades

after the rapid decline in the river's economic and political importance to the capital. The loosening of imperial trading ties and
the lack of long-term investment led to Rotterdam and Dunkirk
superseding London, and the East India Docks, for example, were
forced to close. The number of dock workers fell from 30,000 in
the 1950s to 2000 by 1981.[122] At the same time, many of the new
Caribbean and Asian immigrants settled in areas of London well
away from the East End – in Tottenham, Southall or Brixton. In
previous centuries blacks and Asians in London were rightly linked
with the Thames – it was there that they worked as jack tars,
wharfsmen and dockers; it was near Limehouse and Rotherhithe
that they lived in cheap boarding houses and slowly established
small, inter-racial communities.

Since the Second World War the river's fading importance and
the sheer number of coloured Londoners have led to major
changes. Immigrants are still associated with transport but, nowadays, they aren't found heaving cargoes at Tilbury, but driving
Tube trains on the Northern Line, collecting bus tickets on the
No. 12 from Trafalgar Square to Elephant and Castle, scrubbing
the toilets at Heathrow Airport, cabbying home mullet-haired
clubbers from Old Street at 3 a.m. on a Friday morning, doling
out inedible kebabs to gangs of Asian wideboys from Feltham who
spurn their parents' pleas for filial devotion and stay out late
spending what money they have at glitzy Leicester Square night-
spots. The Thames is no longer the geographic or symbolic centre
of the black and Asian metropolis: it's been replaced by bus routes,
railway lines, A-roads and the British Airway slipstreams over
West London. It's no criticism of D'Aguiar to suggest that
London life has always been so full of turnover, metamorphosis,
and geographic and cultural gerrymandering that any attempt to
associate a sizeable section of its population with a particular landmark or territory – even one so important as the River Thames

– risks obscuring the prolixity and variety of black metropolitan life. The final chapter of *London Calling* seeks to locate precisely some of these more buried and shady byways of black metropolitan literature.

CHAPTER SEVEN

London's Burning

The old *Dreadnought*, one of Nelson's battleships, after having fought the enemies of England, was moored in the Thames, off Greenwich, and became the Seamen's Hospital Ship, a Bethesda in which the sick of all nations were cared for. Here were found Malays, Maoris, Arabs, Javanese, and many from various parts of East India, all with various diseases, suffering in silence because no one could talk to them, or dying without any better knowledge of eternity than heathendom affords.[1]

'HEALING', AS THE PREVIOUS CHAPTER SHOWED, is one of the dominant themes in contemporary black literature on London. The past was a bruising place. Many of those who reached the capital from foreign shores ended up ravaged. To scroll through the back pages of black metropolitan history can be a doleful experience. Such hardships, over and over again. Where are the happy endings? The researcher wishes he could dispense a little medicine, put a little sugar in the bowl. Fred D'Aguiar spoke of wanting to register both his debt to, and admiration for, those post-war Caribbean settlers who seemed 'calcified in their spines'.[2] They'd been reduced 'to a stoop' by a combination of hard labour, pitiful incomes, and racial hostility.[3] D'Aguiar sought to 'cure' these arrivants by allowing them to speak, by rescuing them from the margins of British history and placing them centre-stage.

Central to such a project is the notion of 'respect'. The word, it's true, has become something of a cliché in contemporary black culture. Everyone demands it – from the garage collective member who breaks the jaws of young girls in his spare time, to the barely competent bantamweight boxer who has begun to believe his manager's hype. But earning respect, however inorganic and commercialized the term now is, has always been important in London; the city's ability to render the majority of its inhabitants' lives anonymous and invisible stokes in them the desire to stand out, to escape being overlooked. That this quest has political resonance can readily be seen by the proliferation of street-stall booklets and extra-curricular history classes aimed at making young black Britons proud of their 'heritage'.

Similarly, a recurrent feature of this book has been the persistence with which writers, from Gronniosaw onwards, have sought to show that being poor and dark-skinned doesn't inevitably signal barbarism. This quest for respectability, for improvement and for social approval manifests itself in different ways: Sancho's reluctance to vent his visceral anger about the slave trade; the excruciating politesse of nineteenth-century Indian rajahs when describing their adventures in London; the enduring desire of many of Selvon's characters to buy their own houses and, in doing so, to move up the capital's social ladder; Lamming's need to prove his literary worth to members of the ICA.

However, there's a far less salubrious side to black metropolitan history that has so far escaped recuperation by curators and critics. In their quest to construct a narrative that imputes a special dignity and strength to black people, scholars have often posited an overly dignified and heroic picture of black London that glosses over those voices which are awkward and dissonant. Getting 'respect' can be a bloody business. The quest for cultural capital often leaves a trail of hapless victims in its wake. This final chapter, then, sketches an alternative tradition, a previously uncharted leyline of black urban literature. If the rest of *London Calling* has tended to chart the thrust towards decorum and propriety (Kureishi excluded), this chapter, by contrast, uncovers a series of texts which deal with protest, dissent, impropriety and lawlessness.

The often fractious relationship between dark-skinned Londoners and the courts goes back to the eighteenth century. Many slaves fled their masters and ran away to the East End where they formed criminal alliances with thieves, sailors and the working-class poor. As a result evidence for the black presence in the capital during that period is often found within penal and judicial archives – transportee records, the Newgate Calendar, lost-and-found slave ads in the metropolitan press. Such sources occasionally throw up nuggets like the story of Elizabeth Mandeville who was prosecuted at the Old Bailey for working 'as one of a pair with Ann Grace (a white woman) to steal three half guineas and six shillings from John Pidduck. Grace extracted the money while Mandeville pinned the victims down.'[4]

In June 1780 a number of black men and women were involved in the Gordon Riots. What started off on Friday 2 June as a 50,000-strong march against the repeal of anti-Catholic legislation turned into one of the most destructive few days in London's history as labourers, journeymen and sailors crowded the streets and set fire to dozens of houses, chapels and prisons. The homes of Lord Mansfield and Sir John Fielding (the magistrate who bemoaned the solidarity shown to runaway blacks by the white sub-proletariat) were stripped and burned. The metropolitan constabulary was repeatedly attacked. On 6 June rioters headed to Newgate, London's oldest jail, where some of their friends were imprisoned. Among their leaders were two blacks, Benjamin Bowsey and John Glover, who helped to attack the home of

Akerman, Keeper of the Prison, with pick-axes, sledgehammers and torches. Three hundred prisoners were released, some of them hobbling away in chains. Others burned to death. It was said that jubilant rioters became so drunk on gin and wine that some fell into the flames. A contemporary print shows Bowsey and Glover as part of a mob plundering the jail and carrying furniture from Akerman's house in order to fan the fires. They were duly executed along with a 'pathetic motley' that included two gypsies, 'a demented cross-eyed beggar' and three abscess-covered climbing boys.[5] Charlotte Gardiner, a black servant reputed to be a prostitute, was also hanged for joining in the 'demolition' of a house in Tower Hill.[6]

Throughout the nineteenth century a steady trickle of Africans and Asians were arraigned by East End police courts or locked up for short spells at Coldbath Fields Prison, Horsemonger-lane Gaol and City Prison, Holloway. The majority were lascars and were prosecuted for offences ranging from petty larceny, passing counterfeit money and vagrancy, to trafficking in bhang and hashish. Living in seedy quarters, and out of pocket due to drug habits and gambling debts, the sailors often quarrelled, robbed and fought amongst themselves. They also waged war with local hooligans: 'The vicinity of the docks abounds with roughs, who view the employment of foreign labour with ill feeling, so much so that Asiatics and Africans on coming on shore are exposed to frequent insult and robbery.'[7] Despite the best efforts of city missionaries to impress Christian morality upon dockside residents, Chinese and Indian seamen were regularly imprisoned for smuggling goods such as tobacco and refusing to pay fines when detected.[8]

By the middle of the twentieth century, the heart of the black underworld had shifted westwards from Shadwell to Soho, which a contemporary writer described as 'a centre of racketeering. There are dozens of small cafés where you can "smell" the underworld as soon as you poke your head inside the door.'[9] Having compiled a vivid inventory of 1940s gangster terms – dippers, whizzers, steamers, crimps – the writer admitted:

> there are several Soho cafés which I do not care to enter without Joe Louis or the Big Five [. . .] Here are to be found gamblers, vagabonds and no-good seamen. Hogarth would have been on the beam here. Diseased-looking, scarred mongrel faces, sullen, brooding-drunk; dancers corroded by drink and disease; singers with the drug twitch to their mouths; grey-haired beggars in clothes starched with dirt; thin black girls with frightened eyes. The men sit playing cards with their hats tilted back.

There is a flash of pink gums and a curse if someone says a
word out of place.[10]

The existence of this illicit subculture is confirmed by Ernest
Marke, a Sierra Leonean who first came to this country as a
stowaway in 1917, and spent many of the following decades consorting with London's black lowlife. In his memoirs he recounts
how gun-wielding thugs populated Soho clubs in which drugs,
illegal gambling and drinking were rife: 'Every three months or
so there would be a police raid and a fine or a short prison sentence
imposed on the owners.'[11]

Mike Phillips, a historian and crime novelist of some distinction,
is one of the few black authors to have addressed this submerged
aspect of the black metropolitan past. His commentary to the
photographic book *Notting Hill In The Sixties* (1991) paints an
exhilarating if scary tableau of W11, one full of rowdy shebeens,
blues parties, prostitution rackets, psychotic landlords, gambling
joints, gunslingers, hustlers bootlegging American cigarettes and
rum and whisky: 'Notting Hill was a well established offshoot of
the Soho vice empires, and while many immigrants deeply
resented their propinquity with what they saw as vice and immorality, others plunged enthusiastically into the life they found
there.'[12] He quotes local inhabitants who describe the area as a
frontier town, a metropolitan Klondike: 'it was the Caribbean
immigrants who took hold of Notting Hill, and ironically gave
it its contemporary character, its peculiar cachet. The raffish
undertow.'[13]

The element of romanticization here is unsurprising. Urban
writers have always envied criminals their mastery of the city.
Rogues, gangsters, hustlers – these people trade in secret know-
ledges, occult metropolises. They know the back-streets, the side-
entrances, alternative routes, the paths less travelled. A liar and a

dissimulator, the criminal is a master of narrative: he'll tell you whatever story he wants you to hear and he has ways of making you listen. Like the con artist or dodgy trader, he has street-smart ingenuity, the ability to create revenue streams where none previously existed. He distils the essence of the city: to generate money – brutally, speedily, unfairly. The anonymity and disconti- nuities of urban life, rather than being sources of sorrow, are opportunities; he can hide in them, attack from there. All the time he carries on amassing knowledge: developing contacts, jagging between rich and poor, between the corridors of power and the no-go underbelly. Race is no barrier: he'll deal with anyone when money's at issue. A stop-start, jump-cut life. A Zelig-like trickster.

Along with Edgar Manning, the most famous black criminal in London over the last hundred years was Michael X. He was born Michael de Freitas in Trinidad in 1933 to a Portuguese shopkeeper and a mother who later emigrated to London where she ran a large brothel. He sailed to Tiger Bay as a cargo seaman, doing stints as a mugger, pimp and drug pusher before a botched post-office raid led him to flee to London. His reputation as a hardman endeared him to the slum-landlord Peter Rachman, who hired him in the late fifties as a rent-collector, a job which allowed him to learn the rudiments of media manipulation: he got into the habit of tipping off newspapers at fifty pounds a throw about which houses were being used as brothels. The ensuing publicity triggered police raids and led many disgusted occupants to leave, at which point de Freitas would move in new residents for a sizeable commission. A constant hustler, he went to sea again but was jailed for stealing the ship's paint supplies. On his release he set himself up as a West London drugs baron. Street-sharp, an eloquent dandy who swooshed around town in a red Ford Thunderbird, he soon became well-known among the many writers and painters who hung out in Shepherd's Bush and on the Portobello Road, and for whom he embodied the cool, transgressive sass that Norman Mailer in *The White Negro* (1957) had claimed white bohos habitually seek from black people.

Eager to profit from the rise of colour-consciousness which followed decolonization and the emergence of the American Civil Rights movement, de Freitas changed his name to Michael X and in 1965 created the Racial Adjustment Action Society whose acronym was a Jamaican term for a sanitary towel as well as a popular expletive. It was this vacuously militant Black Power organization – its membership of 150 or so was roughly 60,000 less than officially claimed – that helped Michael X convince the gullible media that he was the chief spokesman and theoretician of a soon-to-be-insurgent black Britain. From then on he was rarely out of the news: encouraged by Alexander Trocchi and William Burroughs, he penned execrable verse, topical examples of which he sent to Chairman Mao who rapidly telexed back his response; when Muhammed Ali came to London for his heavyweight championship fight with Henry Cooper, Michael X escorted him to West Indian playgrounds and community centres in Notting Hill; changing his name once more to Michael Abdul Malik, he wrote pro-sex, pro-dope, pro-revolution copy for hip underground magazines such as *International Times*. He also published an autobiography (ghosted by Stephen John, author of the pornographic *Roman Orgy* for the Olympia Press), and lectured at All Souls.

His most ambitious venture, launched after spending 1967 in jail for inciting racial hatred, was the establishment of the Black House, a complex in Holloway Road run by and for black people, which included a theatre, barber's shop, museum, a place for Muslim worship and a supermarket specializing in West Indian and African products. He solicited donations from US entertainers such as Sammy Davis Jr and the comedian Dick Gregory. He also guilt-tripped John Lennon by claiming that, 'You have stolen the rhythms of the black people you knew in Liverpool'.[14] Soon Yoko Ono was presenting him with £10,000 in £10 notes. Malik also offered Lennon a pair of Muhammed Ali's bloodied shorts in return for a box containing locks of the singer's hair. The plan was to sell them to Beatles fans with the proceeds going to the Black House. This involved far too much petty organizational

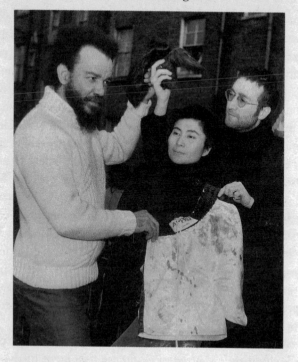

work for Malik and, predictably, his vanity establishment ran out of funds. In 1971 he fled to Trinidad, having been charged with robbing and menacing a Jewish businessman in London.

One of Malik's cronies was Hakim Jamal, a black Muslim with a history of mental instability who, like him, had a penchant for those same white aristocratic women he vituperated from public soapboxes. His lover, Gail Ann Benson, was the daughter of former Tory MP, Captain Sir Leonard Plugge, and a descendant of Sir John Hawkyns, the first English slave trafficker. When Malik set up a commune, the couple joined (Jamal had persuaded Benson that Malik was God). Her growing scepticism riled Malik, who became increasingly tetchy and paranoid. He believed she was a spy and had her killed. Three years later, in May 1975, he was hanged in Port of Spain's Royal Gaol.

Michael X's story is fascinating, as those of con-merchants tend to be. Like all hucksters and charlatans he spent much of his life twisting and shapeshifting. What's especially fascinating is the extent to which he managed to maximize returns on his racial background. The black criminal, according to many autobiographical accounts, is merely enacting the logic of his social marginalization. 'You treat me like an outsider, a criminal? Very well, I'll become one! You say I do not belong here? OK, I'll behave like an interloper!' Trevor Hercules, a former criminal, claimed in *Labelled A Black Villain* (1989) that, 'there was a definite relationship between violence and the black community – a relationship born of frustration at their miserable existence'.[15] Perhaps this is self-serving. He certainly strikes a note of self-satisfaction when recounting what he was like as a teenager growing up in Ladbroke Grove: 'I had an aura of violence, it was in the way I walked, talked, looked.'[16]

An explicit attempt to justify black urban crime appeared in Chris Mullard's *Black Britain* (1973), the first book to be written by a black person born and bred in this country (he later went on to become a professor at the University of London's Institute of Education):

> For us crime has a lure which is more significant than most people think. It is a way of getting our own back on society; it is a way of gaining appreciation from other rejected colleagues whatever their colour; it is a way of proving to ourselves that we are worthy of self-esteem, able to do things and use our talents as well as our next partner in crime. Finally it is a way of surviving, protesting, and forging an identity for ourselves. Warped though this may be, in crime we are equal, we are respected.[17]

One could contest this statement on various grounds: historically, the black propensity towards crime has been no greater than that of other ethnic groups or social classes in London; employing the unnuanced 'we' is highly presumptuous; crime may elicit respect in some quarters, but, on the whole, it attracts widespread opprobrium and has led to whole swathes of the black community – especially young men between the ages of fifteen and thirty-five – being viewed as muggers and hoodlums.

Nonetheless, Mullard's sentiments are interesting because they appear in a book that critiques what its blurb calls 'official race policies, white race experts, and white race institutions'. In other words, *Black Britain* is a work both of political analysis and of social protest. Similarly, all the books to be looked at in this chapter not only chart unlawful activities by black working people, but can also be read as works of political dissent. They are covert manifestos, as much as social reportage. Robert Wedderburn, Linton Kwesi Johnson, Salman Rushdie and Victor Headley all depict and, at some level, *revel in* less varnished black urban experiences over the last two centuries. These authors have not necessarily read each other's work, and this is no wilful, self-reflexive tradition. However their texts all deal sympathetically with – and are expressions of – a disreputable, oppositional, dissenting, and sometimes criminal black metropolis. Tropes that recur throughout their work include a strident masculinity; the use of apocalyptic and eschatological imagery and language; urban entropy; music as both a soundtrack and a harbinger of metropolitan meltdown; rioting.

The father of Robert Wedderburn (c.1761–c.1835) was a Scottish doctor and plantation-holder in Jamaica who sold his son's mother, an African house-slave called Rosanna, when she was five months pregnant. Robert was adopted by his grandmother, 'Talkee Amy', a magic woman 'who earned her livelihood by retailing all sorts of goods, hard or soft, smuggled or not, for the merchants of Kingston'.[18] Around 1778 he joined the merchant navy, coming to England for the first time, where he soon made his way to the rookeries of St Giles where he 'likely became part of a subculture of London's "blackbirds" [. . .] who eked out a living by their wit, strength, agility and cunning – as musicians, entertainers, beggars, thieves and labourers'.[19] In 1785 he travelled to Edinburgh to see his father but was rebuffed; his father 'had the inhumanity to threaten to send me to gaol if I troubled him'.[20] A year later Wedderburn converted to Methodism after hearing a Wesleyan preacher at Seven Dials promising divine mercy to all men who repented their sinful pasts. By the 1790s he'd rejoined the navy, enlisting as a top-station hand aboard a privateer. Wedderburn's lack of respect for authority in later years may have originated in this period during which he toiled in wretched conditions alongside jack tars who were savagely exploited at sea, but still faced the likelihood of penury on being demobbed.[21] Little is known about his activities during the first decade of the nineteenth century. Living amongst the capital's dispossessed – lascars, Irish immigrants, fugitives – in St Giles, it's no surprise that he had at least one spell inside Coldbath Fields prison. He was also charged with theft in 1813, and four years later nearly prosecuted for stealing from a Government-contracted tailor. An intelligence report written in 1818 described him as 'a jobbing Taylor sitting in a kind of bulk near St Matthews Church where he patches clothes and vends cheap seditious publications'.[22]

By this time Wedderburn had become heavily involved with London's Spencean movement whose central tenets included the expropriation of private land, religious toleration, the abolition of slavery, and 'the right of all peoples to freedom of movement, association and trade'.[23] Meetings were held at taverns and inns such as The Nag's Head, The Mulberry Tree and The Minging Jesus in London's seedier districts – Spitalfields, Clerkenwell, Bethnal Green. They were especially popular with sailors, tailors, artisans, and the unemployed. Wedderburn helped to devise debating topics, pressed members to pay their fees, and was himself celebrated for his fiery invective. He also founded and edited two magazines, *Forlorn Hope* and *The Axe Laid to the Root*, which he helped to distribute.

Towards the end of spring in 1818, Wedderburn and a fellow Spencean, Thomas Evans, took out a licence to operate a dissenting chapel in a large basement back-room at 6 Archer Street, a small Haymarket laneway. They called themselves 'Christian Philanthropists', sometimes 'Enquirers after Truth', and met three times a week. Wedderburn quickly became dissatisfied with the venue's lack of atmosphere however. At the end of the year he left the Archer Street chapel taking both its benches and some of its more militant members with him. A furious Evans ran outside and a fight broke out between the two Spenceans that had to be stopped by a local constable.

Wedderburn opened his own chapel in April 1819. It consisted of two back-rooms on the corner of Hopkins and Brewer Streets in Soho, and its main room – 'a ruinous loft' which could hold 300 people – was reached by a stepladder.[24] The behaviour here was far rowdier and gleefully demotic than at Archer Street. The meetings were punctuated with singing, toasting, and speeches sufficiently diabolical to terrify witless the Government spies who frequently attended. Eventually Wedderburn was arraigned for blasphemy and sentenced to two years imprisonment in Dorchester Gaol.

Released in 1823, he started to work for the former Quaker,

William Dugdale, who was about to begin 'a long career as a
publisher of infidel, libertine and ultimately pornographic literature'.[25] He continued to frequent and speak at Spencean haunts
in Moorfields and Soho and, in 1828, presented himself as the
founder of a sect of 'Christian Diabolists', or 'Devil Worshippers',
at the New Assembly Room at 12 White's Alley, Chancery Lane.
The audience for radical Spenceanism had dwindled during the

course of the decade and Wedderburn's lectures were unsuccessful. He turned, like many 'rough artisans' of the period, to running a brothel in Featherbed Lane. In 1830 he was sentenced to two years hard labour at Newgate. Little is known about the final five years of his life.

Tracing the full course of Wedderburn's life and thought is fraught with difficulties. Much of the biographical information about him stems from reports written by Government spies and agents, and must be treated with scepticism. Only a fraction of his journalistic output has survived. There's another crucial complication: he received little education during his childhood and was only partially literate. Much of the material he produced between 1819 and 1821 was secretly ghosted by George Cannon, 'a down-at-heel solicitor, preacher and free-thinker, as well as a fringe revolutionary and putative pornographer'.[26] It may even be Cannon speaking when Wedderburn claims to be 'incapable of delivering my sentiments in an elegant and polished manner'.[27] Nonetheless, a letter written by him has been exhumed by the scholar Iain McCalman, as well as intelligence reports which detail his oratorical style; from these documents it's possible to discern his authentic voice which, harsh and combative, confirms Wedderburn as the founder of a dissenting tradition of literature written about London by black people.

Much eighteenth-century black metropolitan literature is characterized by a sense that teeth are being clenched, tongues bitten, that spleen is being studiously unvented. Gronniosaw, Sancho and Equiano felt they had to couch their criticism of slavery, English foreign policy and the lax morality of their fellow Londoners in guarded terms. They all knew there were limits to the severity of their invective: Gronniosaw's and Equiano's works were published for polemical ends – respectively, Methodist propaganda and the Anti-Slavery Society; it would have been political suicide for them to have antagonized their overwhelmingly middle-class constituencies. Perhaps they tried: their texts certainly underwent a degree of editorial revision: at least one self-reflexive racial comment in Sancho's *Letters* was posthumously interpolated ('Blessed times for a poor Blacky grocer to hang or drown in').[28] It may be significant that he and Equiano both quote – with varying degrees of accuracy – a dictum first voiced in Colley Cibber's *Love's Last Shift* (1696): 'He, who cannot stem his anger's tide,/Doth a wild horse without a bridle ride.'[29] Elsewhere, Sancho denounces the slave trade in a letter to Jack Wingrave only to stop suddenly: 'But enough – it is a subject that sours my blood – and I am sure will not please the friendly bent of your social affections.'[30]

The context in which Wedderburn wrote was rather different. Firstly, his minimal education meant he wasn't versed in the polished vocabularies, lexical formations and literary genres which gave Sancho's and Equiano's work respectability. Secondly, the subscription lists of those two authors included aristocrats, senior politicians and men of letters; Wedderburn, in contrast, targeted labourers and artisans who would have been unimpressed by mellifluous polysyllabics and allusions to Dryden and Pope. Even though black eighteenth-century writers used oral modes of address (sermons for instance), their work was still far more literary than anything Wedderburn could have produced. He performed at Spencean taverns where speakers who used books or prepared speeches were shouted down by ale-sozzled regulars.[31] Their harsh lives, the lowly social settings, and the incendiary nature of the topics up for debate made them warm to rhetorical styles that were direct and knuckle-hard.

Wedderburn didn't let them down: his speech at The Nag's

Head on the American treatment of Indians was described by a Government agent as, 'the most blasphemous, inflammatory, incoherent harangue I ever heard'.[32] Another claimed 'this Mans Language is so Horridly Blasphemous at Archer St every Tuesday afternoon – that the Spenceans themselves are apprehensive of a Prosecution'.[33] In August 1819 the Home Secretary, Lord Sidmouth, wrote to the Prince Regent about the 'notorious firebrand, Wedderburne'.[34]

These descriptions would have pleased him. He believed language was a weapon, something that should be used to cudgel and smite those who promoted the existing social order. When he heard that his white brother had publicly abused his mother he announced that, 'I am forced to take up arms in my own defence'.[35] He liked to come up with military analogies to justify his muscular invective: 'I must give vent, I have commenced my carear, the press is my engine of destruction. I come not to make peace; my fury shall be felt by princes, bidding defiance to pride and prejudice.'[36] There's clearly much bluster here, yet 'must' is an interesting word; it suggests physical compulsion, an almost orgasmic appetite for attack. It also highlights Wedderburn's inability to couch his radical sentiments in honeyed, emollient language. Not that he wanted to: in his memoirs he claimed that he'd inherited his violent temper from his oppressed mother – 'yes, and I glory in her *rebellious* disposition'.[37] The state had made him what he was. Its violence had brutalized him, and now he was turning that brutality back on its creators. (That violent times demand violent creative responses is a notion that also appears in the work of Kwesi Johnson and Rushdie.)

Wedderburn was a vulgarian of the highest order. He loved earthy, excretory language. He wasn't the first black writer to talk about bodily functions – Sancho wrote a funny account of how a fat couple's child had pissed on him in a London stagecoach.

Nowhere in the *Letters*, though, is there so gross and venomous a passage as Wedderburn's description of how his father had slept with most of his Jamaican household's female staff. If one of them became pregnant, 'why, it was an acquisition which might one day fetch something in the market, like a horse or pig in Smithfield. In short, amongst his own slaves my father was a perfect parish bull.'[38] The social and political reality these lines express is sickeningly vile, all the more so for Wedderburn's coarsely pungent language. This is no modulated lament for slavery's routine commodification of humans; the reference to London's own markets makes this a horribly untheoretical and localized piece of invective. It wasn't a one-off performance; a few years earlier *The Times* had reported a speech Wedderburn had made at Finsbury Market Place as being 'fraught with the beauties of Billingsgate slang'.[39]

Such bucking vigour is also seen in an engraving by George Cruikshank which shows Wedderburn in a London tavern mounting a table and waving his fist furiously at Robert Owen, a man he suspected to be a 'tool of the landholders'.[40] It wasn't uncommon at Spencean debating taverns to drink toasts to 'the barren land of our country [being] manured with the blood of our Tyrantry'.[41] Spy reports from the months leading up to Peterloo in 1819 record that Wedderburn constantly invoked armed resistance and offered 'to be placed in the front rank' and 'martyred' as an example to younger radicals.[42]

The violence that features in all black dissenting accounts of London is not unconnected to their authors' rather studied obsessions with male pride and self-assertion. They were probably just reflecting the rage in the souls of many of their unlettered brothers. After all, for much of the seventeenth and eighteenth centuries black Londoners weren't regarded as proper men. They were slaves who could be purchased, auctioned and bequeathed. They were treated as pets or exotic interior furnishings. Even anti-slavery propaganda showed them kneeling, shackled and abasedly crying, 'Am I not a Man? And a Brother?'

Early black writing about London often reads like a catalogue of slights and challenges to male pride. Gronniosaw was coerced into giving a City tradesman half a crown for showing him the way to Whitefield's Tabernacle; Sancho faced racial abuse near Vauxhall Gardens and found stagecoach drivers keen to pass bad coins off on him; Equiano reacted badly to having his authority undermined during the preparations for the Sierra Leone Expedition in 1786; even Jamaican-born William Davidson, one of the five working-class radicals hanged for planning the Cato Street Conspiracy of 1819, was accused of molesting women and schoolchildren.[43] All of these men relied on handouts to survive in the metropolis. So did Wedderburn. Yet he strikes modern readers as more screwface and brawny than the slave autobiographers who came before him. His physical frame was squat and muscular. His debating style was self-confident and rabble-rousing. His language was taut and demotic. The fact that Wedderburn was poor throughout his life, and sought financial assistance from his father in 1785 and, some years later, from his brother, doesn't detract from his image of cocksure autonomy. As a historical character, an orator, and as a writer, Wedderburn embodies the kind of black Londoner – outlaw, shot-caller, ruff-ryder swaggering between portentousness and preposterousness – that Johnson, Headley and, to a lesser extent, Rushdie are all fascinated by.

McCalman argues that the 'Masculine fraternities had been integral to [Wedderburn's] life as a sailor, tailor and criminal', and that he felt an identical camaraderie in Spencean debating clubs.[44] He goes on to suggest that in the tense political atmosphere of late 1819 Wedderburn increasingly exploited the masculine vanity of his followers in order to incite them to acts of rebellion against the state: 'He claimed to be goading his sons to violence by taunting them with their degradation and their cowardice in enduring it.'[45]

Wedderburn's obsession with virility is best seen in *The Horrors of Slavery* (1824). Here he argues against his brother who denied that their father had deceitfully purchased his mother, Rosanna:

> Let my brother COLVILLE deny this if he can; let him bring me into court, and I will prove what I here advance. To this present hour, while I think of the treatment of my mother, my blood boils in my veins; and, had I not some connections for which I was bound to live, I should long ago have taken ample revenge of my father.[46]

Wedderburn's is the language of the fairground prize-fighter. Feisty and roughneck, he'll take on all comers. Slave traders and masters often sundered African fathers from their sons; here, Wedderburn wishes he could rip apart what ties remain. In this passage, and the one that follows, we see how his life is a series of face-offs, of set-piece duels against whichever rival has newly appeared on the scene. There's a fearlessness, partly theatrical, but genuine nonetheless:

> I have to say, that if *my dear brother* means to *show fight* before the Nobs at Westminster, I shall soon give him an opportunity, as I mean to publish my whole history in a cheap pamphlet [...] I have now fairly given him the challenge; let him meet it if he dare.[47]

The pugilistic sparring of the first extract is here made explicit: 'dear brother' is both sarcastic and carries a suggestion of Colville's effeteness. He also introduces a class dimension in referring to the nobs at Westminster. All told, he fairly brims with testosterone. Such conviction is clear in the way Wedderburn talks about himself. In *The Axe Laid to the Root* he claims that, 'Your humble servant being a Spencean Philanthropist, is proud to wear the name of a madman; if the landholders please, they may call me a traitor, or one who is possessed with the spirit of Beelzebub'.[48] Just as he sought to instil panic in the ruling classes with his violent rhetoric, here Wedderburn takes pleasure in shocking the bourgeoisie. He likes to revel in his reputation as social leper and public enemy. Consigned by colour, class and political beliefs to a life of hardship, Wedderburn gets his revenge by becoming the embodiment of all that his enemies fear. Their hatred confirms to him the accuracy of his social critique for, as Victor Headley's novels show, prestige in the urban underground is won by being seen as wicked – the ultimate gangsta, the baddest of the bad.

Only someone steeped in religious language and imagery from an early age would have relished being labelled as diabolic. Wedderburn was often referred to during the second decade of the nineteenth century as the Devil's Engineer.[49] He delighted in another Spencean nickname – 'Black Prince' – which invokes him as a lord of malignity.[50] Many of the dissenting authors to be looked at in this chapter couch their revolutionary rhetoric using Biblical metaphors and allusions. Wedderburn was partly influenced by his 1786 conversion to Methodism which 'was inclined to nurture eschatological hopes and ideas in its early, less stable days'.[51] Defending himself against the charge of blasphemy in 1819 he argued that Christ was a 'Radical Reformer [. . .] this much I know by the same Book that he was born of the very poor parents, who like us felt with him the same as we now feel, and he says I'll turn'.[52] What's more, Wedderburn's calls for popular rebellion and mass uprisings were often expressed chiliastically: 'Prepare for flight, ye planters, for the fate of St Domingo awaits you. Get ready your blood hounds, the allies which you employed against the Maroons'; 'My heart glows with revenge, and cannot forgive. Repent ye Christians, for flogging my aged grandmother before my face, when she was accused of witchcraft by a silly European.'[53]

Wedderburn treated the Bible instrumentally, rather than with reverence or piety. The tendency for establishment clergy to be pious was one reason why he felt they should be 'totally annihilated, suppressed, and abolished'.[54] He compared them to old and established shopkeepers 'who had become *well tiled, warm, fat*, and *saucy*, who in fact cared very little whether his customers came or staid away'; he preferred dissenting preachers who 'delivered with zeal and energy, and directed to the passions instead of the understanding'.[55]

He was equally interested in the Old and New Testaments. The Christ he liked to invoke was a martial figure, a wrathful equalizer. He saw Biblical characters as raw recruits, fellow travellers, potential comrades – and didn't stint from showering them with abuse when they failed to display the levels of radical insurgency he demanded. He promised that Lord Sidmouth and 'jumping fiddling monkey George Canning *will lose their Heads* – they tell us to be quiet like that *bloody spooney Jesus Christ* who like a *Bloody Fool* tells us when we get a slap on one side of the Face turn gently round and ask them to smack the other'.[56]

The impiety of such outbursts is partly fuelled by Spenceanism's exaltation of Reason. Wedderburn, like the creed which had changed his life, believed that large chunks of the Bible were ludicrously muddled and contradictory, and couched his criticism in typically vigorous language:

> Jesus Christ said no man had ever seen God, then what a damned old liar Moses must have been for he tells us he could run about and see God in every Bush [...] then there was Balaam's Ass, oh yes that spoke, and yet they tell us God put the words into his Mouth; then I suppose God got into the Jack Ass – then there was the pretty story they tell us about the Witch of Endor.[57]

Wedderburn, as can be seen here, never could resist a scatological reference: he liked talking about the noise emanating from Balaam's Ass, as well as about the Witch of Endor having 'slip't wind'.[58] Such demotic gusto, popular with his mob audiences, was successfully cited as evidence of his blasphemy in May 1820. No doubt he was aware of the strategic value of using vulgar and idiomatic language – it bolstered his reputation as the Spencean underworld's most fearsome orator. A spy reported that he 'ridiculed Scripture very much. He said he had been endeavouring to offend that they might ring it in the ears of Kings, princes, Lords and commons.'[59] A key feature of all black dissenting literature is the self-conscious desire to be regarded as an author who says the unsayable. This creates a problem: on the one hand, black London authors write teleologically, to critique and register their dissatisfaction with the existing urban regime which they hope to see improved in a variety of ways; at the same time, these critiques often lose focus and become subsumed by the authors' excessive delight in the rhetoric of apocalypse, vengeance and millennialism. The constant invocation of panic and entropy can lead writers to paean conflagration and disorder, though in real life this rarely results in the kind of social amelioration they purport to seek.

Wedderburn's life and rebellions were almost completely forgotten up until his rediscovery in the 1980s. It's fair, then, to say that the most well-known exponent of black urban millennialism is the poet Linton Kwesi Johnson. He was born in rural Jamaica in 1952 and joined his mother in Brixton eleven years later. While a student at Tulse Hill Secondary School he signed up for the youth wing of the Black Panthers and later took a degree in sociology at Goldsmiths' College, University of London. Much of the poetry Johnson wrote in the 1970s marries that discipline's interest in contemporary social structures to the didactic fervour of the Black Power movement.

After 1973 he became a regular contributor to *Race Today*, a journal, originally issued by the Institute of Race Relations in May 1969, which had recently shed its rather academic and non-political approach in favour of an engaged and avowedly polemical stance. Issues now typically contained pieces on police brutality, denunciations of Governmental immigration controls, and reports on local industrial disputes.[60] Johnson's much-reprinted poem 'Five Nights of Bleeding' first appeared between two articles dealing with black women's liberation movements and a historical overview of 'The Deportation Business'.[61]

The savage bleakness of Johnson's early poetry (also a feature of plays by Mustapha Matura and Caryl Phillips) stemmed directly from the dismal prospects open to London's young black population in the 1970s. Over 300,000 manufacturing jobs disappeared from the capital between 1971 and 1976, contributing to the rundown of inner-city areas such as Lambeth, which became characterized by high unemployment, long housing waiting lists, and sink estates.[62] Disproportionate numbers of black people lived in these districts, and it was hardly surprising if in the wake of Enoch Powell's 1968 'Rivers of Blood' speech many of them felt increasingly soured by life in London. According to a contemporary journalist, 'West Indian parties used to be gay. They gave off a sharp joy, snatched sometimes, from the edges of despair. [. . .] But tonight is a different generation, the young, black and English. Immigrants have a past, and therefore the implicit possibility of a future; for the children, there is only now.'[63] Many of these second-generation West Indians refused, unlike their parents, to do what they called 'slave labour' or 'shit jobs'. In 'Yout Rebels', Johnson describes this new breed of blacks as being on the

> rough scene,
> breakin away
> takin the day,
> sayin to capital neva
> movin forwud hevva.[64]

Johnson's socialist politics advertise themselves here in his play on the double meanings of 'capital': (exploitative) capitalist practices; (shoddy) metropolitan governance.

Throughout this period relationships between the police and younger members of London's black communities were fast degenerating. Rucks were almost a daily occurrence. A number of landmark confrontations took place: the Mangrove Trial of 1970 in which nine black people were acquitted followed a pitched battle between the Metropolitan Police and Ladbroke Grove residents who objected to the constant drug raids on a local café; there were further run-ins at the Metro Club in Notting Hill (1971), and at Stockwell and Cricklewood (both 1974), before the riots at the 1976 Notting Hill Carnival. All these were light skirmishes in comparison to the Brixton Riots of 1981.[65]

Many of Johnson's poems address this catalogue of poor relations between the police and sections of the black community. He'd been beaten up himself by three officers when he was just a teenager.[66] In 'Yout Scene' he shows how police would often interrupt social gatherings in Brixton with savage force:

> when nite come
> policeman run dem dung;
> beat dem dung a grug,
> kick dem ass[67]

It's this inability to just get on with things, to carry out day-to-day activities – holding parties, walking along the streets, driving a decent car – without being hassled and hounded that damages both black psychology and metropolitan race relations so severely. In 'Sonny's Lettah (Anti-Sus poem)', Johnson recounts:

> It woz di miggle a di rush howah
> wen everybady jus' a hus'le an' a bus'le
> fi goh home fi dem evenin' showah;
> mi an' Jim stan-up
> waitin' pan a bus,
> nat causin' no fus',
> wen all an a sudden
> a police van pull-up.[68]

Innocence means nothing. Black people are guilty – of being black. Johnson feels no compunction about advocating violence as a legitimate response to police brutality. In 'All We Doin' Is Defendin' he joyfully anticipates the moment when 'de Special Patrol/will fall/like a wall force doun'.[69] Unlike the first generation of Caribbean immigrants, Johnson's characters don't button their lips or turn the other cheek when faced with hostility or aggression. They don't even go in for the crafty revenge depicted in Selvon's short story 'Obeah In The Grove' (1957), where a group of West Indians searching for lodgings discover that they've been exploited by their landlord, and, in retaliation, place a voodoo spell on him. Johnson's solution is direct and forceful, fighting fire with fire: 'choose yu weapon dem,/quick!/all wi need is bakkles an bricks an sticks'.[70] Elsewhere, in 'Street 66', he approvingly quotes the boasts of the reggae DJ, I-Roy: ' "any policeman come yah/will get some righteous raas klaat licks,/yea man, whole heap a kicks" '.[71]

The relish for violence in these two passages, so explicit and visceral, was also present in Wedderburn's speeches which salivated with revolutionary anticipation. This maddening fever seems to infect the bloodstream of every young black person who walks the London streets – 'vibratin violence/is how wi move/rockin wid green riddim'.[72] It also comes, though, from the sense of imminent urban meltdown and accelerating degeneration that many young black Britons felt throughout the 1970s.

> heavy heavy terror
> on the rampage . . .
> o dont you worry
> it is no near . . .
> fratricide is only
> the first phase . . .
>
> yes, the violence of the oppressor runnin wild;
> them pick up the yout them fe suss;
> powell prophesying a black, a black, a black conquest;
> and the National Front is on the rampage
> making fire bombs fe burn we.[73]

In this poem, 'Doun De Road', dread, terror, fury and violence stream like molten lava down London's streets and walkways. The capital is out of control, a place where bloodletting and mayhem are routine, and where both the rhetoric and tactics of warfare now operate. Johnson foresees pavements – rather than Powell's rivers – of blood. It's a sickening vision of the metropolis – literally, for it damages and deforms the mind and body. Johnson's characters know that their skin colour is a source of hatred and contempt, making them vulnerable to physical violence if they leave their homes. This insight asphyxiates them: not only are their freedoms limited according to class, education, wealth and geography, but they are immured by their own flesh. They feel a remorseless compression, psychological incarceration. What can they do? Some go mad. Others quell their anguish – if only partially – by lashing out. The poem 'Rage' makes the connection between the physical pain suffered by contemporary blacks and, in a far more savage form, their plantation forebears. It also hints at the shame

and mental pain induced by contemplating black history –
'Imprisoned in memory/of the whip's sting'.[74] The only release is
the hope that

> Soon some white one will stroll by,
> and strike he will to smash
> the prison wall of his passion
> and let his stifled rage run free.[75]

In 'Doun De Road' Johnson claims that 'the violence damming
up inside/and the violence damming up inside' to such an extent
that

> in the heat
> of the anguish
> you jus turn:
> turn on your brother
> an yu lick him
> an yu lash him
> an stab him
> an kill him[76]

In 'Voices of the Living and the Dead', Death (here personified)
goads those alive to stir themselves and fight for political and
spiritual emancipation:

> Pain pulsing with my blood
> slowly curdling on my brain.
> Death is harsh my brother
> Mine was both harsh and sweet.[77]

The passage above prickles and oozes with relish. It recalls Wedderburn's belief in the nobility of death and self-sacrifice. Johnson
suggests that any corporeal suffering which results from a con-

certed political uprising is a price well worth paying. Death's words serve as an ennobling and orgasmic expiration.

Violence isn't the only motif that Johnson and Wedderburn share: music is also important to both of them. Johnson is commonly cited as the first major dub poet; backed by the Bovell Band, he recorded many of his early poems for vinyl release. 'Voices of the Living and the Dead' was originally performed at the Keskidee Centre in Islington accompanied by drums, bass guitar and flute. By infusing his verse with dub's rhythms and textures, he blurs the distinction between literary and oral art. A socialist and advocate of black solidarity, Johnson has always been keen to reach the broadest possible audience. He even runs a small but successful label – LKJ Records.

Dub and roots reggae were important sources of dynamic religious imagery and metaphors. They helped Johnson to transmit the brooding ambience of London street culture in the 1970s. Rastafarians, as one contemporary journalist noted, could not help but invoke the 'Old Testament language of apocalypse and Armageddon and Revelation. They make Shadrach, Meshach and Abednego or Lot's wife sound as if they happened the day before yesterday, in Jones Town, Kingston.'[78.] Reggae in that decade brimmed with references to hellfire, retribution, thunder, false prophets and Valleys of Death. Record buyers may not have subscribed to such a belief system; most of those flocking to Peckings in W12 to buy a copy of Willie Williams's 'Armagiddeon Time' probably just dug its riddims and would have struggled to articulate a lucid eschatology of their own. Still, the lyrics of such records both mirrored and exacerbated the feelings of panic, tension, dread and the idea of imminent conflagration that marked much black urban culture of the period. Johnson reflects these feelings in poems such as 'Klassical Dub (For The Upsetters)':

> dis is a dreadful bad bass bounce
> blood a leap an pulse a pounce
>
> riddim cuttin sharp[79]

and

> FIRE FE DE WICKED
> venjance on de day
> FIRE FE DE WICKED
> brimstones in deir bones I say
> FIRE FE DE WICKED
> blast dem cast dem doun deh.[80]

Similarly, in 'Dread Beat An' Blood' the volume, cavernous depth and echolalic texture of dub music detonate a terrifying violence: 'Music blazing, sounding, thumping fire, blood./brothers and sisters rocking, stopping, rocking;/music breaking out, bleeding out, bleeding out, thumping out fire: burning.'[81]

Reggae was always seen as a rebel music. Springing from the slums of Kingston, Jamaica, it offered ghetto sonics, urban disaffection. It was less uptempo, more downbeat than ska and rocksteady, the buoyant Caribbean musical forms from which it had developed. The 1970s were straitened, recessionary times. Reggae invoked a militancy and insurrection that appealed to confused, angry young men. Song titles tell the story: Marley's 'Get Up, Stand Up', Delroy Washington's 'Streets of Ladbroke Grove', Tubby Cat Kelly's 'Don't Call Us No Immigrants'.[82] Johnson incites uprising in 'Fite Dem Back', as well as 'Five Nights of Bleeding', in which he savours the prospect of a 'righteous, righteous war' against racists in the Babylonian metropolis.[83] In 'Reggae Sounds', Johnson claims that this music has a dual political function: first, its timbre and lyrics embody a critique of the black past ('bass history is a moving/is a hurting black history'[84]);

secondly, it strives for a redemptive future, pressure drops, a social and political unshackling:

> flame-rhythm of the time of turning,
> measuring the time for bombs and for burning.

> Slow drop. make stops. move forward.
> dig doun to the root of the pain;
> shape it into violence for the people,
> they will know what to do, they will do it.[85]

Johnson's decision to use reggae rhythms and language, and to dedicate particular poems to vocalists, or toasters, such as Big Youth and I-Roy, endorses its status as London's most dissenting and anti-establishment musical form in the mid-1970s, but is also an attempt to mainline similar anger into his own poetry.

Many of Johnson's poems also depict reggae's social setting – the crammed, suffocating world of the South London 'blues'. These were parties at which hundreds of black young Londoners would pack into houses in residential streets, and, squashed up tight with very little room to move – yet alone to dance – soaked in the ganga, sweat and the bass-heavy tunes quaking forth from the massively amplified reggae sound systems. The volume of these all-night 'shebeens' often led to complaints from neighbours which in turn led to run-ins with the police. Too much of a too muchness: righteously incensed Rastafarology, tension and psychosis from days spent pounding Babylon's streets (which these parties were meant to ease), the threat of cops storming in – the snatched pleasure and heady violence of these nights are caught in 'Bass Culture (For Big Yout)': 'muzik of blood/black reared/ pain rooted/heart geared'; 'an is a whole heappa/passion a gather/ like a frightful form/like a righteous harm/giving off wild like is madness'.[86] The 'lick and lash' of the syllables, as they've been described, accumulate and aggregate here.[87] The lines are brusque, jabbing and accusatory. The tremor of dub's bass sounds, its cavernous and rumbling undulations, induce a thirst for change and upheaval:

> for the time is nigh
> when passion gather high
> an the beat jus lash
> when the wall mus smash,
> and the beat will shiff
> as the culture allta
> when oppression scatta.[88]

Roots reggae was certainly not the sole authentic expression of black Londoners during the 1970s. It was often seen as rather po-faced and formulaic. Too much dread, not enough joy. Most black kids weren't even Rastas. Even after the Island-backed campaign to win rock fans over to Bob Marley's freshly remastered LPs, and even after punk groups such as The Clash, The Slits and PiL toured the country with reggae bands as support acts, roots reggae had a cultural resonance far in excess of its limited commercial appeal. Explaining his adolescent love for American soul, film-maker and theorist Isaac Julien has argued that, 'Reggae was more tied up with black nationalism and certain rigidities of sex and race – tough masculine left politics'.[89] By 1980 the harsh didacticism of roots had been supplanted by a softer and more romantic genre, lover's rock, which was especially attractive to black women.

The use of dub aesthetics ensures that Kwesi Johnson's London is a men-only environment. Women make only two appearances in his first four collections: in 'Double Skank', a 'likkle sista' doesn't 'check' for 'bredda Buzza'[90]; 'Sonny's Lettah' deals with a black youth's arrest and death in police custody, and is addressed to his mother. In both poems the women are defined by their relationship to men – object of Buzza's desire, Sonny's mother; neither is vocal, yet alone substantial. Inspired by Rastafarianism's love of Old Testament imagery, Johnson often portrays London's black male population in Biblical and martial terms: 'we young lions roaring rage'[91]; the poem 'Wi A Warriyah (For Rasta Love)'[92]; 'o ye sons an dautas of affliction, o ye warriyahs be,/till yu site de rite tune for de to go to make a show,/an deliver yu blow so fierce to pierce de wicked'.[93] The use of 'we' indicates how deeply the poet identifies with his characters. Casting black youths as lions and warriors confers upon them a bellicosity that in turn renders London a jungle, a battlefield, a gladiatorial arena. The rhetorical inflation in such acts of self-designation is also a common feature of black urban culture: seventies reggae performers had names such as King Tubby, Dice The Boss and Prince Buster, just as many jazz musicians (Duke Ellington, Count Basie, King Oliver) and rappers (Grandmaster Flash, Queen Latifah, The Notorious B.I.G.) have upheld aristocratic and regal pretensions.

Johnson focuses almost exclusively on the damage that urban life inflicts on the black male body. In 'Doun De Road', quoted earlier, London's heat and anguish led brother to turn against brother, 'yu lick him/an yu lash him'.[94] Elsewhere, we read of 'the fire burning within,/his eyes sing pain silently:/twin daggers piercing flesh'.[95] Just as young black men are presented as the sole agents of revolutionary change, so Johnson appears to believe that only they are truly pressured and battered in the capital. One doesn't have to hold essentialist beliefs about the nature of femininity to fear that by concentrating on black men's (often wretched) experiences, Johnson is, whatever his intentions, helping to romanticize a vision of London street culture – full of hustling, dread, strutting machismo – whose social manifestation he deplores.

* * *

To bring Linton Kwesi Johnson and Salman Rushdie under the same thematic heading may seem far-fetched. Although the former spends much of the year touring internationally as a dub poet, and in 2002 became only the second living poet to be published in the Penguin Modern Classics series (the other was Czeslaw Milosz), within the United Kingdom he's still a comparatively little-known writer whose work is believed to have a limited and chiefly black constituency, and is considered by hostile critics to be barely distinguishable from agitprop. GLC chic, if you will. Rushdie, on the other hand, is one of the world's most famous writers. Any upscale Manhattan party on whose dancefloor he hasn't shaken his ass by midnight must be considered a failure. His novels sell in their hundreds of thousands; *Midnight's Children* (1981) was adjudged the Booker of Bookers in 1994. Along with Marquez and Kundera, his writings are often labelled postmodern, global, fabulistic. Another category into which his work is slotted – that of magical realism – has led critics to overlook the historical and geographic specificities which give his fictions such gristle and throb.

Rushdie first visited London in 1961 en route to Rugby School. It wasn't a happy stay – his father became drunk and inexplicably abusive towards him.[96] Subsequent experiences in the city were more enjoyable. In the summer of 1967 he rented a room above the King's Road boutique, Granny Takes A Trip, at World's End: 'it was the Mecca, the Olympus, the Kathmandu of hippie chic. Mick Jagger was rumoured to wear the dresses. Every so often, John Lennon's white limo would stop outside, and a chauffeur would go into the shop, scoop up an armload of gear "for Cynthia", and disappear with it.'[97] Rushdie's own attempts to live such a gilded lifestyle were less successful. He left Cambridge hoping to become an actor and rented a house in Fulham with his sister and some college friends. Work was sporadic and confined to minor walk-on parts. His finest hour was when he appeared as a mustachioed drag queen in the multimedia rock show *Rainy Day Woman* at Kennington Oval House.[98]

In 1971 Rushdie abandoned theatre for another fantasy industry – advertising. He joined Ogilvy and Mather where he displayed his talent for coining slogans and catchphrases (Aero bars were 'irresistabubble'; cream cakes 'naughty but nice') that proved useful in his literary career ('Commonwealth literature does not exist'; 'mongrelization').[99] By 1973 he had moved with his wife to Lower Belgrave Street, an address considerably more exalted than his communal house in Fulham. In *The Jaguar Smile* (1987) he recalled living next door to the wife of the Nicaraguan dictator Anastasio Somoza Debayle whose constant partying filled the SW1 street with expensive cars.[100] Rushdie and his wife next moved to Kentish Town, North London, in the summer of 1976 where, according to Ian Hamilton, they were shocked to encounter 'citizens who hailed from Pakistan or Bangladesh, or even India, [who] were strictly second class and made to know it'.[101] The following year he joined a local project to create jobs for the Bangladeshi community. From then until 1988, when Ayatollah Khomeini issued a fatwah against him, Rushdie lived in various Islington addresses.

His London is more variegated than that of most writers in this study. He has witnessed metropolitan immigrant culture at both extremes: from the glitzy decadence of deposed Latin American tyrants to the violence and poverty faced by families escaping from war-torn Bangladesh. Not only has he worked in the lucrative and creative world of advertising, but he's also made an effort to help those people who could only dream ' 'bout a pile of money' (a line from an advertisement he penned for Burnley Building Society that was later released as a single)[102]; he'd lived in five-storey houses in Highbury Hill, but also in shared digs with students.

Rushdie, like Kureishi (whose 1995 novel *The Black Album* was partly a response to the fatwah against his friend), relishes the messy diversity of metropolitan culture the world over. Discussing the Bombay in which he grew up, Rushdie claims to have prized its monstrous size, its imprecision (the city's frequent power cuts mean that the speaking clock runs six hours late), the way in which it seemed able to incorporate endlessly different peoples, cultures and experiences: 'the West [is not] absent from Bombay. I was already a mongrel self, history's bastard, before London aggravated the condition.'[103] He spotlights this intensely physical appetite for clamour and frisson by contrasting Karachi's 'flat boiled orders of acquiescence' with Bombay's 'highly-spiced nonconformity'.[104] Bombay is spicy, pickled, chutneyed – cooking processes which mix and merge disparate ingredients to create sharp, tangy flavours. Bombay is also dirty and noisy, a city stinkingly material to anyone who has ever visited it, yet which is best known for being the centre of an Indian film industry dedicated to manufacturing hi-gloss fantasies. In short, 'To be a Bombayite (and afterwards a Londoner) was also to fall in love with the metropolis. The city as reality and as a metaphor is at the heart of all my work.'[105]

Reading those critics who dwell on the issue of whether *The Satanic Verses* is a blasphemous text it's easy to forget that the novel, over half of which is set in London, is actually about contemporary urban life. Dealing with the lives of two Indian actors, Saladin Chamcha and Gibreel Farishta, after they fall 30,000 feet from an airliner flying over England, it also grapples with many of those issues that preoccupied Wedderburn and Johnson: the morality of overground, 'straight' London; the need to challenge racist political institutions; the schemers and dreamers who fantasize about forging a new black London order.

Like Lamming and Naipaul, Saladin Chamcha had grown up dreaming of a place called 'Proper London', a dream-city where he'd find 'Bigben Nelsonscolumn Lordstavern Bloodytower Queen'.[106] This metropolis's name inevitably suggests the possibility – and evokes the spectre – of its antithesis, a London that's Improper. As a child Chamcha had 'crept silently up on London, letter by letter, just as his friends crept up to him. *Ellowen deeowen London.*'[107] He prefers to spell out the capital's name rather than to blurt it outright. In doing so, we see the awe in which he holds the city; to say its name aloud might break the spell or invite retribution. His nervousness also brings into view a curious possibility: all it requires is one slip, one stutter while reciting the letters of 'ellowen deeowen' and we are left with a word – and a place – which sounds far less familiar or reassuring. Lobdon? Kondon? Both are wrong Londons, improper Londons. It's precisely this kind of skewing and tilting of the city, the effort to find dissident urban narratives and historiographies, which has prompted some of the most interesting books about the capital during recent years.[108]

Rushdie wants to re-orientate the city and to invert its social order in order that we might peer more closely at the lives of those Londoners on its physical and legal outskirts. This requires him to abandon traditional ways of perceiving the capital. The most obvious of these is 'Geographers' London, all the way from A to Z'.[109] Gibreel, deludedly power-drunk, believes he can go forth and redeem the city armed only with his celestial powers and a London map which, authoritative in its reputation, dotted with illustrations of established landmarks, and listing thousands of street names in alphabetical sequence, will help him to perform his task.

The atlas is Gibreel's 'master-plan', but a combination of his mental instability, the fevered climate, and the reluctance of Londoners to be saved by swarthy strangers eager to plant beatific kisses on them all conspire to scupper his quest. Earlier, Chamcha's hopes of inhabiting Proper London have been dashed when he begins to sprout devil's horns and has to be confined to a spare room above an East End café. To map the city, *The Satanic Verses* suggests, one must first dispense with real maps. Kureishi made the same point in *Sammy and Rosie Get Laid*. Could it be that palimpsests and psychogeographies, ghost-hunting, randomness, chains of association and misbegotten folklore are more effective ways of accessing 'London' than the sequential codification of the *A to Z*? Is imaginative London more real than real London?

Not only does Rushdie show that 'Proper' or 'cartographic' London is, if not mythical, certainly undesirable terrain, he installs in its place a metropolis that is simultaneously more disreputable and more politicized. This insistence that London is far nastier and desperate than official narratives of the city would admit to is fundamental to all the writers in this chapter. In Rushdie's metropolis burglars even steal the guard dogs of the five-storey Notting Hill mansions they raid. In Brickhall NE1 (apparently a conflation of Hackney and Brick Lane in Tower Hamlets), an Asian street trader is deported after eighteen years in England just because he posts a form forty-eight hours late; a fifty-year-old Nigerian woman is tried for assaulting the policeman who has beaten her up. This is not the fantasy London constructed at Shepperton Studios where the city of Dickens's *Our Mutual Friend* has been varnished and heritaged into an American-financed film version, *The Chums*. Rather, it's a wearying and destructive capital where immigrants labour in sweatshops, are attacked on the streets by racist bullyboys, get routinely brutalized by the Metropolitan Police, and put away by the courts. As in Johnson's poetry, this ubiquitous violence drives people insane: one Brickhall resident develops a ritual where for half an hour each evening he rearranges his family's household furniture and pretends to be 'the conductor of a single-decker bus on its way to Bangladesh, an obsessive fantasy in which all his family were obliged to participate'.[110]

Rushdie's London, like that of Wedderburn and Johnson before him, is a place where the forces of law and order are regarded with hostility and suspicion. Wedderburn specifically banished lawyers from his ideal society and compared them to 'tricking gamblers, playing at the game of pricking in the garter'.[111] Johnson believed they and the police were Babylon's stormtroopers; to kill the latter was 'righteous'.[112] Rushdie is equally contemptuous: even the half-Asian lawyer Hanif Johnson, whose job it is to defend the civil liberties of Brickhall's Bangladeshi community, sleeps with the young daughter of the café proprietor above whose premises he has an office, and is described sardonically as being 'in perfect control of the languages that mattered: sociological, socialistic, black-radical, anti-anti-anti-racist, demagogic, oratorical, sermonic: the vocabularies of power'.[113]

The police, meanwhile, busy themselves by framing and beating up innocent members of the public: Uhuru Simba is falsely accused of strangling grandmothers and is later found hanging in a cell; Chamcha is battered in a police van taking him from Dunston to London. In this latter scene, Chamcha's devilish appearance is not only used to embody grandly philosophical ideas about the co-presence of Good and Evil in a sceptical and postmodern era, but to illustrate the attitudes towards dark-skinned peoples that some English men and women still hold. Chamcha wants to – and believes he can – pass as a proper Englishman. Like Mulk Raj Anand, he's read the literature, knows the history, and can speak the language better than many of the country's citizens. Nonetheless, that he's been landed with a satanic form reminds us that immigrants are frequently portrayed as irredeemable aliens, not quite belonging, forever 'them' rather than 'us'. His metamorphosis into a goat also enables Rushdie to satirize racist rhetoric without sliding into polemic: Chamcha's bad breath recalls the standard charge that all Pakis stink of curry, his whinnying voice that foreigners don't even speak the language; his priapic enormity that all blacks are over-endowed and obsessed with white pussy. The police make Chamcha eat the shit that, in his fear, he's expelled in their van. The thought comes flooding into our minds that post-war Asian and Caribbean immigration to this country was largely fuelled by the need for people to do jobs (mopping floors, sluicing down filthy lavatories) that were increasingly unattractive to the English.

As in Wedderburn's and Johnson's work, Chamcha's satanic transformation, far from repelling his fellow citizens, actually attracts many of them. Brickhall's teenagers begin to sport devil's horns as fashion accessories. These give them kudos, subcultural capital. They represent the inversion of standard classifications of good and bad. Those reared on the laws and codes of the urban streets know that virtue is for losers, that the outlaw, the renegade master and the generation terrorist is king: 'While non-tint neo-Georgians dreamed of a sulphurous enemy crushing their perfectly restored residences beneath his smoking heel, nocturnal browns-and-blacks found themselves cheering [this black man] getting off his behind, bad and mad, to kick a little ass.'[114]

Chamcha's monstrous transmogrification also adds to the threat of imminent eruption (actualized in Sancho's account of the Gordon Riots) that develops throughout the second half of the novel, just as it marks not only Wedderburn's and Johnson's writings, but other black urban texts such as Ferdinand Dennis's *The Sleepless Summer* (1989), Kureishi's *Sammy and Rosie Get Laid*, and Two Fingers' and James T. Kirk's *Junglist* (1995). In *The Satanic Verses*, catastrophe and ruination can barely be suppressed: rumours of witchcraft at Brickhall police station begin to circulate; a 'granny-ripper' is on the loose – and is used as a pretext for the corrupt local constabulary to intimidate members of the black community; London is suffering from a terrible heatwave; rats stream over the Strand to Waterloo Bridge; the ravers at Club Hot Wax ecstatically chant 'Meltdown, meltdown, melt';[115] a devil keeps recurring in the dreams of many Brickhall Asians 'rising up in the Street like Apocalypse and burning the town like toast'.[116]

This is summer in the city – piss, sweat, stink; soaring pollen counts, jeep stereos and over-amped in-store sound systems deafening pedestrians already choked by exhaust fumes and maddened by the effort involved in trying to veer clear of rollerbladers, Jesus Army evangelists, posh boys sporting limited-edition primate T-shirts, and the boil-encrusted, dome-headed freak whom the local schoolkids shriek at, and, when on their own, shrink from. With the Brickhall locals – many of them young, bored and jobless (as were Wedderburn's audiences and Johnson's roster of disaffected black teenagers) – already on edge, the news that Uhura Simba has died in a police cell triggers mass rioting. Their resistance and violence seems a valid response to social hardships. It's also infectious. Even Chamcha, so keen to divorce himself from 'your fishing-boat sneakers-in', 'your ugando-kenyattas',[117] finds himself drawn to 'the otherworld, into that undercity whose existence he had so long denied'.[118] Here, at Brickhall Friends Meeting House, he joins schoolchildren, Rastas, and restaurant workers listening to the hellfire sermonizing of Simba's mother who mourns the death of her warrior son and calls for sweeping reforms. The idea that hatred and anger can be enabling had earlier become clear when Chamcha entered Club Hot Wax and noticed that all the dummies bore the face of his fellow Indian, Gibreel Farishta, whom he despised. He became so livid that smoke emanated from his pores and he dissolved all the waxworks with his fetid breath. At the same time, his tail and horns disappeared – hate had humanized him.

This scene at Club Hot Wax is also memorable for featuring a number of the authors who have cropped up in this book: wax models of Gronniosaw, Sancho and Mary Seacole, as well as those of Queen Victoria's beloved Indian private secretary Abdul Karim, and the black clown of Emperor Septimius Severus, appear to bob and shake among the young multi-racial dancers at the venue. Across the dance hall, 'wax villains cower and grimace: Mosley, Powell, Edward Long'.[119] Rushdie has assembled here some of the more vivid characters in the history of black London and given them a radical edge in two ways. First, although many of these figures lived in relatively comfortable parts of London (Sancho in Westminster, Seacole in the West End), Rushdie has relocated them to a dank and anonymous club in rundown Brickhall where prospective ravers 'dive, abruptly, underground, and through [the] unmarked door'.[120] It's a journey not only across metropolitan geography, but also down the social ladder. Secondly, by counterposing them to anti-Abolitionists and fascists, Rushdie lends Sancho and Seacole a righteousness that their writings and lives wouldn't totally support.

The authors in the last chapter also used events and individual figures from the black metropolitan past to critique present-day concerns. However, whilst D'Aguiar saw Equiano as a kind of role model, Rushdie's conception of black London's dissenting past is broad enough to include such unsavoury figures as the fundamentalist Imam. The capital has long served as a haven for political exiles and refugees, from Marx and Mazzini to members of the African National Congress and Mohammed Al-Masari. Hastings Banda was a doctor in the East End after World War Two. Nkrumah studied and militated for West African independence. London has been both an imperial and an anti-imperial city. And while it has always figured in black literature as a bastion of often illegitimate power, from Equiano to the present day, it has been equally cherished for its accommodating attitude towards opposition groups. Douglas Manley, brother of the Jamaican President

Michael, described life as a university student in London during the 1940s as 'like being on the Youth Front of an anti-colonial war.'[121] Regarding the capital as a true cradle of democracy, Manley, and countless political renegades before and after him, gathered in church halls, basements and secret venues, and began to raise funds, print pamphlets, lobby Governments, and disseminate propaganda calling for regional self-determination, equal rights, separate homelands and bloody revolutions. In London free speech is permitted to an extent unknown in many other countries; censorship of the media is minimal; opposition groups aren't harried as brutally as elsewhere.

The unnamed Imam in *The Satanic Verses*, based to some extent on the Ayatollah Khomeini who spent many years exiled in France before returning to Iran after the Shah's death in 1979, exploits London's tolerance towards outsiders by plotting foreign revolutions from his seven-storey block in Kensington. The Imam represents the dark side of dissenting London. He doesn't engage at any level with his urban surroundings. His thick golden velvet curtains are shut all day to ward off 'foreignness, Abroad, the alien nation'.[122] The dissent of all the groups looked at in this chapter – Wedderburn and his ragged Spenceans, Johnson's listless teenagers, Brickhall residents in *The Satanic Verses* – was spawned by the poverty, unemployment and racial hostility by which they had been ravaged in London. None of them rejected urban culture in itself – merely those aspects of it which made their lives unlivable.

The Imam, in contrast, loathes the city's dirt, its disorder and lack of regulation. He exploits its freedom to attack freedom. He drinks a glass of water every five minutes to keep himself clean and despises the city for its slovenliness and impurity. Kureishi believed that anti-urbanism, religious fundamentalism and New Right conservatism were all closely linked. Rushdie agrees: the Imam's metrophobia is tied up with his contempt for history which he regards as 'the blood-wine that must no longer be drunk'.[123] History, like London, is too messy and contingent; both erupt with too many stories for the fundamentalists who, inflexibly dogmatic, lacking interest in individual expression, and preferring theological to chronological time, fear the modern city for precisely the same reasons that it fascinates Otto Cone, father of Gibreel Farishta's lover in *The Satanic Verses*: '[it] is the locus classicus of incompatible realities. Lives that have no business mingling with one another sit side by side upon the omnibus'.[124]

Similarly, the monomaniacal advertising agent Hal Valance, a friend of Mrs Thatcher (or, as he calls her, Mrs Torture/Maggie the Bitch), applauds the Prime Minister's desire to create a new class of people 'without background, without history'.[125] Valance and Thatcher share the same kind of beliefs: reactionary racial attitudes, a distrust of local government, and a limitless faith in laissez-faire economics. All three of these contributed heavily in the 1980s to the rundown of the inner-city neighbourhoods on which Brickhall is based.

The Imam is a pivotal character in the context of this chapter. Wedderburn's scabrous language and hyperbolic rhetoric haven't attracted the condemnation of historians and critics, presumably on the grounds that they were designed to advance progressive and socialistic ideals. Similarly, Johnson's sympathetic descriptions of the will-to-violence of young black Londoners in the 1970s is seen as broadly acceptable – it seems harsh to condemn a writer so keen to expose the manifold social problems faced by those youths. Rushdie, in contrast, shows that the dissent and political opposition of black Londoners aren't always directed towards goals which liberal audiences would find sympathetic. Other authors – Selvon in *Moses Ascending*, Tariq Ali in *Redemption* (1990) – have also written critically about radicals, plotters and troublemakers in London. Their books, however, are comedies. Rushdie is deadly serious in his demonstration that 'Improper' London can be – genuinely – improper. His refusal to sentimentalize or emolliate illicit aspects of black London is a quality he shares with Victor Headley.

Very little is known about Jamaican-born Headley. Interviews and press profiles are scarce. His 'Yardie' trilogy – *Yardie* (1992), *Excess* (1993), *Yush!* (1994) – helped to establish the reputation of a fledgling black publishing company, The X Press, and, through its unexpectedly high sales, encouraged High Street chains such as W.H. Smith to create black literature sections in a number of their shops. Almost all of the early titles from The X Press deal with nineties city life – a loose term encompassing such topics as illegal radio stations, drug-trafficking, dancehall culture, ructions between the police and local communities. The books sported striking covers – close-ups of gun barrels, gold-ringed fists being punched together in criminal solidarity – were promoted through flyers, and sold on tables outside nightclubs. Inspired by the New English Library prole fantasies of Richard Allen in the 1970s (*Skinhead, Suedehead, Knuckle Girls*), the press's co-founder Dotun Adebayo has stated, 'Our readers are working-class blacks, they don't read Ben Okri, but they will read stuff that seems to connect with their lives.'[126]

Headley's ties with improper, dissenting black metropolitan literature are already evident from this brief outline of The X Press. First, as with Wedderburn and Johnson (though not Rushdie), his audience is one largely untapped by mainstream black writers (Okri, D'Aguiar, Gurnah) whose books are issued by well-known publishing houses. Secondly, the titles and covers of the 'Yardie' trilogy signal dissent's recurring preoccupation with thug life. Thirdly, all the authors in this chapter have journalistic backgrounds: Wedderburn edited two journals; Johnson wrote for *Race Today*; Rushdie's output – though chiefly book reviews – has been collected in *Imaginary Homelands* (1991) and *Steps Across This Line* (2002). Adebayo was for many years music editor of *The Voice*, the black weekly paper which his co-partner Steve Pope edited from April 1988 to March 1991, and which, according to a historian of black British newspapers, he tried to locate 'at the heart of a populist market. Populist in the sense of the *Sun* genre of sex, violence and sensationalism'.[127]

Asian and Caribbean authors with journalistic experience have tended to produce accounts of London which are unsentimental, dense with quotidian specificity, and display locality lacking in many of this study's titles written by non-journalists. Examples include *The Indian Eye On English Life* by Behramji Malabari, editor of *The Indian Spectator*; Sam Selvon, formerly of the *Trinidad Guardian*; S.I. Martin who used to write for *The Voice*; Mike Phillips whose Sam Dean detective novels exhibit the same unflinching topographical exactitude already seen in his comments about Notting Hill in the 1960s. That journalists have produced some of the most arresting descriptions of London may be ascribed to their professional need to snout about in the corners and undertows of the capital (often for sensationalistic rather than latitudinarian reasons), to favour substance over form, information over commentary, as well as to keep abreast of shifts in power, fashion and rhetoric.

London's Yardies inhabit precisely the kind of hard-boiled, contemporary and frisson-inducing subculture about which any journalists setting up a new publishing house would love their authors to produce fictions. Yardies hail from Kingston, Jamaica, where they've long ruled large stretches of the city with the help of corrupt police and politicians. By 1987 they had begun to enter London as illegal immigrants and gradually established strongholds in Brixton, Harlesden, Clapham and Stoke Newington. They specialized in extortion, running prostitution rackets, and, above all, selling crack cocaine. Their readiness to use guns and knives, and to torture victims, together with the fact that they've committed far more murders than other London gangs – the Japanese Yakuza, the Triads, the Colombian cartels, and the Sicilian, Russian and Asian mafias – has earned them a notoriety completely out of proportion to their relatively small membership.

Headley's trilogy describes the rise and fall of D. who enters Heathrow under a forged passport and carrying a kilogram of cocaine. Instead of handing over the package to his intended clients, he holds on to the consignment and sets up as a dealer himself. Organized and ruthless, D. is immediately successful, but constantly shadowed by rival gangs. Numerous shoot-outs and turf wars ensue. By the end of *Yardie*, D. has been captured by the police and faces imprisonment. Although the prosecution's evidence is weak, he has been deported back to Jamaica by the time *Excess* begins. He returns to find Hackney cleared out, and takes over a gambling club near Finsbury Park. In *Yush!*, the final volume in the trilogy, Lancey, a corrupt policeman from Jamaica, arrives in the capital and tries to corner a share of the cocaine market, but, together with his accomplice and some of his rivals, is slaughtered in a bloodbath at the end of the novel.

Headley has received much adverse publicity from both black and white commentators who believe his books celebrate and endorse the criminal worlds they describe. This is a charge that has often been levelled at chroniclers of improper London. But some of Headley's characters – Dread in *Yardie*, Chris in *Excess* – do attempt to locate the violence in a social and political context. The latter observes that many youths 'felt unwanted, aliens in the very town they were born in'.[128] Throughout the trilogy Headley not only attacks the Metropolitan Police's unceasing hostility towards young black Londoners, but also schoolteachers who assume their students will underachieve, and, in doing so, effectively consign them to shit jobs or no jobs.

These youths spurn legitimacy. They strut and shuffle through the city checking out the latest dancehall twelve-inchers, hang out in betting shops, stay out late at South London shebeens, or sit at home watching violent videos while freebasing or smoking weed. The work they do revolves around the importation and selling of crack: they set up labs, recruit bodyguards, and stake out rival gangs. Theirs is a deeply brutal and masculine culture. Reputations in the underworld are built around a readiness to carry out violence with equanimity: D. slashes and rapes the girlfriend of his rival, Blue, while her young child sleeps upstairs; in *Excess*, teenage Donovan guns down a Sikh shopkeeper who refuses to sell him alcohol; in *Yush!*, Lancey insouciantly slaughters two dealers, Simon and Cole.

A martial culture operates. D.'s rivals, Bigga and Joseph, are 'soldiers'; his henchman Sticks is a 'lieutenant'; Lancey, an archetypal 'bent copper', regards himself as a 'sheriff'.[129] D. himself is something of a warrior king: he feels 'practically almighty. He was the ruling king, and all the hustlers and players were his subjects and acting as such. Whether through love or through fear, everyone respected D. The constant praises and flattery of the army of sycophants who watched his every move only added to the inflated view he had of himself.'[130] Shame accrues to those unprepared to defend their personal honour: after two gamblers at D.'s club get into a fight, 'a kind of tense vibe had hung over the place. They both had reputations to live up to, and in most cases like that the murmurs, su-su, of the rest of the crowd only egged them on.'[131] Clothing, accessories and transport all become key markers of status:

As a prosperous businessman, D. had invested in his image and bought himself an almost new green Mercedes coupe. Several tailor-made suits, silk shirts, trousers, and expensive soft-leather shoes completed his style and made him one of the sharpest dressers in town. As a final and compulsory touch, he had completed his look with an extensive range of expensive gold jewellery. For a newly arrived 'immigrant', he looked like a million dollars.[132]

Masculine behaviour is precisely defined in the 'Yardie' trilogy: shirking a fight, marrying a white girl, or tolerating 'batty boys' all transgress the codes and norms that regulate gangsta London. In this show-out culture hustlers who show any sign of weakness – an unwillingness to use guns, to avenge dead friends, backing out of fights – plummet down the established criminal hierarchy. Domestic relationships have to be conducted on the same terms as the ballistic affairs between rival gangs: D. is perplexed by Jenny's casual indifference to him – 'That kind of vibes was too unsettling [. . .] It was the same out on the streets; by character,

he didn't like ambiguous situations. He always preferred action to the kind of stand off he was facing now.'[133]

This militarization of the psyche extends into the social realm. There can be no room for ambiguity or imprecision in wartime London. The city is subdivided into home and foreign turf, conflict zones, dangerous terrains, a strictly territorialized landscape which the soldiers and lieutenants must survey, stake out and patrol. Enemy incursions on to someone else's patch, a rival's manor, must be severely punished. In *Excess*, Kevin, chased by a gang of knife-wielding racists, tells himself, 'this was East Ham, the wrong place to get into problems with white guys'.[134] D.'s henchmen, and those of his rivals, need at all times to keep their ears to the ground in order to find out about enemy activities, potential new safe houses or markets. They, like Linton in *Yush!*, are 'used to the streets and constantly tuned in to the most subtle vibrations'.[135] This belief that truth resides on the streets and pavements is also found both in Johnson (a narrator goes 'doun a BRIXTON/an see wha gwane'[136]; 'I woz jus about fe move forwud,/ tek a walk thru de markit,/an suss de satdey scene'[137]), and in Rushdie's analysis of the shortcomings of aerial photography when explaining the cause of the Brickhall riots.[138]

All the writers in this chapter have focused to a greater or lesser degree on coarsening, impoverished quarters of London. While none of them refrains from charting the racial, economic and judicial barriers facing the capital's outcasts, all of them seek to offer solutions. Wedderburn invokes the millenarian creed of Spenceanism; Johnson draws upon reggae's rhetoric of spiritual emancipation; Rushdie at first ironizes the trumpet-blowing Gibreel Farishta's attempts to redeem the fallen city, but then shows him saving his arch-enemy Saladin Chamcha from a burning grocery in Brickhall. There exists, he suggested, a redemptive capacity for goodness and for love – even in the most straitened of circumstances, and in the hearts of the seemingly callous.

Headley, in contrast, offers little scope for transformation. D. is forced to leave the country but, rather than mending his ways, re-enters and takes over a gambling joint. Detective Lancey could have served as a force for moral reformation. The private eye, as one crime writer has pointed out, is a knight errant, a 'lone crusader righting wrongs, rescuing damsels, killing dragons'.[139] But Lancey only wants to lock up D. so that he can take over his share of the crack market. His corruption is another example of the crookedness of the police and judiciary, and is doubly galling as other role models – Dread in *Yardie*, Chris the community worker in *Yush!* – are unable to decelerate the drive of newly-arrived Jamaicans in London towards making quick and illegal profits. Headley's trilogy portrays a segment of black London society so thoroughly cankered that people can only revel in and exploit the sunken environment, rather than try to rail against it. Unlike Wedderburn's millennial polemics, Johnson's fusion of socialism and Rastafarianism, and Rushdie's depictions of East End community activism, there's little belief in resistance and revolution in Headley's work. There are no marches here, no suggestion that politics could effect change. Extra-curricular black history classes are laid on for some of the teenagers but, ultimately, the stress on education and respectable self-improvement they hope to encourage are shown to be flimsy when compared with the instant profits and social cachet offered by getting involved with drug culture.

Nowhere else is London's dystopian violence more evident than in the music scene. Other writers in this chapter treated music as a source of liberation, a soundtrack to the imminent social revolution. Wedderburn's West Indian background instilled in him a love of communal singing; the Soho in which he regularly preached was full of instrument-makers' workshops and hostels for visiting musicians. Together with the tradition of chanting and singing ballads in Spencean debating clubs, it was no wonder that Wedderburn incorporated songs such as 'The Desponding Negro' in his journals; 'Truth Self-Supported' features many Methodist hymns. Johnson effectively deploys reggae rhythms, imagery and topographies in his poetry. Even Rushdie arms Gibreel Farishta with a heavenly trumpet as he strides through the boiling capital attempting to banish wickedness. For other writers in this study, such as Selvon and Kureishi, music – be it calypso or Charlie Hero's punk caterwauling – is also associated with pleasure and delight.

In Headley's trilogy, music has little transformative power. The conscious reggae which Johnson drew on has been supplanted in the affections of the capital's black youth by ragga, a form whose clenched digital phrasing and no-future judderings render aural the precisely demarcated territories of improper London. The gunshots that pepper dancehall tunes are cowboy-regressive rather than barricade-progressive. They're meant to lend both the performers and the DJs who spin the tracks a triumphalist hypermasculinity: at Rocco's the boast rings out, ' "Dis . . . is de wicked, rugged and dangerous Firefly, exclusively on Radical Hi-Powah [. . .] Radical the roughneck sound! Ah we rule." '[140] The venues and clubs are often jammed with 'ravers, hustlers, and players' who create the taut, knife-edge atmosphere that often leads to fights, stabbings and shootings.[141] Though both male and female clubbers in Headley's novels lap up ragga and feel it to be earthy and vital, this shouldn't obscure the fact that in the 'Yardie' trilogy, as compared to the work of the other writers in this chapter, music's function has been degraded. Dancehall serves as a mirror to the culture – black, urban, hardboiled – from which it stems and in which it's popular, but there's no suggestion that it could harbinger possible utopias, stoke a desire for social upheaval.

Paralysis and foredoomedness are distinguishing features of

Headley's London. Poor housing, education and social prospects engender a torpor from which drug dealing offers the most seductive escape route. Narcotics and violence become key currencies, the sole engines of change. There's a certain inevitability when *Yush!* ends in bloody carnage with dealers, rival dealers and policemen all being blown away – the spiralling violence is too great for any truce or let-up. Headley denies his work is amoral, and, certainly, each of his three novels contains characters who are decent and hard-working role models. Nonetheless, the literary conventions of this kind of Hollywood-influenced crime fiction – scant psychological exploration, an inability to portray criminals without lending them a sleazy glamour, clockwork-regular stabbings and shootings – do lead Headley into the trap of exalting the social deformation he claims to lament.

Over 160 years separate *The Horrors of Slavery* from *Yush!* It's legitimate to wonder if the writers in this chapter really have that much in common. Their backgrounds are by no means uniform: Wedderburn, a mulatto, was the son of a slave mother; Rushdie is an upper-class Indian; Johnson comes from rural Jamaica. Equally, the quality, genres and authorial intentions of the four writers vary greatly. Furthermore, the notion of 'improper' London may seem questionable: is it not a rather vague and flabby term? What, after all, is 'proper', yet alone 'improper' London?

Chamcha, in *The Satanic Verses*, thinks he knows. For him proper London consists of famous monuments and landmarks such as Big Ben and the Tower of London. He values these sites, as did the Indian princes of the nineteenth century and many of the characters described in the chapter on Naipaul and Lamming, for the distinction that fame and antiquity lend them. They are symbols of power, order and security. They do England proud.

To be near to them is, in Naipaul's words, to have found the centre, though, as Selvon shows in *The Lonely Londoners*, even physical proximity can't guarantee inner restfulness. The appropriate response to proper London is one of hushed genuflection. One defers to it, and is prepared to forget about the tatty rawness of one's own life. Do not ask questions about history – about money, about power, about how its sacred aura came about. Do not bridle. Admiration, not scepticism, is the order of the day.

 The writers in this chapter prefer to dwell on decentred London. They're drawn to districts and social classes in London that are characterized by a marked lack of order and security – Wedderburn's shifting atlas of plebeian taverns and clubs, Johnson's Railton Road, Brickhall in *The Satanic Verses*, Headley's East London war zones. It could be argued that most of the authors in this book, by topographic necessity, have also looked at insalubrious parts of the capital – Selvon's view of Harrow Road as a modern-day Pompeii, Kureishi's bohemian dives, Phillips's re-creation of dilapidated 1950s London. The difference, then, is that this chapter's four writers home in, not so much on new geographies as on activities within the black metropolis that are largely absent from other accounts: Wedderburn came from, lived amongst, and sought to target the capital's free-floating and quarrelsome criminal and radical underworld; Johnson exposed the ganga-smoking, bass-pumping black outcastes in early 1970s London; Rushdie looks at vicious fundamentalist plotters and tense, insurrectionary second-generation immigrants in the East End; Headley offers coolly non-judgemental portrayals of Yardie drug dealers, rapists and murderers.

 It's not surprising, given the disreputable and slightly scurrilous worlds depicted, that the four authors in this chapter employ literary registers that differ from those in the rest of this study. There's little of Sancho's brio and warmth. The measured respect-

ability of nineteenth-century Indian rajahs is wholly absent. Even
Selvon and Kureishi, neither of whom stint from making polemical
points in their work, write in bitter-sweet modes, and use irony
and humour liberally. The language of Wedderburn and Johnson,
by contrast, is wilfully demotic, inflammatory and violent. All four
authors deal with elements of London in which danger, rioting
and murder are ever-present threats. Although they want to assert
the oft-buffeted humanity of the characters they write about, and
to show how social and economic factors lead to the devaluation
of such concepts in the city, they do so in a brusque and combative
way which, unlike Equiano or Lamming, intimidates and corrals
as much as it reassures or balms the audience.

'Improper' London, then, is as much a voice as a subject matter:
it's colloquial, strutting and street-sharp, verging on the vicious,
and heavily influenced by those cultural forms which also flex their
fire, savvy and toughness – evangelical hymns, pulp fiction, ragga,
hardboiled Hollywood films such as *Mean Streets* and *The Godfather*. Such stylistic debts should forestall any attempt to romanticize this 'improper' London as authentic, the rough-hewn but
genuine metropolis to which other accounts in this study should
be uncritically contrasted. This voice, with its manic calls for urban
revolution, and its invocation of metropolitan cataclysm, entropy
and riotous apocalypse, may not be the sole true voice of black
London. It is, nonetheless, one that reflects the panic, hysteria, and
livid confusion its inhabitants have often felt from the eighteenth
century to the present day.

Afterword

ONE OF THE SCORES OF MEN who boarded the SS *Nautilus* in April 1787 hoping to leave the metropolis and create a new life for himself in Sierra Leone was called Black London. Who was he? His age, profession, even his marital status are all unknown. Undoubtedly poor and desperate, he has left almost no archival mark or trace. Nor do most people, white or black; certainly not the member of eighteenth-century London's underclass. Yet Black London's story (or rather its absence) is especially poignant, because his anonymity symbolizes that gaping void in metropolitan historiography into which black and Asian peoples' lives all too often fall.

Hoping to correct such shortcomings and armed with a copy of his *Letters* and a *London A-Z*, I went searching for Sancho's old shop in Westminster. Duke Street, off which Charles Street used to run, has long been replaced by Horse Guards Road, and on the corner where the two meet there's a huge statue of Clive of India. On the site of Sancho's grocery stands the Foreign and Commonwealth Office. Lacking credentials or ID, I sneaked a look inside only to come up against a large sign announcing: 'The security alert is black'.

Unwittingly ironic as such notices are, they re-emphasize the fact that even such society favourites as Sancho attained fame only fleetingly. It's been the intention of this book to set about restoring Africans and Asians – people like Black London – to metropolitan visibility, and to show that their lives and those accounts written about them merit considerably more attention than they've so far attracted.

It could be argued that I've over-emphasized London's centrality to black writers. It's certainly true that some of them have been drawn to the English countryside in whose hedgerows and ancient estates lay, they suspected, the secret of national identity. Throughout the eighteenth century many slaves were employed in the stables and stately homes of the nobility; over the next two hundred years, a number of authors, among them Sancho, Naipaul, Kureishi and Caryl Phillips, explored the idea that the rural world was more authentic than London, more deep-rooted. They spoke of wanting to flee London's anomie, its homicidal pressure. They wanted to disappear into antiquity.

All of them, however, were to discover that the countryside was no citadel of stability. It did not suddenly make them feel as if they belonged in England: Gronniosaw failed to find steady employment and nearly starved; Sancho spent most of his time there pining for his wife. Naipaul's semi-autobiographical narrator in *The Enigma of Arrival* finds that the Wiltshire landscape to which he has relocated does nothing to alleviate the tyrannical unease and dissatisfaction that hobbled him in the capital; he learns that the countryside is not immune to history and that those who live there also have to cope with flux, change, death. The Brixtonian cricketers in Caryl Phillips's *Playing Away* discover that rural dwellers suffer from the same petty sexual and class-based rivalries as their black opponents. In Monica Grant's comic fantasy, *The Ragga & The Royal* (1994), Leroy Massop is invited to DJ at Eglington Hall, Worcestershire, which has staged the Princess of Wales Horse Trials earlier that day. He has high hopes of tupping the Princess who seems very keen on him. By the end of the evening, though, his mate Rusty has been falsely accused of stealing a wallet. A Royal bodyguard also sides with a bunch of hooray Henrys after they abuse and try to attack Leroy for snogging one of their own, the pony-owning Rebecca who'd come on to him.

In short, London may be grey, anonymous, costly and terrifying; but it also allows for adventure, fortune-making, meeting other black people, self-expansion rather than self-consolidation. Most of all, it offers the possibility of possibility. Rural communities, far from being the bucolic realms many black authors imagined, turn out to be tighter and more exclusive than those in the city: they merely conceal their biliousness a bit more craftily. All forays beyond the metropolis, then, just serve to prove a single, unalterable fact, one that this book has amplified over the course of four hundred pages: namely, from the eighteenth century to the present, London has been the making of black and Asian people. They, in turn, have been the making of London.

Notes

Introduction

1 In A.H. Bullen (ed.), *The Works of George Peele* (London: John C. Nimmo, 1888), vol.1, p.351.

2 Pageants are discussed at greater length by Kris Collins in 'Merchants, Moors and the Politics of Pageantry: The Representation of Africans and Indians in Civic Pageants, 1585–1682', University of Oxford, M.Litt. thesis, 1995.

3 J.A. Giles (ed.), *The Chronicle of Richard of Devizes Concerning The Deeds of Richard The First, King Of England* (London: James Bohn, 1841), p.60.

4 Peter Fryer, *Staying Power. The History of Black People in Britain* (London: Pluto Press, 1984), p.12.

5 Ibid., p.74. One of the rivals for the post of Mayor of London in 1999 was the Guyana-born TV producer – and historian of black Britain – Trevor Phillips.

6 James Walvin, *Passage to Britain: Immigration in British History and Politics* (Harmondsworth: Pelican, 1984), p.6.

7 Peter Fryer, *Staying Power*, p.76.

8 Caroline Adams, *Across Seven Seas and Thirteen Rivers: Life Stories of Pioneer Sylheti Settlers in Britain* (1987 and 2nd ed., London: Eastside Books, 1994), p.46.

9 Examples include Steen Eiler Rasmussen, *London. The Unique City* (1934 and rev. ed., Cambridge, Massachusetts: The MIT Press, 1982); Paul Bailey (ed.), *The Oxford Book Of London* (Oxford: Oxford University Press, 1995); Roy Porter, *London. A Social History* (London: Hamish Hamilton, 1994).

10 Grace Nichols, *i is a long memoried woman* (1983 and London: Karnak House, 1990), p.8. The lack of interest in black writing on London is particularly curious given the 'geographical turn' in recent critical theory. Conference papers and literary textbooks are now full of spatial terms: zones, boundaries and peripheries are routinely invoked. There are 'cartographies of desire', 'landscapes of memory', 'mappings of power'.

One would expect all this to provoke an interest in the historical materiality that post-structuralist criticism is claimed to have shirked. This rarely happens though: spatial rhetoric is often employed loosely and metaphorically. Concepts such as 'centre', 'margin' or, most appositely for this book, 'metropolis', are rarely pinned down. Stephen Slemon, for instance, claims that Third World postcolonial critics are ignored by 'metropolitan theorists' in Paris, New Haven and ... Oxford!; Bill Ashcroft asserts that it's relatively easy to 'obtain the classic texts of colonial discourse theory in metropolitan societies, since they appear in publications widely circulated in these areas'; Homi Bhabha, meanwhile, asks 'what does the narrative construction of minority discourse entail for the everyday existence of the Western metropolis?' Slemon, 'The Scramble For Post-Colonialism', in Chris Tiffin and Alan Lawson (eds), *Re-scribing Empire: Postcolonialism and Textuality* (London: Routledge, 1994), p.31; Ashcroft, Introduction to Ashcroft, Gareth Griffiths and Helen Tiffin (eds): *The Post-Colonial Studies Reader* (London: Routledge, 1995), p.3; Bhabha, *The Location of Culture* (London: Routledge, 1994), p.223.

The metropolis here is being used as shorthand for academic prestige, Europe, the First World. It's surely not pedantic cavilling, however, to point out that all metropolitan societies are *not* alike: they each have different layouts, demographics, (political) climates. Denuding them of specificity and detail may be a requisite of fashioning grandiose theories about the nature of postcoloniality, but it also produces books that are bereft of history or social context. Slemon ignores the fact that Oxford is neither a metropolitan city, nor has a university renowned for its love of Theory. Ashcroft's claim that anyone in Europe and America can easily get hold of primers on

colonial discourse would be news to the jobless Bangladeshi kid on a Tower Hamlets council estate who left his school with only a couple of GNVQs and cannot afford sixty quid for a university press hardback. Bhabha's question not only assumes the existence of 'minority discourse', unnuanced and uninflected, but also of a uniform 'Western metropolis'. To scupper such a fallacy one need only cite Paris whose immigrants are concentrated in the housing projects on the capital's outskirts, its suburbs, rather than in the inner city. The difference this makes to their public visibility and their own sense of national belonging is huge.

11 Rev. John Newton, *Thoughts Upon The African Slave Trade* (London: Printed for J. Buckland, 1788), p.19.

12 It's also interesting that a number of Scottish writers – notably James Kelman – have drawn inspiration from the work of Sam Selvon.

Chapter One

1 *Notes and Queries*, 2nd Series, V, no.123, 8 May 1858, p.375.

2 *The Independent*, 7 August 1995, p.12. Gretchen Gerzina recounts in the first chapter of *Black England. Life before Emancipation* how she encountered similar views while researching her book: 'I entered a well-known London bookshop one day, searching for a paperback edition of Peter Fryer's exhaustive *Staying Power: The History of Black People in Britain*, and instead of assistance received a stern look from the saleswoman. "Madam, there *were* no black people in

England before 1945," she said'
(London: John Murray, 1995), p.3.

3 James A. Rawley, 'London's
Defense of the Slave Trade,
1787–1807', *Slavery and Abolition*,
vol.14, no.2, August 1993, p.53.

4 S.I. Martin, *Britain's Slave Trade*
(London: Channel 4 Books, 1999),
p.37.

5 J. Jean Hecht, *Continental and
Colonial Servants in Eighteenth
Century England*. Smith College
Studies in History, vol.40
(Northampton, Mass.: Department
of History of Smith College,
1954), p.33.

6 Kenneth Little, *Negroes In Britain.
A Study of Racial Relations In English
Society* (London: Kegan Paul,
Trench, Trubner & Co., 1947)
[actually 1948], p.169.

7 Admiralty judge Lord Stowell,
speaking in 1827. Quoted by Fryer,
Staying Power, p.60.

8 Kenneth Little, *Negroes In Britain*,
p.171.

9 J. Jean Hecht, *Continental and
Colonial Servants*, p.36. In Charles
Dunster's *St. James's Street*, at the
head of the parading fashionable
Londoners 'Index of Rank or
Opulence supreme,/A sable Youth
from Aethiopia's climes,/In milk-
white turban dight, precedes the
Train.' Quoted by Wylie Sypher,
*Guinea's Captive Kings: British Anti-
Slavery Literature of the XVIIIth
Century* (Chapel Hill: University of
North Carolina Press, 1942), p.3.

10 David Dabydeen, *Hogarth's Blacks:
Images of Blacks in Eighteenth Century
English Art* (Kingston upon Thames:
Dangaroo Press, 1985), p.26.

11 Aleyn Lyell Reade, *Johnsonian
Gleanings*, Part II. *Francis Barber.
The Doctor's Negro Servant*

(London: Privately Printed for the
Author, 1912), pp.49–51.

12 Peter Fryer, *Staying Power*, p.69.

13 Henry Angelo, *Anglo's Pic Nic; or,
Table Talk* (London: J. Ebers,
1834), p.61.

14 Ibid., p.61.

15 Henry Angelo, *Reminiscences of
Henry Angelo* (London: Henry
Colburn, 1828), vol.1, p.451.

16 Henry Angelo, *Reminiscences of
Henry Angelo, With Memoirs of His
Late Father and Friends* (London:
Henry Colburn, 1828), vol.1,
pp.449–450.

17 Anon, *Nocturnal Revels: Or, The
History of King's-Place, And Other
Modern Nunneries* (2nd ed.,
London: M. Goadby, 1779), vol.1,
pp.222–224.

18 Ibid., pp.226–227.

19 *Lloyd's Evening Post*, vol. XLVI,
no.3539, Friday 25 February–
Monday 28 February 1780, p.194.

20 *The London Gazette*, 7–9 December
1699. Quoted by Maureen Waller,
1700: Scenes from London Life
(London: Hodder & Stoughton,
2000), p.280.

21 Old Bailey Sessions, January 1701.
Quoted by Waller, *1700: Scenes
from London Life*, p.281.

22 Stephen J. Braidwood, *Black Poor
and White Philanthropists. London's
Blacks and the Foundation of the
Sierra Leone Settlement 1786–91*
(Liverpool: Liverpool University
Press, 1994), p.26.

23 Sir John Fielding, *Extracts from
Such of the Penal Laws, As
particularly relate to the Peace and
Good Order of This Metropolis. To
which are added, The Felonies made so
by statute, some general caution to
shopkeepers; And A Short Treatise on
the office of Constable* (New ed.,

London: H. Woodfall and W. Strahan, 1762), p.143.

24 Daniel Defoe, *Serious Reflections During the Life and Surprising Adventures of Robinson Crusoe With His Vision of the Angelic World* (1720 and London: J.M. Dent, 1762), pp.73–74.

25 Quoted by Dabydeen, *Hogarth's Blacks*, p.18.

26 *London Chronicle*, XV, 1116, 14–16 February 1764, p.166.

27 Norma Myers, *Reconstructing The Black Past. Blacks in Britain 1780–1830* (London: Frank Cass, 1996).

28 Maureen Waller, *1700: Scenes from London Life*, p.17.

29 David Dabydeen, *Hogarth's Blacks*, p.18.

30 William Wordsworth, *The Fourteen-Book Prelude*, The Cornell Wordsworth series (Ithaca and London: Cornell University Press, 1985), p.143.

31 Quoted by Norma Myers, *Reconstructing The Black Past*, p.48.

32 Thomas Brown, *Amusements Serious and Comical Calculated for the Meridian of London* (London: Printed by the Booksellers of London and Westminster, 1702), p.27. During the last three centuries, the coffeehouse has been one of the nodal points for the black presence in London. Bryant Lillywhite has explained why so many eighteenth-century metropolitan coffeehouses were called The Black Boy or The Blackamoor's Head: 'Such names and similar ones, with variations in spelling, found in use in London and provincial towns [. . .] were adopted by some traders, and coffeehouses, &c., usually where a black boy commonly known as a blackamoor was employed to advertise the wares of the house. This custom has persisted even to the present day by many establishments where coffee is served by a coloured or dark-skinned person.' *London Coffee Houses. A Reference Book of Coffee Houses of the Seventeenth, Eighteenth and Nineteenth Centuries* (London: George Allen & Unwin, 1963), p.123. Indeed, following the coffee-bar explosion of the 1950s, they can be seen in many of that decade's English films such as *Upstairs and Downstairs* (1959). The eponymous narrator of Andrew Salkey's *The Adventures of Catullus Kelly* also finds himself being sized-up by the owner-manager of a coffee bar in Berkeley Square: 'Tall, good-looking, broad; strong, rich colouring, Marvellous! [. . .] You're the finest Atmosphere Man I've had so far.' Catullus later explains, 'Ralph Ellison's *Invisible Man* is one thing, but my Atmosphere Man is ridiculous. The trouble is everybody sees me only too obviously, zombie flesh and blood' (London: Hutchinson, 1969), p.97 and p.107.

33 Wylie Sypher, *Guinea's Captive Kings*, p.156.

34 Quoted by James Walvin, *Black and White. The Negro and English Society 1555–1945* (London: Allen Lane, 1973), p.173.

35 Ukawsaw Gronniosaw, *A Narrative of the Most Remarkable Particulars in the Life of James Albert Ukawsaw Gronniosaw, An African Prince, Written by Himself* (Bath: W. Gye, [1772]), p.iii.

36 Sandra Burr and Adam Potkay,

Black Atlantic Writers of the Eighteenth Century. Living the New Exodus in England and the Americas (Basingstoke: Macmillan, 1995), p.56.

37 Gronniosaw, *A Narrative*, p.39.

38 Ibid., p.23.

39 Olaudah Equiano, *The Interesting Narrative of the Life of Olaudah Equiano, or Gustavus Vassa, the African* (London: Printed for the Author, 1789), vol.2, p.99.

40 *The Interesting Narrative*, vol.1, pp.211–212.

41 Ibid., vol.1, p.116.

42 Ibid., vol.1, p.132.

43 Ibid., vol.1, pp.134–135.

44 Ibid., vol.1, pp.135–136.

45 Ibid., vol.2, pp.19–20.

46 Ibid., vol.2, p.116.

47 Ibid., vol.2, p.117.

48 James Walvin, *Black and White*, p.61.

49 Vincent Carretta, 'Introduction' to Olaudah Equiano, *The Interesting Narrative And Other Writings* (London: Penguin, 1995), p.ix.

50 Bernard Falk, *The Way of the Montagues: A Gallery of Family Portraits* (London: Hutchinson, 1947), p.274.

51 Ibid., p.285.

52 Ibid., p.277.

53 *The Annual Register, Or A View Of The History, Politics And Literature, For The Year 1775* (4th ed., London: J. Dodsley, 1783), pp.173–174.

54 Josephine R.B. Wright (ed.), *Ignatius Sancho (1729–1780) An Early African Composer in England – The Collected Editions of His Music in Facsimile* (New York and London: Garland Publishing, 1981), p.xxiii.

55 Paul Edwards and Polly Rewt (eds), *The Letters of Ignatius Sancho* (Edinburgh: Edinburgh University Press, 1994), Letter 116, 5 December 1779, p.203.

56 Sancho was quoting from a reprint of Sterne's sermon according to Alan B. Howes (ed.), *Sterne. The Critical Heritage* (London: Routledge & Kegan Paul, 1974), p.175. The source for the quotation itself is Edwards and Rewt (eds), *The Letters of Ignatius Sancho*, p.271.

57 *Letters of Ignatius Sancho*, Letter 36, 21 July 1766 [dated July 1776 – eight years after the death of Sterne – in the first edition], p.85.

58 Letter 36, p.86.

59 Arthur H. Cash, *Laurence Sterne. The Early and Middle Years* (London: Methuen, 1975), pp.37–38.

60 *Sterne. The Critical Heritage*, p.175, p.176, p.176. In volume three of The Florida Edition of the Works of Laurence Sterne, Melvyn New points out that Sterne's attitude to slavery is very different to that of Sancho Panza, after whom Ignatius was named. To prove this he cites the following scene from *Don Quixote*: Sancho considered the fact that if his master's 'Dominions were to be in the Land of the Negroes, and that, consequently, the People, over whom he was to be a Governor, were all to be black', describes that the only remedy is 'loading a ship with 'em, and having 'em into *Spain*, where I shall find Chapmen enow to take 'em off my Hands, and pay me ready Money for 'em . . .' Melvyn New, with Richard A. Davies and W.G. Day, *The Life and Times of Tristram Shandy, Gentleman, Volume II: The Notes* (Gainesville: University of Florida Press, 1984),

p.334. Cervantes' novel was, of course, a significant influence on *Tristram Shandy*.

61 Laurence Sterne, *The Life and Opinions of Tristram Shandy, Gentleman* (1760–67 and Oxford: Clarendon Press, 1983), p.493.

62 Edwards and Rewt (eds), *The Letters of Ignatius Sancho*, p.276.

63 Ibid., 16 May 1767, p.277.

64 Arthur H. Cash, *Laurence Sterne. The Later Years* (1986 and London: Routledge, 1992), p.268.

65 Percy Colson, *Their Ruling Passions* (London: Hutchinson & Co., [n.d., c.1949]), p.140.

66 Reprinted in *The Sermons of Mr Yorick*, vol.1 (Oxford: Basil Blackwell for The Shakespeare Head Press of Stratford-Upon-Avon, 1927), p.29.

67 Laurence Sterne, *The Life and Opinions of Tristram Shandy, Gentleman*, p.58.

68 Hogarth not only repudiated lineality, but was also interested in the story of the Good Samaritan. In 1737 he donated a picture of the parable to St Bartholomew's Hospital in London, of which charitable institution he was a governor.

69 Arthur H. Cash, *Laurence Sterne. The Early and Middle Years* (London: Methuen, 1975), p.123.

70 Letter 43, 27 July 1777, p.94.

71 Letter 29, 4 October 1775, p.77.

72 Letter 58, 27 January 1778, p.122.

73 Letter 76, 4 October 1778, p.150.

74 Letter 56, 20 December 1777, p.119.

75 Letter 25, 12 August 1775, p.72.

76 Edwards and Rewt (eds), *Letters*, p.23.

77 Letter 67, 10 June 1778, p.136.

78 Ibid.

79 Letter 18, 26 November 1776, p.63; Letter 62, 9 May 1778, p.128; Letter 109, 9 October 1778, p.193.

80 Letter 50, 3 September 1777, p.106.

81 Walter Redfern, *Puns* (Oxford: Basil Blackwell, 1984), p.4.

82 Letter 46, 14 August 1777, p.99.

83 Thomas Jefferson, *Notes on the State of Virginia* (1782 and Chapel Hill: University of North Carolina Press, 1955), p.140.

84 Review of the 1783 2nd edition, *The Monthly Review*, vol.69, 1783, pp.492–497. Even in this century, Dorothy George talks of his 'rather painful imitation of the manner of Sterne', in *London Life in the XVIIIth Century* (London: Kegan Paul, Trench, Trubner & Co. Ltd, 1925), p.137; Wylie Sypher meanwhile describes the *Letters* as 'Sterne a little watered', *Guinea's Captive Kings*, p.153.

85 Edward Long, *The History of Jamaica* (London: T. Lowndes, 1774), vol.2, p.383.

86 William Dickson, *Letters On Slavery* (London: J. Phillips, 1789), p.82.

87 Letter 126, 4 January 1780, p.214.

88 Letter 113, 14 November 1778, p.200.

89 Letter 42, 9 February 1777, p.91.

90 Letter 56, 20 December 1777, p.118.

91 Letter 18, 26 November 1776, p.62.

92 John Lennard, *But I Digress. The Exploitation of Parentheses in English Printed Verse* (Oxford: Clarendon Press, 1991), p.94.

93 Letter 157, 27 November 1780, p.257.

94 Letter 20, 26 June 1775, p.65.

95 Letter 62, 9 May 1778, p.129.

96 Quoted by Vincent Carretta in *Letters Of The Late Ignatius Sancho*,

An African (London: Penguin, 1998), p.270.

97 Letter 2, 7 August 1777, p.36.
98 Letter 41, 4 January 1777, p.90.
99 Letter 54, 24 October 1777, p.113.
100 Letter 58, 27 January 1778, p.122.
101 Letter 91, May 1779, p.168.
102 'Sancho expressed his self-awareness in apologetic, complaisant terminology, clothing himself in a cloak of meekness to win immunity which society would allow an unthreatening outsider. Given this self-debasement [...] he conformed [...] to Elkins's American "Sambo" stereotype in a British situation.' Norma Myers, *Reconstructing The Black Past*, p.133.
103 Letter 97, 14 August 1779, p.174.
104 Norma Myers, *Reconstructing The Black Past*, p.173.
105 Letter 33, 14 December 1775, p.81.
106 Letter 88, 11 March 1779, p.164.
107 Letter 56, 20 December 1777, p.119; Letter 100, 31 August 1779, p.179; Letter 17, 9 February 1774, p.61.
108 Letter 15, 8 November 1772, p.58.
109 Letter 32, 20 October 1775, p.81.
110 Letter 106, 18 September 1779, pp.188–189.
111 Letter 32, 20 October 1775, p.81; Letter 33, 14 December 1775, p.82; Letter 53, 20 September 1777, p.110; Letter 46, 14 August 1777, p.100.
112 Letter 66, 31 May 1778, p.134.
113 Letter 49, 27 August 1777, p.104.
114 Richard B. Schwartz, *Daily Life in Johnson's London* (Madison: University of Wisconsin Press, 1983), p.169.
115 Letter 49, 27 August 1777, p.104.

In an earlier letter to his fellow black, Julius Soubise, he laments 'the ill-bred and heart-racking abuse of the foolish vulgar'. Letter 14, 11 October 1772, p.56.

116 *Letters Of The Late Ignatius Sancho*, p.270.
117 Letter 54, 24 October 1777, p.112.
118 Letter 157, 27 November 1780, p.257.
119 Letter 158, 1 December 1780, p.258.
120 Letter 55, 5 November 1777, p.115.
121 Letter 109, 9 October 1778, p.193.
122 Letter 60, 9 April 1778, p.126.
123 Quoted in Edwards and Rewt, *Letters*, pp.3–4.
124 J.T. Smith, *Nollekens And His Times* (1828 and London: Turnstile Press, 1949), p.15.
125 Letter 76, 4 October 1778, p.149.
126 Letter 118, 17 December 1779, p.205.
127 Ibid.
128 Letter 38, 28 August 1776, p.88.
129 Letter 133, 20 May 1780, pp.226–227.
130 Letter 134, 6 June 1780, p.230.
131 Letter 43, 27 July 1777, p.93.
132 Letter 99, 25 August 1779, p.177.
133 Letter 24, 7 August 1775, p.71.
134 Letter 105, 7 September 1779, p.186.
135 Letter 146, 7 September 1780, p.248.
136 Ibid.

Chapter Two

1 Tessa Hosking, *Black People In Britain 1650–1850* (London: Macmillan Education, 1984), p.28.

2 Vita Sackville-West, *Knole and the Sackvilles* (London: W. Heinemann, 1922), p.192.

3 Quoted by Douglas Lorimer, *Colour, Class and the Victorians. English attitudes to the Negro in the mid-nineteenth century* (Leicester: Leicester University Press, 1978), p.41.

4 *Report From Committee On The State of Mendicity in The Metropolis* (11 July 1815), p.51.

5 Ibid., p.51.

6 *The Death, Last Will, and Funeral of 'Black Billy'* (10th ed., London: J. Catnach, 1823).

7 J.T. Smith, *Vagabondiana; Or, Anecdotes of Mendicant Wanderers through the Streets of London, with portraits of the most remarkable drawn from life* (London: 1817), p.19.

8 Cited by Douglas Lorimer, *Colour, Class and the Victorians*, p.41.

9 Pierce Egan, *Boxiana; or Sketches of ancient and modern Pugilism* (London: G. Smeeton, 1812), pp.442–445.

10 Peter Fryer, *Staying Power*, p.446.

11 Harriet Ritvo, *The Animal Estate. The English and Other Creatures In The Victorian Age* (1987 and London: Penguin, 1990), pp.229–230.

12 Marius Kwint, *'Dark Subjects': Race and Performance in the Early English Circus, 1768–1850*, unpublished paper, 1992.

13 Quoted in John M. Turner, *King Pole* I, p.60.

14 John M. Turner, *Victorian Arena – The Performers: A Dictionary of British Circus Biography*, vol.1 (Formby: Lingdales Press, 1995).

15 Peter Fryer, *Staying Power*, p.228.

16 Ibid., p.229.

17 Ibid., p.230. Chris McGreal, 'Coming Home', *The Guardian*, 'G2' section, 21 February 2002, p.6.

18 John Law, *Out of Work* (London: Swan Sonnenschein & Co., 1888), pp.63–64.

19 Henry Mayhew and John Binny, *The Criminal Prisons Of London And Scenes Of Prison Life* (London: Griffin, Bohn & Company, 1862), p.44.

20 General Booth, *In Darkest England and The Way Out* (London: International Headquarters of the Salvation Army, [1890]), p.14.

21 Jack London, *The People of the Abyss* (London: Isbister, 1903), p.228.

22 James Greenwood, *The Wilds of London* (London: Chatto & Windus, 1874), p.1.

23 Quoted by Rev. James Peggs, *The Lascars' Cry To Britain* (London: T. Ward & Co., 1844), p.8.

24 Joseph Salter, *The East in the West. Or Work Among The Asiatics and Africans in London* (London: S.W. Partridge & Co., 1896), p.21.

25 Joseph Salter, *The Asiatic in England* (London: Seeley, Jackson and Halliday, 1873), pp.36–37.

26 Rev. James Peggs, *The Lascars' Cry To Britain*, p.27.

27 G. Laurence Gomme, *London in the Reign of Victoria (1837–1897)* (London: Blackie & Son, 1898), p.133.

28 William Wells Brown, *Three Years In Europe; Or, Places I Have Seen And Peoples I Have Met* (London: Charles Gilpin, 1852), p.xxiii.

29 Harriet Jacobs, *Incidents In The Life Of A Slave Girl* (1861 and New York: Oxford University Press, 1988), p.275.

30 William Wells Brown, *Three Years In Europe*, p.24.

31 Ibid., p.xxi, p.xxiv.

32 Ibid., p.211.

33 Ibid., p.238.

34 Fiona Spiers, 'Black Americans in Britain and the Struggle for Black Freedom in the United States, 1820–70', in Jagdish S. Gundara and Ian Duffield (eds), *Essays on the History of Blacks in Britain. From Roman Times to the Mid-Twentieth Century* (Aldershot: Avebury, 1992), p.98.

35 Ibid., pp.216–217.

36 Ibid., p.208.

37 J.J. Thomas, *Froudacity. West Indian Fables by James Anthony Froude* (1889 and London: New Beacon, 1969), p.19.

38 Ibid., p.55; p.95.

39 *The History of Mary Prince, a West Indian Slave* (London: F. Westley and A.H. Davis, 1831), p.1.

40 *The History of Mary Prince*, 3rd ed., pp.18–19.

41 Ibid., p.19.

42 Ibid., p.i.

43 Ibid., p.41.

44 Quoted by Sukhdev Sandhu, *Slavery, Abolition and Emancipation. Writings in the British Romantic Period*, vol.1: *Black Writers* (London: Pickering and Chatto, 1999), p.344.

45 Ibid., p.344.

46 Mary Seacole, *Wonderful Adventures of Mrs Seacole in Many Lands* (London: James Blackwood, 1853), p.1.

47 Ibid., p.2.

48 Ibid., p.50.

49 Ibid., p.?

50 Ibid., p.?

51 Ibid., p.14.

52 Ibid., pp.79–80.

53 Ibid., p.4.

54 William Wells Brown, *Three Years In Europe; Or, Places I Have Seen And Peoples I Have Met*, p.233.

55 Douglas A. Lorimer, *Colour, Class and the Victorians*, p.60.

56 James D. Hunt, *Gandhi in London* (1978 and rev. ed., New Delhi: Promilla & Co., 1993), p.16.

57 Quoted by Shompa Lahiri, *Indians In Britain: Anglo-Indian Encounters, Race and Identity* (London: Frank Cass, 2000), p.35.

58 S. Satthianadhan, *Four Years In An English University* (Madras: Lawrence Asylum Press, 1890), p.105.

59 B.M. Malabari, *The Indian Eye On English Life Or Rambles Of A Pilgrim Reformer* (Westminster: Archibald Constable and Company, 1893), p.60.

60 M.K. Gandhi, *An Autobiography or The Story Of My Experiments With Truth* (1927 and Ahmedabad: Narajavani Publishing House, 1948), p.70.

61 Quoted by James D. Hunt, *Gandhi in London*, p.xv.

62 From an article in *London Opinion*. Quoted by Lahiri, *Indians In Britain*, p.141.

63 A.M.K. Dehlavi, 'An Indian View Of The Modes Of Living In England. II', in *The Indian Magazine*, vol.24, no.270, June 1893, p.301.

64 Pankaj Mishra, 'You Can't Go Home Again' [review of *The Atlantic Sound* by Caryl Phillips], *The New York Review of Books*, 26 April 2001, p.49.

65 M.K. Gandhi, *An Autobiography*, pp.54–56.

66 T. Ramakrishna, *My Visit To The*

West (London: T. Fisher Unwin, Ltd, 1915), p.3.

67 T.N. Mukharji, *A Visit To Europe* (Calcutta: W. Newman & Co., 1889), p.27.

68 Bhawani Singh, *Travel Pictures. The Record of A European Tour* (London: Longman, Green & Co., 1912), p.vi.

69 Romesh Chunder Dutt, *Three Years In Europe, 1868 To 1871, With An Account of Subsequent Visits To Europe in 1886 And 1893* (4th ed., Calcutta: S.K. Lahiri & Co., 1896), p.i.

70 T.N. Mukharji, *A Visit To Europe*, p.xii.

71 Jehangeer Nowrojee and Hirjeebhoy Merwanjee, *Journal of a Residence of Two Years and A Half In Great Britain* (London: W.H. Allen & Co., 1841), p.xv; T. Ramakrishna, *My Visit To The West*, p.i.

72 T. Ramakrishna, *My Visit To The West*, p.1; Malabari, *The Indian Eye On English Life*, p.8.

73 Malabari, *The Indian Eye On English Life*, p.1.

74 *Travels Of Mirza Abu Taleb Khan In Asia, Africa, And Europe During The Years 1799, 1800, 1801, 1802, And 1803* (2nd ed., London: Longman, Hurst, Rees, Orme and Brown, 1814), pp.195–196.

75 Meredith Borthwick, *Keshub Chunder Sen. A Search for Cultural Synthesis* (Calcutta: Minerva Associates, 1977), p.115.

76 Mirza Khan, *Travels*, vol.1, pp.197–198.

77 Romesh Chunder Dutt, *Three Years In Europe*, p.119.

78 Syed A.M. Shah, 'A Visit To the Tower', *The Indian Magazine*, vol.24, no.268, April 1893, p.208.

79 Bhawani Singh, *Travel Pictures*, p.57.

80 Mirza Khan, *Travels*, vol.2, p.96.

81 B.M. Malabari, *The Indian Eye On English Life*, p.187.

82 Jhinda Ram, *My Trip To Europe* (Lahore: Mufid-I-Am Press, 1893), p.13.

83 Jehangeer Nowrojee and Hirjeebhoy Merwanjee, *Journal of a Residence*, p.106.

84 Capt. Edward W. West (ed.), *Diary Of The Late Rajah Of Kolhapoor, During His Visit To Europe In 1870* (London: Smith, Elder & Co., 1872), p.13.

85 T.N. Mukharji, *A Visit To Europe*, p.99.

86 Ibid., p.324.

87 B.M. Malabari, *The Indian Eye On English Life*, p.28; ibid., pp.31–32.

88 Rev. T.B. Pandian, *England To An Indian Eye: Or English Pictures From An Indian Camera* (London: Elliot and Stock, 1897), p.35; T.N. Mukharji, *A Visit To Europe*, p.149.

89 B.M. Malabari, *The Indian Eye On English Life*, p.120.

90 Ibid., p.39.

91 T.N. Mukharji, *A Visit To Europe*, p.35.

92 Mirza Khan, *Travels*, vol.2, p.233.

93 Rev. T.B. Pandian, *England To An Indian Eye*, p.21.

94 Mirza Khan, *Travels*, p.78.

95 Rev. T.B. Pandian, *England To An Indian Eye*, p.2.

96 T.N. Mukharji, *A Visit To Europe*, p.202.

97 B.M. Malabari, *The Indian Eye On English Life*, p.141.

98 Rao Bahadur Ghanasham Nikanth Nadkarni, *Journal Of A Visit To Europe In 1896* (Bombay: D.B. Taraporevala, Sons & Co., 1903), p.25.

99 B.M. Malabari, *The Indian Eye On English Life*, p.9.

100 As evidenced by such titles as Pandian's *England To An Indian Eye* and Malabari's *The Indian Eye On English Life*.

101 Nowrojee and Merwanjee, *Journal of a Residence*, pp.28–29.

102 T. Ramakrishna, *My Visit To The West*, p.23.

103 T.N. Mukharji, *A Visit To Europe*, p.105.

104 Paul Greenhalgh, *Ephemeral Vistas. The Expositions Universelles, Great Exhibitions And World's Fairs, 1851–1939* (Manchester: Manchester University Press, 1988), p.62.

105 Jhinda Ram, *My Trip To Europe*, p.62.

106 Nowrojee and Merwanjee, *Journal of a Residence*, p.43.

107 Ibid., p.110.

108 Rao Nadkarni, *Journal Of A Visit To Europe In 1896*, p.37.

109 Rev. T.B. Pandian, *England To An Indian Eye*, p.37.

110 B.M. Malabari, *The Indian Eye On English Life*, p.29.

111 Ibid., p.69.

112 Rev. T.B. Pandian, *England To An Indian Eye*, p.93.

113 Jhinda Ram, *My Trip To Europe*, p.14.

114 B.M. Malabari, *The Indian Eye On English Life*, p.46.

115 T.N. Mukharji, *A Visit To Europe*, p.310.

116 Keshub Chunder Sen, *Diary In England*, p.63.

117 Mirza Khan, *Travels*, vol.2, p.41.

118 T.N. Nadkarni, *Journal Of A Visit To Europe*, p.156; ibid., p.381.

119 Rev. T.B. Pandian, *England To An Indian Eye*, p.77.

120 T.N. Mukharji, *A Visit To Europe*, pp.171–172.

121 Bhagvat Sinh Jee, *Journal of A Visit To Europe in 1883*, p.244; *Diary Of The Late Rajah of Kolhapoor*, p.88.

122 Jhinda Ram, *My Trip To Europe*, p.17.

123 Rev. T.B. Pandian, *England To An Indian Eye*, p.19.

124 B.M. Malabari, *The Indian Eye On English Life*, p.192.

125 Ibid., p.188; ibid., p.191.

Chapter Three

1 Jack London, *The People of the Abyss*, pp.147–150.

2 A similar argument is expounded by David Cannadine, *Ornamentalism: How The British Saw Their Empire* (London: Allen Lane, 2001).

3 Jeffrey Green, *Black Edwardians: Black People in Britain 1901–1914* (London: Frank Cass, 1998), p.13.

4 Quoted by Peter Fryer, *Staying Power*, p.295.

5 'East End Riot', *Illustrated Police News*, 24 April 1919, p.2.

6 'More Black and White', *Illustrated Police News*, 19 June 1919, p.4.

7 'Limehouse Race Riots', *Illustrated Police News*, 5 June 1919, p.2.

8 'The Worst Place In The West End', *Illustrated Police News*, 4 October 1923, p.3.

9 *Illustrated Police News*, 1 November 1928, p.7.

10 *Illustrated Police News*, 24 December 1931, p.7.

11 Carlyle Maynard, *East and West of Soho* (London: Hamlin, 1932), p.89.

12 Ibid., p.181.

13 Marek Kohn, *Dope Girls: The Birth of the British Drug Underground* (London: Lawrence & Wishart, 1992), p.155.

14 *Illustrated Police News*, 5 April 1928, p.7.

15 *Illustrated Police News*, 4 September 1930, p.7.

16 Orlando Martin's life is typical in this respect. Born in Nigeria in 1899, he settled in London in 1919, 'earning a living as a porter at Billingsgate fish market, a snake charmer with Lord John Sanger's Circus (Olympia), a night watchman, a kitchen porter, a sailor in the Merchant Navy and a ballet extra at the Lyceum'. He later appeared on stage and screen with Paul Robeson and in *The Four Feathers* (1939), *The Thief of Baghdad* (1939) and later in an early stage version of *Cry, the Beloved Country*. Retiring to Nigeria in the early 1980s, he died in 1986 and was honoured with a state funeral. Susan Okokon, *Black Londoners 1880–1990* (London: Sutton Publishing, 1998), p.12.

17 *Illustrated Police News*, 18 July 1908, p.13.

18 'Coloured Children's Outing to Epsom, Friday, July 14th, 1933', *The Keys*, October 1933, p.24.

19 'Sensitive Black Girl', *Illustrated Police News*, 17 April 1919, p.2.

20 'Negro and Nurse', *Illustrated Police News*, 8 January 1910, p.3.

21 Ibid.

22 Jean Rhys, *Smile Please. An Unfinished Autobiography* (London: André Deutsch, 1979), p.53.

23 Jean Rhys, *Voyage In The Dark* (London: Constable & Co., 1934), p.33, p.62, p.75.

24 Ibid., p.16.

25 Ibid., p.45, p.52.

26 Jean Rhys, *After Leaving Mr Mackenzie* (London: Jonathan Cape, 1931), pp.111–112.

27 Rhys, *Voyage In The Dark*, p.52.

28 Ibid., p.25.

29 In Jean Rhys, *Sleep It Off Lady* (London: André Deutsch, 1976), p.141.

30 In Jean Rhys, *Tigers Are Better-Looking* (London: André Deutsch, 1968), p.12.

31 In *Sleep It Off Lady*, p.132.

32 Rhys, *After Leaving Mr Mackenzie*, p.95.

33 Rhys, *Voyage In The Dark*, p.209.

34 Jean Rhys, 'Till September Petronella', *Tigers Are Better-Looking*, p.36.

35 Rhys, *Voyage In The Dark*, p.51.

36 Ibid., p.26.

37 Ibid., p.41.

38 Rhys, *After Leaving Mr Mackenzie*, p.20.

39 In Rhys, *Sleep It Off Lady*, p.126.

40 Rhys, *After Leaving Mr Mackenzie*, p.146.

41 Rhys, *Smile Please*, p.100.

42 Ignatius Sancho, *The Letters of Ignatius Sancho*, Letter 49, 27 August 1777, p.104.

43 Mary Seacole, *Wonderful Adventures*, p.126.

44 Una Marson, *The Moth and the Star* (Kingston, Jamaica: Printed for the Author, 1937), p.11.

45 Rhys, *Voyage In The Dark*, p.26.

46 Buchi Emecheta, *Head Above Water* (London: Fontana, 1986), p.85.

47 Beryl Gilroy, *Black Teacher* (London: Cassell, 1976), p.165.

48 The first black woman to be published in England, American poet Phillis Wheatley was inspired to seek her freedom after visiting the lions, panthers and tigers at the Tower of London in 1773. She had been taken by Granville Sharp who later helped to set up the Society for the Abolition of Slavery

in 1787. He was also involved with the 1772 Somerset Ruling which stated that all slaves immediately became free on setting foot in England. Phillis, no doubt moved by the sight of African beasts in captivity, was in a position to demand her liberty knowing that if her Boston-based owners Susanna and John Wheatley refused she could stay on in this country.

49 Stanley Jackson, *An Indiscreet Guide To Soho* (London: Muse Arts, 1946), p.105.

50 John Fordham, *Let's Join Hands and Contact the Living: Ronnie Scott and His Club* (London: Elm Tree Books, 1986), p.13.

51 Stuart Hall, 'In Discussion on "British Caribbean Writers"', radio broadcast on BBC Third Programme, 21 April 1958. Typescript held in Hall's radio file at BBC Written Archives Centre, Caversham, Reading, England.

52 Barnabas J. Ramon Fortune, 'Letter To Selvon'. Broadcast as part of the BBC Radio *Caribbean Voices* programme on 13 July 1958. The typescript (no.1365) is found in the *Caribbean Voices* file at the BBC Written Archives Centre, Caversham.

53 In Susheila Nasta (ed.), *Critical Perspectives on Sam Selvon* (Washington: Three Continents Press, 1988), p.78.

54 Naseem Khan, 'The rise of the lonely Londoners', *The Independent*, 12 November 1993, p.23. See also Nasta (ed.), *Critical Perspectives*, p.78, p.91.

55 Sam Selvon, 'Finding West Indian Identity in London' (1988), in Susheila Nasta and Anna Rutherford (eds), *Tiger's Triumph. Celebrating*

Sam Selvon (Hebden Bridge: Dangaroo Press, 1995), p.60.

56 Kenneth Ramchand, 'Preface' to Selvon, *Foreday Morning. Selected Prose 1946–1986* (Harlow: Longman, 1989), p.ix.

57 V.S. Naipaul, 'Preface', in Seepersaud Naipaul, *The Adventures of Gurudeva And Other Stories* (London: André Deutsch, 1976), p.22.

58 Review of *Parian Currents* collection in *Sunday Guardian Weekly*, 14 March 1948, p.12.

59 '"English Goes Abroad". English as Spoken in the West Indies'. Edition of *The English Tongue*, BBC General Overseas Service, 30 August 1957, p.9. Typescript held at BBC Written Archives Centre, Caversham.

60 Sam Selvon, 'Calypso in London', in *Ways of Sunlight* (London: MacGibbon & Kee, 1957), p.127.

61 Selvon, *The Lonely Londoners*, p.81.

62 Selvon, *The Housing Lark*, p.115.

63 Sam Selvon, *Moses Ascending* (London: Davis-Poynter, 1975), pp.6–7.

64 Ibid., p.9.

65 Ibid., p.105.

66 Selvon, *The Lonely Londoners*, p.164.

67 Sam Selvon, *Eldorado West One* (Leeds: Peepal Tree Press, 1988), p.25. This adaptation was published nineteen years after it was first broadcast; 'Come Back To Grenada' in *Foreday Morning*, p.170.

68 Selvon, *The Housing Lark*, p.67; in *Ways of Sunlight*, p.158; *Eldorado West One*, p.20.

69 Selvon, *The Lonely Londoners*, p.170.

70 Selvon, *The Housing Lark*, p.104.

71 In Selvon, *Ways of Sunlight*, p.139.

72 Selvon, *The Lonely Londoners*, p.87.

73 E. Martin Noble, *Jamaica Airman* (London: New Beacon, 1984), p.67.

74 Selvon, *The Lonely Londoners*, pp.77–78.

75 Salman Rushdie, *The Satanic Verses* (London: Viking, 1988), p.38.

76 Selvon, *Moses Ascending*, p.12; *The Housing Lark*, p.81.

77 Selvon, *The Lonely Londoners*, p.104.

78 Selvon, *Moses Ascending*, p.42.

79 Sam Selvon, *An Island Is A World* (London: Allan Wingate, 1955), p.148.

80 Quotes from, respectively, Warren Oster and Beatrice Waters. They are found in Thomas J. Cottle, *Black Testimony. The Voices of Britain's West Indians* (London: Wildwood House, 1978), p.132 and p.138.

81 Mike and Trevor Phillips (eds), *Windrush. The Irresistible Rise of Multi-Racial Britain* (London: HarperCollins, 1998), p.138.

82 Andrew Salkey, *Come Home, Malcolm Heartland* (London: Hutchinson, 1976), p.46.

83 Selvon, *Eldorado West One*, p.37.

84 Interview with Peter Nazereth in Nasta (ed.), *Critical Perspectives*, p.89.

85 In Selvon, *Ways of Sunlight*, p.178.

86 Ibid., p.176.

87 Selvon, *The Lonely Londoners*, p.167.

88 Selvon, *The Housing Lark*, p.9.

89 Selvon, *The Lonely Londoners*, pp.155–156.

90 Nirad Chaudhuri, *A Passage To England* (London: Macmillan, 1959), p.19.

91 Selvon, *The Lonely Londoners*, p.155.

92 Selvon, *Moses Ascending*, p.9.

93 '[Bernard] Miles: What exactly does "lime" mean, Sam?

'Sam Selvon: It's hard to give an exact meaning. As far as I know,

the original lime in Trinidad was the Saturday night dance or party. But the word loosened with usage and now it means any sort of get-together or passing away of time.' ' "English Goes Abroad". English as Spoken in the West Indies' in the BBC Radio General Overseas Service series, *The English Tongue*, 30 August 1957, p.8.

94 Selvon, *The Lonely Londoners*, p.101, p.102.

95 Selvon, *Moses Ascending*, p.27, p.47, p.10, p.8.

96 Selvon, *Moses Migrating*, p.7.

97 Selvon, *Moses Ascending*, p.56.

98 Both are quoted by Edward Pilkington, *Beyond The Mother Country. West Indians and the Notting Hill White Riots* (London: I.B. Tauris, 1988), p.139, p.143. Pearl Jephcott wrote, 'The migrant himself has perhaps written off his expectations of being accepted by Britain and has turned in on himself' – a very perceptive comment, and one borne out by the autonomous cultural activities of the following decade (as evidenced, for instance, by the emergence of the Caribbean Artists Movement).

99 Selvon, *The Housing Lark*, p.32.

100 Ibid., p.49.

101 Ibid., p.47.

102 Ibid., p.117.

103 George Lamming, 'The Occasion for Speaking', in *The Pleasures of Exile* (London: Michael Joseph, 1960), p.45.

104 Selvon, *The Lonely Londoners*, p.34.

105 Ibid., p.101.

106 Ibid., p.97.

107 Ibid., p.115.

108 Ibid., p.115.

109 Mike and Trevor Phillips,

Windrush (London:
HarperCollins, 1998),
pp.116–117.

110 Selvon, The Lonely Londoners,
p.126.

111 Selvon, 'Modern Art . . .', *Sunday
Guardian Weekly*, 18 January
1948, p.12.

112 Selvon, 'Little Drops of Water',
Bim, XI, 44, 1967, p.248.

113 Sam Selvon, *A Brighter Sun*
(London: Allan Wingate, 1952),
p.14.

114 Ibid., p.100.

115 Ibid., p.160.

116 Sam Selvon, *An Island Is A World*,
p.158.

117 Ibid., p.135, p.160.

118 Sam Selvon, *Turn Again Tiger*
(London: MacGibbon & Kee,
1958), p.135.

119 Selvon, *Ways of Sunlight*.

120 Selvon, *Moses Ascending*, p.55, p.60.

121 Andrew Salkey, *Escape To An
Autumn Pavement* (London:
Hutchinson, 1960), p.30. In her
autobiography Cleo Laine recalls
that during the 1920s and 1930s
her Jamaican father would stand
at Hyde Park Corner 'along with
Prince Monolulu of "I've-got-a-
horse" fame and all the political
spouters of the day'. *Cleo*
(London: Simon & Schuster,
1994), p.18.

122 In 1957 *Tonight*, the BBC's daily
news magazine, began to feature
the Guyanese entertainer Cy
Grant who performed a topical
calypso almost every night for
three years. However, he did not
write these himself. That was left
to a youthful Bernard Levin.
Stephen Bourne, *Black In The
British Frame. Black People In
British Film and Television*
1896–1996 (London: Cassell,
1998), p.82.

123 Selvon, *The Lonely Londoners*, p.20.

124 Ibid., p.114.

125 In Selvon, *Foreday Morning*, p.128.

126 Selvon, *The Lonely Londoners*, p.24.

127 John Figueroa, *West Indies in
England. The Great Post-War
Tours* (London: Kingswood Press,
1991), p.99.

128 Selvon, *Moses Migrating*, p.19.

129 Selvon, 'Poem in London' in
Foreday Morning, pp.127–128.

130 In 'We Also Served' (1948),
Selvon drew on his memories of
working for the Trinidad Royal
Naval Volunteer Reserve during
World War Two in recounting
the fear and excitement he felt
during mine-sweeping operations
in which enemy submarines
constantly lurked in Caribbean
waters waiting to attack merchant
ships. 'The Sea', broadcast on
BBC Colonial Services *Caribbean
Voices* series, 14 March 1948,
typescript no. 83, Caversham.
'We Also Served', broadcast on
BBC Colonial Services *Caribbean
Voices* series, 29 August 1948,
typescript no. 274, Caversham.

131 Selvon, 'Tropic (An Excerpt)',
Sunday Guardian Weekly, 5 June
1949, p.12.

132 Selvon, *The Housing Lark*, p.71,
p.71, p.145.

133 Selvon, *The Lonely Londoners*, p.34,
p.121, p.38.

134 Selvon, *The Housing Lark*, p.44.

135 Selvon, *The Lonely Londoners*,
p.167, p.169.

136 Ibid., p.165.

137 Ibid., p.166.

138 Ibid., p.170.

139 Selvon, *Moses Ascending*, pp.43–44.

140 Selvon, *The Lonely Londoners*, p.170.

141 Interview with Michael Fabre in Nasta (ed.), *Critical Perspectives*, p.64.

142 T.S. Eliot, *The Complete Poems and Plays of T.S. Eliot* (London: Faber, 1969), p.62.

143 Selvon, *The Lonely Londoners*, p.165.

144 T.S. Eliot, *The Complete Poems and Plays*, p.77.

145 Selvon, *The Lonely Londoners*, p.170.

146 T.S. Eliot, *The Complete Poems and Plays*, p.73.

147 Interview with Michael Fabre in Susheila Nasta (ed.), *Critical Perspectives*, p.76.

148 Selvon, *The Lonely Londoners*, p.69, p.72, p.30.

149 Selvon, *Moses Ascending*, p.51.

150 Selvon, *Ways of Sunlight*, p.185.

151 Selvon, *The Lonely Londoners*, p.38.

152 Ibid., p.78.

153 Mike Phillips, *London Crossings: A Biography of Black Britain* (London: Continuum, 2001), p.150.

154 Selvon, 'Come Back To Grenada', *Foreday Morning*, p.168.

Chapter Four

1 Paul Edwards and Polly Rewt (eds), *The Letters of Ignatius Sancho*, Letter 60, 9 April 1778, p.126.

2 Olaudah Equiano, *The Interesting Narrative*, vol.1, pp.132–133.

3 Rev. James Peggs, *The Lascars' Cry To Britain. An Appeal To British Christians, On Behalf Of The Asiatic Sailors, Who Resort To The Ports Of London, Liverpool, &c. More Particulars Addressed To The Directors Of The Missionary Societies* (London: T. Ward, 1844), p.32.

4 Donald Hinds, *Journey To An Illusion. The West Indian in Britain* (London: Heinemann, 1966), p.17.

5 Austin Clarke, 'A Personal Reminiscence of Samuel Selvon', in Susheila Nasta and Anna Rutherford (eds.) *Tiger's Triumph: Celebrating Sam Selvon* (Hebden Bridge: Dangaroo, 1995), p.14.

6 Austin Clarke, *Growing Up Stupid Under The Union Jack* (Toronto: McClelland & Hewart, 1980), p.50.

7 Ibid., p.51.

8 Austin Clarke, 'A Personal Reminiscence of Samuel Selvon', p.15.

9 Andrew Salkey, *Escape To An Autumn Pavement*, p.45.

10 George Lamming, *The Emigrants*, p.106.

11 Jack Mapanje, 'Drinking the Water from its Source', in *Of Chameleons and Gods* (London: Heinemann, 1981), p.33.

12 V.S. Naipaul, *The Mimic Men* (London: André Deutsch, 1967), p.12.

13 V.S. Naipaul, *The Enigma of Arrival* (London: Viking, 1987), p.52. *Finding The Centre* (London: André Deutsch, 1984), p.60.

14 Ibid., pp.48–49.

15 V.S. Naipaul, *A Way In The World* (London: Heinemann, 1994), p.209.

16 Naipaul, *The Enigma of Arrival*, p.109.

17 J. Tambimuttu, 'Preface' to *Out Of This War. A Poem* (London: The Fortune Press, c.1940), p.10.

18 V.S. Naipaul, *Finding The Centre*, p.36.

19 Dom Moraes, *My Son's Father* (London: Secker & Warburg, 1967), p.100.

20 George Lamming, *The Pleasures of Exile* (London: Michael Joseph, 1960), p.25.

21 Ibid., p.60.

22 Ibid., p.67.

23 Ibid., pp.66–67.

24 Naipaul, *A Way In The World*, p.83.

25 Ibid., p.88.

26 Naipaul, *The Enigma of Arrival*, pp.124–125.

27 Ibid., p.119.

28 Ibid., p.122.

29 Naipaul, *The Enigma of Arrival*, p.98.

30 Naipaul, *The Mimic Men*, p.267.

31 Ibid., p.22.

32 Naipaul, *Finding The Centre*, p.59.

33 Naipaul, *The Mimic Men*, p.29.

34 Ibid., p.32.

35 Naipaul, *Finding The Centre*, p.45.

36 Nirad Chaudhuri, *A Passage To England* (London: Macmillan & Co., 1959), p.18.

37 Naipaul, *The Mimic Men*, p.55.

38 Naipaul, *Finding The Centre*, p.17.

39 Naipaul, *The Mimic Men*, p.55.

40 George Lamming, *The Pleasures of Exile*, p.51.

41 Mulk Raj Anand, *Conversations in Bloomsbury* (London: Wildwood House, 1981), p.29.

42 Ibid., pp.96–97.

43 Chaudhuri, *A Passage To England*, p.19.

44 V.S. Naipaul, *Mr Stone and the Knights Companion* (London: André Deutsch, 1963), p.59.

45 Lamming, *The Emigrants*, p.137.

46 Ibid., p.139.

47 Ibid., pp.139–144.

48 Jonathan Raban, *Soft City* (London: Hamish Hamilton, 1974), p.205.

49 V.S. Naipaul, *The Mimic Men*, p.9.

50 Dom Moraes, *My Son's Father*, p.223.

51 Dom Moraes, 'The Lost Tribes of India', in *From East and West. A Collection of Essays* (London: Vikas Publications, 1971), p.28.

52 Julian Maclaren-Ross, *Memoirs of the Forties* (London: A. Ross, 1965), pp.145–146.

53 Naipaul, *The Enigma of Arrival*, p.117.

54 Naipaul, *A Way In The World*, p.119.

55 Chaudhuri, *A Passage To England*, p.58.

56 Ibid., p.1.

57 Lamming, *The Pleasures of Exile*, p.91.

58 Chaudhuri, *A Passage To England*, p.188.

59 V.S. Naipaul, in *The Overcrowded Barracoon, and other articles* (London: André Deutsch, 1972), p.16.

60 Naipaul, *The Enigma of Arrival*, p.120.

61 Naipaul, *The Mimic Men*, p.11.

62 Ibid., pp.85–86.

63 P.S. Chauhan, 'V.S. Naipaul: History as Cosmic Irony', in Emmanuel Nelson (ed.), *Reworlding. The Literature of the Indian Diaspora* (New York: Greenwood Press, 1992), pp.13–23.

64 Naipaul, *The Enigma of Arrival*, p.52.

65 Naipaul, *Mr Stone and the Knights Companion*, p.158.

66 Ibid., p.159.

67 Naipaul, *The Mimic Men*, p.22.

68 Jack Mapanje, in *Of Chameleons and Gods*, pp.35–36.

69 Andrew Salkey, *Escape To An Autumn Pavement*, p.48.

70 Ibid., p.145.

71 Naipaul, *Letters Between a Father and Son* (London: Little, Brown, 1999), p.43.

72 V.S. Naipaul, *Half A Life* (London: Picador, 2001), p.52.
73 Sam Selvon, *The Lonely Londoners*, p.99.
74 Naipaul, *Half A Life*, p.120.
75 Ibid., p.33.
76 Naipaul, *Letters Between a Father and Son*, p.9.

Chapter Five

1 Quoted by Robert Hewison, *Too Much. Art and Society in the Sixties 1960–75* (London: Methuen, 1986), pp.41–42.
2 Dilip Hiro, *Black British, White British. A History of Race Relations* (1971 and 2nd ed., London: Grafton, 1991), p.115.
3 Ibid., p.117.
4 Colin Brown, *Black and White Britain. The Third PSI Survey* (1984 and Aldershot: Gower, 1985), p.32.
5 Ray Gosling, *Personal Copy. A Memoir of the Sixties* (London: Faber & Faber, 1980), p.211.
6 For instance, Asian rappers such as Kaliphz and Asian Dub Foundation; the reggae-influenced Apache Indian; drill 'n' bass industrialists 2nd Gen; drum 'n' bass-inflected Talvin Singh, Future State of Bengal and Anjali. The latter is an Asian woman who used to front Voodoo Queens whilst Sonya Aurora-Madan is the lead singer of the otherwise white Echobelly. Leaving aside the chart-topping White Town and Babylon Zoo, one of the most splendidly vital groups – regardless of colour – in this country over the last decade have been Leicester's Cornershop. Led by Tjinder Singh,

their first single (available on the LP, *Elvis Sex-Change*, WIIIJA Records, 1993) included a song called 'Hanif Kureishi Scene', and they feature on the soundtrack to his film *My Son The Fanatic* (1998).
7 He did, however, produce two academic works: *The Nation of Pakistan* (Oxford: Pergamon Press, 1969); *The New Pakistan* (London: Bell, 1977).
8 Norman Stone, 'Through A Lens Darkly', *The Sunday Times*, 10 January 1988, pp.C1–2. Such sleaziness, he argued, had been instigated during the 1960s by The Beatles. He preferred to cite *A Passage to India*, *A Room with a View* and *Hope and Glory* as examples of good cinematic practice.
9 Michael Bracewell, *England Is Mine. Pop Life in Albion from Wilde to Goldie* (London: HarperCollins, 1997), p.111.
10 This antipathy towards suburbia is discussed at length in Paul Oliver, Ian Davis and Ian Bentley (eds), *Dunroamin. The Suburban Semi and its Enemies* (1981 and London: Pimlico, 1994) (London: Barrie & Jenkins, 1981). Suburbia is 'a sort of twilight country, indeterminate between sleeping and waking, muted and barely alive'. Beryl Gilroy, *Black Teacher*, p.110.
11 Oliver et al., *Dunroamin*, p.
12 Hanif Kureishi, *The Buddha of Suburbia* (London: Faber, 1990), p.51.
13 Ibid., p.23.
14 Hanif Kureishi, *The Black Album* (London: Faber, 1995), p.22.
15 Ibid., p.177.
16 Daniel Meadows, *Nattering in Paradise. A Word from the Suburbs*

(London: Simon & Schuster, 1988), p.39.

17 Kureishi, *The Buddha of Suburbia*, p.8.

18 Hanif Kureishi, *Birds of Passage*, in *Outskirts and Other Plays* (London: Faber, 1992), p.178.

19 A.B.C. Merriman-Labor, *Britons Through Negro Spectacles* (London: Imperial and Foreign Co., 1909), pp.175–176.

20 Kureishi, *The Buddha of Suburbia*, p.40.

21 Kureishi, *Birds of Passage*, in *Outskirts and Other Plays*, p.181.

22 Kureishi, *Borderline*, in *Outskirts and Other Plays*, p.100.

23 Ibid., p.117.

24 Meera Syal, *Life Isn't All Ha Ha Hee Hee* (London: Doubleday, 1999), p.13.

25 For example, the introduction to *Outskirts and Other Plays*; the essay, 'Eight Arms To Hold You' in *London Kills Me* (London: Faber, 1991).

26 This theme is discussed thoroughly in Simon Reynolds and Joy Press, *The Sex Revolts. Gender, Rebellion and Rock 'N' Roll* (London: Serpent's Tail, 1995).

27 Quoted by Daniel Meadows, *Nattering in Paradise*, p.82.

28 Jon Savage, *England's Dreaming* (US edition) p.183.

29 Christopher Sandford, *Mick Jagger. Primitive Cool* (London: Victor Gollancz, 1993), p.24.

30 Ibid., p.89.

31 All this information is derived from Piet Schreuders, Mark Lewisohn and Adam Smith, *The Beatles London* (London: Hamlyn, 1994).

32 Kureishi, *The Buddha of Suburbia*, p.68.

33 1976 *Playboy* interview, excerpted

in Patrick Higgins (ed.), *A Queer Reader* (London: Fourth Estate, 1993), p.246.

34 Dick Hebdige, *Subculture*, excerpted by Elizabeth Thomson and David Gutman (eds), *The Bowie Companion* (1993 and London: Sidgwick & Jackson, 1995), p.xxii.

35 Kureishi, *The Black Album*, p.158.

36 Stella to Paul, 'Sydenham's a leaving place.' *Birds of Passage*, p.173; 'it was obviously true that our suburbs were a leaving place', *The Buddha of Suburbia*, p.117.

37 Hanif Kureishi, 'With Your Tongue Down My Throat', *Granta*, no.22, Autumn 1987, p.26.

38 Kureishi, *The Buddha of Suburbia*, p.70.

39 In Mary Hobhouse, 'London Sketched By An Indian Pen', *The Indian Magazine*, February 1890, p.62.

40 In Kureishi, *Outskirts and Other Plays*, p.181.

41 Ibid., p.192.

42 Kureishi, *London Kills Me*, p.52.

43 Daniel Meadows, *Nattering in Paradise*, p.13.

44 London's housing during the 1980s is discussed by Richard Rogers and Mark Fisher, *A New London* (London: Penguin Books, 1992); Andy Thornley (ed.), *The Crisis of London* (London: Routledge, 1992).

45 Hanif Kureishi, 'Finishing The Job', *New Statesman and Society*, 28 October 1988, p.19.

46 Kureishi, *Sammy and Rosie Get Laid*, p.39.

47 Colin Brown, *Black and White Britain*, p.115, p.44.

48 In Kureishi, *Outskirts and Other Plays*, p.124.

49 Kureishi, *My Beautiful Laundrette*, p.104.

50 Ibid., p.51.

51 Kureishi, *The Buddha of Suburbia*, p.43.

52 Kureishi, *The Black Album*, p.3.

53 Kureishi, *My Beautiful Laundrette*, p.53.

54 Kureishi, *Sammy and Rosie Get Laid*, p.55.

55 Kureishi, *The Black Album*, p.2.

56 Kureishi, 'Some Time With Stephen' in *Sammy and Rosie Get Laid*, p.77.

57 Kureishi, *The Buddha of Suburbia*, p.63.

58 Kureishi, *My Beautiful Laundrette*, p.69.

59 Kureishi, *The Black Album*, p.94.

60 Ibid., p.47.

61 Kureishi, *Sammy and Rosie Get Laid*, pp.18–19.

62 Kureishi, *The Black Album*,

63 This response is also articulated on the sleevenotes to *Foxbase Alpha* (1991) by Saint Etienne who hail from the outskirts of London – Croydon – but have come to be viewed as perhaps the most metrophiliac pop stars of recent years. They were also meant to contribute to the soundtrack to *London Kills Me*. Trying to capture the LP's essence, Jon Savage notes,

'June 4 1989. It's a Sunday morning. The weather's not bad enough to be a downer, and in the hard, black economy cash in your pocket puts a spring in your step. On the way into town, you can see London spread out before you: the tombstone skyscrapers of the city and Docklands, the winking lights of the Post Office Tower and Crystal Palace. In the distance, the hills.

'Down in Camden, London in your throat, the lowest point in the city, a sink for pollution, noise, destitution. But it's here that you find the raw materials to make the world in the way that you hear it. Walking through the congested streets and alleys, you're assaulted by a myriad of sounds, looks and smells from all over the world, each with its own memory and possibility [. . .] Stay busy, out of phase, in love.'

64 Kureishi, *Sammy and Rosie Get Laid*, p.33.

65 A notable exception is Sam Selvon: '[W]hen she asked me why I loved London I too shrugged [. . .] The way St Paul's was, half-hidden in the rain, the motionless trees along the Embankment. But you say a thing like that and people don't understand at all. How sometimes a surge of greatness could sweep over you when you see something.' 'My Girl and the City', in *Ways of Sunlight*, p.173.

66 Hanif Kureishi and Jon Savage (eds), *The Faber Book of Pop* (London: Faber, 1995), p.xix.

67 Quoted by Paul Gilroy, *Small Acts. Thoughts on the Politics of Black Cultures* (London: Serpent's Tail, 1993), p.120.

68 Kureishi, *The Buddha of Suburbia*, p.126.

69 Kureishi, *The Black Album*, p.110.

70 Ibid., p.21.

71 Kureishi, *The Buddha of Suburbia*, p.212.

72 Ibid., p.213.

73 Kureishi, 'Introduction' to *Outskirts and Other Plays*, p.ix and p.xvii.

74 Ibid., p.88.

75 David Mellor, *The Sixties Art Scene In London* (London: Phaidon Press, 1993), p.22.

76 A famous example of this, one which is particularly apposite in the light of Charlie's success as a punk

rocker in *The Buddha of Suburbia*, is
the cover to The Sex Pistols' single
'God Save The Queen'. Designed
by Jamie Reid, it showed the
Queen with a safety pin through
her nose. The sleeve's lettering was
put together by tearing strips from
tabloid newspapers to look like a
ransom note. Gaudy yellows and
pinks further enhanced the
intended effect of rebelliousness
and the overstepping of traditional
boundaries of taste and decorum.

77 Kureishi, *The Buddha of Suburbia*,
   p.175.
78 Kureishi, *My Beautiful Laundrette*,
   p.35.
79 Kureishi, 'The Rainbow Sign' in
   My Beautiful Laundrette, p.43.
80 Kureishi, *Sammy and Rosie Get Laid*
   (London: Faber, 1988), p.4.
81 Kureishi, *Outskirts and Other Plays*,
   p.166.
82 Kureishi and Savage (eds), *The Faber
   Book of Pop*, p.xviii.
83 Kureishi, *My Beautiful Laundrette*,
   p.85.
84 Kureishi, *The Buddha of Suburbia*,
   p.15.
85 Hanif Kureishi, 'Erotic Politicians
   and Mullahs', *Granta*, no.17, p.144.
86 Quoted by Patrick Higgins (ed.), *A
   Queer Reader*, p.13.
87 Kureishi, *Sammy and Rosie Get
   Laid*, p.35.
88 Kureishi, *My Beautiful Laundrette*,
   p.105.
89 Kureishi, *The Buddha of Suburbia*,
   p.204.
90 Ibid., p.254.
91 Interview in *Gay Times*, February
   1988. Quoted by Higgins, *A Queer
   Reader*, p.252. Other films during
   this period featuring homosexual
   characters include *Maurice* (1987),
   My Beautiful Laundrette (1986),
   Another Country (1982), and much of
   Derek Jarman's output.
92 Kureishi, *My Beautiful Laundrette*,
   p.84.
93 Ibid., p.100.
94 Kureishi, *Sammy and Rosie Get
   Laid*, p.44.
95 Kureishi, *The Buddha of Suburbia*,
   p.107.
96 Kureishi, *The Black Album*, p.103.
97 Ibid., p.103.
98 Kureishi, *London Kills Me*, p.49.
99 Ibid., p.59.
100 Ibid., p.51.
101 T. Ramakrishna, *My Visit To The
    West*, p.3.
102 Ibid., p.5.
103 Kureishi, *The Buddha of Suburbia*,
    p.24.
104 Yvette Richards, *Single Black Female*
    (London: The X Press, 1994), p.23,
    p.45.
105 Atima Srivastava, *Transmission*
    (London: Serpent's Tail, 1992),
    p.16, p.90, p.53.
106 Andrea Levy, *Never Far From
    Nowhere* (London: Headline
    1996), p.168.
107 Srivastava, *Transmission*, p.152.
108 Ibid., p.19.
109 Ibid., p.16.
110 Ibid., p.56.
111 Vanessa Walters, *Rude Girls*
    (London: Pan, 1996), p.9.
112 Richards, *Single Black Female*,
    pp.188–189.

Chapter Six

1 Steen Eiler Rasmussen, *London. The
  Unique City* (1934 and rev. ed.,
  Cambridge, Massachusetts: The
  MIT Press, 1982), p.76.
2 Romesh Gunesekara, *Reef* (London:
  Granta, 1994), pp.185–186.

3 Jonathan Raban, *Soft City*, p.242.

4 Sam Selvon, *Moses Ascending*, p.12.

5 Angus Calder, 'Wine and wit in English Lit' [obituary of Paul Edwards], *The Guardian*, 12 May 1992, p.37. One of the most important academics in this field – Basil Davidson – hadn't even been to university. Mike Bygrave, 'A Lion for Africa', *The Guardian*, 'Weekend' section, 15 February 1997, p.23.

6 Hugh Trevor-Roper, *The Rise of Christian Europe* (London: 1965), p.9.

7 Ibid., p.9.

8 Quoted by Jonathon Green, *Them. Voices from the Immigrant Community in Contemporary Britain* (London: Secker & Warburg, 1990), p.1.

9 John La Rose, *The New Cross Massacre Story. Interviews with John La Rose* (London: Alliance of the Black Parents Movement, Black Youth Movement and the Race Today Collective, 1984), p.18.

10 Ionie Benjamin, *The Black Press in Britain* (Stoke-on-Trent: Trentham Books, 1995), p.69. In her introduction to the book, Benjamin claims that 'London is fast becoming the Black newspaper capital of the world. At the last count there were more than a hundred newspapers and periodicals owned and controlled by Asians, Africans and West Indians and published in Britain today, mostly in London.' p.3.

11 Quoted in unsigned article, 'The Black Art Group', *Artrage*, no.14, Autumn 1986, pp.28–29. The Group's aesthetic goals are also briefly analysed by Kobena Mercer, *Welcome to the Jungle. New Positions in Black Cultural Studies* (New York: Routledge, 1994), p.14.

12 John Akomfrah, 'Black Independent Film-making: A statement by the Black Audio/Film Collective', *Artrage*, nos3/4, Summer 1983, p.29. See also Manthia Diawara, 'Power and Territory: The Emergence of Black British Film Collectives', in Lester Friedman (ed.), *British Cinema and Thatcherism. Fires Were Started* (London: UCL Press, 1993), pp.147–160.

13 John La Rose, *The New Cross Massacre Story*, p.16.

14 Examples include Nigel File and Chris Power, *Black Settlers in Britain, 1555–1958* (London: Heinemann Educational Books, 1981); James Walvin (ed.), *Slavery and British Society 1776–1846* (London: Macmillan, 1982); Peter Fryer, *Staying Power*; Tessa Hosking, *Black People In Britain 1650–1850*; David Dabydeen, *Hogarth's Blacks: Images of Blacks in Eighteenth Century English Art*.

15 Fine examples include Sylvia L. Collicott, *Connections. Haringey Local-National-World Links* (London: Haringey Community Information Service in association with the Multi-Cultural Curriculum Support Group, 1986); *Forty Winters On. Memories of Britain's Post-War Caribbean Immigrants* (London: Lambeth Council, 1988).

16 Peter Fryer, *Staying Power*, p.ix.

17 Roy Kerridge, *The Story of Black Britain* (London: Claridge Press, 1998), p.39.

18 Ibid., p.38.

19 Raphael Samuel has argued that much of the impetus for the upsurge of interest in local history over the last twenty years 'so far as writing and often even readership was concerned' was 'so often in the

hands of newly settled residents [. . .]; family history seems to have had a particular appeal to the geographically and socially mobile – i.e. those who, without the aid of history, were genealogical orphans. "Feelings of rootlessness", as the family history societies themselves acknowledge, animated the new enthusiasm. It gave to the territorially mobile the dignity of ancient settlement, to the limited nuclear family a far-flung kinship network.' *Theatres of Memory. Volume 1: Past and Present in Contemporary Culture* (London: Verso, 1994), p.150. There are obvious parallels here with the emergence of black English history which satisfied a need for ballast and belonging after centuries of travel and criss-crossing of the oceans.

20 Bernardine Evaristo, *The Emperor's Babe* (London: Hamish Hamilton, 2001), p.10 and p.4.

21 Ibid., p.201.

22 Gbenga Agbenugba, *Another Lonely Londoner* (London: Ronu Books, 1991), p.218.

23 Caryl Phillips, *The European Tribe* (London: Faber & Faber, 1987), p.5.

24 The first example is from *The Shelter*; the other two from *Crossing The River*. Phillips has presented television features on the nineteenth-century black actor Ira Aldridge, and delivered a speech to the Royal Society of Literature on Ignatius Sancho.

25 Interview with Kay Saunders, *Kunapipi*, vol.9, no.1, 1987, p.51.

26 Rosalind C. Bell, 'Worlds Within. An Interview with Caryl Phillips', *Callaloo*, vol.14, no.3, Summer 1991, p.578. 'My ignorance probably came about as a result of my education and my own lack of a coherent sense of identity in 1970s Britain. In British schools I was never offered a text that had been penned by a black person, or that concerned the lives of black people.' *The European Tribe*, p.1.

27 Maya Jaggi, 'Crossing The River: Caryl Phillips talks to Maya Jaggi', *Wasafiri*, no.20, Autumn 1994, p.29. Phillips is not alone among writers of Caribbean extraction in commenting upon that region's lack of a sense of the past. In *The Pleasures of Exile* (1960) George Lamming feelingly quotes James Joyce's claim that, 'History is a nightmare from which I am trying to awaken'. He added that, 'one characteristic of the West Indian is the tendency to forget'. This led '[us] to feel a sense of exile by our inadequacy and our irrelevance of function in a society whose past we can't alter, and whose future is always beyond us'. Quotes taken from, respectively, p.9, p.26, p.24.

28 Caryl Phillips, *Where There Is Darkness* (Ambergate: Amber Lane Press, 1983), p.25.

29 Caryl Phillips, *Playing Away* (London: Faber & Faber, 1987), p.ix. The film itself was premièred at the London Film Festival in November 1986.

30 Ibid., p.79.

31 Caryl Phillips, *Higher Ground* (London: Viking, 1989), p.192.

32 Phillips, *Where There Is Darkness*, p.25; *The Final Passage* (London: Faber, 1985), p.160.

33 Caryl Phillips, *The European Tribe* (London: Faber, 1987), p.119.

34 Phillips, *The Final Passage*, pp.200–201.

35 Ibid., p.170.

36 Phillips, *Where There Is Darkness*, p.62.

37 Ibid., p.58.

38 Caryl Phillips, *The Shelter* (Oxford: Amber Lane Press, 1984), p.43.

39 Phillips, *Higher Ground*, p.193.

40 Phillips, *Playing Away*, p.39.

41 Phillips, *Higher Ground*, p.214.

42 Phillips, *The Shelter*, pp.46–47.

43 Phillips, *The Final Passage*, p.121.

44 Phillips, *Higher Ground*, p.216.

45 Many of the black film collectives which emerged during the 1980s also eschewed linear narrative. 'Whilst early [black British] films relied on realist narratives, *Passion of Remembrance* disrupted naturalistic conventions by breaking up a family narrative with a dialogue between a man and a woman in abstract space. Likewise fragmentary collage and dream-like narratives are employed in both *Handsworth Songs* and *Territories* to reinforce the complexities and intersections of cultural difference and identity.' Gargi Bhattacharyya and John Gabriel, 'Gurinder Chadha and The *Apna* Generation', *Third Text*, no.27, Summer 1994, p.56.

46 Salman Rushdie, *Midnight's Children* (London: Jonathan Cape, 1981), p.150.

47 Salman Rushdie, 'On Palestinian Identity: A Conversation With Edward Said', in *Imaginary Homelands* (London: Granta Books, 1992), p.168.

48 David Dabydeen, *Disappearance* (London: Jonathan Cape, 1993), p.75.

49 Fred D'Aguiar, 'A Jamaican Airman Foresees His Death', in Yvonne Brewster (ed.), *Black Plays 3* (London: Methuen, 1995), p.279.

50 Phillips, *The European Tribe*, p.103.

51 Phillips, *Playing Away*, p.23.

52 Phillips, *The Final Passage*, p.139, p.123, p.158, p.148.

53 Phillips, *The Shelter*, p.50.

54 Phillips, *The Final Passage*, p.166; *The Shelter*, p.50.

55 Phillips, *The Final Passage*, p.121.

56 Phillips, *The Shelter*, p.35.

57 Caryl Phillips, 'Following On: The Legacy of Lamming and Selvon', in *A New World Order: Selected Essays* (London: Secker & Warburg, 2001), p.232.

58 Phillips, *The Final Passage*, p.160.

59 Sam Selvon, *The Lonely Londoners*, p.76.

60 Ibid., p.77.

61 Phillips, *The Final Passage*, p.124.

62 Ibid., p.124.

63 In Anna Rutherford and Kirsten Holst Peterson (eds), *Displaced Persons* (Mundelstrup: Dangaroo Press, 1988), p.146.

64 First broadcast on Channel 4, 8 July 1996. Video available for consultation at BFI.

65 Allister Harry, 'Time the tale were told', *The Voice*, 2 July 1996, p.26.

66 S.I. Martin, *Incomparable World* (London: Quartet, 1996), p.2.

67 Ibid., p.20.

68 Ibid., pp.3–4.

69 Peter Linebaugh and Marcus Rediker, *The Many-Headed Hydra: Sailors, Slaves, Commoners, and the Hidden History of the Revolutionary Atlantic* (Boston: Beacon Press, 2000), pp.332–333.

70 S.I. Martin, *Incomparable World*, p.162.

71 Ibid., pp.63–64.

72 Ibid., p.65.

73 Ibid., p.87.

74 Ibid., p.66, p.130.

75 Ibid., p.96.

76 Ibid., pp.100–101.
77 Ibid., pp.92–93.
78 Ibid., p.136.
79 Ibid., p.166.
80 Ibid., p.40.
81 Fred D'Aguiar, 'Black British Poetry', in Gillian Allnutt, Fred D'Aguiar, Ken Edwards, Eric Mottram (eds), *The New British Poetry 1968–88* (London: Paladin, 1988), p.4.
82 Fred D'Aguiar, 'Editorial', *Artrage*, no.18, Autumn 1987, p.1.
83 'Sweet Thames is rich, satisfying and stimulating. This collaborative effort captures the bitter-sweet history of immigration to this country and what it means to be black and British.' Commission for Racial Equality official citation.
84 J.M. Weylland, *Round The Tower*, p.83.
85 Ernest Marke, *Old Man Trouble* (London: Weidenfeld & Nicolson, 1975), p.22.
86 Ibid., p.23.
87 Michael Banton, *The Coloured Quarter. Negro Immigrants in an English City* (London: Jonathan Cape, 1955), pp.47–48; Roy Kerridge, *Real Wicked, Guy. A View of Black Britain* (Oxford: Basil Blackwell, 1983), p.5.
88 Roland Vane, *Girl from Tiger Bay* (Stoke-on-Trent: The Archer Press, 1954), p.5.
89 D'Aguiar, *Sweet Thames*, p.13.
90 Ibid., p.13, p.13, p.14.
91 Ibid., p.15.
92 Ibid., p.1; Sam Selvon, *The Lonely Londoners*, p.32.
93 Collected on the CD, 'Root and Branch 1: A New World' (1999).
94 D'Aguiar, *Sweet Thames*, p.6.
95 Ibid., p.6.
96 Caryl Phillips, *Crossing The River*

(London: Bloomsbury, 1993), p.237.
97 David Dabydeen, *A Harlot's Progress* (London: Jonathan Cape, 1999), p.3 and p.34.
98 D'Aguiar, *Sweet Thames*, p.7.
99 Ibid., p.8.
100 Ibid., p.8.
101 Ibid., p.8.
102 Ibid., pp.9–10.
103 Ibid., p.1, p.12, p.16.
104 Ibid., p.6.
105 Ibid., p.6.
106 Ibid., pp.16–17.
107 Ibid., p.17.
108 Ibid., p.20.
109 Ibid., p.7 and p.4.
110 Ibid., p.4.
111 Ibid., pp.8–9.
112 Ibid., p.25.
113 Ibid., p.6 and p.4.
114 Ibid., p.23.
115 Salman Rushdie, *The Wizard of Oz* (London: BFI, 1992), p.23.
116 D'Aguiar, *Sweet Thames*, p.4, p.9, p.22.
117 Ibid., p.11.
118 *Collected Poems and Plays of T.S. Eliot*, p.69.
119 D'Aguiar, *Sweet Thames*, p.26; T.S. Eliot, *Collected Poems*, p.171.
120 Eliot, *Collected Poems*, p.67.
121 Ibid., p.75.
122 Roy Porter, *London: A Social History* (London: Hamish Hamilton, 1994), p.349.

Chapter Seven

1 Joseph Salter, *The East In The West. Or Work Among The Asiatics And Africans In London* (London: S.W. Partridge & Co., 1896), p.97.
2 Fred D'Aguiar, *Sweet Thames*, p.6. Elsewhere D'Aguiar has claimed

that, 'Cure resides in knowing the facts and rehabilitating the pain associated with them. And by a trick of the mind brought about by the agency of art, that pain becomes a source of pride and strength.' 'The Last Essay About Slavery', in Sarah Dunant and Roy Porter (eds), *The Age of Anxiety* (London: Virago Press, 1996), p.136.

3 *Sweet Thames*, p.6.

4 Ibid., p.87.

5 Christopher Hibbert, *King Mob: The Story of Lord George Gordon and the Riots of 1780* (London: Longman, Green & Co., 1958), p.80.

6 *The Annual Register* (London: J. Dodsley, 1781), p.276.

7 Salter, *The East In The West*, p.112.

8 E.S. Valentine, 'His Majesty's Customs', in George R. Sims (ed.), *Living London*, vol.1 (London: Cassell & Company, 1901), p.288.

9 Stanley Jackson, *An Indiscreet Guide To Soho* (London: Muse Arts, 1946), p.113.

10 Ibid., p.109.

11 Ernest Marke, *Old Man Trouble* (London: Weidenfeld & Nicolson, 1975), p.144.

12 Mike Phillips, *Notting Hill In The Sixties* (London: Lawrence & Wishart, 1991), p.50.

13 Ibid., p.44.

14 Derek Humphry and David Tindall, *False Messiah. The Story of Michael X* (London: Hart-Davis, MacGibbon, 1977), p.91.

15 Trevor Hercules, *Labelled A Black Villain* (London: Fourth Estate, 1989), p.29.

16 Ibid., p.34.

17 Chris Mullard, *Black Britain* (London: George Allen & Unwin, 1973), pp.151–152.

18 'The Horrors of Slavery', in Iain McCalman (ed.), *The Horrors of Slavery and Other Writings by Robert Wedderburn* (Edinburgh: Edinburgh University Press, 1991), p.48.

19 Iain McCalman, *Radical Underworld. Prophets, Revolutionaries and Pornographers in London, 1795–1840* (Cambridge: Cambridge University Press, 1988), p.54.

20 Wedderburn, 'The Horrors of Slavery', p.60.

21 Iain McCalman, *Radical Underworld*, pp.53–54.

22 Ibid., p.55.

23 Ibid., p.24.

24 Intelligence report, *The Horrors of Slavery*, p.116.

25 McCalman, 'Anti-Slavery and Ultra-Radicalism in Early Nineteenth-Century England: The Case of Robert Wedderburn', *Slavery and Abolition*, vol.7, no.2, September 1986, p.113.

26 Introduction, pp.4–5.

27 'The Address of the Rev. R. Wedderburn', *The Horrors of Slavery*, p.138.

28 In Paul Edwards and Polly Rewt (eds), *The Letters of Ignatius Sancho*, Letter 114, 16 November 1779, p.200. This line does not appear in the original manuscript which is owned by Professor J.R. Willis, Princeton.

29 Edwards and Rewt (eds), *The Letters of Ignatius Sancho*, Letter 8, 21 March 1776, p.46. The quote also appears in *The Interesting Narrative of the Life of Olaudah Equiano*, vol.2, p.210.

30 *Letters*, vol.2, p.5.

31 McCalman, 'Anti-Slavery and Ultra-Radicalism', p.110.

32 Iain McCalman, *Radical Underworld*, p.117.

33 Ibid., p.131.

34 Robert Wedderburn, *The Horrors of Slavery*, p.23.

35 Robert Wedderburn, 'The Horrors of Slavery', p.45.

36 Robert Wedderburn, 'The Axe Laid to the Root', no.4, 1817, *The Horrors of Slavery*, p.96.

37 Robert Wedderburn, 'The Horrors of Slavery', p.59.

38 Ibid., p.46.

39 Iain McCalman, *Radical Underworld*, p.137.

40 Ibid., p.127.

41 Ibid., p.151.

42 Ibid., p.134.

43 George Theodore Wilkinson, *An Authentic History of the Cato-Street Conspiracy* (London: Thomas Kelly, 1820), p.411.

44 Iain McCalman, *Radical Underworld*, p.69.

45 Ibid., p.137.

46 Robert Wedderburn, *The Horrors of Slavery*, p.47.

47 Ibid., p.60.

48 Ibid., p.83.

49 Iain McCalman, *Radical Underworld*, p.50.

50 Ibid., p.123.

51 Ibid., p.62.

52 Robert Wedderburn, *The Horrors of Slavery*, p.124.

53 Robert Wedderburn, 'The Axe Laid to the Root', no.1, *The Horrors of Slavery*, p.86.

54 Robert Wedderburn, 'Cast-Iron Parsons', *The Horrors of Slavery*, p.147.

55 Ibid., pp.144–145.

56 *The Horrors of Slavery*, p.122.

57 Ibid., p.124.

58 Iain McCalman, *Radical Underworld*, p.149.

59 Robert Wedderburn, *The Horrors of Slavery*, p.115.

60 The transition is explained in an editorial, 'Race Today – And Tomorrow?', *Race Today*, April 1972, p.109.

61 *Race Today*, May 1973, p.170.

62 Jeff Rodrigues, 'The Riots of '81', *Marxism Today*, October 1981, p.20.

63 Chris McGlashan, 'The Sound System', *The Sunday Times Magazine*, 4 February 1973, p.14.

64 In Linton Kwesi Johnson, *Dread Beat An' Blood* (London: Bogle-L'Ouverture, 1975), p.21.

65 Joshua Harris and Tina Wallace, *To Ride The Storm. The 1980 Bristol 'Riot' and the State* (London: Heinemann, 1983), pp.59–61.

66 Sharon Atkin, 'Finally there was Linton Kwesi Johnson himself', *Caribbean Times*, 6 May 1995, p.16.

67 *Dread Beat An' Blood*, p.13.

68 In Linton Kwesi Johnson, *Inglan Is A Bitch* (London: Race Today Publications, 1980), p.7.

69 'All Wi Doin' Is Defendin', in *Dread Beat An' Blood*, p.27.

70 Ibid., p.27.

71 'Street 66', in ibid., p.19.

72 Ibid., p.19.

73 'Doun De Road', in ibid., p.22.

74 'Rage', in ibid., p.18.

75 Ibid., p.18.

76 'Doun De Road', in ibid., p.22.

77 Linton Kwesi Johnson, *Voices of the Living and the Dead* (1974 and 2nd ed., London: Race Today Publications, 1983), p.21.

78 Colin McGlashan, 'The Sound System', p.17. See also Ken Pryce, *Endless Pressure* (Harmondsworth: Penguin, 1979), p.147.

79 'Klassikal Dub', in *Dread Beat An' Blood*, p.61.

80 Ibid., p.61.

81 'Dread Beat An' Blood', in *Dread Beat An' Blood*, p.55.

82 Simon Jones, *Black Culture, White Youths. The Reggae Tradition from JA to UK* (Basingstoke: Macmillan, 1988), p.95.

83 'Five Nights of Bleeding', in *Voices of the Living and the Dead*, p.31.

84 'Reggae Sounds', in *Dread Beat An' Blood*, p.56.

85 Ibid., p.56.

86 Ibid., p.57.

87 Farrukh Dhondy, Introduction to *Inglan Is A Bitch*, p.5.

88 *Dread Beat An' Blood*(?), p.59.

89 Isaac Julien and Colin MacCabe, *Diary of a Young Soul Rebel* (London: BFI Publishing, 1991), p.2.

90 *Dread Beat An' Blood*, p.14.

91 *Voices of the Living and the Dead*, p.28.

92 *Dread Beat An' Blood*, p.66.

93 'To Show It So', in ibid., p.67.

94 Ibid., p.22.

95 'Rage', in ibid., p.18.

96 Ian Hamilton, 'The First Life of Salman Rushdie', *The New Yorker*, 25 December 1995 and 1 January 1996, p.94.

97 Rushdie, 'Heavy, man', *The Guardian*, 'Weekend' section, 28 January 1995, p.26.

98 Ian Hamilton, 'The First Life of Salman Rushdie', p.100.

99 Ibid.

100 Salman Rushdie, *The Jaguar Smile* (London: Picador, 1987), p.11.

101 Ian Hamilton, 'The First Life of Salman Rushdie', p.102.

102 Line from advertisement for Burnley Building Society penned by Rushdie and later released as a single. Quoted by Alkarim Jivani, 'Eastern Eye', *Time Out*, 9–16 March 1988, p.28.

103 Salman Rushdie, 'In Good Faith',

104 Salman Rushdie, *Midnight's Children* (London: Jonathan Cape, 1981), p.308.

105 Rushdie, 'In Good Faith', p.404.

106 Rushdie, *The Satanic Verses* (London: Viking, 1988), p.38.

107 Ibid., p.37.

108 For example Rachel Lichtenstein's *Rodinsky's Room* (London: Granta, 1998); Christopher Ross, *Tunnel Visions* (London: Fourth Estate, 2001); Angela Carter, *Wise Children* (London: Chatto & Windus, 1991); Iain Sinclair, *Downriver* (London: Paladin, 1991).

109 Rushdie, *The Satanic Verses*, p.322.

110 Ibid., p.283.

111 Ibid., p.94.

112 Linton Kwesi Johnson, 'Fite Dem Back', *Voices of the Living and the Dead*, p.31.

113 Rushdie, *The Satanic Verses*, p.281.

114 Ibid., p.286.

115 Ibid., p.292.

116 Ibid., p.285.

117 Ibid., p.140.

118 Ibid., p.412.

119 Ibid., p.294.

120 Ibid., p.293.

121 Darrell E. Levi, *Michael Manley. The Making of a Leader* (London: André Deutsch, 1989), p.60.

122 Rushdie, *The Satanic Verses*, p.206.

123 Ibid., p.210.

124 Ibid., p.314.

125 Ibid., p.270.

126 George Barber, 'X Press Yourself', *The Independent Magazine*, 9 July 1994, p.42.

in *Imaginary Homelands* (1991 and new ed., London: Granta, 1992), p.404.

127 Ionie Benjamin, *The Black Press in Britain* (Stoke-on-Trent: Trentham Books, 1995), p.77.

128 Victor Headley, *Excess* (London: The X Press, 1993), p.5.

129 Victor Headley, *Yardie* (London: The X Press, 1992), p.5; Victor Headley, *Yush!* (London: The X Press, 1994), p.4; *Yush!*, p.73.

130 Headley, *Yardie*, p.103.

131 Headley, *Excess*, p.219.

132 Headley, *Yardie*, p.44.

133 Headley, *Excess*, p.107.

134 Ibid., p.120.

135 Headley, *Yush!*, p.43.

136 Kwesi Johnson, *Dread Beat An' Blood*, p.13.

137 Kwesi Johnson, 'Double Skank', in ibid., p.14.

138 Rushdie, *The Satanic Verses*, pp.454–455.

139 H.R.F. Keating, *Writing Crime Fiction* (1986; 2nd ed., London: A. & C. Black, 1994), p.45.

140 Headley, *Excess*, p.9.

141 Headley, *Yardie*, p.26.

Bibliography

Part 1 of this bibliography has been arranged chapter-by-chapter each of which has been divided according to the following four subsections:

* Archival and unpublished material.
* Primary material.
* Uncollected work by the author.
* Selected reviews, biographies, interviews and criticism.

Part 2 lists some of the other works consulted.

PART ONE

CHAPTER ONE Archival Material

Unpublished letters by Ignatius Sancho, Elizabeth Sancho, William Sancho. Personal collection of J.R. Willis, Princeton, USA.

St Margaret's Parish Register [containing baptismal and burial records], 1761–1780. City of Westminster Archives Centre.

Westminster Poll Books, 1774 & 1780. Original registers held at Greater London Corporation Record Office. WR/PP/1774/1–4 & WR/PP/1780/1–3.

St Margaret's Grand Division Poors Rate records, 1774–1804. Held at City of Westminster Archives Centre. Microform reels E 471, E 475, E 478, E 481, E 485, E 488, E 492, E 496, E 499, E 502, E 504, E 508, E 512, E 516, E 519, E 523, E 527,

E 530, E 533, E 536, E 539, E 542, E 545, E 548, E 551, E 554, E 557, E 560, E 563, E 566, E 569, E 572.

Needham, W.E. (compiler): *The Broadway [Burial] Ground at Christ Church in the Parish of St Margaret Westminster* (1846). Manuscript book held at City of Westminster Archives Centre.

CHAPTER ONE **Primary Material**

Edwards, Paul (ed.): *Letters of the Late Ignatius Sancho*, Colonial History Series (London: Dawsons of Pall Mall, 1969).

Edwards, Paul and Polly Rewt (eds): *The Letters of Ignatius Sancho* (Edinburgh: Edinburgh University Press, 1994).

Equiano, Olaudah: *The Interesting Narrative of the Life of Olaudah Equiano, or Gustavus Vassa, the African*, 2 vols (London: Printed for the Author, 1789).

Equiano, Olaudah: *The Interesting Narrative And Other Writings*, ed. Vincent Carretta (New York: Penguin, 1995).

Gronniosaw, Ukawsaw: *A Narrative of the Most Remarkable Particulars in the Life of James Albert Ukawsaw Gronniosaw, An African Prince, Written by Himself* (Bath: W. Gye, [1772]).

Sancho, Ignatius: *Letters of the Late Ignatius Sancho: an African, to which are Prefixed, Memoirs of his Life*, 2 vols (London: J. Nichols, 1782).

Sancho, Ignatius: *Letters of the Late Ignatius Sancho: an African, to which are Prefixed, Memoirs of His Life by Joseph Jekyll, Esq., M.P.*, (5th ed., London: William Sancho, 1803).

Sancho, Ignatius: *Letters Of The Late Ignatius Sancho, An African*, ed. Vincent Carretta (New York: Penguin, 1998).

Wright, Josephine (ed.): *Ignatius Sancho (1729–1780) An Early African Composer in England – The Collected Editions of His Music in Facsimile* (New York and London: Garland, 1981).

CHAPTER ONE **Selected Biography and Criticism**

Anim-Addo, Joan: *Sugar, Spices And Human Cargo. An Early Black History of Greenwich* (London: Greenwich Leisure Services, 1996).

The Annual Register, Or A View Of The History, Politics And Literature, For The Year 1775 (4th ed., London: J. Dodsley, 1783), pp.173–174.

Brown, Lloyd: review of 1969 reprint, *Eighteenth-Century Studies. An Interdisciplinary Journal*, vol.3, no.3, Spring 1970, pp.415–419.

Dabydeen, David: 'Freedom's Slave' [Equiano profile], *The Observer*, 8 August 1999, p.23.

Dathorne, O.R.: 'African Writers of the Eighteenth Century', *London Magazine*, vol.5, no.6 (new series), October 1965, pp.51–58.

Dictionary of National Biography, vol.L (London: Smith, Elder & Co., 1897), pp.243–244.

Edwards, Paul and James Walvin (eds): *Black Personalities in the Era of the Slave Trade* (London: Macmillan, 1983).

The European Magazine, And London Review; Containing the Literature, History, Politics, Arts, Manners and Amusements of the Age. For Sep, 1782 (London: John Fielding, 1782), vol.2, pp.199–202.

The Gentleman's Magazine, September 1782, pp.437–439.

'Gillespie': 'Some Old Tobacco Labels', *Tobacco. A Monthly Trade Journal For The Importer, Exporter, Manufacturer, and Retailer of Tobacco*, no.86, 1 February 1888, pp.36–38.

'Gillespie': 'Some Old Tobacconists', *Tobacco. A Monthly Trade Journal For The Importer, Exporter, Manufacturer, and Retailer of Tobacco*, no.90, 1 June 1888, pp.156–158.

Girdham, Jane, Reyahn King, Sukhdev Sandhu and James Walvin: *Ignatius Sancho. An African Man Of Letters* (London: National Portrait Gallery Publications, 1997).

Gregoire, H.: *An Enquiry Concerning The Intellectual and Moral Faculties, and Literature of Negroes; Followed With an Account Of The Life and Works of Fifteen Negroes and Mulattoes, Distinguished in Science, Literature and the Arts* (1808 and Brooklyn: Thomas Kirk, 1810).

Jefferson, Thomas: *Notes on the State of Virginia* (1782 and Chapel Hill: University of North Carolina Press, 1955).

Mason, W.: *An Occasional Discourse, Preached In The Cathedral of St Peter In York, January 27, 1788. On The Subject of the African Slave Trade* (York: Printed by A. Ward for the Author, 1788).

Notes and Queries: 7th series, vii, p.325 and p.457; 7th series, viii, pp.32–33 and pp.296–297.

Ogude, S.E.: *Genius in Bondage. A Study of the Origins of African Literature in English* (Ile-Ife, Nigeria: University of Ife Press, 1983).

Peckard, Peter: *Piety, Benevolence, and Loyalty, Recommended. A Sermon Preached Before The University of Cambridge, January the 30th, 1784. Published At The Bequest of the Vice-Chancellor and Heads of Colleges* (Cambridge: J. Archdeacon, 1784).

Peckard, Peter: *Am I Not a Man? And a Brother? With All Humility Addressed To The British Legislature* (Cambridge: J. Archdeacon, 1788).

Phillips, Caryl: 'Hard times of the "outside" writers' [edited version of a lecture, 'Extravagant Strangers: the "Other" Voices in English Literature', in the Radio 3/Royal Society of Arts series, *These Islands Now*, broadcast 11.11.95], *Daily Telegraph*, 11 November 1995, p.A3.

R[athbone]., R[ichard].: review of 1969 reprint, *African Affairs*, vol.69, no.274, January 1970, p.88.

Sandiford, Keith: *Measuring the Moment: Strategies of Protest in Eighteenth-Century Afro-English Writing* (Selinsgrove: Susquehanna University Press, 1988).

Vincent, Theo: 'Two Eighteenth Century African Writers: Ignatius

Sancho and Ottobah Cugoano', *Black Orpheus. A Journal of the Arts in Africa*, vol.2, nos 5 and 6, 1970, pp.20–30.

Walvin, James: *An African's Life: The Life and Times of Olaudah Equiano 1745–1797* (London: Cassell, 1998).

W[illis], J.R.: 'New Light on the Life of Ignatius Sancho. Some Unpublished Letters', *Slavery and Abolition. A Journal of Comparative Studies*, vol.1, no.3, December 1980, pp.345–358.

CHAPTER TWO **Primary Material**

Alexander, Ziggi and Audrey Dewjee (eds), *Wonderful Adventures of Mrs Seacole in Many Lands* (Bristol: Falling Wall Press, 1984).

Brown, William Wells: *Three Years In Europe; Or, Places I Have Seen And Peoples I Have Met* (London: Charles Gilpin, 1852).

Carpenter, Mary (ed.): *The Last Days In England of Rajah Rammohun Roy* (Calcutta, 1915).

Chatterjee, A.R.: *A Peep Through The Veil* (London: Arthur H. Stockwell, [1914?]).

Collet, Sophia Dobson (ed.): *Keshub Chunder Sen's English Visit* (London: Strahan & Co., 1871).

Collet, Sophia Dobson: *The Life and Letters of Raja Rammohun Roy* (1900 and 3rd ed., Calcutta: Sadharan Brahmo Samaj, 1962).

Dehlavi, A.M.K.: 'An Indian View Of The Modes Of Living In England', *The Indian Magazine*, vol.24, no.269, May 1893, pp.246–249.

Dehlavi, A.M.K.: 'An Indian View Of The Modes Of Living In England. II', *The Indian Magazine*, vol.24, no.270, June 1893, pp.298–307.

Douglass, Frederick: *My Bondage and My Freedom* (New York: Miller, Orton and Mulligan, 1855).

Douglass, Frederick: *The Life and Times of Frederick Douglass, from 1817–1882, Written by Himself* (Hartford, Connecticut: Park Publishing Co., 1881).

Dutt, Romesh Chunder: *Three Years In Europe, 1868 To 1871, With An Account of Subsequent Visits To Europe In 1886 And 1893* (4th ed., Calcutta: S.K. Lahiri & Co., 1896).

Ferguson, Moira (ed.): *The History Of Mary Prince. A West Indian Slave Related by Herself* (London: Pandora Press, 1987).

Gandhi, M.K.: *An Autobiography or The Story Of My Experiments With Truth* (1927 and Ahmedabad: Narajivan Publishing House, 1948).

Hobhouse, Mary: 'London Sketched By An Indian Pen', *The Indian Magazine*, vol.21, no.230, February 1890, pp.61–73.

Hobhouse, Lady: 'Further Sketches by an Indian Pen', *The Indian Magazine*, vol.21, no.231, March 1890, pp.139–152.

I' Tesanuddin, Mirza Sheikh: *The Wonders of Vilayet: Being the Memoir, originally in Persian, of a visit to France and Britain in 1765* (Leeds: Peepal Tree, 2002).

Jacobs, Harriet: *Incidents In The Life Of A Slave Girl* (1861 and New York: Oxford University Press, 1988).

Jee, Bhagvat Sinh, Thakore Saheb of Gondal: *Journal of A Visit To England in 1883* (Bombay: Education Society's Press, 1886).

Karaka, D.F.: *I Go West* (London: Michael Joseph, 1938).

Khan, Mirza Abu Taleb: *Travels Of Mirza Abu Taleb Khan In Asia, Africa, And Europe, During The Years 1799, 1800, 1801, 1802, And 1803*, 3 vols (1810 and 2nd ed., London: Longman, Hurst, Rees, Orme and Brown, 1814).

Mahomed, S.D.: *Shampooing; Or, Benefits Resulting From The Use Of The Indian Medicated Vapour Bath, As introduced to this Country* (Brighton: E.H. Creasy, 1822).

Malabari, Behramji M.: *The Indian Eye On English Life Or Rambles Of A Pilgrim Reformer* (Westminster: Archibald Constable & Company, 1893).

Mukaza, Ham: *Uganda's Katikiro in England; Being the Official Account of his Visit to the Coronation of His Majesty King Edward VII* (London: Hutchinson & Co., 1904).

Mukharji, T.N.: *A Visit To Europe* (Calcutta: W. Newman & Co., 1889).

Nadkarni, Rao Bahadur Ghanasham Nikanth: *Journal Of A Visit To Europe In 1896* (Bombay: D.B. Taraporevala, Sons & Co., 1903).

Nowrojee, Jehangeer and Hirjeebhoy Merwanjee: *Journal of a Residence of Two Years and A Half In Great Britain* (London: W.H. Allen & Co., 1841).

Pandian, Rev. T.B.: *England To An Indian Eye: Or English Pictures From An Indian Camera* (London: Elliot and Stock, 1897).

Personal Adventures Of 'Prince Ananda' (E.A.R.C.) For the first time presented to the British Public (Deansgate: John Heywood, [1904?]).

Prince, Mary: *The History of Mary Prince, a West Indian Slave, Related by Herself* (London: F. Westley and A.H. Davis, 1831).

Prince, Mary: *The History of Mary Prince*, ed. Sara Salih (London: Penguin, 2000).

Ram, Jhinda: *My Trip To Europe* (Lahore: Mufid-I-Am Press, 1893).

Ramakrishna, T.: *My Visit To The West* (London: T. Fisher Unwin Ltd, 1915).

Roper, Josiah: *A Narrative Of The Adventures And Escapes Of Moses Roper From American Slavery* (2nd ed., London: Darton, Harvey and Darton, 1838).

Satthianadhan, S.: *England and India. Lectures* (Madras: Addison & Co., 1886).

Satthianadhan, S.: *Four Years In An English University* (Madras: Lawrence Asylum Press, 1890).

Satthianadhan, S.: *A Holiday Trip To Europe And America* (Madras: Srinivasa, Varadachari & Co., 1897).

Seacole, Mary: *Wonderful Adventures of Mrs Seacole in Many Lands* (London: James Blackwood, 1857).

Sen, Keshub Chunder: *Diary In England* (2nd ed., Calcutta: Brahmo Tract Society, 1894).

Shah, Syed A.M.: 'A Visit To The Tower of London', *The Indian Magazine*, vol.24, no.268, April 1893, pp.208–210.

Singh, Bhawani: *Travel Pictures. The Record of A European Tour* (London: Longman, Green & Co., 1912).

Sorabji, Cornelia: *India Calling. The Memoirs of Cornelia Sorabji* (London: Nisbet, 1934).

Ward, Samuel Ringgold: *Autobiography Of A Fugitive Negro: His Anti-Slavery Labours In The United States, Canada, & England* (London: John Snow, 1855).

Washington, Booker T.: *The Man Farthest Down: A Record of Observation and Study in Europe* (New York: Doubleday, Page & Company, 1912).

West, Capt. Edward W. (ed.): *Diary Of The Late Rajah Of Kolhapoor, During His Visit To Europe In 1870* (London: Smith, Elder & Co., 1872).

CHAPTER TWO **Selected Biography and Criticism**

Alexander, Ziggi: 'Let it Lie Upon the Table: The Status of Black Women's Biography in the UK', *Gender and History*, vol.2, no.2, Spring 1990, pp.22–33.

Borthwick, Meredith: *Keshub Chunder Sen. A Search for Cultural Synthesis* (Calcutta: Minerva Associates, 1977).

Burton, Antoinette: 'A "Pilgrim Reformer" at the Heart of the Empire: Behramji Malabari in Late-Victorian London', *Gender and History*, vol.8, no.2, August 1996, pp.175–196.

Burton, Antoinette: 'Making a Spectacle of Empire: Indian Travellers in Fin-de-Siecle London', *History Workshop Journal*, no.42, Autumn 1996, pp.126–146.

Craft, William and Ellen: *Running A Thousand Miles For Freedom; Or, The Escape Of William And Ellen Craft From Slavery* (London: William Tweedie, 1860).

Craig, Christine: 'Wonderful Adventures of Mrs Seacole In Many Lands. Autobiography as literary genre and a window to character', *Caribbean Quarterly*, vol.30, no.2, June 1984, pp.33–47.

Dutta, Krishna and Andrew Robinson: *Rabindranath Tagore. The Myriad-Minded Man* (London: Bloomsbury, 1995).

Gandhi, M.K.: 'From The London Diary', in *The Collected Works Of Mahatma Gandhi, vol.1 (1884–1896)* (Delhi: The Publications Division, Ministry of Information And Broadcasting, 1958), pp.3–21.

Hay, Stephen: 'The Making Of A Late-Victorian Hindu: M.K. Gandhi In London, 1888–1891', *Victorian Studies*, vol.33, no.1, Autumn 1989, pp.74–98.

Henson, Josiah: *The Life of Josiah Henson, Formerly A Slave, As Narrated By Himself* (London: Charles Gilpin, 1851).

Hinnells, John R. and Omar Ralph: *Sir Mancherjee Merwanjee Bhownagree K.C.I.E., Order of the Lion and the Sun of Persia 1851–1933* (London: Hansib, 1995).

Hunt, James D.: *Gandhi in London* (1978 and rev. ed., New Delhi: Promilla & Co., 1993).

Karaka, D.F.: *Then Came Hazrat Ali* (Bombay: D.F. Karaka, 1972).

Lahiri, Shompa: 'British Policy Towards Indian Princes in Late Nineteenth and Early Twentieth Century Britain', *Immigrants and Minorities*, vol.15, no.3, November 1996, pp.214–232.

Spiers, Fiona: 'Black Americans in Britain and the struggle for Black freedom in the United States, 1820–70', in Jagdish Gundara and Ian Duffield (eds), *Essays on the History of Blacks in Britain. From Roman Times to the Mid-Twentieth Century* (Aldershot: Avebury, 1992), pp.81–98.

Sundquist, Eric J. (ed.): *Frederick Douglass. New Literary And Historical Essays* (Cambridge: Cambridge University Press, 1990).

CHAPTER THREE **Archival and Uncollected Material**

Selvon, Sam: 'Modern Art . . .', *Sunday Guardian Weekly*, 18 January 1948, p.12.

Selvon, Sam: 'The Sea', short story broadcast on BBC Colonial

Service *Caribbean Voices* radio series, 14 March 1948.
Typescript no.183 in *Caribbean Voices* file at BBC Written
Archives Centre, Caversham, Reading, England.

Selvon, Sam: Review of Barnabas J. Ramon Fortune's *Parian
Currents*, *Sunday Guardian Weekly*, 14 March 1948, p.12.

Selvon, Sam: 'We Also Served', short story broadcast on BBC
Colonial Service *Caribbean Voices* radio series, 29 August 1948.
Typescript no.274 in *Caribbean Voices* file, Caversham.

Selvon, Sam: 'Tropic (An Excerpt)', *Sunday Guardian Weekly*,
5 June 1949, p.12.

Selvon, Sam: Contributor to '"English Goes Abroad". English as
Spoken in the West Indies', *The English Tongue* radio series,
General Overseas Service, 30 August 1957. Typescript kept in
Selvon's radio file, Caversham.

Fortune, Barnabas J. Ramon: 'Letter To Selvon', poem broadcast
on BBC Overseas Service *Caribbean Voices* radio programme,
13 July 1958. Typescript in *Caribbean Voices* file.

Hall, Stuart: 'In Discussion on "British Caribbean Writers"', radio
broadcast for BBC Third Programme, 21 April 1958.
Typescript kept in Hall's radio file, Caversham.

Selvon, Sam: 'Little Drops of Water', *Bim*, XI, 44, 1967,
pp.245–252.

Selvon, Sam: *Bringing In The Sheaves* (22 January 1969), drama
script held at BBC Radio Drama Library, Caversham.

Selvon, Sam: *Mary Mary Shut Your Gate* (6 January 1971), BBC
Radio Drama Library, Caversham.

CHAPTER THREE **Primary Material**

Rhys, Jean: *After Leaving Mr Mackenzie* (London: Cape,
1930).

Rhys, Jean: *Tigers Are Better-Looking* (London: André Deutsch,
1968).

Rhys, Jean: *Sleep It Off Lady* (London: André Deutsch, 1976).

Rhys, Jean: *Smile Please. An Unfinished Autobiography* (London: André Deutsch, 1979).

Selvon, Sam: *A Brighter Sun* (London: Allan Wingate, 1952).

Selvon, Sam: *An Island Is A World* (London: Allan Wingate, 1955).

Selvon, Sam: *The Lonely Londoners* (London: MacGibbon & Kee, 1956).

Selvon, Sam: *Ways of Sunlight* (London: MacGibbon & Kee, 1957).

Selvon, Sam: *Turn Again Tiger* (London: MacGibbon & Kee, 1958).

Selvon, Sam: *I Hear Thunder* (London: MacGibbon & Kee, 1963).

Selvon, Sam: *The Housing Lark* (London: MacGibbon & Kee, 1965).

Selvon, Sam: *The Plains of Caroni* (London: MacGibbon & Kee, 1970).

Selvon, Sam: *Those Who Eat The Cascadura* (London: Davis-Poynter, 1972).

Selvon, Sam: *Moses Ascending* (London: Davis-Poynter, 1975).

Selvon, Sam: *Moses Migrating* (1983 and Washington: Three Continents Press, 1992).

Selvon, Sam: *Eldorado West One* (Leeds: Peepal Tree Press, 1988).

Selvon, Sam: *Foreday Morning. Selected Prose 1946–1986* (Harlow: Longman, 1989).

Selvon, Sam: *Highway In The Sun and Other Plays* (Leeds: Peepal Tree Press, 1991).

CHAPTER THREE **Selected Criticism**

Angier, Carole: *Jean Rhys. Life and Work* (London: André Deutsch, 1990).

Birbalsingh, Frank: 'Samuel Selvon: The open society or its enemies?', in *Frontiers of Caribbean Literature in English* (London: Macmillan, 1996), pp.54–67.

Chen, Willi: 'A Night With Sam Selvon', *London Magazine*, vol.34, nos5 and 6, August/September 1994, pp.99–103.

Clarke, Austin: *A Passage Back Home. A Personal Reminiscence of Samuel Selvon* (Toronto: Exile Editions, 1994).

Dance, Daryl Cumber: *New World Adams. Conversations with Contemporary West Indian Writers* (1984 and Leeds: Peepal Tree Press, 1992).

Emery, Mary Lou: *Jean Rhys at 'World's End'. Novels of Colonial and Sexual Exile* (Austin: University of Texas Press, 1990).

Gardiner, Judith Kegan: 'The Exhilaration of Exile. Rhys, Stead, and Lessing', in Mary Lynn Broe and Angela Ingram (eds): *Women's Writing in Exile* (Chapel Hill: University of North Carolina Press, 1989), pp.133–150.

James, Louis: Obituary of Selvon, *The Independent*, 20 April 1994, p.14.

Jarrett–Macauley, Delia: 'Putting the black woman in the frame: Una Marson and the West Indian challenge to British national identity', in Christine Gledhill and Gillian Swanson (eds), *Nationalising Femininity. Culture, Sexuality and British Cinema in the Second World War* (Manchester: Manchester University Press, 1996), pp.119–126.

Joseph, Margaret Paul: *Caliban In Exile. The Outsider In Caribbean Fiction* (New York: Greenwood Press, 1992).

Jussawalla, Feroza and Reed Way Dasenbrock (eds): *Interviews With Writers of the Post-Colonial World* (Jackson: University Press of Mississippi, 1992).

Khan, Naseem: 'The rise of the lonely Londoners', *The Independent*, 12 November 1993, p.23.

Looker, Mark: *Atlantic Passages: History, Community, and Language in the Fiction of Sam Selvon* (New York: Peter Lang, 1996).

Nasta, Susheila (ed.): *Critical Perspectives on Sam Selvon* (Washington: Three Continents Press, 1988).

Nasta, Susheila: 'Lighting the bleak city streets', *The Guardian*, Section 2, 19 April 1994, p.21.

Nasta, Susheila and Anna Rutherford (eds): *Tiger's Triumph. Celebrating Sam Selvon* (Hebden Bridge: Dangaroo Press, 1995).

Ramchand, Kenneth: 'The Love Songs of Samuel Selvon', in *Ariel. A Review of International English Literature* [special issue, 'Tribute To Sam Selvon'], vol.27, no.2, April 1996, pp.77–88.

Salkey, Andrew: 'Here's Thinking of You Sam-Sam', *Kyk-Over-Al*, no.46/47, December 1995, pp.240–249.

Thomas, Sue: 'Modernity, Voice, And Window-Breaking. Jean Rhys's "Let them call it jazz"', in Carole Boyce Davies, *Black Women, Writing and Identity* (London: Routledge, 1994), pp.185–200.

Wyndham, Francis and Diana Melly (eds): *Jean Rhys. Letters 1931–66* (London: André Deutsch, 1984).

CHAPTER FOUR **Primary Material**

Anand, Mulk Raj: *Conversations in Bloomsbury* (London: Wildwood House, 1981).

Chaudhuri, Nirad: *A Passage To England* (London: Macmillan & Co., 1959).

Lamming, George: *The Emigrants* (London: Michael Joseph, 1954).

Lamming, George: *The Pleasures of Exile* (London: Michael Joseph, 1960).

Moraes, Dom: *My Son's Father* (London: Secker & Warburg, 1967).

Moraes, Dom: *Between East and West. A Collection of Essays* (London: Vikas Publications, 1971).

Naipaul, V.S.: *Mr Stone and the Knights Companion* (London: André Deutsch, 1963).

Naipaul, V.S.: *The Mimic Men* (London: André Deutsch, 1967).

Naipaul, V.S.: *The Overcrowded Barracoon, and other articles* (London: André Deutsch, 1972).

Naipaul, V.S.: *Finding The Centre. Two Narratives* (London: André Deutsch, 1984).

Naipaul, V.S.: *The Enigma of Arrival. A novel in five sections* (London: Viking, 1987).

Naipaul, V.S.: *A Way In The World. A Sequence* (London: Heinemann, 1994).

Naipaul, V.S.: *Letters Between a Father and Son* (London: Little, Brown, 1999).

Naipaul, V.S.: *Reading and Writing: A Personal Account* (New York: New York Review Books, 2000).

Naipaul, V.S.: *Half A Life* (London: Picador, 2001).

Naipaul, V.S.: *The Writer and The World: Essays* (London: Picador, 2002).

CHAPTER FOUR **Selected Criticism and Interviews**

Gurr, Andrew: *Writers In Exile: The Identity of Home in Modern Literature* (Sussex: Harvester Press, 1991).

Khair, Tabish: *Babu Fictions: Alienation in Contemporary Indian English Novels* (New Delhi: Oxford University Press, 2001).

Levy, Judith: *V.S. Naipaul: Displacement and Autobiography* (New York: Garland, 1995).

Munro, Ian and Reinhard Sander (eds): *Kas-Kas. Interviews with Three Caribbean Writers in Texas. George Lamming, C.L.R. James, Wilson Harris* (Occasional Publications of the Afro-American Research Institute, University of Texas at Austin, 1972).

Nightingale, Peggy: *Journey Through Darkness. The Writing of V.S. Naipaul* (St Lucia, Queensland: University of Queensland Press, 1987).

Nixon, Rob: *London Calling. V.S. Naipaul, Postcolonial Mandarin* (New York: Oxford University Press, 1992).

Theroux, Paul: *V.S. Naipaul: an introduction to his work* (London: Heinemann, 1972).

Theroux, Paul: *Sir Vidia's Shadow: A Friendship Across Five Continents* (London: Hamish Hamilton, 1998).

Weiss, Timothy: *On The Margins: the art of exile in V.S. Naipaul*
(Amherst: University of Massachusetts Press, 1992).

CHAPTER FIVE **Primary Material**

Tomorrow-Today! (London: Calder, 1983).
My Beautiful Laundrette and The Rainbow Sign (London: Faber,
1986).
Sammy and Rosie Get Laid, the Script and the Diary [i.e. *Some Time
With Stephen*] (London: Faber, 1988).
'Esther', *New Statesman and Society*, 1 September 1989,
pp.19–23.
The Buddha of Suburbia (London: Faber, 1990).
London Kills Me (London: Faber, 1991).
Outskirts and Other Plays [inc. *The King and Me, Outskirts,
Borderline, Birds of Passage*] (London: Faber, 1992).
The Black Album (London: Faber, 1995).
Kureishi Hanif and Jon Savage (eds): *The Faber Book of Pop*
(London: Faber, 1995).
Love In A Blue Time (London: Faber, 1997).
Intimacy (London: Faber, 1998).
My Son The Fanatic (London: Faber, 1998).
Sleep With Me (London: Faber, 1999).
Midnight All Day (London: Faber, 1999).
Gabriel's Gift (London: Faber, 2001).
Intimacy and Other Stories (London: Faber, 2001).
The Body (London: Faber, 2002)

CHAPTER FIVE **Uncollected Articles by Hanif Kureishi**

'Syphilitic Septimus' [review of Kikki Ducornet, *Entering Fire*],
Times Literary Supplement, 21 February 1986, p.198.
'Erotic Politicians and Mullahs', *Granta* (Cambridge: Spring 1986),
no.17, pp.139–151.

'How our laundrette cleaned up the US', *The Guardian*, 6 May
    1986, p.9.

'Away from the family' [review of Joseph Olshan, *Clara's Heart*],
    TLS, 16 May 1986, p.536.

'Saved by ambition' [review of Ved Mehta, *Sound-Shadows of the
    New World*], *TLS*, 30 May 1986, p.589.

'A Feast Of Words' [review of Amitav Ghosh, *The Circle of Reason*],
    The New Republic, 4 August 1986, pp.40–41.

'Without Deference' [review of John Street, *Rebel Rock*; David
    Widgery, *Beating Time*; Bob Geldof, *Is That It?*], *TLS*,
    8 August 1986, p.874.

'The cold eye of Joe Orton' [review of John Lahr (ed.), *The Orton
    Diaries*], *The Guardian*, 7 November 1986, p.13.

'Stations of the liberal cross' [review of Dervla Murphy, *Tales from
    Two Cities*], *The Guardian*, 13 November 1987, p.16.

'Outrage unforced' [review of Robert Chesshyre, *The Return of a
    Native Reporter*], *TLS*, 27 November 1987, p.1312.

'England, bloody England', *The Guardian*, 15 January 1988, p.19.

'Saatchi and Thatcher' [review of Ivan Fallon, *The Brothers: The
    Rise and Rise of Saatchi and Saatchi*], *New Statesman and Society*,
    2 September 1988, pp.33–34.

'Finishing The Job', *New Statesman and Society*, 28 October 1988,
    pp.19–24.

'England, Your England', *New Statesman and Society*, 21 July 1989,
    pp.27–29.

'High societies' [review of Richard Rudgley, *The Alchemy of
    Culture*], 'Night and Day' [*The Mail on Sunday* review section],
    5 December 1993, p.34.

'My father's gift', *The Sunday Telegraph Magazine*, 26 April 1998,
    pp.14–18.

CHAPTER FIVE **Selected Interviews and Criticism**

Babuscio, Jack: Review of *Sammy and Rosie Get Laid*, in *Gay Times*, January 1988, p.70.

Bald, Suresht Renjen: 'Images of South Asian migrants in literature: differing perspectives', *New Community*, vol.17, no.3, April 1991, pp.413–431.

Barron, Janet: 'Weird Sex and Good Karma in S.E.20', *GQ*, April 1990, pp.40–42.

Burton, Peter: 'The price of free speech may be vilification and abuse' [interview], *Gay Times*, no.139, April 1990, pp.24–26.

Desert Island Discs, BBC Radio 4, 22 April 1996.

Dodd, Philip: 'Requiem For a Rave' [interview], *Sight and Sound*, vol.1, no.5, 1991, pp.9–13.

Fuller, Graham: 'Battle For Britain: The Empire Strikes Back', *Film Comment*, vol.24, no.4, July–August 1988, pp.62–68.

Hennessy, Kesewa: 'A girl from nowhere' [interview with Andrea Levy], *The Voice*, 6 August 1996, pp.23–24.

Jack, Ian: 'Brutish way of life' [review of *My Beautiful Laundrette*], *TLS*, 2 May 1986, p.470.

Jaggi, Maya: 'A buddy from suburbia' [interview], *The Guardian*, Section 2, 1 March 1995, pp.6–7.

Jamal, Mahmoud: 'Dirty Linen' [review of *My Beautiful Laundrette*], *Artrage*, no.17, Summer 1987, p.40.

Jarman, Derek: 'Freedom fighter for a vision of the truth' [response to Norman Stone article, 10 January 1988], *The Sunday Times*, 17 January 1988, p.c9.

Jena, Seema: 'From Victims To Survivors: The Anti-Hero and Narrative Strategy in Asian Immigrant Writing', *Wasafiri*, no.17, Spring 1993, pp.3–6.

Julian, Ria: 'Brecht and Britain: Hanif Kureishi in Interview with Ria Julian', *Drama: the Quarterly Theatre Review*, no.155, Spring 1985, pp.5–7.

Kaleta, Kenneth C.: *Hanif Kureishi: Postcolonial Storyteller* (Austin: University of Texas Press,

Kauffmann, Stanley: 'London Broils' [review of *My Beautiful Laundrette*], *The New Republic*, 7 April 1986, pp.24–26.

Kauffmann, Stanley: 'Made in Britain' [review of *Sammy and Rosie Get Laid*], *The New Republic*, 30 November 1987, pp.24–26.

Kermode, Frank: 'Voice of the almost English' [interview], *The Guardian*, 10 April 1990, p.42.

Lee, A. Robert: 'Changing the Script: Sex, Lies and Videotapes in Hanif Kureishi, David Dabydeen and Mike Phillips', in A. Robert Lee (ed.), *Other Britain, Other British* (London: Pluto Press, 1995).

Marcus, Greil: 'Greil Marcus' Top Ten Real Life Rock', *Artforum International*, vol.32, no.3, November 1993, p.13.

Mathews, Tom Dewe: Review of *London Kills Me*, in *Sight and Sound*, December 1991, pp.180–181.

Moore-Gilbert, Bart: *Hanif Kureishi* (Manchester: Manchester University Press, 2001).

Robinson, Andrew: 'Boys From The Currystuff', *Sight and Sound*, Winter 1985/1986, p.15.

Schwarz, Walter: *The New Dissenters. The NonConformist Conscience In The Age of Thatcher* (London: Bedford Square Press of the National Council for Voluntary Organizations, 1989).

Spivak, Gayatri Chakravorty: 'Sammy and Rosie Get Laid', in *Outside In The Teaching Machine* (New York and London: Routledge, 1993), pp.243–254.

Stone, Norman: 'Through A Lens Darkly' and 'Sick Scenes From English Life', *The Sunday Times*, 10 January 1988, pp.c1–2.

Syal, Meera: Review of *The Buddha of Suburbia* on *Kaleidoscope*, BBC Radio 4, 5 November 1993.

Wheen, Francis (ed.): 'Hackney-ed' [review of *The Buddha of Suburbia*], in *Lord Gnome's Literary Companion* (London: Verso, 1994).

Youngs, Tim: 'Morality and Ideology: The Arranged Marriage In

Contemporary British-Asian Drama', *Wasafiri*, no.9, Winter 1988/1989, pp.3–6.

CHAPTER SIX **Archival Material**

Phillips, Caryl: *The Final Passage*. Broadcast 7 and 8 July 1996. 2-part video available for consultation at British Film Institute, programme numbers 8.032 663 AA and 8.032 716 AA.

D'Aguiar, Fred: *Sweet Thames*. Broadcast 3 July 1992, BBC2. Script held at BBC Written Archives Centre, Caversham, Reading. Video available for consultation at British Film Institute, programme no.1 NBS J 146F/71X.

CHAPTER SIX **Primary Works**

Dabydeen, David: *A Harlot's Progress* (London: Jonathan Cape, 1999).

D'Aguiar, Fred: *Mama Dot* (London: Chatto & Windus, 1985).

D'Aguiar, Fred: *Airy Hall* (London: Chatto & Windus, 1989).

D'Aguiar, Fred: *British Subjects* (Newcastle upon Tyne: Bloodaxe, 1993).

D'Aguiar, Fred: *The Longest Memory* (London: Chatto & Windus, 1994).

D'Aguiar, Fred: 'A Jamaican Airman Foresees His Death', in Yvonne Brewster (ed.), *Black Plays 3* (London: Methuen, 1995).

D'Aguiar, Fred: *Dear Future* (London: Chatto & Windus, 1996).

D'Aguiar, Fred: *Feeding The Ghosts* (London: Chatto & Windus, 1997).

D'Aguiar, Fred: *Bill of Rights* (London: Chatto & Windus, 1998).

D'Aguiar, Fred: *An English Sampler: New and Selected Poems* (London: Chatto & Windus, 2001).

Evaristo, Bernardine: *The Emperor's Babe* (London: Hamish Hamilton, 2001).

Martin, S.I.: *Incomparable World* (London: Quartet, 1996).

Phillips, Caryl: *Strange Fruit* (Ambergate: Amber Lane Press, 1981).

Phillips, Caryl: *Where There Is Darkness* (Ambergate: Amber Lane Press, 1982).

Phillips, Caryl: *The Shelter* (Oxford: Amber Lane Press, 1984).

Phillips, Caryl: *The Final Passage* (London: Faber, 1985).

Phillips, Caryl: 'The Wasted Years', in *Best Radio Plays of 1984: The Giles Cooper Award Winners* (London: Methuen/BBC Publications, 1985).

Phillips, Caryl: *A State of Independence* (London: Faber, 1986).

Phillips, Caryl: *The European Tribe* (London: Faber, 1987).

Phillips, Caryl: *Playing Away* (London: Faber, 1987).

Phillips, Caryl: *Higher Ground* (London: Viking, 1989).

Phillips, Caryl: *Cambridge* (London: Bloomsbury, 1991).

Phillips, Caryl: *Crossing The River* (London: Bloomsbury, 1993).

Phillips, Caryl: *Extravagant Strangers. A Literature of Belonging* (London: Faber, 1997).

Phillips, Caryl: *The Nature of Blood* (London: Faber, 1997).

Phillips, Caryl: *The Right Set: The Faber Book of Tennis* (London: Faber, 1999).

Phillips, Caryl: *The Atlantic Sound* (London: Faber, 2000).

Phillips, Caryl: *A New World Order* (London: Secker & Warburg, 2001).

CHAPTER SIX **Uncollected Articles**

D'Aguiar, Fred: 'Twenty Five Years On The Parallel Bars. An Appraisal of the Work of Wilson Harris', *Artrage*, no.9/10, Autumn 1985, pp.2–3.

D'Aguiar, Fred: Review of Caryl Phillips, *The European Tribe*, *Artrage*, no.16, Spring 1987, pp.25–26.

D'Aguiar, Fred: Signed editorial, *Artrage*, no.18, Autumn 1987, p.1.

D'Aguiar, Fred: Introduction to 'Black British Poetry' in Gillian

Allnutt, Fred D'Aguiar, Ken Edwards and Eric Mottram (eds), *The New British Poetry 1968–88* (London: Paladin, 1988), pp.3–4.

D'Aguiar, Fred: 'Zigzag Paths', in E.A. Markham (ed.), *Hinterland. Caribbean Poetry From The West Indies And Britain* (Newcastle upon Tyne: Bloodaxe, 1989), pp.314–316.

D'Aguiar, Fred: 'Against Black British Literature', in Maggie Butcher (ed.), *Tibisiri. Caribbean Writers and Critics* (Mundelstrup, Denmark: Dangaroo Press, 1991), pp.106–114.

D'Aguiar, Fred: 'Ambiguity Without A Crisis? Twin Traditions, the Individual and Community in Derek Walcott's Essays', in Stewart Brown (ed.), *The Art of Derek Walcott* (Bridgend: Seren Books, 1991), pp.157–168.

D'Aguiar, Fred: 'Have You Been Here Long? Black Poetry in Britain', in Robert Hampson and Peter Barry (eds), *New British Poetries: The Scope of the Possible* (Manchester: Manchester University Press, 1993), pp.51–71.

D'Aguiar, Fred: 'The Last Essay About Slavery', in Sarah Dunant and Roy Porter (eds.), *The Age of Anxiety* (London: Virago Press, 1996), pp.125–147.

Phillips, Caryl: '1978', in *21 Picador Authors Celebrate 21 Years of International Writing* (London: Picador, 1993), pp.65–70.

Phillips, Caryl: 'Black & White Television', *Artrage*, no.12, Spring 1986, pp.34–36.

Phillips, Caryl: 'Living and Writing in the Caribbean: An Experiment', *Kunapipi*, vol.11, no.2, 1989.

Phillips, Caryl: 'Mariner, Renegade and Castaway' [review of Kent Worcester, *C.L.R. James: A Political Biography*], *The New Republic*, 5 August 1996, pp.32–39.

Phillips, Caryl: 'Talkback' [memoir of his Birmingham secondary school], *The Guardian*, 'Education' section, 20 August 1996, p.19.

Phillips, Caryl: 'So let's just leave out the ones everybody's heard of' [review of Alison Donnell and Sarah Lawson Welsh (eds),

The Routledge Reader in Caribbean Literature], *The Observer*, 'Review' section, 5 January 1997, p.16.

Phillips, Caryl: 'Staying Power', *The Times Magazine*, 13 June 1998, pp.34–38.

Phillips, Caryl: 'Strangers in a Strange Land', *The Guardian*, 17 November 2001.

CHAPTER SIX **Selected Interviews and Criticism**

Bell, C. Rosalind: 'Worlds Within. An Interview with Caryl Phillips', *Callaloo*, vol.14, no.3, Summer 1991, pp.578–606.

Birbalsingh, Frank: Interview with Caryl Phillips in Anna Rutherford and Kirsten Holst Peterson (eds), *Displaced Persons* (Mundelstrup, Denmark: Dangaroo Press, 1988).

Birbalsingh, Frank: 'An Interview with Fred D'Aguiar', *Ariel*, no.24, January 1993, pp.133–145.

Crewe, Candida: 'Caryl Phillips. Leeds' [interview for 'Hometown' column], *The Times Magazine*, 6 July 1996, p.54.

Cumberbatch, Sylvan: 'Memories Of The Windrush Generation', *The Voice*, 23 July 1996, pp.16–17.

Harry, Allister: 'Time the tale were told' [interview with Phillips], *The Voice*, 2 July 1996, pp.25–26.

Ilona, Anthony: 'Crossing the River: A Chronicle of the Black Diaspora', *Wasafiri*, no.22, Autumn 1995, pp.3–9.

Jaggi, Maya: 'On being here' [interview with D'Aguiar], *The Guardian*, Section 2, 4 August 1993, pp.4–5.

Jaggi, Maya: 'Crossing The River. Caryl Phillips talks to Maya Jaggi', *Wasafiri*, no.20, Autumn 1994, pp.25–29.

Jaggi, Maya: 'The new Brits on the block', *The Guardian*, 13 July 1996, p.31.

Sander, Reinhard: 'Caryl Phillips', in Bernth Lindfors and Reinhard Sander (eds), 'Twentieth-Century Caribbean and Black African Writers', *Dictionary of Literary Biography*, vol.157 (Detroit: Gale Research Company, 1996).

Saunders, Kay: Interview, *Kunapipi*, vol.9, no.1, 1987, pp.44–52.

Sharpe, Kay: 'Of This Time, of That Place' [interview with Phillips], *Transition*, no.68, Winter 1995, pp.154–161.

Sewell, Tony: 'Finding our feet', *The Voice*, 9 July 1996, p.9.

Stewart, Robert J.: 'Fred D'Aguiar', in Bernth Lindfors and Reinhard Sander (eds), 'Twentieth-Century Caribbean and Black African Writers', *Dictionary of Literary Biography*, vol.157 (Detroit: Gale Research Company, 1996).

CHAPTER SEVEN **Primary Material**

Headley, Victor: *Yardie* (London: The X Press, 1992).

Headley, Victor: *Excess* (London: The X Press, 1993).

Headley, Victor: *Yush!* (London: The X Press, 1994).

Headley, Victor: *Fetish* (London: The X Press, 1995).

Headley, Victor: *Off Duty* (London: Hodder & Stoughton, 2001).

Johnson, Linton Kwesi: *Voices of the Living and the Dead* (1974 and 2nd ed., London: Race Today Publications, 1983).

Johnson, Linton Kwesi: *Dread Beat An' Blood* (London: Bogle-L'Ouverture Publications, 1975).

Johnson, Linton Kwesi: *Inglan Is A Bitch* (London: Race Today Publications, 1980).

Johnson, Linton Kwesi: *Tings an Times. Selected Poems* (Newcastle upon Tyne: Bloodaxe Books, 1991).

McCalman, Iain (ed.): *The Horrors of Slavery and Other Writings by Robert Wedderburn* (Edinburgh: Edinburgh University Press, 1991).

Perkins, Erasmus (ed.): THE TRIAL OF THE REV. ROBt. WEDDERBURN, (A Dissenting Minister of the Unitarian persuasion,) FOR BLASPHEMY, *Before Sir Charles Abbott, Knight, Lord Chief-Justice, and a Special Jury*, IN THE COURT OF KING'S BENCH, WESTMINSTER, The Sittings after Hilary Term, 1820;

Containing a Verbatim Report of the DEFENCE (London: Printed for the Editor, 1820).

Rushdie, Salman: *Midnight's Children* (London: Jonathan Cape, 1981).

Rushdie, Salman: *The Jaguar Smile* (London: Picador, 1987).

Rushdie, Salman: *The Satanic Verses* (London: Viking, 1988).

Rushdie, Salman: *Imaginary Homelands* (1991 and new ed., London: Granta, 1992).

Rushdie, Salman: *The Wizard of Oz* (London: BFI Publishing, 1992).

Rushdie, Salman: *East, West* (London: Jonathan Cape, 1994).

Rushdie, Salman: *The Moor's Last Sigh* (London: Jonathan Cape, 1995).

Rushdie, Salman: *The Ground Beneath Her Feet* (London: Jonathan Cape, 1999).

Rushdie, Salman: *Fury* (London: Jonathan Cape, 2001).

Rushdie, Salman: *Step Across This Line: Collected Nonfiction 1992–2002* (London: Jonathan Cape, 2002).

CHAPTER SEVEN **Uncollected Articles**

Johnson, Linton Kwesi: 'Education?', *Race Today*, vol.6, no.3, March 1974, p.81.

Johnson, Linton Kwesi: 'Against All Flags', *Race Today*, vol.11, no.2, February–March 1979, pp.42–44.

Johnson, Linton Kwesi: 'Speaking in tongues' [review of Richard Allsop (ed.), *Dictionary of Caribbean English Usage*], *The Guardian*, Section 2, 19 April 1996, p.15.

Johnson, Linton Kwesi: 'Influences', *New Statesman*, 9 August 1996, p.30.

Rushdie, Salman: 'Heavy, man', *The Guardian*, 'Weekend' section, 28 January 1995, p.26.

CHAPTER SEVEN **Selected Criticism**

Adebayo, Dotun: 'On the write track', *The Voice*, 6 September 1994, p.12.

Ahsan, M.M. and A.R. Kidwai (eds): *Sacrilege versus Civility. Muslim Perspectives on The Satanic Verses Affair* (Leicester: The Islamic Foundation, 1991).

Appignanesi, Lisa and Sara Maitland (eds): *The Rushdie File* (London: Fourth Estate, 1989).

Atkins, Sharon: 'Finally there was Linton Kwesi Johnson himself', *Caribbean Times*, 6 May 1995, pp.16–17.

Bedford, Carmel (ed.): *Fiction, Fact and the Fatwa. 2,000 Days of Censorship* (London: Article 19, 1994).

Caesar, Burt: 'Interview' [with Kwesi Johnson], *Critical Quarterly*, vol.38, no.4, Winter 1996, pp.64–77.

Cohn-Sherbok, Dan (ed.) *The Salman Rushdie Controversy In Interreligious Perspective* (Lewiston/Queenston/Lampeter: The Edwin Mellen Press, 1990).

D'Aguiar, Fred: 'Linton Kwesi Johnson', in Bernth Lindfors and Reinhard Sander (eds), 'Twentieth-Century Caribbean and Black African Writers', *Dictionary of Literary Biography*, vol.157 (Detroit: Gale Research Company, 1996), pp.123–130.

Edwards, Paul and David Dabydeen (eds): *Black Writers In Britain 1760–1890* (Edinburgh: Edinburgh University Press, 1991).

Edwards, Paul: *Unreconciled Strivings and Ironic Strategies: Three Afro-British Authors of the Georgian Era; Ignatius Sancho, Olaudah Equiano, Robert Wedderburn*, Occasional Papers no.34 (Edinburgh: Centre of African Studies, Edinburgh University, 1992).

Fletcher, D.M. (ed.): *Reading Rushdie. Perspectives on the fiction of Salman Rushdie* (Amsterdam: Editions Rodopi B.V., 1994).

Grundy, Gareth: 'Guns 'N' Proses', *Select*, October 1994, p.13.

Hamilton, Ian: 'The First Life of Salman Rushdie', *The New Republic*, 25 December 1995 and 1 January 1996, pp.90–113.

Inglefield, Mark: 'Rushdie's early verses found', *The Sunday Telegraph*, 9 August 1998, p.32.

McCalman, Iain: 'Anti-Slavery and Ultra-Radicalism in Early Nineteenth-Century England: The Case of Robert Wedderburn', *Slavery and Abolition*, vol.7, no.2, September 1986, pp.99–117.

McCalman, Iain: *Radical Underworld. Prophets, Revolutionaries and Pornographers in London, 1795–1840* (Cambridge: Cambridge University Press, 1988).

Odell, Michael: 'Thriller that pulls no punches', *The Voice*, 12 May 1992, p.25.

Patel, Jitin H.: 'is inglan still a bitch?', *2nd Generation*, issue 9, Summer 1998, pp.30–32.

Phillips, Caryl: 'Prophet in another land', *The Guardian*, 'Weekend' section, 11 July 1998, pp.28–33.

Pidcock, David Musa: *Satanic Voices Ancient and Modern. A Surfeit of Blasphemy Including The Rushdie Report. From Edifice Complex to Occult Theocracy* (Milton Keynes: Mustaqim, 1992).

Rreder, Michael (ed.): *Conversations with Salman Rushdie* (Jackson: University Press of Mississippi, 2000).

Ruthven, Malise: *A Satanic Affair: Salman Rushdie and the Wrath of Islam* (1990 and revised and updated ed., London: The Hogarth Press, 1991).

Sissay, Lemn: 'Still bitchin', *Dazed & Confused*, July 1998, pp.130–133.

Weatherby, W.J.: *Salman Rushdie. Sentenced To Death* (New York: Carroll & Graf Publishers, 1990).

PART TWO

Selection of Other Works Consulted

Ackroyd, Peter: *Blake* (London: Sinclair-Stevenson, 1995).

Adair, Gilbert: 'Capital Letters', in *The Postmodernist Always Rings Twice. Reflections on culture in the 90s* (London: Fourth Estate, 1992), pp.201–204.

Adams, Caroline: *Across Seven Seas and Thirteen Rivers: Life Stories of Pioneer Sylheti Settlers in Britain* (1987 and 2nd ed., London: Eastside Books, 1994).

Adi, Hakim: *West Africans in Britain 1900–1960. Nationalism, Pan-Africanism and Communism* (London: Lawrence & Wishart, 1998).

Agbenugba, Gbenga: *Another Lonely Londoner* (London: Ronu Books, 1991).

Ahmed, Rollo: *I Rise: The Life Story of a Negro* (London: J. Long, 1937).

A Late Secretary of Legation. To The Court of St James's, &c., &c.: *Nocturnal London* (London: S.E. Stanesby, 1890).

Ali, Beatrice: *The Good Deeds Of A Good Woman* (London: Dennis Dobson, 1976).

Ali, Tariq: *Redemption* (London: Chatto & Windus, 1990).

Ali, Tariq and Susan Watkins: *1968: Marching In the Streets* (London: Bloomsbury, 1998).

Alibhai-Brown, Yasmin: *No Place Like Home. An Autobiography* (London: Virago, 1995).

Alibhai-Brown, Yasmin: *Who Do We Think We Are? Imagining The New Britain* (London: Allen Lane, 2000).

Alibhai-Brown, Yasmin: *Mixed Feelings: The Complex Lives of Mixed-Race Britons* (London: The Women's Press, 2001).

Altick, Richard: *The Shows of London* (London: The Belknap Press, 1978).

Anand, Sushila: *Indian Sahib. Queen Victoria's Dear Abdul* (London: John Murray, 1996).

Anonymous: *Nocturnal Revels: Or, The History of King's-Place, And Other Modern Nunneries*, 2 vols (2nd ed., London: M. Goadby, 1779).

Anonymous: *Memoirs and Opinions of Mr Blenfield*, 2 vols (London: Printed for W. Lane, 1790).

Anonymous, *The Death, Last Will, and Funeral of 'Black Billy'* (10th ed., London: J. Catnach, 1823).

Anwar, Farrah: 'A mirror of Britain', *The Guardian*, Section 2, 19 January 1995, pp.12–13.

Ashcroft, Bill, Gareth Griffiths and Helen Tiffin: *The Post-Colonial Studies Reader* (London: Routledge, 1995).

Augustus, Patrick: *Baby Father* (London: The X Press, 1994).

Augustus, Patrick: *Baby Father 2* (London: The X Press, 1995).

Augustus, Patrick: *When A Man Loves A Woman* (London: The X Press, 1996).

Bachelard, Gaston: *The Poetics of Space* (1958 and Boston: Beacon Press, 1994).

Bailey, Paul (ed.): *The Oxford Book Of London* (Oxford: Oxford University Press, 1995).

Bandele, Biyi: *The Street* (London: Picador, 1999).

Banton, Michael: *The Coloured Quarter. Negro Immigrants in an English City* (London: Jonathan Cape, 1955).

Barber, George: 'X Press Yourself', *The Independent Magazine*, 9 July 1994, pp.42–43.

Barker-Benfield, G.J.: *The Culture of Sensibility. Sex and Society in Eighteenth-Century Britain* (Chicago: University of Chicago Press, 1992).

Barrett, Norman and Mel Watman: *Daley Thompson* (London: Virgin Books, 1984).

Bayne-Powell, Rosamond: *Travellers in Eighteenth-Century England* (London: John Murray, 1951).

Beaton, Norman: *Beaton But Unbowed: An Autobiography* (London: Methuen, 1986).

Benjamin, Ionie: *The Black Press in Britain* (Stoke-on-Trent: Trentham Books, 1995).

Bennett, A.G.: *Because They Know Not* (Phoenix Press, [1959]).

Bentley Jr, G.E.: *A Bibliography of George Cumberland (1754–1818) Comprehending his Published Books (1780–1829) and Articles (1769–1847) and his Unrecorded Works in Manuscript – including a Novel (?1800), a Play (?1800), a Biography (?1788, ?1816, ?1820)* (New York: Garland Publishing, Inc., 1975).

Benyon, John (ed.): *Scarman and After: Essays Reflecting on Lord Scarman's Report, the Riots and their Aftermath* (Oxford: Pergamon Press, 1984).

Berry, James (ed.): *Bluefoot Traveller. Poetry by Westindians in Britain* (1976 and 2nd ed., London: Harrap, 1981).

Berry, James (ed.): *News For Babylon. The Chatto Book of West-Indian British Poetry* (London: Chatto & Windus, 1984).

Bhabha, Homi (ed.): *Nation and Narration* (London: Routledge, 1990).

Bhabha, Homi: *The Location of Culture* (London: Routledge, 1994).

Bhattacharyya, Gargi and John Gabriel: 'Gurinder Chadha and The *Apna* Generation', *Third Text*, no.27, Summer 1994, pp.55–63.

Bidisha: *Seahorses* (London: Flamingo, 1997).

Bidisha: *Too Fast To Live* (London: Duck Editions, 2000).

Binyon, T.J.: *'Murder Will Out'. The Detective in Fiction* (Oxford: Oxford University Press, 1989).

Bishton, Derek and John Reardon: *Home Front* (London: Jonathan Cape, 1984).

Black, Clementine (ed.): *The Cumberland Letters. Being the Correspondence of Richard Dennison Cumberland and George Cumberland between the Years 1771 and 1784* (London: Martin Secker, 1912).

Blair, John G.: 'Blackface Minstrels as Cultural Export: England,

Australia, South Africa', in George Mckay (ed.), *Yankee Go Home (& Take Me With U): Americanization and Popular Culture* (Sheffield: Sheffield Academic Press, 1997), pp.53–66.

Blake, John: *Memories of Old Poplar* (1977 and 2nd ed., London: Stepney Books, 1985).

Boehmer, Elleke: *Colonial and Post-colonial Writing: Migrant Metaphors* (Oxford: Oxford University Press, 1995).

'Books, Libraries And Racism', *Race Today*, vol.5, no.10, October–November 1973, pp.301–305.

Booth, Chris, Jane Darke and Susan Yeandle (eds): *Changing Places. Women's Lives In The City* (London: Paul Chapman Publishing, 1996).

Booth, General: *In Darkest England and The Way Out* (London: International Headquarters of the Salvation Army, [1890]).

Bourne, Stephen: *Black In The British Frame. Black People In British Film and Television 1896–1996* (London: Cassell, 1998).

Bracewell, Michael: *England Is Mine. Pop Life in Albion from Wilde to Goldie* (London: HarperCollins, 1997).

Bradbury, Malcolm (ed.): *The Atlas of Literature* (London: Agostini Editions, 1996).

Bradley, Lloyd: *Bass Culture* (London: Viking, 2000).

Brah, Avtar: *Cartographies of Diaspora. Contesting Identities* (London: Routledge, 1996).

Braidwood, Stephen J.: *Black Poor and White Philanthropists. London's Blacks and the Foundation of the Sierra Leone Settlement 1786–91* (Liverpool: Liverpool University Press, 1994).

Bratton, J.S.: 'English Ethiopians: British Audiences and Black-Face Acts, 1835–1865', *The Yearbook of English Studies*, no.11, 1981, pp.27–43.

Brewis, Kathy: 'Take it to the bridge' [interview with Tjinder Singh], *The Sunday Times Magazine*, June 1998, pp.12–15.

Brown, Colin: *Black and White Britain. The Third PSI* [Policy Studies Institute] *Survey* (1984 and Aldershot: Gower, 1985).

Brown, Thomas: *Amusements Serious and Comical Calculated for the Meridian of London* (1700 and 2nd ed., London: Printed by the Booksellers of London and Westminster, 1702).

Bullen, A.H. (ed.): *The Works of George Peele*, vol.1 (London: John C. Nimmo, 1888).

Burr, Sandra and Adam Potkay: *Black Atlantic Writers of the Eighteenth Century. Living the New Exodus in England and the Americas* (Basingstoke: Macmillan, 1995).

Buruma, Ian: *Voltaire's Coconuts, or Anglomania in Europe* (London: Weidenfeld & Nicolson, 1999).

Bush, Julia: 'Moving On – and Looking Back', *History Workshop Journal*, Issue 36, Autumn 1993, pp.183–194.

Byrd, Max: *London Transformed. Images of the City in the Eighteenth Century* (New Haven and London: Yale University Press, 1978).

Calvino, Italo: *Invisible Cities* (1972 and London: Secker & Warburg, 1974).

Campbell, Christy: *The Maharajah's Box: An Imperial Story of Conspiracy, Love and A Guru's Prophecy* (London: HarperCollins, 2000).

Campbell, Sheri: *Wicked In Bed* (London: The X Press, 1995).

Cannadine, David: *Ornamentalism: How The British Saw Their Empire* (London: Allen Lane, 2001).

Carey, A.T.: *Colonial Students. A Study of the Social Adaptation of Colonial Students in London* (London: Secker & Warburg, 1956).

Carr, Rocky: *Brixton Bwoy* (London: Fourth Estate, 1998).

Carter, Erica, James Donald and Judith Squires (eds): *Space and Place: Theories of Identity and Location* (London: Lawrence & Wishart, 1993).

Cash, Arthur H.: *Laurence Sterne. The Early and Middle Years* (London: Methuen, 1975).

Cash, Arthur H.: *Laurence Sterne. The Later Years* (1986 and London: Routledge, 1992).

Cathcart, Brian: *The Case of Stephen Lawrence* (London: Viking, 1999).

Certeau, Michel de: *The Practice of Everyday Life* (Berkeley: University of California Press, 1988).

Chaudhuri, Nirad: *The Autobiography of an Unknown Indian* (London: Macmillan, 1951).

Clarke, Austin: *Growing Up Stupid Under The Union Jack. A Memoir* (Toronto: McClelland & Hewart, 1980).

Cobham, Rhonda and Merle Collins (eds): *Watchers and Seekers. Creative Writing By Black Women In Britain* (London: The Women's Press, 1987).

Collicott, Sylvia: *Connections. Haringey Local-National-World Links* (London: Haringey Community Information Service, 1986).

Collins, Kris: 'Merchants, Moors and the Politics of Pageantry: The Representation of Africans and Indians in Civic Pageants, 1585–1682', University of Oxford, M.Litt. thesis, 1995.

Collins, Merle: *Rotten Pomerack* (London: Virago Press, 1992).

Colson, Percy: *Their Ruling Passions. A Study in Wire-Pulling Baron Stockmar[.] A Study in Fanaticism Lord George Gordon[.] A Study in Egoism Dr Samuel Parr[.] A Study in Avarice Joseph Nollekens[.] A Study in Ambition The Young Disraeli* (London: Hutchinson & Co., [1949]).

Conrad, Peter: *Imagining America* (London: Routledge & Kegan Paul, 1980).

Constantine, Learie: *Colour Bar* (London: Stanley Paul, 1954).

Conway, E. Buxton: 'London's Police Courts', in George R. Sims (ed.), *Living London*, vol.2 (London: Cassell & Company, 1902), pp.139–144.

Cooke, Alan: *Shades of Grey* (London: Undercover, 1991).

Copy of The Poll For The Election Of Two Citizens To Serve In The Present Parliament For The City and Liberty of Westminster, Begun on Thursday the 7th, And Ended On Saturday the 23rd September 1780. Thomas Corbett, Esq. High Bailiff (London: W. Richardson, 1780).

Cottle, Thomas J.: *Black Testimony. The Voices of Britain's West Indians* (London: Wildwood House, 1978).

Craig-Martin, Michael: *Drawing the Line. Reappraising drawing past and present* (London: The South Bank Centre, 1995).

Creaton, Heather (ed.): *The Bibliography of Printed Works on London History* (London: Library Association, 1994).

Cross, Wilbur: *The Life and Times of Laurence Sterne* (1925 and 3rd ed., New Haven: Yale University Press, 1929).

Cugoano, Ottobah: *Thoughts and Sentiments on the Evil and Wicked Traffic of the Slavery and Commerce of the Human Species* (London: T. Becket, 1787).

Cumberland, George: 'An African Tale', in *Original Tales*, vol.2 (London: Miller and Pople, 1810).

Cunningham, Laza: *Seen: Black Style UK* (London: Booth-Clibborn Editions, 2001).

Dabydeen, David (ed.): *The Black Presence in English Literature* (Manchester: Manchester University Press, 1985).

Dabydeen, David: *Hogarth's Blacks: Images of Blacks in Eighteenth Century English Art* (Kingston upon Thames: Dangaroo Press, 1985).

Dabydeen, David: *Disappearance* (London: Jonathan Cape, 1993).

Dabydeen, David: *Turner: New and Selected Poems* (London: Jonathan Cape, 1994).

D'Archenholz, M.: *Containing A Description Of The Laws, Customs, And Manners of England*, vol.1 (London: Edward Jeffery 1789).

David, Saul: *The Indian Mutiny: 1857* (London: Viking, 2002).

Davies, Christie: *Ethnic Humour Around The World. A Comparative Analysis* (Bloomington and Indianapolis: Indiana University Press, 1990).

Davies, Nick: 'How the Yardies duped the Yard', *The Guardian*, Section 2, 3 February 1997, pp.2–5.

Davies, Ray: *X-Ray* (London: Viking, 1994).

Davison, John: *Gangsta. The Sinister Spread of Yardie Gun Culture* (London: Vision, 1997).

Defoe, Daniel: *Serious Reflections During the Life and Surprising Adventures of Robinson Crusoe With His Vision of the Angelic World* (1720 and London: J.M. Dent, 1762).

Deleuze, Gilles and Guattari, Felix: *Kafka. Towards A Minor Literature* (1975 and Minneapolis: University of Minnesota Press, 1986).

Dennis, Ferdinand: *Behind The Frontlines. Journey into Afro-Britain* (London: Victor Gollancz, 1988).

Dennis, Ferdinand: *The Sleepless Summer* (London: Hodder & Stoughton, 1989).

Dennis, Ferdinand: *The Last Blues Dance* (London: HarperCollins, 1996).

Dennis, Ferdinand: *Duppy Conqueror* (London: HarperCollins, 1998).

Dennis, Ferdinand: 'The Prince and I', in *Granta*, no.65, Spring 1999, pp.311–323.

Dennis, Ferdinand and Naseem Khan (eds): *Voices of the Crossing: The Impact of Britain on Writers from Asia, the Caribbean and Africa* (London: Serpent's Tail, 2000).

Dhanjal, Beryl: 'Asian housing in Southall: some impressions', *New Community*, vol.6, nos1–2, Winter 1977/1978, pp.88–93.

Dhondy, Farrukh: *C.L.R. James: Cricket, the Caribbean, and World Revolution* (London: Weidenfeld & Nicolson, 2001).

Dickens, Charles: 'The Black Man', *All The Year Round*, new series, XIII, 6 March 1875, pp.489–494.

Dickson, William: *Letters On Slavery* (London: J. Phillips, 1789).

Digby, John and Joan: *The Collage Handbook* (London: Thames and Hudson, 1985).

Does The Sun Rise Over Dagenham? And Other Stories. New Writing From London (London: Fourth Estate, 1998).

Dromey, Jack and Graham Taylor: *Grunwick: The Workers' Story* (London: Lawrence & Wishart, 1978).

Duffield, Ian: 'From Slave Colonies to Penal Colones: The West

Indian Convict Transportees to Australia', *Slavery and Abolition*, vol.7, no.1, May 1986, pp.25–45.

Duffield, Ian: 'Billy Blue. A Legend of Early Sydney', *History Today*, vol.37, February 1987, pp.43–48.

Dyer, Geoff: *The Colour of Memory* (London: Jonathan Cape, 1989).

Dyer, Geoff: *Paris Trance* (London: Abacus, 1998).

Dyer, Richard: *White* (London: Routledge, 1997).

Eagleton, Terry: *Exiles And Émigrés. Studies In Modern Literature* (London: Chatto & Windus, 1970).

Edun, Ayune M.: *London's Heart-Probe And Britain's Destiny* (London: Arthur H. Stockwell, c.1934).

Edwards, Paul: *Black Personalities in the Era of the Slave Trade* (London: Macmillan, 1983).

[Egan, Pierce]: *Boxiana; or Sketches of ancient and modern Pugilism* (London: G. Smeeton, 1812).

Ekpenyon, E.I.: *Some Experiences of an African Air-Raid Warden* (London: Sheldon Press, 1943).

Eliot, T.S.: *The Complete Poems and Plays* (London: Faber, 1969).

Ellis, Markman: *The Politics of Sensibility. Race, Gender and Commerce in the Sentimental Novel* (Cambridge: Cambridge University Press, 1996).

Ellmers, Chris: *City & River* (London: Museum of London, 1989).

Ellmers, Chris and Alex Werner: *Dockland Life. A Pictorial History of London's Docks 1860–1970*, Museum of London (Edinburgh: Mainstream Publishing, 1991).

Emecheta, Buchi: *In the Ditch* (London: Barrie & Jenkins, 1972).

Emecheta, Buchi: *Second-Class Citizen* (London: Allison & Busby, 1974).

Emecheta, Buchi: *Head Above Water* (London: Fontana, 1986).

Eshun, Kodwo: *More Brilliant Than The Sun: Adventures In Sonic Fiction* (London: Quartet, 1998).

Evaristo, Bernardine: *Lara* (Kent: Angela Royal Publishing, 1997).

Falk, Bernard: *The Way of the Montagues: A Gallery of Family Portraits* (London: Hutchinson, [1958]).

Farson, Daniel: *Soho In The Fifties* (London: Michael Joseph, 1987).

Fielding, Sir John: *Extracts from Such of the Penal Laws, As particularly relate to the Peace and Good Order of This Metropolis. To which are added, The Felonies made so by statute, some general caution to shopkeepers; And A Short Treatise on the office of Constable* (New ed., London: H. Woodfall and W. Strahan, 1762).

Figueroa, John: 'The Flaming Faith of These First Years: Caribbean Voices', in Maggie Butcher (ed.): *Tibisiri. Caribbean Writers and Critics* (Sydney: Dangaroo Press, 1989), pp.59–80.

Figueroa, John: *West Indies in England. The Great Post-War Tours* (London: The Kingswood Press, 1991).

Figueroa, John: 'Supply Teaching', *London Magazine*, vol.36, nos 7 and 8, October–November 1996, pp.104–109.

Fingers, Two: *Bass Instinct* (London: Boxtree, 1996).

Fingers, Two and James T. Kirk: *Junglist* (London: Boxtree, 1995).

Fishman, William: *East End Jewish Radicals, 1875–1914* (London: Duckworth, 1975).

Fitzgerald, Percy: *A Famous Forgery Being The Story of 'The Unfortunate' Doctor Dodd* (London: Chapman & Hall, 1865).

Flanagan, Bud: *My Crazy Life. The Autobiography of Bud Flanagan* (London: Frederic Muller, 1961).

Forbes, Deidre: 'Throwing the book at mainstream publishing', *The Voice*, 11 August 1992, p.22.

Fordham, John: *Let's Join Hands and Contact the Living: Ronnie Scott and His Club* (London: Elm Tree Books, 1986).

Francis, Vivienne: *With Hope In Their Eyes* (London: Nia, 1998).

Fraser, George MacDonald: *Black Ajax* (London: HarperCollins, 1997).

Fryer, Peter: *Staying Power. The History of Black People in Britain* (London: Pluto Press, 1984).

Fulcher, The Late George Williams: *Life of Thomas Gainsborough, R.A.* (London: Longman, Brown, Green and Longman, 1856).

Fuller, Vernella: *Going Back Home* (London: The Women's Press, 1992).

Gates, Henry Louis: 'Black flash', *The Guardian*, 'The Week' section, 19 July 1997, pp.1–2.

George, M. Dorothy: *London Life in the XVIIIth Century* (London: Kegan Paul, Trench, Trubner & Co. Ltd, 1925).

Gerzina, Gretchen: *Black England. Life before Emancipation* (London: John Murray, 1995).

Ghose, Zulfikar: *Confessions Of A Native-Alien* (London: Routledge & Kegan Paul, 1965).

Giles, J.A. (ed.): *The Chronicle of Richard of Devizes Concerning The Deeds of Richard The First, King Of England* (London: James Bohn, 1841).

Gilroy, Beryl: *Black Teacher* (London: Cassell, 1976).

Gilroy, Beryl: *Boy Sandwich* (London: Heinemann, 1989).

Gilroy, Paul: *Small Acts. Thoughts on the Politics of Black Cultures* (London: Serpent's Tail, 1993).

Gilroy, Paul: *The Black Atlantic: Modernity and Double Consciousness* (London: Verso, 1993).

Glancey, Jonathan: *London* (London: Verso, 2001).

Gomme, G. Laurence: *London in the Reign of Victoria (1837–1897)* (London: Blackie & Son, 1898).

Gorgon, Donald: *Cop Killer* (London: The X Press, 1994).

Grant, Monica: *The Ragga & The Royal* (London: The X Press, 1994).

Green, Jeffrey: *Black Edwardians: Black People in Britain 1901–1914* (London: Frank Cass, 1998).

Green, Jonathon: *Days In The Life: Voices from the English Underground 1961–1971* (London: Heinemann, 1988).

Greenhalgh, Paul: *Ephemeral Vistas. The Expositions Universelles, Great Exhibitions And World's Fairs, 1851–1939* (Manchester: Manchester University Press, 1988).

Greenwood, James: *The Wilds of London* (London: Chatto & Windus, 1874).

Griffiths, Peter: *A Question of Colour?* (London: Leslie Frewin, 1966).

Grimshaw, Anna (ed.): *The C.L.R. James Reader* (London: Blackwell, 1992).

Gundara, Jagdish S. and Ian Duffield (eds): *Essays on the History of Blacks in Britain. From Roman Times to the Mid-Twentieth Century* (Aldershot: Avebury, 1997).

Gunesekara, Romesh: *Reef* (London: Granta, 1994).

Gupta, Sunil: 'Correct Singularities', *Gay Times*, no.131, August 1989, pp.40–41.

Hall, Stuart: 'Reconstruction Work. Images of Post-War Black Settlement', in Jo Spence and Patricia Holland (eds), *Family Snaps. The Meanings of Domestic Photographs* (London: Virago Press, 1991), pp.152–164.

Haque, Shaheen: 'The Politics of Space. The Experience of a Black Woman Architect', in Shabnam Grewal, Jackie Kay, Liliane Landor, Gail Lewis and Pratibha Parmar, *Charting The Journey. Writings By Black And Third World Women* (London: Sheba Feminist Publishers, 1988), pp.34–39.

Hare, Nancie: 'The Prospects For Coloured Children In England', *The Keys*, July–September 1937, pp.11–12 and pp.25–27.

Harris, Joshua and Tina Wallace with the assistance of Heather Booth: *To Ride The Storm. The 1980 Bristol 'Riot' and the State* (London: Heinemann, 1983).

Hebdige, Dick: *Cut 'N' Mix: Culture, Identity and Caribbean Music* (London: Methuen & Co., 1987).

Hecht, J. Jean: *Continental and Colonial Servants in Eighteenth*

Century England (Northampton, Massachussetts: Department of History of Smith College, 1954).

Henderson, Mae G. (ed.): *Borders, Boundaries, and Frames. Essays in Cultural Criticism and Cultural Studies* (New York: Routledge, 1995).

Hercules, Trevor: *Labelled A Black Villain* (London: Fourth Estate, 1989).

Heron, Liz (ed.): *Streets of Desire: Women's fictions of the twentieth-century city* (London: Virago, 1993).

Hewison, Robert: *Too Much. Art and Society in the Sixties 1960–75* (Oxford: Oxford University Press, 1986).

Hibbert, Christopher: *King Mob: The Story of Lord George Gordon and the Riots of 1780* (London: Longman, Green & Co., 1958).

Higgins, Patrick (ed.): *A Queer Reader* (London: Fourth Estate, 1993).

Hinds, Donald: *Journey To An Illusion. The West Indian in Britain* (London: Heinemann, 1966).

Hiro, Dilip: *Three Plays: To Anchor A Cloud. Apply, Apply, No Reply. A Clean Break* (London: Madison Books, 1985).

Hiro, Dilip: *Black British, White British. A History of Race Relations in Britain* (1971 and new ed., London: Grafton Books, 1991).

'The History of Blacks in Britain'. Special issue of *History Today*, vol.31, September 1981, pp.33–51.

Honigsbaum, Mark: 'UK Jihad', *GQ*, June 1995, pp.100–103 and p.180.

Hosking, Tessa: *Black People In Britain 1650–1850* (London: Macmillan Education, 1984).

Howe, Darcus: 'See you in court, brother', *New Statesman and Society*, 31 May 1996, p.14.

Howells, W.D.: *London Films* (London: Harper and Brothers, 1905).

Howes, Alan B. (ed.): *Sterne. The Critical Heritage* (London: Routledge & Kegan Paul, 1974).

Huggan, Graham: *The Postcolonial Exotic: Marketing The Margins* (London: Routledge, 2001).

Humphry, Derek and David Tindall: *False Messiah. The Story of Michael X* (London: Hart-Davis, MacGibbon, 1977).

Hussain, Abdullah: *Émigré Journeys* (London: Serpent's Tail, 2000).

Huxley, Elspeth: *Back Street New Worlds. A Look at Immigrants in Britain* (London: Chatto & Windus, 1964).

Hyde, Ralph (introductory note by): *The A to Z of Georgian London* (London: Harry Margary Lympne Castle, Kent in association with Guildhall Library, London, 1981).

Imlay, Gilbert: *A Topographical Description of the Western Territory of North America: Containing A Succinct Account of its Soil, Climate, Natural History, Population, Agriculture, Manners, and Customs. With an ample description of the several divisions into which that country is partitioned* (1794 and 3rd ed., London: J. Debrett, 1797).

Ingledew, John: 'Samuel Johnson's Jamaica Connections', *Caribbean Quarterly*, vol.30, no.2, June 1984, pp.1–17.

Innes, C.L.: A History of Black and Asian Writing in Britain, 1700–2000 (Cambridge: Cambridge University Press, 2002).

Ireland, John: *Letters and Poems, By The Late Mr John Henderson. With Anecdotes Of His Life, By John Ireland* (London: Printed for J. Johnson, 1786).

Jackson, Stanley: *An Indiscreet Guide To Soho* (London: Muse Arts, 1946).

Jacobs, Jane M.: *Edge of Empire. Postcolonialism and the City* (London: Routledge, 1996).

James, C.L.R.: *Beyond A Boundary* (London: Hutchinson, 1963).

James, Lawrence: *Raj: The Making and Unmaking of British India* (London: Little, Brown & Company, 1997).

Jephcott, Pearl: *A Troubled Area. Notes on Notting Hill* (London: Faber & Faber, 1964).

Jones, Eldred: *Othello's Countrymen. The African in English Renaissance Drama* (London: Oxford University Press, 1965).

Jones, Jennifer: 'The Face Of Villainy On The Victorian Stage', *Theatre Notebook*, vol.L, no.2, 1996, pp.95–108.

Jones, Simon: *Black Culture, White Youths. The Reggae Tradition from JA to UK* (Basingstoke: Macmillan, 1988).

Jones, Steve: *When The Lights Went Down: Crime in Wartime London and Manchester* (1995 and new ed., Nottingham: Wicked Publications, 2000).

Julien, Isaac and Colin MacCabe: *Diary of a Young Soul Rebel* (London: BFI Publishing, 1991).

Kerridge, Roy: *Real Wicked, Guy. A View of Black Britain* (London: Basil Blackwell, 1983).

Kerridge, Roy: *The Storm Is Passing Over. A Look at Black Churches in Britain* (London: Thames and Hudson, 1995).

Kerridge, Roy: *The Story of Black History* (London: Claridge Press, 1998).

Kerridge, Roy: *Subjects of the Queen* (London: Gerald Duckworth & Co., 2002).

Killingray, David (ed.): *Africans In Britain* (Ilford: Frank Cass, 1994).

King, Anthony D. (ed.): *Re-presenting The City. Ethnicity, Capital and Culture in the 21st-Century Metropolis* (Basingstoke: Macmillan, 1996).

Kohn, Marek: *Dope Girls: The Birth of the British Drug Underground* (London: Lawrence & Wishart, 1992).

Kwint, Marius: *Dark Subjects: Race and Performance in the Early English Circus, 1768–1850*, unpublished paper.

Lahiri, Shompa: *Indians In Britain: Anglo-Indian Encounters, Race and Identity* (London: Frank Cass, 2000).

Lahr, John: *Prick Up Your Ears: The Biography of Joe Orton* (London: Allen Lane, 1978).

Laine, Cleo: *Cleo* (London: Simon & Schuster, 1994).

Lamming, George: *In The Castle of My Skin* (London: Michael Joseph, 1953).

Lamming, George: *Of Age and Innocence* (London: Michael Joseph, 1958).

Lamming, George: *Water With Berries* (London: Longman Caribbean, 1971).

Lamming, George: *Natives of My Person* (London: Longman Caribbean, 1972).

Langford, Paul: *Englishness Identified: Manners and Character 1650–1850* (Oxford: Oxford University Press, 2000).

La Rose, John: *The New Cross Massacre Story. Interviews with John La Rose* (London: Alliance of the Black Parents Movement, Black Youth Movement and the Race Today Collective, 1984).

Larwood, Jacob and John Camden Hotten: *English Inn Signs. Being a Revised and Modernized Version of History of Signboards by Jacob Larwood and John Camden Hotten with a Chapter on the Modern Inn Sign by Gerald Miller* (1866 and Exeter: Blaketon Hall, 1985).

Law, John: *Out of Work* (London: Swan Sonnenschein & Co., 1888).

Leapman, Michael: *London's River. A History of The Thames* (London: Pavilion, 1991).

LeBor, Adam: 'Halfway house for the hopeful', *The Guardian*, 'The Week' section, 7 September 1996, p.5.

Leech, Kenneth: *Through Our Long Exile: Contextual Theology and the Urban Experience* (London: Darton, Longman & Todd, 2001).

Lennard, John: *But I Digress. The Exploitation of Parentheses in English Printed Verse* (Oxford: Clarendon Press, 1991).

Leslie, David Stuart: *Two Gentlemen Sharing* (London: Secker & Warburg, 1963).

Levi, Darrell E.: *Michael Manley. The Making of a Leader* (London: André Deutsch, 1989).

Levy, Andrea: *Every Light In The House Burnin'* (London: Headline, 1994).

Levy, Andrea: *Never Far From Nowhere* (London: Headline, 1996).

Lewis, Jeremy: *Adrift in Literary London* (London: John Murray, 1995).

Lewis, Peter: *The Fifties* (London: Heinemann, 1978).

Lillywhite, Bryant: *London Coffee Houses. A Reference Book of Coffee Houses of the Seventeenth, Eighteenth and Nineteenth Centuries* (London: George Allen & Unwin, 1963).

Lillywhite, Bryant: *London Signs. A Reference Book of London Signs From Earliest Times to About the Mid-Nineteenth Century* (London: George Allen & Unwin, 1972).

Lindfors, Bernth: 'The Signifying Flunkey: Ira Aldridge as Mungo', *The Literary Griot*, vol.5, no.2, Fall 1993, pp.1–11.

Lindfors, Bernth (ed.): *Africans on Stage* (Bloomington: Indiana University Press, 1998).

Linney, A.G.: *The Peepshow Of The Port Of London* (London: Sampson Low, Marston & Co., [1929]).

Little, Kenneth: *Negroes In Britain. A Study of Racial Relations In English Society* (London: Kegan Paul, Trench, Trubner & Co., 1947) [actually 1948].

Litvinoff, Emanuel: *Journey Through A Small Planet* (London: Michael Joseph, 1972).

Lively, Adam: *Masks. Blackness, Race and the Imagination* (London: Chatto & Windus, 1998).

London, Jack: *The People of the Abyss* (London: Isbister, 1903).

Long, Edward: *The History of Jamaica. Or, General Survey Of The Antient And Modern State of That Island: with Reflections on its Situation, Settlements, Inhabitants, Climate, Products, Commerce, Laws, and Government*, 3 vols (London: T. Lowndes, 1774).

Lorimer, Douglas: *Colour, Class and the Victorians. English attitudes to the Negro in the mid-nineteenth century* (Leicester: Leicester University Press, 1978).

[Macaulay, Zachary]: *The Black Prince, A True Story: Being An Account Of The Life And Death of Naimbanna, An African King's Son, who arrived in England in the Year 1791, and set Sail on his*

Return in June, 1793, Cheap Repository for Moral and Religious Tracts (London, n.d. [c.1797]).

McCann, Graham: *Woody Allen. New Yorker* (Cambridge: Polity Press, 1990).

MacDonald, Ian: *Revolution In The Head. The Beatles' Records and the Sixties* (London: Fourth Estate, 1994).

McGlashan, Colin: 'The Sound System', *The Sunday Times Magazine*, 4 February 1973, pp.12–21.

McGreal, Chris: 'Coming Home', *The Guardian*, 'G2' section, 21 February 2002, p.6.

McKay, Claude: *A Long Way From Home* (1937 and London: Pluto Press, 1985).

Maclaren-Ross, Julian: *Memoirs of the Forties* (London: A. Ross, 1965).

Makonnen, Ras: *Pan-Africanism From Within*, recorded and edited by Kenneth King (Nairobi: Oxford University Press, 1973).

Malik, Michael Abdul: *From Michael DeFreitas to Michael X* (London: André Deutsch, 1968).

Malik, Sarita: 'Beyond "the cinema of duty?" The Pleasures of Hybridity: Black British Film of the 1980s and 1990s', in Andrew Higson (ed.), *Dissolving Views. Key Writings on British Cinema* (London: Cassell, 1996), pp.202–215.

Mapanje, Jack: *Of Chameleons and Gods* (London: Heinemann, 1981).

Markandaya, Kamala: *The Nowhere Man* (London: Allen Lane, 1972).

Marke, Ernest: *Old Man Trouble* (London: Weidenfeld and Nicolson, 1975).

Marshall, Herbert and Mildred Stock: *Ira Aldridge: The Negro Tragedian* (London: Rockliff, 1958).

Marson, Una: *The Moth and the Star* (Kingston: Published by the Author, 1937).

Marson, Una: *Towards The Stars* (Bickley: University of London Press, 1945).

Martin, S.I.: *Incomparable World* (London: Quartet, 1996).

Martin, S.I.: *Britain's Slave Trade* (London: Channel 4 Books, 1999).

Martin-Jenkins, Christopher: *Ball by Ball. The Story of Cricket Broadcasting* (London: Grafton Books, 1990).

Massey, Doreen: 'A Place Called Home?', *New Formations*, no.17, Summer 1992, pp.3–15.

Matar, Nabil: *Islam In Britain 1558–1685* (London: Cambridge University Press, 1998).

Matura, Mustapha: *Six Plays* (London: Methuen, 1992).

Maxted, Ian: *The London Book Trade 1775–1800. A Preliminary Check List of Members* (Folkestone, Kent: Dawson, 1977).

Mayhew, Augustus: *Paved With Gold. Or The Romance and Reality Of The London Streets. An Unfashionable Novel* (London: Chapman & Hall, 1858).

Mayhew, Henry and John Binny: *The Criminal Prisons Of London And Scenes Of Prison Life* (London: Griffin, Bohn & Company, 1862).

Maynard, Carlyle: *East and West of Soho* (London: Hamlin, 1932).

Meadows, Daniel with additional interviews by Sara Tibbetts: *Nattering in Paradise. A Word from the Suburbs* (London: Simon & Schuster, 1988).

Mehta, Ved: *Delinquent Chacha* (London: Collins, 1967).

Mellor, David: *The Sixties Art Scene In London* (London: Phaidon Press, 1993).

Mercer, Kobena: 'Black Gay Men in Independent Film', *Cineaction: Radical Film Criticism and Theory*, no.32, Fall 1993, pp.51–62.

Mercer, Kobena: *Welcome to the Jungle. New Positions in Black Cultural Studies* (New York: Routledge, 1994).

Merrimann, Nick (ed.): *The Peopling of London. Fifteen Thousand Years of Settlement From Overseas* (London: Museum of London, 1993).

Merriman-Labor, A.B.C.: *Britons Through Negro Spectacles, or, A Negro on Britons* (London: Imperial and Foreign Company, 1909).

Mew, Charlotte: *Collected Poems and Prose* (Manchester: Carcanet Press, 1981).

Mirza, Heidi Safia (ed.): *Black British Feminism. A Reader* (London: Routledge, 1997).

Mishra, Pankaj: 'You Can't Go Home Again' [review of Caryl Phillips, *The Atlantic Sound*], *The New York Review of Books*, 26 April 2001, pp.49–51.

Mo, Timothy: *Sour Sweet* (London: André Deutsch, 1982).

Monolulu, Ras Prince: *I Gotta Horse* (London: Hurst and Blackwell, 1950).

The Monthly Review: or, Literary Journal: From January to December, inclusive, 1783, vol.69 (London: R. Griffiths, 1783), pp.492–497.

Moraes, Henrietta: *Henrietta* (London: Hamish Hamilton, 1994).

Morley, Dave and Ken Worpole (eds): *The Republic of Letters. Working class writing and local publishing* (London: Comedia Publishing Group, 1982).

Morris, Dennis: *Southall – A Home From Home: A Photographic Journey Through Little India* (London: Olympus Cameras, 1999).

Morris, Sam: 'Black Studies in Britain', *New Community*, vol.2, no.3, Summer 1973, p.245–248.

Morton, James: *East End Gangland* (London: Little, Brown, 2000).

Moss, Arthur B.: 'Waterside London', in George R. Sims (ed.), *Living London*, vol.1 (London: Cassell & Company, 1901), pp.68–73.

Mullard, Chris: *Black Britain* (London: George Allen & Unwin, 1973).

Mulvey, Laura: *Visual and Other Pleasures* (London: Macmillan, 1989).

Mungo, Paul: 'A power in the land', *The Guardian*, 'Weekend' section, 1 June 1996, pp.20–25.

Murray, Charles Shaar: *Crosstown Traffic. Jimi Hendrix and Post-war Pop* (London: Faber, 1989).

Murray-Brown, Jeremy: *Kenyatta* (1972 and 2nd ed., London: George Allen & Unwin, 1979).

Musgrave, Sir William: *Obituary prior to 1800 (As Far As Relates to England Scotland and Ireland)* (London: The Publications of the Harleian Society, 1901).

Myers, Norma: *Reconstructing The Black Past. Blacks in Britain 1780–1830* (London: Frank Cass, 1996).

Myers, Walter Dean: *At Her Majesty's Request: An African Princess In Victorian England* (New York: Scholastic Press, 1999).

Naipaul, Seepersaud, *The Adventures of Gurudeva And Other Stories. With a Foreword by V.S. Naipaul* (London: André Deutsch, 1976).

Naipaul, Shiva: *An Unfinished Journey* (London: Hamish Hamilton, 1986).

Nangle, Benjamin Christie: *The Monthly Review First Series 1749–1789. Indexes of Contributors and Articles* (Oxford: Clarendon Press, 1934).

Nelson, Emmanuel (ed.): *Reworlding. The Literature of the Indian Diaspora* (New York: Greenwood Press, 1992).

Newland, Courttia: *The Scholar* (London: Abacus, 1997).

Newland, Courttia: *Society Within* (London: Abacus, 1999).

Newland, Courttia and Kadija Sesay (eds): *IC3: The Penguin Book of New Black Writing in Britain* (London: Penguin, 2000).

Newton, Rev. John: *Thoughts Upon The African Slave Trade* (London: Printed for J. Buckland, 1788).

Ngcobo, Lauretta: *Let It Be Told* (London: Pluto Press, n.d. [c.1987]).

Nichols, Grace: *Leslyn in London* (London: Hodder & Stoughton, 1984).

Nichols, Grace: *The Fat Black Woman's Poems* (London: Virago Press, 1984).

Nightingale, Peggy (ed.): *A Sense of Place in the New Literatures in*

English (St Lucia, Australia: University of Queensland Press, 1986).

Nkrumah, Kwame: *The Autobiography of Kwame Nkrumah* (Edinburgh: Thomas Nelson & Sons, 1959).

Noble, E. Martin: *Jamaica Airman. A black airman in Britain 1943 and after* (London: New Beacon, 1984).

Nord, Deborah Epstein: *Walking the Victorian Streets. Women, Representation, and the City* (Ithaca: Cornell University Press, 1995).

Okoko, Susan: *Black Londoners 1880–1990* (London: Sutton Publishing, 1998).

Oldfield, J.R.: *Popular Politics And British Anti-Slavery. The mobilisation of popular opinion against the slave trade 1787–1807* (Manchester: Manchester University Press, 1995).

Oliver, Paul, Ian Davis and Ian Bentley (eds): *Dunroamin. The Suburban Semi and its Enemies* (1981 and London: Pimlico, 1994).

Omissi, David (ed.): *Indian Voices of the Great War: Soldiers' Letters, 1914–18* (Basingstoke: Macmillan, 1999).

Oyinlola, Rufus: *Britain and Colour Prejudice* (Ibadan: Printed by Omotayo Printing Works, [1956]).

Palmer, Paulina: 'The City in Contemporary Women's Fiction', in Anna Massa and Alistair Stead (eds), *Forked Tongues? Comparing Twentieth-Century British and American Literature* (London: Longman, 1994).

Palmer, Paulina: 'The Lesbian Thriller: Transgressive Investigations', in Peter Messent (ed.), *Criminal Proceedings: The Contemporary American Crime Novel* (London: Pluto, 1997).

Patterson, Sheila: *Dark Strangers. A Study of West Indians in London* (1963 and abridged ed., Harmondsworth: Pelican, 1965).

Paulson, Ronald: *Hogarth. High Art and Low, 1732–1750* (1971 and 2nd ed., Cambridge: Lutterworth Press, 1992).

Peggs, Rev. James: *The Lascars' Cry To Britain. An Appeal To British Christians, On Behalf Of The Asiatic Sailors, Who Resort To The Ports Of London, Liverpool, &c. More Particulars Addressed To The Directors Of The Missionary Societies* (London: T. Ward, 1844).

Perera, Shyama: *Haven't Stopped Dancing Yet* (London: Sceptre, 1999).

Perera, Shyama: *Bitter Sweet Symphony* (London: Sceptre, 2000).

Perera, Shyama: *Do the Right Thing* (London: Sceptre, 2002).

Phillips, Charlie (photos) and Mike Phillips (words): *Notting Hill In The Sixties* (London: Lawrence & Wishart, 1991).

Phillips, Mike: *Blood Rights* (London: Michael Joseph, 1989).

Phillips, Mike: *The Late Candidate* (London: Michael Joseph, 1990).

Phillips, Mike: *An Image To Die For* (London: HarperCollins, 1995).

Phillips, Mike: *The Dancing Face* (London: HarperCollins, 1997).

Phillips, Mike and Trevor Phillips (eds): *Windrush. The Irresistible Rise of Multi-Racial Britain* (London: HarperCollins, 1998).

Phillips, Mike: *London Crossings: A Biography of Black Britain* (London: Continuum, 2001).

Philpott, Trevor: 'Would You Let Your Daughter Marry A Negro?', *Picture Post*, 30 October 1954, pp.21–23.

Pilkington, Edward: *Beyond The Mother Country. West Indians and the Notting Hill White Riots* (London: I.B. Tauris, 1988).

Pinnock, Winsome: 'A Rock in Water', in Yvonne Brewster (ed.), *Black Plays 2* (London: Methuen, 1989).

Piper, Alan: *A History of Brixton* (London: The Brixton Society, 1996).

Pirani, M.: 'Aspirations and expectations of English and immigrant youth', *New Community*, vol.3, nos 1–2, Winter/Spring 1974, pp.73–78.

Poologasingham, P.: *Poet Tambimuttu – A Profile* (Colombo, Sri Lanka: P. Tambimuttu, 1993).

Porter, Roy: *London: A Social History* (London: Hamish Hamilton, 1994).

Powell, J. Enoch: *Reflections Of A Statesman. The Writings and Speeches of Enoch Powell*, selected by Rex Collings (London: Bellew, 1991).

Prendergast, Christopher: *Paris and the Nineteenth Century* (Oxford: Blackwell, 1992).

Proctor, James (ed.): *Writing black Britain 1948–1998: an interdisciplinary anthology* (Manchester: Manchester University Press, 2000).

Pryce, Ken: *Endless Pressure. A Study of West Indian Life-styles in Bristol* (Harmondsworth: Penguin, 1979).

Raban, Jonathan: *Soft City* (London: Hamish Hamilton, 1974).

Rasmussen, Steen Eiler: *London. The Unique City* (1934 and rev. ed., Cambridge, Massachusetts: The MIT Press, 1982).

Rawley, James A.: 'London's Defense of the Slave Trade, 1787–1807', *Slavery and Abolition*, vol.14, no.2, August 1993, pp.48–69.

Reade, Aleyn Lyell: *Johnsonian Gleanings*. Part II. *Francis Barber. The Doctor's Negro Servant* (Strand, London: Privately Printed for the Author at the Arden Press, 1912).

Redfern, Walter: *Puns* (Oxford: Basil Blackwell, 1984).

Rehin, George F.: 'Blackface Street Minstrels in Victorian London and its Resorts: Popular Culture and its Racial Connotations As Revealed in Polite Opinion', *Journal of Popular Culture*, vol.15, no.1, Summer 1981, pp.19–38.

Report From Committee On The State of Mendicity in The Metropolis (11 July 1815).

Reynolds, David: *Rich Relations: The American Occupation of Britain 1942–1945* (New York: Random House, 1995).

Reynolds, Simon: *Blissed Out. The Raptures of Rock* (London: Serpent's Tail, 1990).

Reynolds, Simon and Joy Press: *The Sex Revolts. Gender, Rebellion and Rock 'N' Roll* (London: Serpent's Tail, 1995).

Richards, Yvette: *Single Black Female* (London: The X Press, 1994).

Richardson, Henry: *Greenwich: Its History, Antiquities, Improvements And Public Buildings* (London: Simpkin and Marshall, 1834).

Riley, Joan: *The Unbelonging* (London: The Women's Press, 1985).

Ritvo, Harriet: *The Animal Estate. The English and Other Creatures In The Victorian Age* (1987 and London: Penguin, 1990).

Rodrigues, Jeff: 'The Riots of '81', *Marxism Today*, vol.25, no.10, October 1981, pp.18–22.

Rogers, Pat: 'Ziggerzagger Shandy: Sterne and the Aesthetics of the Crooked Line', *English: The Journal of the English Association*, vol.42, no.173, Summer 1993, pp.97–107.

Rogers, Richard and Mark Fisher: *A New London* (London: Penguin Books, 1992).

Rohlehr, Gordon: *Calypso and Society in Pre-Independence Trinidad* (Port of Spain: Gordon Rohlehr, 1990).

Rohmer, Sax: *The Mystery of Dr Fu-Manchu* (London: Methuen & Co., 1913).

Ross, Karen: *Black and White Media. Black Images in Popular Film and Television* (Cambridge: Polity Press, 1996).

Routes and Beyond: Voices From Educationally Successful Bangladeshis (1993 and rev. ed., London: Centre for Bangladeshi Studies, 1997).

Rowe, Colin and Fred Koetter: *Collage City* (Cambridge, Massachussetts: The MIT Press, 1978).

Ruck, S.K. (ed.): *The West Indian Comes To England. A Report Prepared for the Trustees of the London Parochial Charities by the Family Welfare Association* (London: Routledge & Kegan Paul, 1960).

Rudet, Jacqueline: 'Basin', in Yvonne Brewster (ed.), *Black Plays* (London: Methuen, 1987).

Rugg, Akea: *Brickbats and Bouquets* (London: Race Today Collective, 1984).

Sabin, Margery: 'The Beast in Nirad Chaudhuri's Garden', *Essays In Criticism*, vol.44, no.1, January 1994, pp.26–48.

Sala, George Augustus: *Gaslight And Daylight. With Some London*

Scenes They Shine Upon (London: George Chapman & Hall, 1859).

Sala, G.A.: *Twice Round the Clock: Or, The Hours Of The Day And Night In London* (London: Houlston and Wright, [1859]).

Salkey, Andrew: *Escape To An Autumn Pavement* (London: Hutchinson, 1960).

Salkey, Andrew: *Come Home, Malcolm Heartland* (London: Hutchinson, 1976).

Salter, Joseph: *The Asiatic in England; Sketches of Sixteen Years' Work Among Orientals* (London: Seeley, Jackson and Halliday, 1873).

Salter, Joseph: *The East in the West. Or Work Among The Asiatics And Africans in London* (London: S.W. Partridge & Co., [1896]).

Samuel, Raphael: *Theatres of Memory. Volume 1: Past and Present in Contemporary Culture* (London: Verso, 1994).

Sander, Reinhard: *The Trinidad Awakening. West Indian Literature of the Nineteen-Thirties* (New York: Greenwood Press, 1988).

Sanderson, Tessa: *Tessa. My Life In Athletics* (London: Willow Books, 1986).

Sandford, Christopher: *Mick Jagger. Primitive Cool* (London: Victor Gollancz, 1993).

Sandhu, Sukhdev (ed.): *Slavery, Abolition and Emancipation. Writings in the British Romantic Period*, vol.1: *Black Writers* (London: Pickering and Chatto, 1999).

Savage, Jon: *The Kinks. The Official Biography* (London: Faber, 1984).

Savage, Jon: *England's Dreaming. Sex Pistols and Punk Rock* (London: Faber, 1991).

Savage, Jon: 'March of the Modes', *The Guardian*, 23 November 1992, p.22.

Schneer, Jonathan: *London 1900: The Imperial Metropolis* (New Haven: Yale University Press, 1999).

Schreuders, Piet, Mark Lewisohn and Adam Smith: *The Beatles London* (London: Hamlyn, 1994).

Schwartz, Richard B.: *Daily Life in Johnson's London* (Madison: University of Wisconsin Press, 1983).

Schwarz, Bill: 'Black Metropolis, White England', in Mica Niva and Alan O'Shea (eds), *Modern Times. Reflections on a Century of English Modernity* (London: Routledge, 1996), pp.176–207.

[Scott, Sarah]: *The History of Sir George Ellison, etc.* (London: A. Millar, 1766).

Sealey, Mark (ed.): *Vanley Burke: A Retrospective* (London: Lawrence & Wishart, 1993).

Sharp, James: *The Life and Death of Michael X* (Waterford: Uni Books, 1981).

Shepherd, T.B.: *Methodism and the Literature of The Eighteenth Century* (London: The Epworth Press, 1940).

Sherwood, Marika: *Many Struggles: West Indian Workers and Service Personnel in Britain, 1939–45* (London: Karia Press, 1985).

Sherwood, Marika: *Kwame Nkrumah: the years abroad 1935–1947* (Legon, Ghana: Freedom Publications, 1996).

Shields, John (ed.): *The Collected Works of Phillis Wheatley* (New York: Oxford University Press, 1988).

Short, Philip: *Banda* (London: Routledge & Kegan Paul, 1974).

Shyllon, F.O.: *Black Slaves in Britain* (Oxford: OUP for Institute of Race Relations, 1974).

Shyllon, F.O.: *Black People in Britain 1555–1833* (Oxford: OUP for Institute of Race Relations, 1977).

Silverstone, Roger (ed.): *Visions of Suburbia* (London: Routledge, 1997).

Simmel, Georg: 'The Metropolis and Mental Life', in K.H. Wolff (ed.), *The Sociology of Georg Simmel* (New York: Free Press, 1950).

Sinclair, Iain: *Lights Out For The Territory. 9 Excursions In The Secret History Of London* (London: Granta, 1997).

Singh, Sikander: *Udham Singh* (Amritsar: B. Chattar Singh Jiwan Singh, 1998).

Sizemore, Christine Wick: *A Female Vision of the City. London in the*

Novels of Five British Women (Knoxville: University of Tennessee Press, 1989).

Smith, Garland Garvey (ed.): *Thomas Holcroft's A Plain and Succinct Narrative of the Gordon Riots, London, 1780* (Atlanta: Emery University Library, 1944).

Smith, Graham: *When Jim Crow Met John Bull. Black American Soldiers In World War II* (London: I.B. Tauris, 1987).

Smith, John Edward, *A Catalogue of Westminster Records Deposited At The Town Hall, Caxton Street In The Custody of The Vestry of St Margaret and St John with an Introductory essay, illustrations and extracts* (London: Wightman & Co., 1900).

Smith, J.T.: *Nollekens And His Times: Comprehending a Life of That Celebrated Sculptor, From The Time of Roubiliac, Hogarth, and Reynolds, To That of Fuseli, Flaxman, And Blake*, 2 vols (1828 and London: Turnstile Press, 1949).

Smith, J.T.: *An Antiquarian Ramble In The Streets of London; with anecdotes of their more celebrated residents* (ed. C. Mackay), 2 vols (London: Richard Bentley, 1846).

Smith, Zadie: *White Teeth* (London: Hamish Hamilton, 2000).

Soja, Edward: *Postmodern Geographies. The Reassertion of Space in Critical Social Theory* (London: Verso, 1989).

Soja, Edward: *Thirdspace. Journeys to Los Angeles and Other Real-and-Imagined Places* (Oxford: Blackwell, 1996).

Soper, Donald: *Calling for Action: An Autobiographical Enquiry* (London: Robson, 1984).

Spivak, Gayatri Chakravorty: *The Post-Colonial Critic. Interviews, Strategies, Dialogues. Edited by Sarah Harasym* (New York: Routledge, 1990).

Spivak, Gayatri Chakravorty: *Outside in the Teaching Machine* (New York: Routledge, 1993).

Squier, Susan M.: *Virginia Woolf And London. The Sexual Politics Of The City* (Chapel Hill: University of North Carolina Press, 1985).

Srivastava, Atima: *Transmission* (London: Serpent's Tail, 1992).

Statt, Daniel: *Foreigners and Englishmen. The Controversy over Immigration and Population, 1660–1760* (Newark: University of Delaware Press, 1995).

Sterne, Laurence: *The Life and Opinions of Tristram Shandy, Gentleman* (1759–67 and Oxford: Clarendon Press, 1983).

Sterne, Laurence: *A Sentimental Journey Through France and Italy* (Oxford: Basil Blackwell, Publisher to the Shakespeare Head Press of Stratford-Upon-Avon, 1927).

Sterne, Laurence: *The Sermons of Mr Yorick*, vol.1 (Oxford: Basil Blackwell, Publisher to the Shakespeare Head Press of Stratford-Upon-Avon, 1927).

Sulter, Maud: *As A Blackwoman. Poems 1982–1985* (1985 and Hebden Bridge: Urban Fox Press, [1989?]).

Sulter, Maud (ed.): *Passion. Discourses on Blackwomen's Creativity* (Hebden Bridge: Urban Fox Press, 1990).

Summers, Judith: *Soho. A History of London's Most Colourful Neighbourhood* (London: Bloomsbury, 1989).

Sypher, Wylie: *Guinea's Captive Kings: British Anti-Slavery Literature of the XVIIIth Century* (Chapel Hill: University of North Carolina Press, 1942).

Tabili, Laura: *'We Ask For British Justice': Workers And Racial Difference in Late Imperial Britain* (Ithaca: Cornell University Press, 1994).

Tajfel, Henri and John L. Dawson: *Disappointed Guests. Essays by African, Asian, And West Indian Students* (London: Institute of Race Relations for OUP, 1965).

Tambimuttu, J.: *Out Of This War. A Poem* (London: The Fortune Press, [c.1940]).

Tambimuttu, J.: *Natarajah. A Poem for Mr T.S. Eliot's Sixtieth Birthday* (London: Editions Poetry Limited, [c.1949]).

Thomas, Helen (ed.): *Dance in the City* (London: Macmillan, 1997).

Thomas, J.J.: *Froudacity. West Indian Fables by James Anthony Froude* (London: T. Fisher Unwin, 1889).

Thompson, Tony: 'Gangland London', *Time Out*, 8–15 November 1995, pp.12–21.

Thompson, Tony: 'The harder they come...', *Time Out*, 12–19 August 1998, pp.12–13.

Thomson, Elizabeth and David Gutman (eds): *The Bowie Companion* (1993 and London: Sidgwick and Jackson, 1995).

Thornley, Andy (ed.): *The Crisis of London* (London: Routledge, 1992).

Timothy, Bankole: *Kwame Nkrumah from cradle to grave* (Dorchester: The Gavin Press, 1981).

Turner, John M.: 'Pablo Fanque "an Artiste of Colour"', *King Pole*, no.89, December 1990, pp.5–9; and no.90, March 1991, pp.3–5.

Turner, John M.: *Victorian Arena. The Performers. A Dictionary of British Circus Biography*, vol.1 (Formby: Lingdales Press, 1995).

Tyau, Min-Ch'ien T.Z.: *London Through Chinese Eyes; Or My Seven And a Half Years in London* (London: The Swarthmore Press, 1920).

Vadgama, Kusoom: *India in Britain: The Indian Contribution to the British Way of Life* (London: Robert Royce, 1984).

[Vague, Tom]: *London Psychogeography: Rachman Riots And Rillington Place* (London: Vague, 1998).

Valentine, E.S.: 'His Majesty's Customs', in George R. Sims (ed.), *Living London*, vol.1 (London: Cassell & Company, 1901), pp.286–291.

Vane, Roland: *Girl from Tiger Bay* (Stoke-on-Trent: The Archer Press, 1954).

Visram, Rozina: *Ayahs, Lascars, and Princes. Indians in Britain, 1700–1947* (London: Pluto Press, 1986).

Visram, Rozina: *Indians in Britain* (London: B.T. Batsford, 1987).

Visram, Rozina: *The History of the Asian Community in Britain* (Hove: Wayland, 1995).

Visram, Rozina: *Asians in Britain: 400 Years of History* (London: Pluto Press, 2002).

Voltaire, François Marie Arouet de: *The Henriade* (1728 and London: William Sancho, 1807).

Wagner, Leopold: *Saunterings In London: With A Few Bars' Rest* (London: George Allen & Unwin, 1978).

Wain, John: *Frank* (Oxford: Amber Lane Press, 1984).

Wake, Joan: *The Brudenells of Deene* (1953 and rev. 2nd ed., London: Cassell & Company, 1954).

Walkowitz, Judith R.: *City of Dreadful Delight: Narratives of Sexual Danger in Late-Victorian London* (London: Virago, 1992).

Waller, Maureen: *1700: Scenes from London Life* (London: Hodder & Stoughton, 2000).

Walters, Vanessa: *Rude Girls* (London: Pan, 1996).

Walvin, James: *Black and White. The Negro and English Society 1555–1945* (London: Allen Lane, 1973).

Walvin, James: *Passage To Britain: Immigration in British History and Politics* (Harmondsworth: Pelican, 1984).

Walvin, James: *Black Ivory: A History of British Slavery* (London: HarperCollins, 1992).

Walvin, James: *Making The Black Atlantic: Britain and the African Diaspora* (London: Cassell, 2000).

Wambu, Onyekachi (ed.): *Empire Windrush. Fifty Years of Writing About Black Britain* (London: Gollancz, 1998).

Weinreb, Ben and Christopher Hibbert (eds): *The London Encyclopaedia* (1983 and rev. ed., London: Papermac, 1993).

Weintraub, Stanley: *The London Yankees. Portraits of American Writers and Artists in England 1894–1914* (London: W.H. Allen, 1979).

Western, John: *A Passage To England: Barbadian Londoners Speak of Home* (London: UCL Press, 1992).

Weylland, John Matthias: *Round The Tower; or, the Story of the London City Mission* (London: 1875).

Weylland, John Matthias: *Our Veterans; or, life-stories of the London City Mission* (London: S.W. Partridge, [1881]).

Wheatle, Alex: *Brixton Rock* (London: Black Amber Books, 1999).

Wheatle, Alex: *East of Acre* (London: Fourth Estate, 2001).

Wheen, Francis: *The Battle for London* (London: Pluto Press, 1985).

Whitlark, James and Wendell Aycock (eds): *The Literature of Emigration and Exile* (Texas: Texas Tech University Press, 1992).

Wilkinson, George Theodore: *An Authentic History of the Cato-Street Conspiracy* (London: Thomas Kelly, 1820).

Willett, Ralph: *Hard Boiled Detective Fiction* (Keele: B[ritish] A[ssociation for] A[merican] S[tudies] Pamphlets in American Studies 23, 1992).

Williams, Eric: *British Historians and the West Indies* (1964 and London: André Deutsch, 1966).

Williams, Jane: *Tambimuttu: Bridge between two worlds* (London: Owen, 1989).

Williams, Patrick and Laura Chrisman: *Colonial Discourse And Post-Colonial Theory. A Reader* (New York: Harvester Wheatsheaf, 1993).

Wilmer, Val: 'Skanking Ahoy!', *Mojo*, July 1998, pp.52–57.

Wilson, Amrit: *Finding A Voice. Asian Women In Britain* (London: Virago, 1978).

Wilson, Elizabeth: *Hallucinations. Life In The Postmodern City* (London: Radius, 1988).

Wilson, Elizabeth: *The Sphinx In The City. Urban Life, the Control of Disorder, and Women* (London: Virago Press, 1991).

Wilson, Kathleen: *The sense of the people. Politics, culture and imperialism in England, 1715–1785* (New York: Cambridge University Press, 1995).

Wilson, Peter: *Crab Antics. The Social Anthropology of English-Speaking Negro Societies of the Caribbean* (New Haven: Yale University Press, 1973).

Wilt, Judith: 'The Imperial Mouth: Imperialism, the Gothic and

Science Fiction', *Journal of Popular Culture*, vol.14, no.4, Spring 1981, pp.618–628.

Winfield, Pamela: *Bye Bye Baby. The Story of the Children the GIs Left Behind* (London: Bloomsbury, 1992).

Women and Geography Study Group of the IBG: *Geography and Gender. An Introduction to feminist geography* (London: Hutchinson, 1984).

Woolf, Virginia: 'Street Haunting: A London Adventure', in Rachel Bowlby (ed.), *The Crowded Dance Of Modern Life. Selected Essays: Volume Two* (London: Penguin, 1993), pp.70–81.

Worpole, Ken: 'Mother to legend (or going underground): the London novel', in Ian A. Bell (ed.), *Peripheral Visions. Images of Nationhood in Contemporary British Fiction* (Cardiff: University of Wales Press, 1995).

Wright, Patrick: *On Living In An Old Country* (London: Verso, 1985).

Wright, Patrick: *The Thames in Our Time* (London: BBC Books, 1999).

Yamanouchi, Hisaaki: 'The Spleen of London 1900–1902: A Japanese Writer's Encounter With Late Victorian English Culture', *Studies in Travel Writing*, no.3, 1999, pp.102–112.

Yee, Chiang: *The Silent Traveller In London* (London: Country Life, 1938).

York, Peter: *Modern Times* (1984 and London: Futura, 1985).

Young, Lola: *Fear of the Dark. 'Race', Gender and Sexuality in the Cinema* (London: Routledge, 1996).

Zangwill, Israel: *Children of the Ghetto* (London: W. Heinemann, 1892).

Acknowledgements

This book would have been inconceivable without the pioneering scholarship of Michael Banton, Vincent Carretta, Paul Edwards, Peter Fryer, and Rozina Visram.

On a personal note, I would like to thank the following individuals, all of whom helped me – by forwarding obscure references, offering institutional space, reading versions of the manuscript, or just by being good and true human beings – during the years, far too many of them, I have spent on this study: Pallavi Aiyar, Tariq Ali, Harinder Bains, John Barrell, David Beard, Thomas Bender, Val Cunningham, James Davidson, David Godwin, Jeremy Harding, Lara Heimert, Ian Jack, Reyahn King, Robert Mason, Nicholas Pearson, Arabella Pike, Kay Sandhu, Pritam Sandhu, Rebecca Saraceno, Richard Symonds, Jack Tchen, Thuy Linh Nguyen Tu, Anne Walmsley.

Special thanks to Paul Laity: true brick.

Index

P.S.

Ideas,
interviews
& features ...

About the author

Read on

A Conversation with Sukhdev Sandhu

by Will Woodward

WE MEET IN an office in Clerkenwell, near the City, in sun-and-showers season. The day before, Sukhdev Sandhu spent three hours walking in and around Cable Street, near his home in East London, with the writer Manzu Islam.

'We were going round these railway arches, going to Watney Market and checking out street corners, angling for particular views,' Sandhu says. 'Manzu wrote this really good book called *The Mapmaker of Spitalfields*. He was telling me about the special forms of terror that he would face growing up there in the mid-seventies, how far up a certain street you could go without getting your head kicked in, pointing out the micro-zones in which different populations live.

'We were mapping the changes, looking at butchers that had been turned into sweatshops and then transformed by Bengali entrepreneurs into internet cafés. We were just trying to evoke a sense of the past. Even the recent past. It's disappearing so quickly. If you look up, you see all these corporate Fabergé eggs, these gleaming Gherkins in the distance. Pricey real-estate developers have moved into the area in a big way, and many of the Bangladeshis, those people who lived through the dark years of the 1970s and 1980s, are moving on ...'

Over the fifteen years I've known him, quite a few of Sandhu's stories have sounded something like this, as he races at

Schumacher speed through descriptions of the sights, sounds and smells of the city, with short-stopover ruminations on the bands Belle and Sebastian and Saint Etienne. 'I have a kind of idiot glee about London. I used to get off the coach at Marble Arch and literally skip down Oxford Street,' he says.

London Calling has been researched, written, published, reviewed and put out in paperback, but the emotions that drove his 'love letter' to the capital remain, and if anything are reinforced. 'For me the book is what I would do anyway. My idea of a good time is just to go on pointless, drifting, noodly walks around still relatively derelict, bust-up parts of London, which tend to be congregated in the East End, hoping to bump into ghosts of the past, trying to see what value it has in the current day.

'London's so deep it can be mined endlessly. London's an ongoing project. It's incomplete and so it should be. That's what all good cities are, otherwise they'd be dead. I sometimes worry that I'm getting more obsessive and antiquarian, more microscopic. But this is a period of accelerated transformation when classic cafés, allotments, public spaces are being razed. The present-day city gets privatized and whole zones get regulated and kept under surveillance. Meanwhile its history becomes streamlined, a commodity. Even immigrant history is saleable, background texture for hipster realtors. It's important ▶

> ❝ For me the book is what I would do anyway. My idea of a good time is just to go on pointless, drifting, noodly walks around still relatively derelict, bust-up parts of London. ❞

LIFE
at a Glance

BORN
....
Chiswick, 1970

EDUCATED
....
University of Oxford
(BA, PhD)
University of Warwick
(MA)
Research Fellow,
International Center for
Advanced Studies, New
York University

CAREER
....
Currently the chief film
critic for the *Daily
Telegraph*, he has also
taught at New York
University, and written
extensively for
publications including the
London Review of Books,
Times Literary Supplement
and *Modern Painters*.

A **Conversation** *(continued)*

◀ to root down and cleave to an earthy,
distressed version of what the past was like
so that you aren't left with an excessively
polite narrative.'

So it is that his justification for writing
London Calling has hardened. Its big bang
came when Sandhu, already infused with
passion for Hanif Kureishi's work,
discovered, 'in a flea-bitten second-hand
bookstore', Sam Selvon's first book, *The
Lonely Londoners*. He was put off by Selvon's
title at first. 'It sounds incredibly bleak, as if
it's going to be a version of the collective
immigration story which you've seen so
many times from Pathé newsreels. Hard
times – and more hard times. But when you
read Selvon's novel, within a sentence or two
it's just aflame. It's needy and it's desperate.
But it's also funny and vulgar. It prefigures
better-known books like Colin MacInnes's
Absolute Beginners. It has a lot in common
with The Streets' album or Dizzee Rascal. It's
avant-urchin.

'Selvon traffics between high and low
culture; he's influenced by people like Eliot,
but he's also writing about scuzzy runaways
and pimps. In a way that reflects the extremes
of London. You get the whole circumference
of the city in his book. And he makes you
laugh. You could read it in conjunction with
the Ealing film *Hue and Cry*; they're equally
charming, equally vivid portals into post-war
English art and culture.

'So I wanted to write about people I liked,
who I thought were worth reading, and not
just by people sitting in seminar rooms. A fair
few of the authors I look at have been written

about before, but all too often out of a sense of duty, or in post-colonial or academic terms that end up betraying their spirit. I also wanted to convey a sense of them as individuals, as shysters, hustlers. The lives they described are often fairly picaresque or down-at-heel; their own lives matched that. I wanted to do justice to them.'

If Sandhu's book had a manifesto, it was, at least at first, a relatively limited one. 'I was really examining the idea that ethnicity is an add-on when we're thinking about London. It's not this secondary or tertiary element that you can haul in when imagining or writing about what makes the city what it is. I was pleading for an acknowledgement that black and Asian people had for centuries contributed not just economically, but imaginatively, to the capital, and that within their texts there was way more variety and sadness and depth and gaiety than had ever been commemorated.

'It's only now that I've written the book that I realize the central story of London, rather than the secondary one I thought I was writing, could be constructed around people like Selvon, Naipaul, Rushdie, Zadie Smith, Equiano and Sancho. It's UFO Central. Aliens have been invading it for millennia: the Romans, the Normans, people coming in from the countryside, the Huguenots, and Germans, the Irish and Jewish, Eritreans in Southall, the Portuguese in Stockwell today. We have a particular idea that in order to create history you need something that is fixed and stable, and maybe we do, but that stability can be composed of discontinuity ▶

❛ I was pleading for an acknowledgement that black and Asian people had for centuries contributed not just economically, but imaginatively, to the capital. ❜

A Conversation (continued)

◀ and fragmentation. In many ways, it's not just black and Asian writers but all outsiders and immigrant voices who have actually been the key narrative of the city.'

A decade ago, when the *Faber Book of London* failed to include any black or Asian writers, this thought was submerged; that's changed now, Sandhu says. 'This capital city has only recently been accepted for the international, globalized, cosmopolitan city it always has been.' We wonder what an updated version of *London Calling* might look like in ten years' time; it might have to talk even more about music, and would certainly have to explore the internet. 'Some of the best writings of the current day, if I were to update it, would be blogs written by car park attendants working in Stratford and the Romford Road. I could easily have made the book 2,000 pages long.

'Maybe the book marks the outer contours of a tradition of black writing about the city. The status of black and Asian people is changing, especially as more Iraqis, Latin Americans and East Europeans start to come in. The new migration is increasingly white. Colonialism didn't shape their relationship to London. Also, there are so many new books, dramas, poetry collections coming out, all splintering and fizzing, all with so many different lenses and takes on the city, that it gets harder to try and delineate any kind of broad patterns.'

The city is changing too, in ways which Sandhu returns to again and again with a slightly elegiac air. 'There've never been particular ghettos in this city. There

❝ Some of the best writings of the current day, if I were to update the book, would be blogs written by car park attendants working in Stratford. ❞

have always been nodes of particular concentration, but they've never been formalized in the way they've been in the States. In New York, there are still loads of people who won't go into Harlem. Even the lure of cheap property hasn't yet been enough of an incentive. Manhattan's a self-enclosed grid city, Victorian in many ways, and many parts of it are, both imaginatively and in real life, cordoned off from each other.'

Now new communities are increasingly being separated from Inner London, finding homes at the far ends of the Central or Metropolitan lines. In Spitalfields, near Sandhu's home, 'for the first time in its history it's not poorer people than the last immigrant group moving in. Now even the artists are struggling to afford it; it's really businessmen who are seizing the soil. Immigrant stories are moving out to the edge of the city.

'In terms of the ecology of the city, the promiscuity and chance encounters, the cultural collisions that we come here for, there's a growing threat that immigrants become less visible. A case of out of sight, out of mind. You have people ferried in just for the work that they do rather than to indulge in the full range of their desires and longings. London might become more like Paris or LA. That would be really regrettable, if seemingly inevitable, especially as it was the redemptive energy of immigrants that made the city, all the way through the 1970s and 1980s when it was damned and neglected by Conservative politicians, so ultimately alluring.' ▶

> 6 Immigrant stories are moving out to the edge of the city. 9

A Conversation *(continued)*

◄ Sandhu's parents moved to London from a village near Ludhiana, northern India, in the 1960s, but in the early 1970s relocated to Gloucester, a city with no Sikh temples and not much of a Punjabi community, for work. He has spent most of his life outside London. The book is for, and because of, his parents, he says in the dedication. It is also, in some ways, to them. 'My parents don't quite see why anybody sane would want to live in London. And sometimes when you are stuck in a sweltering tube train at three o'clock in the afternoon in August and some lunatic guy is gobbing in your face, or you've just split up with someone and you're sobbing on a rainy November night, transport's down because of some terrorist alert, and you stagger home but can't find your key because you've been drinking too much, London is particularly dire. It's increasingly a young person's city with 24/7 merry-making and high house prices meaning families would rather live elsewhere. Your relationship with London is really intense when you're younger because you've got more energy, more desire to get out and see the place, but less money.'

Nowadays, emigrants from the Punjab are moving to the US and Canada, he says. 'England is slightly on the wane for many of them; you probably have to have a certain kind of old-fashioned sensibility to come here. There's the idea that you can't really make it big in quite the same way any more.' For all that, he remains a true believer. 'My book is a form of PR, saying London still counts, it's still valid,' he confesses. 'My book is dogmatic in a certain way. It insists that

> ❝ London is increasingly a young person's city with 24/7 merry-making and high house prices meaning families would rather live elsewhere. ❞

you should like London . . . For all the bad things there is still a sense of possibility and hope and remaking, a begrudging generosity about life here. It's an endlessly porous city. London is still a place where you can be reborn, where you can feel as if you're living for the first time.' ■

⸢ My book is dogmatic in a certain way. It insists that you should like London . . . For all the bad things there is still a sense of possibility and hope and remaking. ⸥

You Should
Listen to ...
by Sukhdev Sandhu

A Selection of Music Composed by Ignatius Sancho (1998)
This is a rare recording of the eighteenth-century grocer-aesthete's music. Available from Jean Boylan, Greenwich Education Service, 10th Floor, Riverside House, Woolwich High Street, London SE18 6DT.

Black British Swing (Topic, 2002)
Rousing collection of London's own hot jazz scene during the 1930s and 1940s with great vintage recordings from West Indian maestros such as Ken 'Snakehips' Johnson and Leslie Thompson.

'87 Sundays', Ruth, on *Dream Babes*, vol. 5: *Folk Rock and Faithfull* (RPM, 2003)
Recorded in the late 1960s, but never released, this song was discovered in acetate form in a Glasgow charity shop. If Morrissey was to pen a lyric for one of Jean Rhys's characters it would sound like this beautiful and shockingly sad folk-plaint.

Foxbase Alpha, Saint Etienne (Heavenly, 1991)
For this three-piece every day is a holiday, every summer a summer of love. Moving effortlessly between dub, Northern soul, sixties Euro chansons and football samples, this is one of the definitive London albums of all time.

Routes from the Jungle: Escape Velocity
(Virgin, 1995)
Kodwo Eshun, author of the superb *More
Brilliant Than the Sun* (1999), curated this
cerebrum-cranking, bodyrocking
compilation of urban astronomics from
London's drum'n' bass scene. Body Snatch, 4
Hero and Doc Scott keep it unreal.

When I Was Born for the Seventh Time,
Cornershop (Wiiija, 1997)
Released during the summer in which
eighteen years of Conservative rule came to
an end, this drunken, affirming, funky
album, full of wit and beauty, captured the
sense of possibility that coursed through the
streets of the capital on 2 May: 'My friends,
we'll be wearing dungaree cords again'.

Your Favourite London Sounds, Peter
Cusack (LMC, 2000)
Improv musician Cusack asked his friends
which sounds they associated with London.
Gaggia coffee machines, beigel shops on
Brick Lane, swallows over Stoke Newington –
they're all here. Listened to on a Discman
while walking through the capital, what
emerges is a fascinating sound clash between
the real city and this pre-recorded auditory
London. ∎

You Should Read . . .

by Sukhdev Sandhu

Children of the Ghetto
Israel Zangwill (1892)
Zangwill coined the phrase 'melting pot'
that has become a metaphor for multi-ethnic
urbanism, but this is his most famous work,
a novel about the East End. At once
sentimental and realistic, it was the first
Anglo-Jewish bestseller, and prefigures other
E1 fiction such as Monica Ali's *Brick Lane*.

Out and About: A Note-Book of London in
War-Time
Thomas Burke (1919)
G.W. Sala, G.R. Sims, H.V. Morton – London
used to have lots of chroniclers pounding the
streets and wearing out shoe leather as they
explored the nooks and crannies of the city.
An earlier short story by Burke, 'The Chink
and the Child', was remade by D.W. Griffiths
as *Broken Blossoms* (1919).

The Seventh Man: A Book of Images and
Words about the Experience of Migrant
Workers in Europe.
John Berger and Jean Mohr (1972)
Its subtitle alone shows what a prescient
book this is. A literary version of a jump-
cutting Godard film, it leaps between the
personal and the political, eye-opening
statistics and heart-opening poetry.

***The World of Our Fathers: The Journey of
the East European Jews to America and the
Life They Found and Made***
Irving Howe (1976)
Written by one of the most prominent New
York intellectuals of the post-war period, this
wonderful book could serve as a template for
anyone wishing to write or understand the
cultural history of immigrants.

Troutfishing in Leytonstone
(late 1980s)
Graffiti, club flyers, magazines: literature
about London does not have to come in book
form. As a child I used to send concealed 50-
pence pieces to get copies of this fanzine
whose messily photocopied pages were
packed with ideas about how to have a great
time in the city: rule no. 1 – rip up your A–Z;
rule no. 2 – run down the streets pretending
to be a fighter plane.

The Colour of Memory
Geoff Dyer (1989)
One of the best London novels of the last
twenty years, this is a funny and dreamy
account of slacking dolewallahs getting high
on grass, jazz and bohemian idealism. At
once crepuscular and sunny, tough and
lushly lyrical.

Duppy Conqueror
Ferdinand Dennis (1998)
A really ambitious novel by one of this
country's best writers, about a young man's
quest to shake off a long-standing family ▶

13

You Should Read ... *(continued)*

◄ curse by returning to Africa. The book moves around all parts of the black Atlantic and works as a twentieth-century diasporic history. The scenes set in the clubland of wartime London are especially good.

Southall – A Home from Home
Dennis Morris, with text by Satinder Chohan (2000)
An evocative collection of black-and-white photographs from 1972 to 1978, taken by a lensman better known for his pictures of punk musicians, about the West London suburb that since the 1950s has become the main home of Sikhs in England.

'My Lost City'
Luc Sante, republished as 'Afterword' to *Low Life: Lures and Snares of Old New York* (2004)
The book itself is a riot of rogues, winos and Bowery bums at the start of the twentieth century. This essay is a wonderfully textured and happy-sad account of the way that young artists and adventurers forged their identities in the recessionary Manhattan of the 1970s.

http://heronbone.blogspot.com
Luke Young is the nearest contemporary London has to William Blake. He lives on Romford Road, raves about grime, and in his spare time keeps a blog that is as funny, poetic and trippy as anything currently being written. No one straddles the ornithology/eski dance divide like he does. ■

You Should Visit ...

by Sukhdev Sandhu

Corner of Archer and Rupert Street, Soho, W1

Nearby lurk clumps of adult video stores and scantily clad women beckoning passers-by into basement clubs. In 1818, in the basement of 6 Archer Street, future brothel-keeper Robert Wedderburn and his fellow Spencean radicals met to plot the overthrow of the government.

Jamme Masjid, Brick Lane, E1

This mosque, opened at the end of the 1970s, started out in 1742 as a chapel for those thousands of Huguenot refugees, many of them silk weavers, who were fleeing French persecution. After being taken over by local Methodists, in 1898 it became a synagogue for Jews escaping the pogroms in Russia and Poland.

Internet cafés

Often open all hours, they attract a mixed and ragged crowd of autodidacts, the cash-strapped, and international students. A single keystroke allows one to access the hopes and desires of a cross-section of Londoners that evening: cheap flights, CV-writing companies, purveyors of lady-boy porn.

Little Britain, EC1

This small street in the middle of the City is given over to offices and international businesses. In the evenings it is deserted, until a bevy of West African and Eastern European cleaners, most of them living in ▶

You Should Visit . . . *(continued)*

◄ Haringey or New Cross, arrive to polish the desks and pick up the Styrofoam cups of people who earn more in a week than they do in a year.

www.derelictlondon.com

A site dedicated to mapping faded, spotted, run-down areas in the capital. It induces a certain melancholy, but also an understanding of the way in which the city operates asynchronously, flowing and ebbing at different rates in different streets or boroughs. It shows how London is an unfinished project, a mercifully incomplete city.

Don's Café, 150 Lower Clapton Street, E5

The owners are in their seventies, French accordion music plays continuously, and the décor is strictly old school. Throughout the centuries, cafés have served as business opportunities, drop-in centres, knocking shops and betting joints for new immigrants. It is in places such as these that communities come into being.

Vietnamese DVD sellers

Immigrants are portable cartographies. To follow them around is to appreciate how many metropolises co-exist side by side. Some are underground and illicit. Vietnamese vendors are increasingly familiar on the city's streets, where they traipse into pubs and restaurants hoping to offload some of the bootleg Hollywood films they carry in their small rucksacks. A modern-day Henry Mayhew would track their routes.

New Beacon Bookshop, 76 Stroud Green Road, N4

Stocking a number of the titles discussed in this volume, New Beacon was the first Caribbean bookstore in London. It was set up in 1966 by John La Rose, the Trinidadian poet, scholar, publisher and social activist. It has been at this site since 1973 and remains one of the first ports of call for anyone interested in learning more about the history, politics and literature of diasporic London.

Leicester Square, W1

Londoners often scoff at this place because they think it's overrun by thousands of international tourists in dodgy checked trousers. It is, sometimes. That's what makes it so great. English reserve and diffidence is inappropriate here. Witnessing the families, the backpackers, the student throngs, it's hard not to revel in the excitement that London engenders in people from abroad.

Lunar House, Croydon, SE23

This is where chancers and desperadoes, the stateless and the brutalized go to apply for visas, leave to stay, asylum. It is where they embark on another journey, as tortuous and tantalizing in its own way as the one they made to get to London in the first place. ∎

You Should Watch ...
by Sukhdev Sandhu

Piccadilly (1929)
Before World War Two international film-makers such as D.W. Griffiths were drawn to Limehouse in East London by the presence there of an apparently exotic Chinese community. This jazz age melodrama, directed by German director E.A. Dupont and starring silent-era siren Anna May Wong, is a ravishing and Scorsese-lauded classic.

Hue and Cry (1947)
One of the most lovable Ealing films, this captures post-war London in all its rubble and blackmarket spivvery. It's hard not to envy the gang of East End schoolboys, led by Harry Fowler, as they dash across bombsites trying to catch the crooks who have been using Alastair Sim's comic to plan their dastardly crimes.

The London That Nobody Knows (1967)
Norman Cohen's documentary, based on the writing of Geoffrey Fletcher, features James Mason traipsing around the catacombs, market stalls and decayed music halls of a London that is definitely not Swinging.

The Elephant Man (1980)
David Lynch's portrait of the unfortunate John Merrick is a fine example of London gothic, a genre that has also thrown up gems such as *The Dark Eyes of London* (1939) and *The Sorcerers* (1967).

Exodus (1992–1997)
It lasts for only 65 seconds, but this is a

delightful and casually artful super-8 film by
the 1999 Turner Prize winner Steve McQueen.
Two old West Indians walk across Brick Lane
carrying potted palms that seem to sprout
from their heads. As they're about to get into
a bus, they look back, laugh, and wave to the
camera.

London (1994)
Patrick Keiller's important documentary, at
once psychogeography, architectural satire
and threnody for a Tory-blighted urbanism,
makes a great companion piece to Iain
Sinclair's book *Lights Out For the Territory*
and has influenced the work of young
filmmakers such as Nick Relph and Oliver
Payne, and Kieron Evans and Paul Kelly.

Wonderland (1999)
Michael Winterbottom's refugee epic *In this
World* (2003) reveals London as a kind of
New Jerusalem for the world's dispossessed.
This earlier film is an intimate and beauti-
fully tender portrait of the interconnected
lives of a group of strangers in South London.
It is, in its understated way, as romantic as
Woody Allen's *Manhattan* (1979).

Skin Deep (2001)
Yousaf Ali Khan's thirteen-minute short film
is set in the 1970s and shows a half-white,
half-Pakistani boy trying to ingratiate
himself with local bully boys who would pulp
him if they discovered his ethnicity. A dark
and upsetting film, it's a powerful example
of the aesthetics of Asian abjection. ▶

You Should Watch ... *(continued)*

◄ **Weekender** (1992)
This is actually a video directed by Wiz for
the song of that name by Flowered Up.
Clocking in at eighteen minutes, it's a
hallucinogenic, bludgeoned and
bludgeoning vision of forty-eight hours in
the life of a young guy as he snorts amyl
nitrate and boffs pills to the sound of laddish
rave-era club sounds. At one point he finds
himself being chased by a needle. A fetching
period document.

The Gleaners and I (2000)
This must surely be one of the most
delightful and moving documentaries ever
made. Using cheap digital cameras, Agnès
Varda roams around France filming
migrants, vagrants and farm workers who
bend down to make a living. It is a
meditation on memory and on growing old,
and an unforgettable ode to the beauty and
goodness that may be found on the margins
of society. ■